W9-CMB-838

Bad Ol' Boy

Bad Ol' Boy

A novel by

Harold Miles

Humana Press • Totowa, New Jersey

Library of Congress Cataloging in Publication Data

Miles, Harold.
    Bad Ol' Boy : a novel / by Harold Miles.
        376 pp.
    ISBN 0-89603-267-1
        I. Title.
PS3563.I3718B3   1993
813'.54—dc20

Contents

Will's Last Days

I left work at the General Shoe Factory for the four-and-a-half mile ride home with my buddy and coworker, Harvey Wright. On the way home me and Harvey talked about what pissy jobs we had.

He sewed in the sole department. His job was stitching the three-piece sole together all the way around the edge, which he didn't like very much. I liked my job even less. I was in the baby heel department. I took a thin wedge of rubber, made a sandwich with two pieces of leather, and poked the whole business in a big press. When I pushed a lever with my left foot, the press came down and squeezed all that stuff together.

The foreman was constantly on my back about this one was okay, and that one was not okay. He took great pleasure in telling me how many heels I'd ruined in any particular eight hour shift. And to tell the truth, I never did know by looking at one when it was right or when it was wrong. It was the biggest damn mystery to me that ever was, how he could pick out two pieces looking exactly alike and tell me one of 'em was good and one of 'em was bad. He almost convinced me that summer that I was stupid. I hated the job.

Before the shoe plant, I had worked for Dryden Brothers Lumber Company delivering board all over three counties. It was heavy, hard work, but at least I got to move around and had the fresh wind blowing in my face. I could stick my head out the window of that old truck going 50 miles an hour and keep cool. In the shoe factory, it stayed a hundred degrees all day long, plus the boss I worked for had to be one of the biggest sons-of-bitches in the world.

When I told him I couldn't see the difference in a good shoe and a bad shoe, he'd say I wasn't paying attention, when, as a matter of fact, I was looking just as hard as I could. He thought his job was just to bitch at folks. That was what he sometimes opined made a good foreman, one who bitched all the time. If that was so, he was the best damn foreman God ever made.

Harvey let me out at the road, and I walked up the path to the house. It was late summer; the house was as hot as hell.

1

Ma said, "Bremen Hospital called a while ago. They tol' me Uncle Will was dying, said he wanted to see you before he died."

"Can I have the car to go up there?"

"You ain't got no business up there. Let the son-of-a-bitch die."

"Ma, you ought not talk that way about Uncle Will, he's your blood kin. He's closer to you than he is to me. He's my great uncle, but he's your blood uncle, your mother's brother. Why do you...?"

"He's a good for nothing, foul mouth, son-of-a-bitch. I'll be glad when he's dead. You know how I feel about him."

"Yeah, Ma, I know how you feel about him, but he ain't been no harm to nobody for years, not since the war. He's just a sick ol' man. You know that him and me had some good times fishing and hunting. He's done a lot of stuff, he's been all over, he's traveled."

"Yeah," she said, "he travels—robbing, stealing, sluttin' around all over the whole world—he did that alright. Now his time comes for judgment, and he wants to cry on his nephew's shoulder. Let the son-of-a-bitch die."

"Ma, can I borrow the car to go see him?"

"I don't think so; there ain't no gas in the car. I don't think there's enough gas to get to town."

"There's enough gas to get over to Bud Cole's store. I'll fill it up if you'll let me have the car to go see him."

"You think so much of Will, you must gonna be just like him when you grow up. I don't know why God Almighty decreed it so, but I knowed exactly what you was gonna be like before me and your Pa was ever married. We went to a fortuneteller—her name is Mayhayley Lancaster down in Heard County—the last year we courted, before we got married. I wasn't but 17 years old; that old woman took my hand, looked at my life line, and said, 'Child, your first born is gonna bear the mark of Cain.'

"I snatched my hand away. 'I ain't gonna marry no colored.'

"'Child, the mark of Cain ain't black; the mark of Cain is having a soul so rebellious, a spirit so wild, he'll wreak a wide path of heart-break and destruction his whole life. You'll rue the day he was born.'

"I didn't believe her when she told me that, but watching your sassy ass grow up, yep, you got the mark of Cain. Go see that no good son-of-a-bitch and leave us here."

"Ma, I'm growed up. I'm 18 years old."

"You ain't no such thing, you're 17 years old."

"Well, I'm past 17, I'm going on 18."

"See there, you just lie about everything."

"Ma, I didn't lie, I'm going on 18 years old. Are you gonna let me have the car?"

"I'll let you have the car if you'll fill it up with gas, provided it's alright with your Pa. If you won't go nowhere but to the hospital and come straight home after you've talked to the son-of-a-bitch."

"Ma, I wish you wouldn't say that about Uncle Will. He's a sick old man, and he's sorry for a lot of the things he did."

"He can't be sorry enough for all the damn heartaches he caused my Ma and the rest of the family. I wish he was already dead."

"Ma, can I have the car?"

"I already told you you could have the car if you'll fill it up with gas, just go to Bremen and back."

"But Ma, that won't take but a gallon of gas. I've got to buy ten gallons of gas to use one gallon?"

"Well, there's wear and tear on the car, young man. Your Pa worked hard for that...."

"Ma, I helped Pa pay for the car. I don't see why it ain't half mine anyway."

"Young man, you just look to see whose name is on the bill of sale."

"I know whose name is on the bill of sale, Ma."

"If you go, and I ain't said you could yet, you got to do the milking, slop the hogs, feed the mules, do all the other chores before you go—Pa might want to plow the garden when he gets home."

"It's five o'clock, Ma. I can milk the cow and be ready to go when Pa gets home. You know visiting hours are seven to nine. I've got plenty of time to do all that stuff. Are you gonna let me use the car? I can't walk to Bremen and back; it's ten miles. I wouldn't be there by the time visiting hours are over."

"You get the things done and if it's alright with your Pa, and if you'll fill the car full of gas, I'll let you use it."

That's the way Ma was; I guess she couldn't help it. She used to talk about "so-and-so was so stingy he'd skin a damn gnat for its tallow." She never could see that in herself.

k bucket and went to the barn, set down under the
nd started milking. Right away, Snowflake stuck her
e corner of the stable and let out a little meow.
is our barn cat. She stayed there and kept the rats
in the crib down. She was black as a quarter past twelve, but we
called her Snowflake. I thought that was a right nice touch, and
had a lot of fun with it; nobody ever guessed her name.

Anyway, I took one of the cow's tits and aimed a stream of milk
at Snowflake's mouth. It hit her dead center all the way across the
barn's hall. She started purring and licking her face, lapping the
milk off her fur. Then she took a couple of steps closer, sat down,
and meowed till I gave her another squirt of warm milk. She shut
her eyes while licking herself clean. A backslappin' look of ecstasy
crossed her face as I gave her still another swig while her eyes were
shut. When she finished licking that off her face and fur, she came
over, squeezed between my legs as I set on the milk stool, and
marked my britches' legs with her scent. Then with a flick of her
tail, she wandered off to the feed room.

I put the mule's corn in his trough. When Ol' Jack went in the
stable, I shut the door on him in case Pa wanted to plow when he
got home from work. He was still working for Dryden Brothers Lumber Company. I didn't see any reason to do any plowing; the veg-
etable garden was already made, but Ma, like always, wanted to
have plenty of jobs for everybody.

I carried the milk back to the house. Ma looked in the bucket
and said, "You been feeding that damn cat again, ain't you?"

"No ma'am," I lied to her, wonderin' all the time how she could
miss those three little squirts.

"I know damn well you're lyin'. Your Pa said that old cat has
gotten so lazy she won't kill no rats. You're gonna have to help
him set a drowning trap for 'em if you don't quit feeding that cat
milk." She knew how I hated drowning traps; it made me sick to
think about 'em. I hated rats, but nothing deserved the drowning trap.

I remember the first time I helped Pa fix one; I thought it was
an ingenious invention as he told me how it worked. We had a big
ol' 30-gallon cast iron washpot we cooked lard in, and every Monday morning we boiled the family wash in it. It was during the

Depression, and I wasn't more than 9 years old, but I helped him wrestle that old pot up into the crib.

We climbed up on the pile of corn and dug out a hole. Then we buried the washpot level with the top of the corn. I watched fascinated as Dad cut a chunk of salty meat out of a cured ham from the meat box. He stretched a wire from one handle of the washpot to the other, tying it to each handle. In the middle he tied a piece of ham; next we toted water from the well and filled the washpot to within about six inches of the top. Then Pa took some cottonseed hulls and tossed them in till they covered the water. It looked like the pot was full of cottonseed hulls as they floated on the water.

He explained to me as he went along how the rat would go out on the wire and try to tear a piece of ham off. When he couldn't get himself noplace to set, he'd hop down on what appeared to be cottonseed hulls. He'd go right to the bottom and drown.

I was horrified. I protested it was a cruel way to kill an animal. He explained, "Son, it's either them or us. They're gonna have all our corn et up before spring gets here. Come on, we'll climb up in the loft and watch 'em. It won't take 'em long. They'll smell the ham and go right to work. Come on up and we'll watch through the cracks in the loft."

I climbed the ladder and watched horrified, but fascinated, as two rats, one from each side, approached the piece of ham we'd tied securely to the hay baling wire stretched across the middle of the pot. Each one eased out on the thin slippery wire. They met at the piece of ham. A fight immediately started, and they toppled off the wire, to disappear beneath the floating cottonseed hulls. They both paddled frantically through the hulls to the side of the washpot. Since the pot sloped back toward the center as the neck rose, they couldn't get no toehold. They paddled pathetically until they were exhausted and then slipped beneath the cottonseed hulls. In the meantime, they'd been joined by two others.

The next morning, it was my gruesome task to take a bucket and dip them out. There must have been 40 pounds of drowned rats I carried behind the barn and dumped out in an old dry ditch for the buzzards. We left the traps set for several weeks until finally we got no more rats. Funny how the dumb things never got wise to it—when we put a fresh piece of ham on the wire, they'd just keep coming. I think we must've killed every rat in the crib that winter, but, God, I hated the job.

I guess I'd stood in a trance thinking about it too long. Ma said suddenly, "If you are going to see the son-of-a-bitch, you better clean up. You ain't going up there looking like no tramp. Some people know us in Bremen and think we're a respectable family. I'd hate for them to know we're kin. If you see anybody up there we know, you don't tell 'em why you're up there."

I heated a bucket of water on the cookstove and took a sponge bath. Even though it was 1947, we still didn't have any indoor plumbing, like a lot of our neighbors. Things were scarce after the war, and it seemed we never had any money for the things other folks had even though Ma scrimped and saved. Sometimes I wondered where she put all the money.

I had to give her half my paycheck every week even though I was 17 years old. In her eyes, I was still a kid. She threatened to make me give it all to her from time to time. I think if Pa had stood for it, she would have.

Pa was a strong believer that you were a man of your own when you were 21 years old, but had to do what your Ma and Pa told you to as long as you stuck your feet under their table. At least that's what he said. Ma took full advantage of that—she was the tyrant.

Even though I gave her half my paycheck every Friday, she'd still order me to buy milk, bread, or other things I had to pay for myself. Usually, I was broke well before the next payday. But it was better than it used to be.

I got cleaned up, put on my Sunday-go-to-meeting clothes, and went in to get the car keys. She made a big to-do about where the keys were, looking around in her satchel-like handbag, acting like she was giving me the key to the safe where the crown jewels are kept. Finally she produced a key and told me the car'd better be full of gas the next morning. She was gonna go out and check herself. "If you don't, you'll never use it again," she said.

I snatched the key out of her hand and stomped out of the house, went to Bud Cole's store, took the old hand pump and pumped ten gallons of gas up into the glass bubble, and then let it run into the tank. It still wasn't full; it took another five gallons. The gas cost $2.25. That left me just one quarter till next payday, four days away.

Dr. King's hospital in Bremen was no more than an old dwelling house. One of the partitions had been cut out and a counter put across it. That was where the nurses stayed when they weren't doing rounds with the doctors.

I told the nurse on duty I'd come to see Uncle Will. She said, "He's a mighty sick man, boy, but he's been asking for you all day, so I guess it won't hurt none."

"Ma'am, is he gonna die?"

"Son, I don't know that. I don't think he's gonna die this time, but his days are short. He has awful trouble sleeping; has terrible nightmares. He must've done something fierce. Sometimes at one in the morning, he'll wake the whole hospital with his screaming and groaning, just like the Devil himself is chasing him."

"Boy, you wouldn't have any idea what he's done to make him like that, would ya?"

I tried to think of a good answer that wouldn't be a lie, but I finally decided I couldn't think of one, and so I told her he'd had an awful lot of bad luck in his life. Lots of folks didn't understand him. I wasn't sure I did, but he wasn't no harm to anybody now. The nurse agreed, but she still wondered what he'd done to so trouble his sleep.

"He's in room #4. Turn to the right, go down the hallway, it's the second door on the left. Now mind ya, try not to upset him."

I followed her instructions and knocked. A feminine voice invited me in. A nurse was giving Uncle Will some kind of shot. He feebly raised his head off the pillow and motioned me to come on in. The smell of camphor, menthol, and alcohol hung heavy in the room.

The young nurse withdrew the needle from his arm, gave me a big smile, and said, "Mr. Will was worried you weren't coming. He was afraid your Ma wouldn't let you. Is your Ma as mean as he says she is?"

It embarrassed me a little that he would tell strangers about our family. I guess it didn't matter, though; she was a pretty little thing. He motioned with the side of his head for me to sit while she was taking his pulse. I was shocked looking at Uncle Will. Only a shadow of hisself just three months ago, this six-foot-six giant of a man now looked so tiny and fragile. I didn't speak until the nurse left.

"Ma said you wanted to see me."

"Yeah, I did, nephew. I need to talk to you. I was afraid your Ma wouldn't let you come."

"Do you remember how me and you used to sit down on the Tallapoosa River fishing and hunting? And how I'd tell you about my hell-raising days?"

"Yeah, Uncle Will, we spent a lot of good times together, but it ain't been that long ago. Ya know it was just this past spring when we moved from Bremen. We went fishing back in March; it's only August now. It ain't been all that long."

"You're right, it ain't been that long, but I've had a problem with my asthma this summer, and it seems like a hundred years."

I sat there looking at him. His hair was snow white; his complexion was pale, lookin' like cheap putty. I could hear the old rattling he'd had in his chest ever since I could remember. It was hard for him to catch his breath. As a matter of fact, back early in the spring once, on a warm day, he just plumb talked hisself out of breath telling me about one of the men he'd killed. Even with no medical knowledge, I knew he was a sick man.

He looked at me weak-eyed and said, "Nephew, how've you been?"

"I've been doing good, Uncle Will. You don't look so good though."

"That's why I've called you, Nephew, I ain't doing too good. My time draws nigh, Nephew. I powerfully dread knocking on them Pearly Gates and asking Pete and Gabe to let me in.

"You remember all them tales I told you since the war about what I did when I was young? I told you a lot, but I didn't tell you all of it. I've been reading the scriptures lately, and I figured out I need to tell somebody before I get to see the Old Man. The way I read the scriptures, I'm gonna have to explain everything I've done to the Almighty Hisself. So I think it's a thin thread I'm hanging by."

"Uncle Will, don't you think you ought to talk to a preacher? I don't know about confession or nothing like that, but I remember one time you told me you didn't believe it made any difference whether you confessed or not."

"I said that, Nephew, but the last several weeks I've been readin' up on this, and I think I was wrong for more than one reason. The Book says if we want to go off to Heaven we've got to confess our

sins. On top of that, every time I close my eyes I start dreaming about Ol' Ebo, I gotta keep running, trying to get away from him. I can't hardly breathe when I ain't running. There is something I gotta do to get this burden off of my soul. I don't think I can go another night, 'cause every time I shut my eyes, I see that fire-belching monster calling me.

"Remember one time you asked me why I called Satan, Ol' Ebo. You remember that?"

"Of course, I remember that, Uncle Will. Nobody else I've heard ever called him that. Only you—everybody else says 'devil.' But you said you wasn't gonna tell me why, so I took you at your word."

"I said that, and at the time I meant it. But I think the Almighty Hisself is sending me these terrible dreams every night. That same dream I had on the train after me and Willy split up. I think the Almighty is giving me one last chance to put my life in order before I cross over. According to the Scriptures I'm readin', the only way I can do it is to confess to somebody. I've got a lot to confess, and I ain't got much time to do it.

"The reason I called you, Nephew, is you're the only person on the face of this earth who'll take a spell and listen to what I got to say. Ain't no preacher gonna do it—I ain't got no money. So I ain't gonna be around to put my coins in the collection plate every Sunday. No, there ain't no preacher who's gonna listen."

"Uncle Will, you don't know that, and I don't know how to listen to no confession. Ain't nothing I can do for you. I ain't even had a lot of experience at it myself. I always start praying when I get in trouble, but, so far, I don't remember it ever doing me any good.

"I remember one time when I was 6 or 7 years old, I went to let the chickens out of the coop. The skunks and the weasels were catching and killing all of 'em. So we built a little coop to put the chickens in. They were just more or less boxes with some slats placed close together so the weasels or skunks couldn't climb through—you've seen 'em.

"It was pretty heavy for me when I picked the coop up. The old hen and the little biddies started out from under it, and they took their own time. It got so heavy I couldn't hold it no longer, so I dropped it and squashed one of them baby chickens.

"Right away, I set to praying that Ma wouldn't beat me. I mean I was praying hard. Would you believe she just happened to walk out the door and see that little chicken's head stickin' out from under the coop. She came over and beat the livin' shit out of me, with me praying as hard as I could, right up to the time she started whacking me. So either prayer ain't no good or I don't know how to do it. I'll be glad to listen to what you've got to say because I've always liked to hear the tales you tell, but I ain't makin' no promises about it doin' any good. I just want you to understand that."

"Nephew, I understand that. You don't have to make any promises to me. I just feel like it's something I hafta do. I'd like for my soul to rest easy when passing over, and it ain't gonna be long. I'd hate to go with Ol' Ebo chasing me through the alleys of all hell.

"Let me tell you, Nephew, there's alleys, tunnels, and rooms in Hell. It's something like you ain't never seen. I've seen it in my dreams. I know what it's like and you don't want to go there. Never kill nobody. I ain't never had no peace since I killed that Pinkerton detective. But you know, Nephew, if I was back in the same circumstances I'd still kill the son-of-a-bitch."

"Now Uncle Will, don't get yourself excited, you know it ain't good for you. The nurse is gonna run me out of here if she has to come in while we're talking."

"Nephew, I know I need to get better control of my temper. I swear I am standing at death's door still getting all mad and upset about something that happened 50 years ago. It's always been my downfall; it's what caused me to kill those folks. That and liquor together just made me a wild man. And some of them juices are still flowing, though they ain't flowing much.

"I guess you could say I got you up here partially under false pretenses. You see, I plumb run out of money. I can't pay the hospital, can't pay the doctor bill. It's expensive to stay in this hospital; they charge $12 a day just for the room. My doctor bill and medicines are probably going to cost me close to $20 a day, and I ain't got no money. One thing I never did, Nephew, I never begged. I stole, I lied, and I held up banks, but I never did beg.

"Remember when me and you went fishing down on the Tallapoosa River and I showed you the old farm I owned, where

me and Fannie Hawk spent about two years together; do you remember that place?"

"Of course, I do, Uncle Will; you took me down there this past
spring. Both of us damn near drowned. The river got up over the
wheels of that old bus we were in. If it wasn't for that farmer, we
both would have drowned."

"You remember, we got there before dark and I showed you
around the house me and Fannie lived in. There was an old churn
sitting on the hearth of the fireplace. Remember, I told you about
burying all the money from that poker game up in Maine. I also
told you about digging it up and moving it—more than once—
because I was wearing a trail through the weeds and people could
see there was something going on. Every time I'd walk the grass
and weeds down, I'd dig it up and bury it somewhere else."

"I remember that, Uncle Will."

"Well, here's the part I didn't tell you. I've still got $10,000 buried
down there on that old farm. Ain't nobody but you and me in this
world who knows about it. Remember, I told you I built a room
onto the house when Fannie Hawk moved in?"

"I remember."

"Before we built that room onto the house, I buried it right in
front of the fireplace. It's down about two feet deep. You're gonna
have to go get the money for me. There ain't nobody else in the
world I'd trust with that much money.

"You have to take the floor up and dig two feet away from the
edge of the hearth. It's about two feet deep and it's dead in the
middle of the hearth. You think you can get me the money so I
can pay my hospital bill? I'd rather go to Hell than owe these sons-
of-bitches for one day. If you'll promise me you'll do that, and do
it quick, then I'll rest easier. Do you remember how to get there?"

"Yes, sir, I remember how to get there. But Uncle Will, I'll have
to wait until Saturday or Sunday. I know Ma won't let me have
the car before then, and maybe not even then. I may have to get
somebody else to take me; that's 25 miles from home."

"Will you do it this weekend? As soon as you dig the money up,
I want you to put it in a sack, drop it in the trunk, go back home,
and hide it good. I'll tell you how much to bring me because I'll be

so weak I ain't gonna be able to go nowhere. So I'm gonna need somebody to take me everywhere, but if I got money, there's somebody'll do what I want.

"I was saving that $10,000 for my old age, I never once thought about how, when I got old, I ain't gonna be able to dig it up. Right now I couldn't dig it up if it was two inches under the ground—I ain't got the strength. Nephew, you are the only one I got in the whole world. Ain't nobody else in the family who'd even speak to me. If I sent any of my other nephews down there, they'd take the money and tell me to go to Hell, but I know you won't. I know you'll do what I ask ya. Will you go this weekend?"

"Yessir."

"You ain't got no idea what a burden you've lifted off my mind, but it's important you don't tell another living soul. It's also important you don't take anybody down there with you. And it's important when you get there, you tell Josh Webster you're going fishin'. Tell him I'm near dead is the reason I ain't with you. I think he bought the land; I'm not even sure who owned it after I sold it, but you gotta be careful. You ain't stealing nothing, it's mine, but if somebody caught you getting it out, it'd be hard to explain how a 17-year-old boy has $10,000. And if the sheriff knowed about it, and knowed it was mine, he'd know I stole it.

"The old floor was pretty rotten when we were down there. I think you can just knock a hole through the floorboards with a pick, dig it up, and get out of there quick. And if Josh asks why you came out so quick, tell him the fish ain't bitin'."

"Yessir."

"Now, I got to tell you why I call the Devil, Ol' Ebo. I first had this dream 50 years ago, but I'm having it every night now—it's the same dream. Last night I had the dream as usual. The nurses woke me up and said I was screaming and howling like the hounds of Hades were chasing every step I took. As a matter of fact, it was worse than that. I'd had my old dream alright, but after they woke me up, I started off on a new dream when sleep came again.

"In the new dream I looked down on my body—and it was stone dead. The next thing I knew, I was standing in front of a marble building. It looked like a government warehouse of some kind.

There was a huge door, big enough you could drive six trucks through it at one time. It had angels and all sorts of artwork carved all over the door.

"There was a long set of steps up to the building and I was standing at the bottom. At the top of the steps were two old men in togas—I think that's what they call them. Anyway, some kind of long flowing robes. Each had a staff in his hand and each had a long white beard. Standing there talking to these men was Ol' Ebo in all of his splendor—and he is one imposing bastard.

"I ain't told you nothing about Ebo, nothing of why I call him Ebo. I'm coming to that, I'm gonna tell you my dream, but I gotta tell you this new dream first. This is what made me have the hospital call you.

"Nephew, I thought I was fearful from the dream about Ebo, but my heart knew no fear till them two old men and Ebo motioned me to come on up them steps. My feet felt like lead. I could barely lift one foot to the next step. I didn't want to go, but I couldn't keep from it, step, by step, by step—it must've been a hundred steps.

"Finally, I was on a big veranda in front of that enormous golden door. I took a closer look at the door; it had pearls all amongst the gold and diamonds and other precious jewels.

"In one of the softest, kindliest voices I've ever heard, the old man on the right said, 'Will, we've been waiting for you, come in.'

"Without any visible signal, the doors opened just wide enough for the four of us. Nephew, it looked like it was a mile to the front of the room. Sitting in the middle of the room was an elevated platform. On the platform was a chair, and in that chair looking out over the room was a man who looked just like pictures of Jesus you see in the churches.

"The four of us walked down the long aisle. Looking around, the seats were filled with people on both sides. I knowed a lot of those people. Some of 'em I hadn't seen for 40 years, but everyone I'd knowed for a fact was dead. Dead and buried. But they was sittin' there, and it appeared they were waitin' for me.

"We walked all the way to the front. One of the old men took me by the arm, and guided me to a table off to the left. A table just like I'd sat at when they tried me for murder. He said, 'I'm gonna try to defend you, Will, but your eternal soul is about to be put on trial. Ebo's come for your soul, and I need to know anything you can tell me that might help us to save you.'

"I was paralyzed. I couldn't utter a word. That's when the nurse woke me the second time.

"'Mr. Will, I swear I don't know what we're going to do with you. What on earth have you done to give you such terrible nightmares?'

"That, Nephew, is when I told her to call and get you to come. And Lord, I'm glad you come. But now let me tell you my dream about Ebo.

"It happened long, long years ago, I've dreamed it a thousand times. It's always been the same, and this is why I call Ebo—Ebo."

Will Meets Ebo

"Nephew, I was laying drunk in my private compartment on the train across New York State that first night after I killed the Pinkerton detective. I woke up near 11 o'clock in a cold sweat. I couldn't shake a horrible recurring vision of that Pinkerton man tumbling from brace to brace down into the bottomless ravine. When I'd pushed him off the back of the observation car, he'd fallen head first. His head struck the rail, and his momentum carried him over the side of the trestle where the first wooden cross-brace caught his body, and then tossed it onto the next brace. Down, down he went, spinning from brace to brace until he literally disappeared from view. That damned sight is burned into my brain.

"I got out of my compartment and looked up a porter who sold me a quart of whiskey for $10. I drank the liquor, went back to sleep, and the dream started right up again.

"Now my dream shifted, and I was transported high above the earth, with a gentle breeze caressing every nerve in my body. Looking side-to-side, I saw a giant wing on my right side, and looking to the other side, saw a second great wing whose feathers were flaked with gold. I wiggled my arms, but now they were wings, and I could feel the breeze caressing every feather on my arms. The soft breezes took me higher and higher, but I was unafraid, and could see for miles.

"I turned and cartwheeled off to the right in great swooping dives. The land seemed to roll under me. Ahhh, the sight was as pretty as the pink on a gourd vine.

"Far below, I caught a glimpse of a farmer plowing a field. My eyesight was unbelievably sharp—it was Pa in that field. He stopped Ol' Jack, his mule, looked up at me, took off his big straw hat, and waved at me like he knowed who I was. Pa can't know who I am. Why is he waving at me?

"I thought maybe my eyesight was playing tricks, so I folded my wings tight against my body, and went diving toward the ground. I had to be sure I saw what I thought I saw. When I was still 400 or

500 feet up, I spread those amazin' wings, and gently as a baby's breath, they brought me almost to a stop.

"It was Pa alright. He was in the cornfield, where the stalks was just a little more than knee high. He was sittin' on the crossbar of the plowstock, rolling himself a cigaret from a Prince Albert can. Every once in a while, he would glance up at me, taking his hat off and wave to me. I couldn't understand how he knowed it was me, but he did.

"This troubled me, so I let the winds carry me higher again while I tried to figure out how Pa knew that I was the eagle he saw soaring above. Gliding in a big lazy circle, I watched as Pa went about his plowing.

"Then I saw Pa going to the edge of the woods. He turned Ol' Jack around, stopped, left the plow, and walked into the trees where I couldn't see him. A minute later, he came back with a rifle, pointed it at me, and suddenly a great pain gripped my chest. I started tumbling end over end, watching the feathers rip from my wings one at a time as I went spinning to the ground, unable to move a muscle. With feathers flying everywhere, I lost consciousness.

"I landed on the ground with a thud, and now I was just me again, this time walking along behind the plow following Ol' Jack across a rocky field. How could I be two things at the same time? First, I was flying high up, and the next moment, I was back plowing in the fields. Both were surely me. But how can you do that? Well you can do anything in a dream, nephew. There ain't no rules for dreams. I tell you, there ain't no rules for dreams.

"I went on plowing the field, and watched the rocks roll over and break the cornstalks. Every time I passed a stalk, a rock rose out of the ground, rolled over, and broke it. Looking behind me, there wasn't a single stalk of corn standing. Every one had been broken by a rock the plow had pulled up.

"I told Ol' Jack, 'Haw,' to move toward the middle of the row. But the plow just kept snatching up rocks as it passed each stalk of corn, and the rocks rolled over the stalks, popping each one off at the joint just above the ground. No matter where I plowed the row, there was always a rock just beneath the ground that rolled up and broke the stalks.

"I said 'Whoa' to Ol' Jack, and turned to look at the field be-hind me. The cornstalks were wilting—first the ones closest to me, then further on back, they were curling up, turning brown, crum-bling to dust. Looking ahead again, the corn was still lush and green. But behind me it was flying away in dust.

"I left Ol' Jack standing there, and walked ahead a hundred feet through the green corn. Looking back at Ol' Jack standing in the furrow, I saw he hadn't moved. But the corn between us, and on beyond, had wilted, crumbled to dust, and the wind was wafting it away. So I began to understand it was me who was destroying every-thing—not the rocks, not the mule, not the weather, just me.

"Off in the distance I could see dark smoke rising slowly from what looked like a low hill. And I felt an uncontrollable desire to head off toward that column of smoke. As I got to the end of the corn rows, I entered a meadow of wildflowers. When I had gone only a couple of hundred feet, I turned and saw how the wildflow-ers too were now beginning to droop and wither away.

"Presently, I topped a little ridge. Stretched out before me was a meadow shaped like a shallow basin where a stream ran some ten or fifteen feet wide. By now, daylight was fading.

"Alongside the brook a figure in a black cape stood with his back to me. He appeared to be stirring a huge washpot, a black cast iron pot, like the one Ma always washed our clothes in. I didn't want to go one step further, but I had no choice. I approached within a foot. The figure never turned, but I could tell that, whoever or whatever it was, it knew I was there.

"From the back, the cape was fan-shaped at the top, small at the neck but widening out above. I shuffled crab-like to get around so I could see who it was. When I stood full-face in front of the giant, I saw why. There was a huge horn growing out of each side of his head. The skin and the horns were as black as the ace of clubs. His eyes were round glowing embers of fire, the same as Ol' Jack's.

"He smiled at me and said, 'Greetings, Will,' with the most evil looking grin I'd ever seen.

"Standing there in sheer terror, dreading the answer I knew would come, I stammered, 'Who are you?' But the answer still startled me. 'Call me Ebo,' the apparition said.

"The first reply didn't startle me as much as the one I was about to hear. I thought maybe he'd say I am the Devil, Ol' Scratch, Lucifer, Ruler of the Other Realm, or some such. But instead he responded, 'No, those are all different names by which my father is known— but now he works for me!'

"I looked down for the first time into the pot of bubbling, stinking broth he was constantly stirring. It was greenish yellow with the consistency of thick corn meal mush. Bubbles burst and spewed bilious droplets over the surface of the brew. The escaping steam caused my eyes to burn, my throat to gag, my lungs to rebel.

"I said hoarsely, 'You mean you're in charge of Hell, you have power over Satan?'"

"'Will, word travels slowly in your world, and it's really none of your business. But since we're going to be spending eternity together, there's no reason why you shouldn't know my genealogy. I am Ebo, the firstborn from the passions of Pandora and Lucifer.'

"'When my mother, Pandora, arrived in Hell to begin her punishment for the wickedness everybody knows about, the passion that sprung up between Lucifer and her was so overwhelming they copulated continuously for forty days and forty nights. I was conceived during the first hour, and the fire of their passion during that forty days and forty nights burned every cell in my being as black as ebony. Pandora swore everlasting and eternal fidelity to Lucifer, but nine months later when I was born, Lucifer flew into a towering rage. Because I was black and they were white, he was convinced I was the result of Pandora's infidelity, and he tried to destroy me.

"'Pandora managed to send me to the temperate zone of his domain and hide me until I was fully grown. But he searched endlessly, and I lived in terror of the day I would have to confront him. That day arrived in time, but so powerful had I become in surviving raw nature that I defeated him with a single blow, and took him captive. Dante told of Satan's imprisonment, but nobody's ever believed him except for a pitiful few Catholics. Now I, Ebo, have him staked down in the deepest pit, the lowest ring of Hell, where icicles form from his tears and freeze his eyelids to the ground. He'll stay there welded in that terrible rigid position as long as I want. That, Will, is what I've done to my own father. Can you imagine what I now have in store for you?'

"A hellfire grin spread across Ebo's face, and I awoke in a terrible trembling sweat. Afraid to close my eyes, afraid that Ebo's dreadful apparition would visit my dreams again, I refused to sleep for days. But we mortal folk can only stay awake so long, and so three days later, when fatigue overcame me, and I could no longer hold my eyes open or resist any longer, my eyes closed while I was still riding the train. No sooner had sleep smeared my thoughts, than I was transported back to the desolate meadow where all the corn and wildflowers lay still crumbling to dust, blowing away in the wind. And Ebo was once again staring at me eye to eye.

"He wheeled and said, 'Follow me,' pointing in the direction of a tiny stream emerging from a cave in the face of a high cliff. I could see a flickering light that seemed to come from deep within the cave—Ebo headed straight for it. Much against my will, I followed. We crossed the little brook, scrambled up the side of the cliff, and went in.

"Deeper and deeper we went into the bowels of the earth, coming eventually to an opening in what seemed to be a solid rock wall. Emerging onto a small ledge, I gazed down on a huge lake of bilious, green soup that stank of death. There I could see many people I knew, and many I didn't know, swimming frantically. An enormous shark with white teeth, looking much like Ebo, leapt in and out of that soup, diving after the frantic swimmers one after another. As the ferocious creature captured each helpless victim, you could see it's teeth slice through the body, then with one great gulp, the beast swallowed both pieces of the hapless victim. I couldn't look, and turned away.

"'No stomach for such amusement?' Ebo asked.

"We continued down the passageway we had just entered. Every few moments we would pass other openings in the tunnel's walls from which poured the most terrifying screams of humans in agony I've ever heard.

"Nephew, I never was much at school. Our teacher, Miss Yates, read aloud from a book every day just before recess, and I remember the terrifying things that happened to the people in that book.

I thought in those days, it's a fairytale story, but in my dream's now, those events are real.

"The strangest thing is that I knew I was dreaming, yet I couldn't believe I was dreaming. I was sleeping in another level of consciousness, and I couldn't do anything about it but marinate in my own terror. I couldn't command myself to wake, and so down, down we descended. I could feel the temperature fall, and I began to shiver, not just from my fear, but from the terrible cold that seemed to penetrate my bones, even as I knew I was dreaming. Suddenly, the tunnel ended, and a vast glacial expanse stretched before me. Some chunks of ice canted crazily, like Indian teepees. In the far distance, I could see a lone figure bent beneath a heavy accumulation of ice and snow. Icicles thick as walking sticks stretched from the floor to his head.

"As we started across that forbidding icescape, I knew in my heart I was about to come face to face with Ebo's father. I wondered whether Dante himself had been here in another dream, a thousand years earlier. Ebo strode resolutely forward. In a few moments, we stood before an ice-draped creature whose profuse tears were hardening even as they poured down the icicles to the cave's floor.

"Ebo turned to me with those burning, red eyes and said, 'Will, this is my father, better known as Satan, Lucifer, Scratch, the Devil, the Ruler of the Underworld. What a laugh. They should change all of the books and give me proper credit. Behold the Devil. I, Ebo, rule the Underworld.'"

"Nephew, I couldn't stand the dream any longer. I fought with every fiber in my body to open my eyes. Succeeding, I looked out the pullman car window and felt such terrible, tired exhaustion as you will never know while the North Carolina countryside slid by.

"I got up and walked the length of the train. I didn't think I could stand to shut my eyes ever again and risk seeing that awful scene, though I knew I couldn't stay awake forever. I had a huge sum of money in my bags, but was truly the most miserable human on the face of this earth. The train pulled into the Winston-Salem station. Even though I had a ticket to Atlanta, I stepped off and went to Salem, North Carolina.

"I took a brisk walk to a nearby hotel where I checked the bag with most of the money in the hotel safe. I rented a room and followed the porter up the stairs. As soon as he unlocked the room, and handed me the key, I asked him where I could get a bottle of liquor. He said, 'North Carolina is a dry state. There ain't no whiskey in a 100 miles of here.' I pulled out a roll of money and peeled off a $100 bill. I thought his eyes would pop right out of his head. I said, 'Young man, I've got the Devil's own thirst, and I aim to have some liquor. Are you going to get it for me, or am I going to have to go out and get it for myself?'"

"He said, 'It will cost you $10, it's homemade, but it's good.'"

"'Get me a gallon. Have it back here in 15 minutes.'"

"Fifteen minutes later, the porter was back at my door carrying a little market basket with a couple of sandwiches on top. He picked up the towel he had over it, and underneath was four quart fruit jars of the magic elixir that was going to take me out of Ebo's reach. I offered the young man an opportunity to join me in a drink. He said, 'No sir, momma and daddy tell me that's the Devil's own brew.'

"'Your momma and daddy's right young man; I hope you'll believe them. But I'm gonna use the Devil's brew to get away from him.'"

"Wide-eyed, he asked, 'Will that be all, sir?'

"I dismissed him with the wave of my hand as I gulped down half-a-quart of the meanest liquor that ever crossed these lips. I pushed three quarts under the bed, then finished off the first one. Ten minutes later, I passed out. I would be free of Ebo for one night ...I thought.

"No sooner were my eyes closed, than I was back with Ebo, gazing at his pathetic father encased in his icy prison. The tears were running freely down the stony stalks drooping from his eyelids. They seemed to grow bigger by the moment. He walked around Lucifer until he stood directly in front of those white, frozen eyes. With a mocking tone and gesture, he waved his hands and said, 'Remember me, pop, Pandora's son, Ebo, your first born. Remember me?'

"Then he motioned me to follow him. We got only a few steps away when he turned and hissed to me, 'Just in case you're thinking I might have a little streak of pity or compassion, remember that's my father.'

"Soon, Ebo made a left turn through the tunnel wall, and I followed. Cowering in one corner with his hand held up in front of his face, I now saw a frail, spent man lying in bed amidst the most luxurious pillows and counterpanes I've ever seen. A powerful handsome woman beckoned, and then pointed to a pathetic creature cowering in the corner. Ebo said, 'Meet my mother, Pandora. That shriveled husk in the corner is her lover, Don Juan. Pandora, with her infinite, insatiable passion, has long since sucked all the juice from him, but he's obliged to keep on marching like an army through a whorehouse.' Pandora waved warmly as we left the bed chamber.

"Coming to another door, Ebo said, "This is where our rapists are rewarded. As far as I could see, there was a huge gathering of vultures, the great condors, and spread-eagled before each giant bird was a man. The ravenous condors tore a testicle from each man's sack, while the poor souls let out the most hideous screams imaginable. As each condor swallowed the testicle, another grew in its place, and the process was endlessly repeated. With a shudder, I turned my head. Ebo pushed me rudely back into the tunnel, and we proceeded upward.

"A little further ahead, I heard screams even more terrible than those we had just escaped. Ebo turned, his fiery eyes on me. 'Will, the next room is where the murderers are kept, and of course you're numbered among those. As a matter of fact, the man you killed, Steve Young, is also here. He, too, was a murderer, and you, Will, are scheduled to be his assistant throughout eternity. Would you like a little preview of what you will be doing?'

"My terror was so great that not even the liquor could keep me unconscious. I bolted up in bed; my clothes were soaked. They stank of alcohol—decaying, rotten alcohol."

I could contain myself no longer, and innocently asked, "Uncle Will, did you ever look at the place where you're gonna be?"

"Nephew, I did look, but I won't burden your mind with what I saw. But Nephew, hear me well. Despite all the terrible things I've done since I killed Steve Young, despite having toured Hell with Ebo hisself, I still did all the terrible things I'm about to tell you. And as my time comes nigh, Nephew, I feel a powerful dread."

When Uncle Will finished relating his awful story, the room was quiet for several minutes except for his labored breathing. I was overwhelmed, and couldn't imagine anybody living in that kind of terror for 50 years. I wanted so badly to do something to help this feeble giant know at least a trace of peace before he departed this life. To me, that event looked to be coming soon.

He was the first to break the silence.

"Now, Nephew, can you understand the urgency of my situation? Do you understand why I have to have some relief? I've become convinced over the past few weeks that the only way I can get any relief from these terrible nightmares is to confess my sins. And you're the only one who will listen."

I couldn't help it, but my mind drifted back to a time years before when he'd had a wonderful opportunity to confess to a preacher, somebody who could do him good. Not me, just a boy, who didn't know anything and never had much faith in prayer, simply because for me it never had worked.

About this time the nurse came in and said, "Mr. Will, you're not tiring yourself out, are you?"

"No, young lady, I'm fine. Me and my nephew here, we're just talkin' over old times. It's awful good to have somebody you can talk to and trust, tell 'em about times in your life, and know they listen and care. It's important to have friends who will listen to you and talk to you. Don't forget that, young lady."

While she was working with Uncle Will, my mind drifted back to a summer night, seven or eight years earlier when I was just a little kid helping him do some work on his farm. We had decided one time to go to Wednesday night prayer meeting to hear a traveling evangelist.

The reverend had stopped alongside the road and spoken to Uncle Will a while before sundown. I remember him giving Uncle Will a business card and introducing himself as Preacher Harmon. He said something about him being a fisherman of men. I sat there reconstructing that afternoon and evening in my mind while the nurse was working.

It was about 4 o'clock when the preacher drove up and stopped. He had a white horse, a white surrey, and was dressed in white from head to toe. He was peddling salvation, something Uncle Will sorely needed at this very moment, but had refused then.

On that day long ago, I stood next to Uncle Will while Brother Harmon, dressed in his flamboyant white suit and panama hat, pulled out a card and handed it to him. The card read, 'Reverend Jacob Harmon, Graduate of the 1902 Class, Asbury Seminary, Kentucky, Dr. Divinity.' There was something on the back of the card that caught Uncle Will's attention. A circle an inch in diameter, inside of which was a fish. All around the circle were stars—many, many stars. Over on one side in very fine print it read, 'Fisher of Men.'

As Brother Harmon stood there chatting, the sun slipped lower while a bank of clouds in the west raised up a little bit. He turned around, pointed to the black bank of clouds, and said, "I thought I saw the lightning dancing across the top of those clouds. Did you see that?"

Uncle Will said, "Yes, I caught a flash out of the corner of my eye."

"Brother Will, does that suggest anything to you? That dark bank of clouds lying there with lightning dancing along the top edge of it?"

"Yeah, it suggests to me that we might be gettin' a shower, and we sure do need it."

Brother Harmon, more persistent, "But does it suggest anything of a spiritual nature to you, such as the handiwork of the Almighty?"

Uncle Will said, "I never thought that much about a thunderstorm. They make me nervous when they get to poppin' too close to me. I've seen balled lightning a time or two, but I never really thought too much about God setting loose a thunderstorm. I just thought it was some upheaval in the atmosphere that caused them. I don't really know what causes them. I suppose God's got something else to do besides skatin' thunderstorms around all over the country. If He's got his hand on all of 'em, He's busy as hell in the summertime."

Brother Harmon asked, "Do you not believe in God?"

"Oh, yes I believe in God. Sure do. I'd have a hell of time if I didn't. There's a lot of things I'd do, but I don't want to spend all eternity breathing sulfur and sizzling in a lake of fire."

"You know how you can avoid that, don't you, Will?"

"Preacher, why don't you worry about your own soul and leave me be."

'Will, promise me you'll be at the service tonight, will you?'

"I'll be there."

That night as we walked to church, the bank of clouds was still lying back tight on the horizon, but by then there were big flashes of lightning. Uncle Will watching the lightning said, "We could sure use a good rain. It'll make them strawberries produce twice as long, but that cloudbank's been lying back there for hours. It may have already rained itself out."

Aunt Beth said, "Will, if the Lord thinks we need rain, we'll get a rain."

"Beth, the Lord ain't got a damn thing to do with it. Nobody knows what causes thunderclouds; it sure ain't the Lord. He's got better things to do than fool around with little summer thunderstorms."

"Will, I do declare. Some day you are gonna learn that you don't know everything, though I don't know what it's going to take."

Old Shiloh Church was built like a lot of churches in those days. There were two front doors and an alcove at the front of the sanctuary that looked something like a bay window. There were two windows on either side of the pulpit, and the lectern sat just in front of those windows. There was a bench for visiting ministers or other dignitaries that extended around the alcove.

Brother Harmon took charge of everything. By the time we got there, the church was half full, and they were singing hymns so loud, you could hear them for half a mile in any direction. At the back of the alcove, about 6 feet high, there was a shelf that extended all the way across between the windows, and on which there were three kerosene lamps.

As they finished the hymn, Brother Harmon requested that the windows be raised. "It's getting awful stuffy. It appears there is a thunderstorm approaching us from the west, and maybe it will give us a cooling breeze."

He mounted the platform. It seemed as if he looked every soul in the congregation directly in the eye. He turned his back on the flock for a moment, and then facing them again with a flourish, he said in a booming voice, "I hope the Almighty God never does to you what I just did...turns His back on you. I promise you there is a way to prevent that from ever happening. I am going to talk to you, people of God about that very thing for the next hour. I'll tell

you right now, my sermons last exactly one hour. Not one minute
more, not one minute less. Anybody who ain't got that much time
to spend here tonight in worshiping the Lord, get up and leave now.

"I don't want nobody fidgeting around, looking out the windows,
or looking up at the ceiling. I want you looking at me. I want your
undivided attention for the next hour. If not, the hours you are
going to spend in Hell are immeasurable. Especially when it only
takes one hour to guarantee...it's guaranteed by this book," as he
slaps the Bible across his hand, 'that you will spend eternity in
adoration and praising the Lord for what you can do in this one
hour. If you don't do that, and if you don't have another chance,
you are going to burn in Hell forever and ever. I can't impress on
you how long forever is. I got my calling from God Almighty himself to go forth across this land and spread the word of how you get
salvation. Without it, you pitiful creatures are doomed. Nothing
more than chaff blowing in the wind."

As Brother Harmon walked back and forth across the stage, the
shadows cast by the altar lamps grew darker, then lighter, rippling
across the back wall as if there were some moving spirit disturbing the
surface of a quiet pond. His thunderous voice called on all souls present
to repent of their sins. The sound of distant thunder began to echo
across the sanctuary whenever the preacher paused in his sermon.

Now a gentle wind began to waft through the open windows,
making the flames from the lamps dance still more wildly, dou-
bling the mesmerizing flicker of the shadows they cast as they flit-
ted back and forth across the back of the pulpit. For the first time,
Preacher Harmon seemed to take notice of the gathering storm.
He called the congregation to observe the handiwork of God. And
as if in response to this attention, a mighty clap of thunder crashed
down on the sanctuary. It shook the building, as if to punctuate so
awe-inspiring a moment, and a gale-force wind rushed through the
sanctuary, extinguishing all the kerosene lamps. Out of the darkness, the thunderous voice of Reverend Harmon roared, "Behold,
the awesome power of the Almighty!"

Once again, lightning danced across the countryside. The tomb-
stones around Old Shiloh Church stood like ghostly soldiers in
perfect order. Preacher Harmon kept going full force through ev-

ery thunderclap, "The Almighty is doing this to water the corn. Think what He would do if He were angry with us."

Another explosion of thunder shook the church to its foundation. "How can any sinner witness this awesome display of the power of the Almighty and not confess his sins? It doesn't make sense. How can a man harden his heart before such a demonstration of the power of the Almighty? I invite each and every one of you to come forward, to reaffirm your faith in the Almighty. Those of you who have stepped forward before, and those of you have not, I urge you to come at this moment, repent of your sins, and join the brotherhood of the children of God, so that one day we shall all gather at the river and cross over into that land where there will be no more sorrow. There will be no death. There will be nothing but brotherly love for each of you. Come now."

The entire church—filed forward to the altar and knelt down. The young and the old, the crippled, and the lame gathered in front of the altar. Each of them in his own way was confessing and repenting of his sins and asking Brother Harmon for the right hand of fellowship to join Jesus Christ and walk amongst the saved. But Uncle Will sat like a stone in the back of the church. I got up, went to the alter, and knelt with the rest of the congregation. Reverend Harmon scared the shit out of me.

By then the thunder was almost a continuous roar, and the lightning danced about outside almost brighter than high noon. As the congregation stood huddled in a prayerful attitude, Brother Harmon descended from the pulpit and went straight to Uncle Will's pew. Bending down on one knee, he pointed a finger at Uncle Will's face and said, "Sinner, repent. I offer you salvation this moment." Once again, with a mighty blast, thunder rocked the church's foundation. I didn't see how he could sit quiet the way he did with Brother Harmon yelling at him, "Accept salvation, Will." The third time he said it, he stood up and marched back to the front of the church as the storm reached its full fury. Then he walked back along the edge of the stage, knelt among the congregation, and uttered up a prayer asking the Almighty to intercede and quiet the storm. He begged the Almighty to restore some measure of calm to the troubled people, to throw oil upon the troubled waters.

Almost as suddenly as the storm had burst upon us, it passed on. Brother Harmon asked the members closest to the lamps to relight them and close the windows. Then he finished his sermon.

"Brothers and sisters, I extend the right hand of fellowship from God Almighty Himself. Those of you who take my hand as I march between your kneeling figures will save yourself from the fury of the Almighty come judgment day. The demonstration tonight has been just a tiny sample of the awesome power and wrath of the Almighty. You do not wish to provoke His wrath. Those souls who refuse the gift of everlasting life will reside forever in damnation.

"And what is your name? Bless you, bless you. Bless you. I count twelve people who have accepted the right hand of fellowship, who have accepted eternal salvation. But I would point out to you that tonight you have only fulfilled half of your contract. You must still be baptized, so the cleansing blood of Jesus can remove from you the taint of original sin and guarantee you a ticket to the Promised Land. I am going to hold a baptizing on Indian Creek at the old wash hole Sunday morning at nine AM. For those of you who have come part way, come on in and enjoy the full fellowship. I'm going to issue an invitation now for anybody who would like to think it over."

The pretty little nurse smelling of alcohol and ether brushed past me as she left the room, plucking my mind back to the present from that night long ago. But I was thinking, "Why didn't he accept salvation then; why wait till now? And why do I have to hear his confession? I don't know nothing 'bout such things, I'm just a kid. But I remembered how the preacher said every Sunday, 'Why not confess your sins today—you may not live to have another chance.'"

I never once thought that might apply to me, but now as I sat there looking at Uncle Will, I remembered how just two weeks earlier the prettiest little girl in my class, was killed in a car wreck. Sitting there in the hospital room with Uncle Will, I realized the preacher was right. Maybe I ought to think more seriously about some of the things I did. Maybe I, too, ain't immortal.

I guessed the shot the nurse gave Uncle Will was finally taking effect on him. He weakly raised his hand and said, "Nephew, I feel like I can go to sleep now, but promise me you'll come back tomorrow night and we'll get this business over with."

The Flood

On the way home, my mind was scattering like a fart in a whirlwind. Somehow I had to get Ma to let me use the car to go over to Alabama and retrieve Uncle Will's $10,000. Ten thousand dollars was a sum of money I could not comprehend. The great uncle I half despised and half loved, but everybody else straight out hated, had chosen me to be his father confessor, a role I did not relish.

How could I hide his money, then get it to him when he wanted it? Even though I was strong and able-bodied, I was still pretty much at the mercy of Ma's whims. I sure couldn't take somebody down to the Tallapoosa River, and let them watch me dig up $10,000.

By the time I got home, it was 10 o'clock. Everybody was already sleeping as I tumbled into bed, and I worried about all these complications. Uncle Will, why couldn't you keep things simple like everybody else? But eventually I drifted off to a dreamless sleep.

The next morning I asked Ma for the car again that night. As before, she said the only way I could get it was to fill it back up with gas. She'd already been out to check the fuel gage, and it showed only three quarters full. She wasn't sure I'd filled it up before I went to Bremen; if I had, I'd also gone somewhere else.

Of course, Ma knew better than anybody in the world how to set me off. I yelled back at her, "You'd skin a gnat for it's tallow, Ma. You can see it in everybody else, but you can't see it in yourself. I did fill the car up! And someday you will be old and near dead, I hope folks'll be kinder to you than you want me to be to Uncle Will."

Immediately I wished I hadn't said it. Maybe I didn't like Ma very much, but I really didn't want to cause her pain. Sometimes, when I flared up like that, it reminded me of something Uncle Will would do. Believe me, I didn't want all the trouble he had; no siree, that I didn't need.

As soon as I finished breakfast I grabbed the milk bucket and headed for the barn to milk the cow. When I finished the chores

29

for Ma, I took a bath, and finished just in time to catch Harvey's ride back to my job at the shoe factory.

The only reason I kept the stinkin' job at General Shoe was a little girl named Julie New. She was 17 years old, the same as me. We'd go off under the trees outside the plant and eat our lunch and drink a soda pop together. But I was so bashful around her I could hardly talk. After several weeks, I felt at ease while she was around, except when she got too close and I smelled her perfume. I'd get sort of dizzy-headed. After lunch, we'd sit and talk, and I'd have to walk around with my hands in my pocket holding ol' Pete down till I could get my mind off Julie.

Every day I'd ask her for a date, and every day she'd tell me her daddy said she wasn't old enough to date. Every day I'd ask her how she could work and earn her own money, and still always have to do what her Ma and daddy told her. She'd point out she didn't have any other place to live, except at her Ma and daddy's; so she had to do what they told her.

Looking back years later, I figured out Julie liked me as much as I liked her. Every time she turned me down for a date, she did it in a way that said, "Why don't you marry me and make me a house. I'll be glad to marry you. But right now daddy won't let me date you." All that went right over my head. I never could take a hint about nothing. Something had to jump up and slap me in the face before I realized what was going on. I never could pick up the little things most folks had no trouble with.

I described to Harvey on the way home just how seriously sick Uncle Will was and how I had to go back and sit with him until bedtime that night. I tried to feel out, without directly asking him, whether he'd be interested in taking me to Alabama, knowing I was gonna have one heck of a time persuadin' Ma to let me have the car. As a matter of fact, I knew I was gonna have to lie to her in order to get the damn car.

I didn't really want to do that, but then, on the other hand, I couldn't let Harvey take me down there, either. If I came out of the shack with a croker sack in my hand, Harvey would sure want to know what was in it. What was I gonna tell him? I had to figure out a way to get a car, dig up the money, and sneak it home without anybody knowing about it but me. When we reached the house, Harvey turned right, I jumped out, went and fetched the milk bucket, and headed for the barn to do my chores.

Ma was out in the garden picking string beans. I asked her if she was gonna let me have the car again to go see Uncle Will. Just to soften her up a bit, I also told her I wanted to visit a friend in Tallapoosa that coming weekend.

She immediately started yelling at me. "You're wearing the car out and we don't have enough money to buy another one. What do you need to go to Tallapoosa for?" I really didn't like to lie to Ma, but I figured if I told her I was doing something for Uncle Will, the first thing she'd want to know is what it was. I knew I was going to have to lie, so I took a short cut and said, "There's a little girl who works at the plant and I want to go and meet her family. She's got a car of her own, but I don't want to seem like no pauper by having her come and get me."

I took a calculated gamble, "She said she'd come pick me up if I couldn't get our car." We had been poor all our life, but Ma sure didn't want nobody thinking we was poor. So she said, "I'll let you go there Saturday morning, provided you drop by Bud Cole's and fill the car up as soon as you get back. Me and your Pa are thinking about taking a little trip Sunday and I want the car to be full of gas. That's the only way I'm gonna let you have it, do you hear that young man?"

"Yes ma'am, I'll do it."

I made a mental note to ask Uncle Will if I couldn't use some of his $10,000 to pay my expenses since I was doing all this for him. Meanwhile, to keep Ma happy, I went to the barn, put old Bossy's feed in the trough, set down on the milk stool, stuck my head in her flank, washed her sack off, and started milking.

Snowflake showed up as she always did, and I gave her the usual pop of warm milk, just enough to make her whole day. You could almost tell the cat was smiling and wishing the blessings of the Lord on me. She lapped every drop of it off her mouth, so I gave her another shot.

Just about that time, old Bossy picked up her right hoof and set it down right in the middle of the milk bucket. As you might expect she had cowshit all over her hoof, so I had to pour the milk out. I poured it in the bowl for Snowflake, went back to the house, washed the bucket, and got some more water to clean her sack off again. While I was gone, Bossy finished her feed and wandered back to the pasture, so when I got back to the barn, I had to run her down. All the time I was thinking, "Uncle Will, why can't you be like everybody else. I don't need the trouble. Now I'm gonna catch hell because I ain't got a full bucket of milk."

I went to the house with only half a bucket of milk, and Ma lit right in on me. I told her Bossy'd stuck her hoof into the milk bucket, but she started telling me about how careless I was. So I told her if she didn't shut up, next time I'd finish milking right on top of the cowshit and let her drink it. As usual, me and Ma got in a cuss fight. I still had to slop the hogs and get in the stove wood for cooking breakfast the next morning. When my chores were done, I finally got to take a sponge bath.

When Pa came home from work, we sat down to supper while I fussed with my young brother and sister about why they couldn't go to the hospital. My sister pointed out that she was 15 years old; my little brother pointed out he was 11 and they wasn't kids no more, they were all grown up.

Finally, Ma put a stop to the feudin' and told us if we didn't shut up she wasn't gonna let us have no supper. As soon as I finished dinner, I started washing the dishes, which was another one of the many penalties Ma'd made me pay for getting use of the car again that night.

When I finally stepped into the car to head off for the hospital, I was feeling pretty good. At least I had a promise from Ma that I could use the car Saturday, so now I could tell Uncle Will I'd made progress. But I dreaded seeing him if he was as sick as he'd been the night before. I sort of wished he was dead, then felt ashamed of myself for wishing it. But it didn't look like he was much good to anybody anymore, and it seemed to me he'd lived a full life. He got into more mischief than any ten men. Little did I realize what I knew about Uncle Will still only scratched the surface of his life.

I arrived at the hospital just before visiting hours started. So I went into the waiting room to while away the time until the clock rolled round to seven. When I walked in, there sat one of my cousins, the only nitwit we had in the family. He was 25 years old, but had the mind of (they said) a 6 year old.

I asked him where Aunt Mae was 'cause I knew he wasn't there by himself. They didn't trust him no further than the hog lot by himself. I don't guess he was really born a nitwit. He'd got kicked in the head by a mule when he was but 6 years old. That arrested his brains; they never developed another bit. Leastwise that's what they said.

Sometimes when I was talking to him I thought he must've been kicked in the head when he was four because I knew a lot of 6 year olds who had more sense. Maybe that kick had sort of jarred something loose that wouldn't quite fit back together. I knew you couldn't say anything around him you didn't want repeated 'cause he was just like a gramophone; he repeated everything he heard.

"Ma is in talking to Uncle Will. They won't let me go in there. They're afraid I'll start some kind of ruckus with him. You know that son-of-a-bitch beat me out of my labor when I was a kid. I worked for him for two weeks and never got a dime. That son-of-a-bitch promised me a bunch of money."

I asked him how much money Uncle Will beat him out of.

"Oh, it was a fortune! I forgot now, it's been a long time ago, but he owed me $10 or $12 and the son-of-a-bitch ain't never offered to pay me. I've asked him for it every time I've seen him."

"Well, Timmy, Uncle Will was probably doing the best he could. Back in those days it was hard. I worked for him a few days myself and didn't get paid, but I always thought he would have paid me if he could have. Did you ever feel that way?"

"No, he was a big man. He had money. He's just a sorry son-of-a-bitch."

Having nothing better to do, I said, "If he's that sorry of a son-of-a-bitch, why are you up here to see him, why is your Ma up her to see him, if you don't like him no better than that?"

"Well, Ma said he was kin and he was dying, even though he is a son-of-a-bitch, we'll have to go to his funeral. To tell you the damn truth, I'll be glad to go to the son-of-a-bitch's funeral. I hope he dies tonight."

"Timmy, you don't really mean that. You don't wish nobody dead do you?"

"Damn sure do! The son-of-a-bitch went around lyin', cheatin', and stealin'. You know he killed several men? Did you know that?"

"Yeah, I know a good bit about him."

"What are you doing up here to see him anyway?"

"We spent a lot of time together over the past two or three years. I guess I sort of hate to see him go."

"Didn't you say he beat you out of money?"

About that time Aunt Mae came into the waiting room. I stood up, hugged her, and she kissed me with a mouthful of snuff. It seemed like all of my great aunts dipped snuff or chewed tobacco. Every time any one of them saw me, they wanted to kiss me right in the mouth. Damn! I hated it. Of course the men dipped snuff and chewed tobacco, too, but at least they didn't want to kiss me. She took Timmy by the hand and they walked out. I went down the hall to Uncle Will's room. He was sittin' up with a pillow behind his back eating a bowl of soup. He looked a right smart better than the night before. I thought maybe I could get away early.

No sooner had I sat down than the nurse came in, took his food away, and told me not to let him exert himself too much. She wasn't the same pretty little creature who'd been there the night before, so I asked her what happened to the other nurse. She said, "Oh, it's Bonnie's night off. She'll be back tomorrow night."

"Pretty little thing, ain't she," she said, as she swept by me. I knowed my face turned red. Uncle Will started grinning; which made it get even redder. I'm fair complected, blush at almost anything, and hate it. Usually people make fun of me when I do, and that just makes it worse.

No sooner she was gone, than Uncle Will was back down to business.

"Well, Nephew, are you gonna be able to do what I asked you to do last night?"

I told him Ma'd promised me I could have the car Saturday. Of course, I pointed out, he knew how unreliable Ma was. She'll tell you one thing today, then change her mind tomorrow. So her promise wasn't a guarantee, but was better than nothing.

Half afraid, I asked, "How'd you sleep last night?"

"I slept real fine until the shot wore off about 2 o'clock this morning, then the dreaming started all over again."

Not knowing what was coming next, I tried to change the subject. I told him about meeting Timmy out in the waiting room. I told him Aunt Mae was afraid to bring him in the room with her because she didn't never know what he was going to say.

"That little sucker is the biggest pain in the ass I ever saw."

I decided before Uncle Will got serious in telling me something I didn't want to hear, I'd better clear up the money situation. So I came right out and asked him, "Can I use some of your $10,000 to pay some of my expenses? Ma said I have to fill the car back up after I go to Tallapoosa. That was where I told her I was going, even though I'm going several miles beyond. I have to leave the car full of gas for her and Pa Sunday morning."

"Of course you can, Nephew. Whatever money you spend on me, take that amount. You don't know how I appreciate you doing this for me. I'll tell you, Nephew, whatever's left when I cross over is yours, but you need to hide it. You need to be careful about where and how you spend it. Don't ever let folks see you spending more than they know you can make.

"I know from experience, and that's part of the story I'm gonna tell you. When you start throwing money around, folks begin to wonder how you got it. When they begin to wonder how you got it, they start trying to find out where you got it because there might be more where it come from. And there might be something you don't want folks to know. It's awful important you don't flash a lot of money around unless you can prove how you made it honest.

"I'm gonna tell you. The money came from that poker game in Maine I told you about last spring. So you know the history of the money. That still don't matter. If I leave you $7000 or $8000, you gotta be mighty careful of how you spend it. But it'll be a good start for you."

"Uncle Will, I don't want any of your money. I want to help you. But I still think you ought to talk to a preacher."

"Nephew, I'm telling you there ain't none of them damn preachers gonna spend no time with a man who's about to cross over.

They want to get the young folks who come to church and Sunday School every week, and fill their collection plates. That's what makes them preachers look good, that's what makes them money."

"Uncle Will, the preachers want to save your soul. That's what they tell you every time you go to church, if you'd just let them. I remember one time at Old Shiloh when I was visiting you, the preacher begged you to join the church and save your soul. If you'd have done it then, you wouldn't be in such a pickle now."

"You talkin' about that Preacher Harmon, all dressed in white? Had the white surrey, and white horse?"

"Yes, sir."

"Well, Nephew, I ain't so sure that son-of-a-bitch wasn't the Devil himself masquerading as a preacher. I never did like the way he looked at you, nor the way he talked. Things ain't always what they appear. The son-of-a-bitch seemed more interested in lining his pockets than saving anybody's soul."

"Uncle Will, I don't remember Brother Harmon mentioning money one time during that service."

"Well, maybe he didn't, but if he'd stayed around long enough, he sure would have. That's all them damn preachers want anyway."

"You got something you want to tell me? I'm ready to listen."

"Boy, I'm feeling better. I think maybe now I'll be able to get up and leave the hospital. We'll go back out in the woods when I get up and around. I still got some things I need to get off my chest, but tonight I'm feeling better. Let's just talk about the good times we've had together.

"It sure is good to have you here. I've been so lonesome these last two and half months, sleeping in that old bus."

"Uncle Will, if you ain't got nothing to say, I've been thinking about last spring when me and you were down at the river, right where I'm supposed to get your money. It come that awful flood. The water was six or seven feet deep in that place. I've been wondering if it might have washed your money away or got it sopping wet. Water must've stood there for two or three days after we left."

At that moment, there was a knock on the door. Bill Warren, one of Uncle Will's great nephews on the other side of the house, stuck his head in the hospital room and asked, "Are you talking private stuff?"

"No, come on in and have a seat."

As soon as Bill sat down, Uncle Will took over the conversation.

"Me and Gene here were talking about an adventure we had last spring." He asked Bill, "Did you ever see any balled lightning?"

Bill allowed as how he hadn't, although he'd heard about it all of his life. Then Uncle Will launched into the story about the time me and him saw the balled lightning. He acted impatient. He wanted Bill to go away. Since he didn't want to talk about nothing personal, he just started right in on the story.

"We were down on the big Tallapoosa River last spring, I guess it was early March. We got there shortly after sundown. No sooner was we parked than we began to hear thunder roll in the northwest while lightnin' danced over the top of the clouds. The cloud was almost on top of us before it caused us any concern. Suddenly a brilliant burst of lightnin' lit up the whole countryside. I could see every fishline on our trotline just as clear as if it was midday, even after the flash died away. Seemed like it burned the image of that trotline on my brain. With my eyes shut, I could still see it stretched across the river with 15 to 20 lines hanging from it.

"I remember saying to Gene, 'That was pretty close. Maybe we ought to move into the old bus. It's probably just a quick spring rain, be gone in a minute.' Before I got that out of my mouth, another flash of lightnin' lit up the skies, then the rain came. The heavens opened like I'd never seen before. We made a mad dash to my old school bus.

"All the storms I ever saw before was just a little sigh of the elements compared to what we saw that night. Me and Gene turned our chairs around toward the back of the bus so we could see the trotline. There was a fish on one of the lines. He was jerking the whole trotline up and down like you wouldn't believe. He must've weighed ten pounds cause he was really shaking the line. Gene wanted to get out of the bus and wade out into the river. I could tell the river was already up two feet, so I wouldn't let him go.

"I remember saying that I didn't rightly know I'd ever been in a cloudbust, but I thought that was what we were witnessing right then. By that time the lightning was continuous. The river was lit up like it was daylight. Thundercrashes raised a constant roar.

"When the storm reached its full fury, we couldn't hear anything except the thunder. We could see the river rising, maybe two or three inches every minute. It was coming up that fast.

"I've heard it argued back and forth all my life that there ain't no such thing as balled lightning. My daddy swore there was such a thing, and my mama swore there wasn't. The people who'd seen balled lightning believed in it just as much as they believed in judgment day. But I didn't believe there was any such thing.

"As we sat there in the old bus and watched a huge bolt of lightnin' come down, it split the tree where the trotline was fastened from top to bottom. It looked like there was a huge ball of fire on the end of the lightnin' bolt. The ball was as big as a number three washtub. It started rolling down the fishing line headed straight towards the back of the bus. I watched frozen in my fascination. I couldn't move a muscle as that thing came nearer and nearer. The center of it was rollin' right down the trotline, and it made a funny little sound, sort of like when a lady files her finger nails with an emery board.

"When it bumped the bus, it exploded with a noise that was so horrendous it made all the rest of the thunderclaps seem like a whisper. When it hit, it split into three balls. They rolled around the floor making that noise like somebody using an emery board, just a gentle grinding noise. As they rolled around, each bumped into the wall or into this or that. But they all headed toward the front door. As they dropped off into the stepwell of the bus, each one exploded in turn. I thought for sure I'd be as deaf as an adder.

"During the short time it took for all that to happen, the trotline was gone, and the water had already come level with the banks of the river. It must have been fifteen or twenty feet deep at that point, and still rising.

"I was terrified. But I didn't want to let my terror seep over into the boy's mind. So, as calmly as I could, I lit my old corncob pipe. While stuffing the tobacco in the bowl of the pipe, my trembling hands weren't so noticeable. But as I stuck the pipe between my teeth, I was shaking so bad I spilled all the tobacco. I had to start all over, and all of the time he was watching me. He knew I was scared, but it hadn't seemed to affect him."

"Uncle Will, I was terrified. When I saw your pipe jumping up and down between your teeth I didn't think my hide could hold me. If you were scared that bad, big man that you are, Lord I ain't never been as scared."

I looked back out the window, annoyed that I'd interrupted him, "the flood waters had already come up over the bank. I said to the boy, 'We better get out of here while the gettin' is good, the water has done left the banks of the river.' I went up, sat in the driver's seat, turned the switch on, pushed the starter, and all I got was, 'rarrrh, rarrrh, rarrrh.' The battery had died.

"I reached over and opened the door of the bus. The water was done up to the step. I shut the door, still trying to look as calm as I could, and then walked back, sat down, and once again started filling my pipe with tobacco. My hand was still shaking, but I finally got my old pipe loaded, took a match out of a box I had sitting there, and tried to light it. I was shaking so bad that I broke that match right in half. I tried it three more times, striking the match on the face of the drawer as gentle as I could, but I broke each match. Finally, I peered over at Gene, and could tell by his eyes he knowed I was scared to death.

"Gene then took a match, struck it on the box, and held it while I was still shakin' and tremblin'. I'd take a puff and cut my eyes up to his; he was standing there as calm as you please.

"But the storm didn't slow down, it just kept raging. Pretty soon the water was six inches deep in the bus. When the lightning flashed, as far as we could see was a huge lake. The river was rushing by with an awful roar. We watched trees come around the bend that must have been a hundred feet long. One almost hit the old bus. If it had, it would've knocked us in the river and carried us away sure as the world.

"About that time I looked out the front window, and saw a man coming through with a team of mules. The water was up to their bellies, and he was struggling toward the bus. The driver was holding a doubletree in his hand, guiding the mules with a pair of checklines.

"I immediately stepped out into the water, which came up to my waist or higher, and waded out to meet our rescuer. He drove the mules right up to the front of the bus and turned them around. By the flash of the lightning, I could see it was Josh, who lived in the big house up on the main road.

"'Neighbor, you picked a terrible night to go fishing,' Josh said. 'I never see'd a bigger cloudbust in my life. If we don't get out of here in a hurry, we may have to ride these mules. We ran across some water coming in that was up to their shoulders. Didn't I see a youngun with you when you drove in?'

'Yeah, he's there in the bus.'

"I took the trace chain, reached down under the water, hooked it to the front bumper of the bus, and then fastened it to the doubletree, waded back around, and got into the bus as he started whipping the mules. It was a powerful turn for them to pull, but they got the old bus rollin'. We started down a little incline, and the water got almost up to the windows of the bus. But them mules finally managed to drag us out on top of the hill."

Uncle Will surprised me telling Bill he was scared. And even though I'd been there, and knew everything was true, it was still exciting. But Bill had a rather bored look on his face. Impolitely, I thought, he stood up, and told Uncle Will he had to be going.

"I'm glad to see you're doing as well as you are," he said. Then he walked out of the room.

No sooner was he off than Uncle Will said, "You see, Nephew, that's what my kin think of me. I'm an old man and that's one of the most exciting events in my life—including some gun battles, and not to speak of all the dives I've been in and out of, in all my life. That stupid son-of-a-bitch ain't got time to listen."

"Speaking of time," I butted in, "tomorrow's Friday, and I don't know if I can come to see you. Saturday I've got to go to your old home place and get your money. It's almost time for visiting hours to be over. We were talking about what kind of shape the money might be in when Bill walked into the room. What do you think? If it has been there as long as you say, it may be rotted by now."

"No, nephew, that money ain't rotted. It's buried in some fruit jars with lids sealed on them. I knew stuff like that could deterio-

rate, so when you find one, don't quit digging 'cause that ain't all of it. There's three half-gallon fruit jars. Before I put the money in, I heated them up on the stove to reduce the moisture. As soon as I poked the money in, I heated them a little more, slapped the lid on, and sealed them. I guarantee you the money is alright.

"I took each fruit jar, wrapped it in several layers of newspaper, and put them in brown paper sacks. The dirt is sort of sandy under the house; it ain't gonna be hard digging, but when you find newspapers, dig carefully because you'll bust the fruit jar if you don't. When you get one, you just grabble around with your hands until you find all three of them. There should be all together about $10,000 in them three fruit jars.

"Dr. King come by last night. Told me he'd let me go home next Monday if I keep improving. I sure hope you'll get me some money here by that time, so I can pay my bills. If you dig it up Saturday and get back home before visiting hours Saturday night, I sure would appreciate it if you would bring $200 or $300.

"Remember, Nephew, it's awful important that nobody but me and you know about the money. Because of the life I've lived, people around here don't like me; the family don't like me. They'll damn sure take it away—either the sheriff in Carroll County or the one here in Haralson County will claim I stole it somewhere. They'll get it away from us if they know we've got it. The only way we're gonna be able to keep it, is for you not to let them know we've got it."

"Okay, Uncle Will, I'll do the best I can, but if you're gettin' well enough to go home, why don't you start going to church and see if you can't confess to the church, get saved, and be baptized?"

"Aw, hell, Nephew, don't worry about that. I'm feeling much better, I've got several more good years yet. You'll do fine."

I told him good night, and walked out of the room with a heavy heart. Here he was begging me to hear his confession just last night, now he's done changed his mind. I don't understand grown folks. I sure don't understand Uncle Will. I wish he had another nephew or somebody besides me.

Out on the street, I got into the old Ford, and started home, thinking about how complicated this world had turned out to be just about the time I got growed up. I never once thought there was any such goings on, like an Uncle Will who tempts the gods by refusing to do what you're supposed to do to save yourself from Hell. That surely pleased Ol' Ebo. God! If I had a dream like that, I'd join the church and get baptized before sun up. I don't understand Uncle Will.

As a matter of fact, I thought about going and joining the church myself next Sunday, but I'm a long way from where Uncle Will is. I've got plenty of time. Besides, Pa says joining the church don't guarantee you going to Heaven no how. Lord, this is a complicated world.

By the time I got home and to bed, it was near 10:30. I fell dead asleep, and the next thing I knowed, Ma was in there shaking me to get me up, and telling me I was going to be late for work. "Today's Friday, I get paid today. Then tomorrow I've got to get Uncle Will's money," I thought as I pulled my socks on to start another day.

Treasure Hunt

I wanted to use the car Friday night to go see Uncle Will and to make sure I could use it Saturday to get his money. And I wanted Ma to promise me use of the car Friday night and Saturday in front of Pa. I knew if she said I could use it with Pa sitting there, he wouldn't let her back out. Once again, when I asked her she laid down the same conditions, "You got to take the car over to Bud Cole's and fill it up. And you've got to have it back here ready to go Sunday morning full of gas. You've done enough traveling this week, so don't even ask me to go along with us."

Ma was gifted at those spiteful little barbs. She knew she was just showing me who was boss. It didn't matter who went with them or who didn't. She really enjoyed being hateful. She also knew that I'd got the commitment out of her in front of Pa, so she'd have to do what she'd promised me she'd do. I felt certain I was going to be able to recover Uncle Will's money on Saturday. He was feeling so much better I half expected him to want to go. He still looked awful feeble to me. I didn't know how to judge those things.

That day at lunch, for the fiftieth time, I asked Julie New for a date that night. When she said, "Okay," I almost fainted.

I stammered, "Are you sure it's okay with your folks?"

She said, "I asked them."

I thought I'd have a little fun, "How did you know I was going to ask you?"

She said, "I thought somebody would."

"Oh."

That sort of let the wind out of me just a little. She's told me a dozen times where she lived.

"What time can I pick you up?"

"Are you sure you can get your car?"

"I asked this morning." Then I remembered I'd asked to go see Uncle Will, not to see my date. Flushed with success, and on a sudden impulse, I said, "Could you go out tomorrow night, too?"

43

"I've never been out with you. I don't know if I'll want to go tomorrow night or not."

"Well, if you do, can you?"

"I don't know; it was hard enough to get Ma and Pa to let me go tonight. I don't know whether two nights in a row with the same boy will go over so good."

She said, "About 7:30." As she did, she bent over and kissed me on the nose. She had on a loose frock, and when she did that, I saw down her dress all the way to Christmas. Old Pete jumped straight up and I had to stick my hand in my pocket and walk sideways to get back in the building to pick up my check before returning to work that afternoon. It took ten minutes before he behaved himself, and I could take my hand out of my pocket and go back to running that hateful press.

My paycheck was $15.70. I had to give Ma half of that, so I wasn't going to be a big spender that night. But at least I had a date with Julie. We could go to a movie. Then I remembered, "I've got to see Uncle Will! But I haven't promised him for sure I'd go." I wrestled with my conscience all afternoon about just saying the heck with it and not visiting him until Saturday night.

When the whistle blew, I went over and asked Julie if she'd mind stopping by the hospital a minute to see Uncle Will so he'd know I had better things to do than just sit around with him for two hours. She said that would be fine. If I picked her up at 7:30, I'd miss half of the visiting hours anyway because I couldn't get to the hospital before 8 o'clock.

When I walked into the room with Julie, Uncle Will's eyes got as big as saucers. He said, "Lord help me, boy, what have we here?"

I couldn't help but turn red whenever grown folks talked to me like that. I was glowing a bright cherry red. Julie reached up bold as brass and put her hand on my forehead like she was taking my temperature. Uncle Will got a big thrill out of that.

"Well, nephew," he said, "where'd you find her? She's as pretty as the pink on a gourd vine."

"Uncle Will, this is Julie New. We work together at General Shoe." Without thinking, and just to be saying something for the embarrassment of the moment, I went on, "I put on the lowers and she puts on the uppers." He paused for a minute and said, "Wouldn't it be better if it was the other way around?"

For a minute it didn't sink in that he was making a sex joke out of it. But when I did, I turned bright red, and stammered, "Uncle Will! She's a nice girl."

"Nephew, nice girls got pussies."

Lord, I could have died.

We were standing right before him and instinctively, I raised my hand to strike him. Julie grabbed my arm and said, "It's okay, Gene, we do," as she pushed me down in the easy chair beside the bed. I smoldered. Uncle Will saw that I was really furious. I squinted my eyes up and looked at him like Ma used to look at me when I'd done something bad, and she wanted me to know that she was fixing to beat the shit out of me.

I made up my mind I was leaving, stood up, and said to Julie, "let's go."

Uncle Will said, "Nephew, don't be that way. What's the matter with you?"

"Uncle Will, I ain't never heard anybody talk like that in front a lady. How dare you! I like Julie...I love Julie," I stammered out.

"That's alright. Nephew, you don't know nothing about girls, and she don't know nothing about boys, but I got a feeling before this night's over, ya'll are going to find out. Just consider what I said an ice breaker. Julie accepted it in good grace, so don't be an old stick in the mud. Just sit down and let's talk until visiting hours are over. It won't be but 30 more minutes, then ya'll can go do whatever it is you want to do. Remember, I'm a sick old man, and you've got your whole life in front of you."

"Uncle Will, don't pull that stuff on me. You're sick one day, you're well the next day, and you just done got me about half mad."

"Now simmer down, just simmer down. Tell me where Julie's from and let's just forget this."

He looked over at Julie and said, "Are you willing, Julie?"

She gave him a big smile and said yes.

When she smiled like that and said it was okay, Lord, it was okay with me. So I said, "okay," and felt my wrath ease up. I was so lovesick, I must've looked like a dying calf in a hailstorm.

When visiting hours were over, I asked Uncle Will to excuse us and we left. It was too late to go to the picture show by now, so I asked Julie what we should do.

She said, "Well, I've got to be home at 11 o'clock. Why don't we just park somewhere and talk." That sounded like a wonderful idea to me.

We started back in the direction of Tallapoosa from Bremen, driving very slowly. She snuggled up next to me, so I put my arm around her and felt I was in hog heaven. Pretty soon we came to an old logging road. I eased off the main road. The logging road ended in a wide spot. I turned the car around and pointed it back toward the main road.

Julie suggested that we sit in the back seat. She said that without the steering wheel it would be more comfortable, which sounded fine to me. We crawled over the front seat into the back without opening the doors, and before I knew it, she had her arms around me and gave me a long juicy kiss. By now I was panting like a dog, so swimmy-headed I might as well have been drunk. I begin to feel one of her little breasts. She made some peculiar movements under me and the first thing I knew, she'd unzipped my pants, and my tool popped out as stiff as a crowbar. She grabbed it and got it between her legs and right inside her. In less than a minute, it felt just like a covey of quail flew out of my ass. The whole world exploded!

"When I let her out at her place at one minute to eleven o'clock and started back home, I realized why her folks didn't let her date. And on the way home, I couldn't stop thinking, if all women have things like that, why would ever a man want to divorce a woman? God, she was the most wonderful thing in the world to me.

By the time I got home, I'd settled down enough to think about something other than Julie. I started planning the way I would get Uncle Will's money for him. I decided I'd get up early, milk the cow, do all my chores, and leave about daylight. That way I'd look more like a real fisherman when I got to Josh Webster's house early in the morning. I didn't want anything to seem suspicious.

The next morning, thinking about Julie every step of the way to the barn, I milked the cow before Ma and Pa got up. They usually slept in a little on Saturday morning, sometimes as late as 6:30. When I got back to the house Pa had already built a fire in the cook stove. Ma was making biscuits. I told Pa I'd fed the mule and left the stable door open so it could get out. He didn't need to go to the barn unless he just wanted to. I gave the hogs 12 ears of corn. Ma told me to take them a bucket of slop, which was her way of rewarding me for having everything else done. She couldn't stand idle hands. As a matter of fact, her favorite saying was, "An idle mind is the devil's workshop. I can't do nothing about your mind, but I can keep you hands busy, boy." She could and did.

As soon as I finished breakfast I got up and left. Before heading off, I reminded Ma I wanted the car again to see Julie that night. She said, "You can't go. I want that car full of gas and parked in the front yard before I go to bed. You get back here this afternoon in time to fill it up at Bud Cole's. And you didn't give me but $7 out of your check. You owe me 75 more cents." Since I hadn't spent my money on Julie, I reached in my pocket, threw a $1 bill on the table, and stomped out.

All I could think about on my trip to Josh Webster's place was Julie. I'd lost my virginity the night before, but I wasn't mourning. What I 'd found was ten times finer! To say that I was love-sick was the understatement of all time. As a matter of fact, while driving to Josh Webster's place I had to pass right by the road to Julie's house. I wanted to go by and see her so bad, I could hardly keep the car going straight. But I passed by and shortly arrived at Webster's farm.

Mr. Webster lived on a little hill across the road from the property Uncle Will'd once owned. There was an old farm road almost directly across from his front door where we had to let a wire gate down to get into the pasture. I had to go across the pasture for the better part of a mile and a half to reach the house where Uncle Will had lived with Fanny Hawk. As I drove in Josh's yard, two red bone hounds came out to greet me with a great deal of barking and growling. I talked to them all the way to the side door where I knocked. Presently, the man who'd once rescued us from the flood waters presented his jovial face to the screen.

"What can I do for you, boy?" was his greeting.

"Mr. Webster, I'd like to go fishing over on the Tallapoosa River where Uncle Will and I were fishing the night you pulled us out."

"Sure," he said. "Where's Will," he asked looking out at the car.

"Uncle Will's in the hospital. He's near dead; but he seemed to perk up a little bit last night." I'd already forgiven him for what he said to Julie that'd embarrassed me so terribly. Mostly, I guess because of the things that happened with her later on that same night.

Josh walked out on the porch, looked up at the sky, winked at me, and said, "Looks like if you'll be fishing today you might not get yourself in such a pickle as the last time you were here. Sure, boy, go on and fish till your heart's content. But if you catch a big mess of fish, more than you can eat, bring me one or two when you come out. Be sure you close the gap when you come out, if I ain't here. I've got about 40 head of cows in that pasture and some of 'em are bullin'. Make sure you don't get between one of them cows and that old bull because he's as mean as a rattlesnake on a griddle."

"Yes, sir," I replied as I got back in the car. I crossed the meadow and headed down the bumpy road. The road was pretty rough, but I was able to drive right to the old house. There was a bed of cannas in full bloom running the entire length of the east side of the house. Out from that a little way, there was a crabapple tree Uncle Will'd told me the spring before. Fanny Hawk had planted it, and it looked like it had a million crabapples.

There were three unkept holly bushes higher than my head along the south side of the house. I walked around on the west, the river side of the house, where I entered the kitchen door. The floor was rotted enough there were weeds growing up through it. The churn was still there, with the cloth that once had kept dust out of the milk all tattered and torn, setting on the hearth just like it had the spring before. I couldn't understand how all those floodwaters hadn't moved it off the hearth. I guess the walls of the building had slowed the waters enough. You could clearly see the high water mark of the flood most of the way up the wall.

I walked in and tested the floor by stomping my feet. I'd be able to kick all the way through. I carefully made my way through the kitchen to the fireplace, and stood directly in front of it. Backing away from the hearth two feet, I guessed I was standing directly over the money. I stomped hard on the floor and was able to bust out a good size chunk of rotten wood. The ground beneath was dry and firm.

Looking around the room, I could see the Bruton snuff box me and Uncle Will had noticed on the mantleboard the spring before was still there. The door to Uncle Will and Fanny Hawk's bedroom was still hanging by one hinge at a drunken angle. I thought about his description of Fanny Hawk, and how she must have looked like my Julie. After last night, I wondered how he could beat her up the way he'd told me. He'd bloodied her nose, and given her two black eyes the last night she lived with him. I wondered how a man could do that. Then I remembered he'd said he was blind drunk. I needed to try that sometime, I thought, but I sure didn't want to do it around Julie. I didn't want to touch her with any anger at all. God, she was wonderful!

As I sat there on the floor and watched the rays of sunlight bathe bits and pieces of the rotten floor, I could almost hear Fanny Hawk's screams as she tried to get out of a drunken giant's way. The sounds as he went crashing into the bedroom door. And how he must have felt the next morning when he woke up, as he said with the granddaddy of all hangovers, knowing he'd never see her again.

And I remembered all the family legends about Uncle Will, and my own very different experience with him. How is it that everybody in the family, everybody where we lived, hated him—and why did I love him?

I remembered one night, when I couldn't have been over three and a half years old, Pa told me to get stovewood in so we'd have some dry wood to cook breakfast with the next morning. I'd played and forgotten about it until after dark. Pa went by, looked at the woodbox behind the stove, and saw there was no stovewood in it. He told me I had to go out in the dark and get it, though he knew I was powerful afeared of the dark. Uncle Will had been sitting with us, so he took me by the hand and led me out to the stovewood pile. He stayed with me to protect me, and when we came back in with the wood, Pa was furious. He told Uncle Will that I'd never mind him if I had somebody to do things for me that I was supposed to do, and that he didn't appreciate Uncle Will one bit. Pa then ordered him out of the house. I had never seen Pa so mad. He sent me to bed, and I heard Uncle Will crank up his old motor-cycle and leave. I couldn't understand why Pa would be so mean to that kindly man. Even though Uncle Will had cheated me when I helped on his farm, and never paid me what he'd promised to, he made me feel sorry he didn't have the money. It was alright with me, and I never forgot what he'd done for me that night.

I thought to myself, is that all it takes to win a kid's affection forever? Am I an idiot to love a man for one lonely act of kindness that made my Pa so furious? Lord, this is a complicated world.

Hearing a twig break outside the house somewhere, I glanced at the windows and there standing outside was Josh Webster. He took his fist and popped out one of the window panes. "Boy, I thought you wanted to go fishing."

"I do, Mr. Webster, but I got interested in the mark of the flood-waters almost up to the ceiling, the churn is still setting on the hearth the way it was when me and Uncle Will were here last spring, that old Bruton snuff box is still sitting on the mantle. I don't see how it managed to stay there with the waterline two or three feet above, but it looks just like it did last spring. I got inter-ested in that and was sitting here thinking about some of the sto-ries Uncle Will's told me about this place. About him and Fanny Hawk...you ever hear of Fanny Hawk, Mr. Webster?"

"Yeah, boy, there was talk about her around here. She was quite a gal from what I hear. But she was before my time; I never saw the lady. They say she was a good looking thing though. They said she and Will did some more hell-raising on that motorcycle of his. Wasn't much bigger than your fist from what I hear tell. Is that what Will says?"

"Yes, sir. He says she was a tiny thing."

"You know, boy, she just up and vanished one time. She was here one day and gone the next. There was talk about he killed her somewhere and throwed her in the river. Did you ever hear that kind of talk?"

"No, sir, I never heard anything like that. Uncle Will told me he beat her up one night; the next morning he woke up and she was gone."

"Boy, why don't you ask him sometime how she left. There wasn't no way to travel except for his old motorcycle. Nobody around here ever saw her. They didn't see her going anywhere; just suddenly one day they quit seeing her. Up until that day Will was riding up and down everywhere, raising hell, getting drunk, and she was too. What did you say Will told you about her, boy?"

"Uncle Will said he got drunk one night and beat her up. As a matter of fact, see that door hanging half on the hinges? He busted that door in. It's still hanging that way, according to what he told me. Beat the hell out of her—gave her two black eyes and bloodied her nose. He woke up the next morning with the grandpaw of all hangovers, and she was gone. He never saw her again."

"Well, according to what I hear, Will was one hell-raiser. And if Fanny Hawk had of been anything except a carnival girl he picked up in Tallapoosa, there would have been a helluva lot of nosin' around when she disappeared. You know that's how he met her don't you?"

"Yes, sir. He told me about that. Said she had two black eyes and had been living with the man who owned the carnival. He made a regular habit of beating her up. At that time Uncle Will had a brand new Harley-Davidson. He just talked her into living with him."

"She was a loose woman alright. That is the story everybody tells around here. That's how they got together. If she'd not have been that kind, I guarantee they'd have looked into her disappearance more than what they did. I wouldn't be a damn bit surprised if she ain't buried right there under the floor of this house."

When Josh Webster said that, a cold chill went up my spine. Surely Uncle Will didn't kill her. I know he killed some other folks, but he loved Fanny, and he hadn't killed her. Josh was not going to let it rest. He saw that I was disturbed.

"Boy, I'd bet the whole damn farm that Fanny Hawk is buried within 200 feet of where me and you are right now. And if it wasn't such hard labor, if I had one of them new-fangled backhoes like I see out digging holes in the ground, I'd tear up this whole place just to see if I couldn't find her bones. There was also some talk, mind you, when I bought this place, that Will'd buried some gold. When we went off the gold standard in '33, he had a bunch of gold he stole from somewhere up north...he didn't send you down here to dig up some of his ill-gotten gains did he boy? Seeing he's about dead, he might be broke. That ain't why you're down here, is it boy?"

I was taken by surprise, but I recovered quickly I thought. "No, sir, Uncle Will didn't say nothing to me about no buried gold," which was the truth. I didn't mention the fact that I was down here to dig up money. Things were getting a little bit complicated for me. I got back up on the floor and walked outside where Josh Webster was standing.

He said, "The reason I got curious, I didn't see any fishing poles on your car. I said to myself, why would a young lad come fishing early on Saturday morning without any fishing poles."

I said, "Well, Mr. Webster, me and Uncle Will always cut our own fishing poles alongside the river. I got my sinkers and fish-hooks in the car. We always dig our bait on the side of the river, then we cut our poles."

He grudgingly admitted that was a reasonable thing to do as I took my pocket knife out and walked to the edge of a cane break. I picked out a cane that looked to be 12 or 14 feet long and cut it, started trimming the leaves off, then went to the car, opened the trunk, and took my shovel out deliberately. Walking close to the riverbank, I started digging fishbait in a mirey, mucky place. While Josh Webster watched me with what appeared to be diminishing interest, I immediately found a couple of big earthworms and dropped them into a #3 tin can I'd brought along just in case some passerby got curious why I was down on the river. I broke one of the worms half-in-two, put a lead weight on the line, and tossed it out in the river. I punched the pole into the bank, and went back to the cane break to cut me another. I made sure I stayed in a line of sight so I could watch my cork float in the event the fish were accommodating.

Webster eventually announced, "Boy, I'm going to leave you to your fishing. Don't forget, if you catch more than you can eat, stop by and leave me a mess. I'll be at the house." He sauntered off up the old logging road.

I glanced up in time to see the cork dragged under the water, raced over to the bank, and pulled out the prettiest two-pound bass a fellow ever saw. Any other time it would have been a very exciting event. But the last thing on earth I wanted to do today was catch a mess of fish. I was hoping I didn't even get a bite. But I cut a stringer off of a nearby blackgum bush, and stuck one leg of the stringer in the creek bank so the bass wouldn't die. Food was still precious, and I wouldn't dare throw any away. But I hoped I wouldn't catch anymore.

I could only see Josh going back up the logging road for about 200 yards, and kept feeling eyes in the back of my neck. I started thinking he might slip back around so he could watch me, so I kept myself busy cutting poles, baiting the hooks, and setting them in the bank. About every five minutes, I caught another fish. If I'd wanted fish, I couldn't have caught one every two hours. I just kept popping them on the stringer.

"Finally, when I thought Mr. Webster had time to be back to the house, I climbed up a big oak tree all the way to the top to see whether he'd reached his house. When I got almost to the top of the tree, I could see him walking across the road. He'd really gone back to the house, so I scampered down the tree, went inside, made the hole I'd stomped in the floor earlier big enough so I could crawl under the house, and started digging furiously. I'd dig for about a half a minute, stick my head up through the floor to make sure nobody had slipped up to watch me through any of the windows, then go back down and dig a little more.

The ground was soft and sandy like Uncle Will said it would be. After about two or three minutes, I knew Josh Webster couldn't have run and got back here so quickly. The pick dragged across a newspaper. It was dry as a bone, but I could tell it had been wet many times. I took my hands and started grabbling, and sure enough, there was a half-gallon fruit jar. I pulled it out, and just like he'd said, it was full of money! I kept grabbling very quickly and found two more half-gallon fruit jars wrapped in newspapers. I dragged once more with my hand to make sure that was all, and felt the straight edge of a metal box. Uncle Will hadn't said anything about a metal box!

I quickly put the three half-gallon fruit jars in the croker sack I'd brought with me, and covered up the crumbly bits of newspaper in the hole. I pushed all the dirt down and swept it as clean as I could with my hands to make it look like nobody'd been there. I'd knocked a hole in the floor directly above where the treasure was buried. I hoped if Josh Webster came back down he wouldn't go inside the house. I tried to scatter bits and pieces of the floor over the fresh dirt so as not to raise his curiosity, and then took the croker sack and locked it in the trunk of the car.

I went out to check my fishing poles. I'd caught two more big ones, and put them on the stringer. But I was badly shaken. What was that box doing there? Uncle Will'd told me earlier that spring he'd buried a metal box with the money from the poker game in Maine. But when he said the rest of his money'd been put in fruit jars, he hadn't said anything about a metal box. It was disturbing.

I cut the lines off my fishing poles and laid them alongside the riverbank, got my pick and shovel and put them in the trunk. Then I split the twelve fish I had on two stringers. One was to leave with Mr. Webster so he wouldn't get suspicious of me leaving so early.

I drove back out to the main road and knocked on the door at Mr. Webster's house. He came to the door grinning as I held up six big fish for him. "Mr. Webster, here's your half. I've got enough to make us supper and breakfast. I sure appreciate you letting me fish, and I wonder if I might do it again sometime."

"Sure, boy, anytime you want to fish, come on down. Bring Will back when he gets to feeling better."

I promised him I would as I got in the car and left. I was so upset about what happened that morning, I didn't even think of Julie once. I was headed for the Bremen Hospital, and I had to talk to Uncle Will!

I went to the hospital with the three fruit jars locked in the trunk and marched into Uncle Will's room. He had a noon meal sitting across his legs, and Aunt Minny was talking to him. She was another one of my snuff-dipping great aunts. She was not his sister, 'cause she was on my Grandpa's side of the house. She jumped up, acting proud to see me, and kissed me right in the mouth with snuff dripping out of both corners. I hated snuff, and wiped my mouth off with the back of my hand. Momentarily her eyes clouded, she looked hurt, but only for a moment. Uncle Will seemed surprised.

"Fancy you being here, lad," he said, "I wasn't expecting you before visiting hours tonight."

Since the business I had couldn't be discussed in the presence of company, I asked him how he was feeling. He allowed how he was just a mite better than he'd been last night. He thought he would be ready to go home come Monday, which is when Dr. King said he could go.

I sat there fidgety and bored while he and Aunt Minny talked about their younger days, and how they had grown old a lot quicker than they thought they would. I sat there fuming, wondering what all the things that happened this morning meant. I kept hearing Josh's words over and over, "I'd dig the whole damn place up if it wasn't so much labor and if I had one of them newfangled back-hoes. I betcha I'd find her bones."

I looked at Uncle Will so gray and spent. How could he have murdered his true love? And most of all, his not telling me about it! My belly began to burn as if the acid it was making was cutting a hole in it. I couldn't wait for Aunt Minny to get out of there.

Slowly but surely, their conversation came to a halt. She sat there for several minutes, but finally feeling the spirit move her, she stood up and said, "Well, Will, I'm glad you're doing as well as you are. If any of us can help you, you let us know." With that, she started by me. I stood up out of politeness just in time to get another juicy snuff kiss. Then she was gone.

As soon as she closed the doors, I said, "Uncle Will, I've got a bone to pick with you. I don't like what happened down on the Tallapoosa River this morning a bit. Josh Webster says he thinks you murdered Fanny Hawk and buried her down there near your old house. Not only that, he thinks you've got a bunch of gold buried around the house. He's even thinking about getting a back-hoe and digging the whole place up. We need to talk."

The orderly came in to pick up his meal tray, and I had to shut up until he left. As soon as the aide shut the door, Uncle Will said, "Now, now, Nephew, simmer down, just simmer down. What's all this business about murder and bones?"

I repeated what Josh Webster had said to me. Then half-heartedly I stated, "What he says makes sense. He said there wasn't no way

of traveling except her walking or on your motorcycle. One day
she was there, and the next day she was gone. How did she leave?
And something else, I got scared when I was digging up that money
of yours. There's a metal box buried with the fruit jars! You didn't
say nothing about a metal box being there."

His eyes lit up, "You mean you got the money? Did you count it,
nephew?"

"No, it's out in the trunk. Three half-gallon fruit jars inside a
croker sack. I ain't had time to count it. I want to know what you
have to say about what Josh Webster told me before I count it. I
may just take it and throw it back in the damn river!

"You need to give me some answers. Maybe you're as mean as
folks say you are. You've always been good to me, and I've always
thought highly of you, even though you say you killed those people.
I know you killed those people, but you sort of made it alright with
me because of the things they'd done to you. But Fanny Hawk never
done nothing to you but love you, and if you killed her, Uncle
Will, I ain't got no use for you never, no more!"

"Nephew, I promise you, I never killed Fanny Hawk."

"Uncle Will, you know just two nights ago you were begging me
to listen to you so you could purge your soul. So you could stand a
chance of going to heaven. And now you're acting like the man
who murdered all those people. You've forgotten your soul's in
danger of hellfire. What's in that metal box? All the time I was
digging under the house, I kept thinking what if Josh Webster
comes back and catches me here, and I got all that money you say
is under there. What's he going to do? Is he an honest man? Will
he let me go? Will he take it away? Will he shoot me and drop me
in the river? What about the ideas he had about Fanny Hawk? He
said you might have shot her and dropped her in the Tallapoosa
because you're too damn lazy to bury her. How're you going to prove
you didn't kill Fanny Hawk? Do you know where she is today? Is
she still alive? The only way I'll believe you didn't kill her now is
for me to see her. For her to tell me herself that she's the same
woman you batted around. And you ain't said what's in that box!"

"Nephew, I don't know about the box, the only thing I can guess
is I just happened to bury the fruit jars close to it. I don't know

anything about a metal box. I told you this spring, I buried the money I got out of the poker game in a metal box. I kept digging it up and moving it. Unless one of the times when I buried it back, I just happened to bury it there and forgot it, I don't know what's in the box. And if you just ran your fingers down the side of it, how do you know it wasn't a piece of lumber buried there. How do you know it was a metal box if you just felt it?"

"Uncle Will, I know how metal feels. I bumped my fingernail against it, it was a metal box. I felt one edge of it. It was maybe a foot long. When you took the money out of the metal box the last time, did you take all of it out, did you leave the box under the ground? What did you do with the metal box that you buried? And how big was the box?"

"It was an old dynamite box, nephew. They used to sell dynamite in a metal box. You were supposed to turn the boxes over from time to time so the nitroglycerine could run back through the guncotton. The box had a buckle on each side. It came in two pieces. You could unbuckle it and pick the top up, and the dynamite stood on end. Every few months, if you didn't use it, you turned it over. Now they put it in wax paper and wooden boxes. The wooden boxes get oily and gooey, but wood is cheaper than metal, so they quit putting it in metal boxes. Didn't you ever see any of those old metal dynamite boxes?"

"No, sir, I never did. They always put dynamite in wooden boxes since I've been seeing dynamite."

"Did you open up any of the fruit jars, nephew?"

"No, sir."

"Well, how do you know there's money in them?"

"I could see the money through the glass. There's money in them, I don't know how much. Looks like they are stuffed full. What I mostly saw was $10 and $20 bills."

"There will be some $50 bills, some $100 bills, and some $20s, $5s, and $10s. There ain't no $1 bills."

"Prove to me Fanny Hawk's still alive if you ever want me to believe anything else you say."

"Nephew, you know where Muscadine Junction, Alabama, is?"

"Yes, sir."

"Alright, go to Fruithurst, Alabama and turn left. At Muscadine Junction, where the railroad crosses a dirt road?"

"Yes, sir. I know where that is."

"Go to the next road to the left. Then to the second house on
the left. It's an old, old house, with the outside siding boards running up and down. Knock on the door, and a tiny lady, just a little
over five feet tall, will answer the door. You ask her anything you
want to ask her."

I stood up, and started for the door.

"You going now, Nephew?" he said.

"I'm going now," I said.

"Nephew," he said as I closed the door, motioning me inside,
and closing the door. He said, "Hide the money before you go, count
it, and tell me tonight how much there is."

Without saying anything I turned again and walked out. I got in
the old Ford and headed for Alabama.

Forty-five minutes later I crossed the railroad at Muscadine Junction. There was an old red bonehound laying on the front porch of the
general store that constituted the entire town of Muscadine Junction.
I didn't see a car or a wagon for the couple of miles to the first road to
the left, as Uncle Will had directed me. The road was a washboard and
the Ford bounced all over it. The first road to the left was even smaller
than the one through Muscadine Junction.

When I turned, totally out of view of any houses, I stopped and unlocked the trunk. I took the fruit jars out, screwed the lid off the first
one, and dumped the money in the trunk. In the first jar there was 100
$50 bills, 100 $20s, and 100 $10s. I couldn't believe it! I didn't know
that much money existed in the whole world! There was already $8000
and I hadn't even opened the other two jars. When I finished counting the money, there was $23,500! Uncle Will thought there was
$10,000. Something was wrong. How could he have more than twice
the amount of money he'd thought he had, and what was in that metal
box under the floor?

But I had another more urgent mystery on my hands. What had
happened to Fanny Hawk? I was supposed to be able to solve that
mystery when I went to the second house down this godforsaken
road. Now I put 20 of the $20 bills in my pocket. In the trunk of

the car were two spare innertubes we always carried in those days. One of them had been patched several times. There was also a patching kit, another essential we always carried. I took my pocket knife, made a slit in the innertube about three inches long, and poked the money through until all the rest of it was in the innertube. I worked the money around until there were no lumps anywhere. It looked just like any deflated innertube, and I carefully repaired the slit with the patching kit. Now I was certain nobody would suspect there was anything unusual about the car.

I headed to the second house on the left. A short time later I was knocking on the door. A tiny lady I estimated to be in her mid-sixties opened the door. From Uncle Will's prior description, I was almost certain I was speaking to Fanny Hawk. Her hair was totally white. She said, "What can I do for you, young man?"

I said, "First of all, do you know Will Stogner?"

She said, "I once did. Why do you ask?"

"Would you tell me your name?"

"My name is Fanny Hawk."

"Will is my great uncle, and it's important to me that I know you're okay. Could I ask you some questions about you and Uncle Will?"

"Sure. Come on in, have a seat."

I walked into a nicely furnished small sitting room with some very comfortable chairs and sat down. She sat next to me. "What would you like to know, young man?" she said as soon as she was seated.

"Would you mind telling me about Uncle Will?"

Fanny Hawk

"Tell me boy, what's your name?" Fanny Hawk asked.

"My name is Gene."

"What does Will call you?"

"Will calls me 'nephew', 'son', 'boy'. Mostly he calls me Nephew."

"What kin are you to Will; why is this important to you?"

"Well, Uncle Will is really my grandma's brother, so he is my great uncle, but I've always sort of liked him and ain't none of the rest of the family ever cared much about him. He's sick now. As a matter of fact, I thought Tuesday night he was going to die, but he's a lot better today.

"To tell you the truth, Miss Fanny, the gossip around where you and Uncle Will lived, is that he killed you and tossed you into the river. He wants me to do some things for him and before I did, I had to find out if that was so."

"Lord no, boy. Will beat the hell out of me a few times. That's what caused me to leave him, but I still love him. It's been 40 years since I left him and I still love him. But exactly what is it you want to know, Gene?"

"Well, Miss Fanny, I just need to know if you are the same woman he told me some stories about. For instance, do you remember being at an embarrassing baptizing? I just need to know it's you."

"Oh yeah, I remember very well. That was down on Indian Creek."

"I always have been interested in peoples' stories and if you've got time, just tell me how you met Uncle Will, tell me whatever you can or will about your life."

"Gene, I'm 65 years old. That's gonna take a spell."

"Miss Fanny, I've got three or four hours before I've got to go."

"I guess Will's told you some things about me. I don't know where to start. I guess you'd have to understand why I'm the way I am. That's no excuse, mind you, but my life just sort of happened.

"Most girls in my time had a planned life. They'd go to school until they got old enough and pretty enough for some man to offer

60

them matrimony. Then they'd get married, have younguns, and grow old. That wasn't much of a plan, but at least it was some kind of plan. But I didn't even have that.

"I'm not trying to get your sympathy young man. I'm just telling you the way it was. I came to accept my life long, long ago. My Pa was a bootlegger and a gambler. Pa would make liquor, then he would wholesale it out to other people, and they would sell it in quart, pint, and half-pint bottles.

"Till I was 10 or 12 years old, Pa was always a good provider. Everybody knowed he made liquor, but he provided for his family. I went to school just like all the other little girls, but when I was 11 my maw died. She was the prettiest thing you ever saw. I was heartbroken and life began to change around our house.

"Pa began to go off at night and leave me by myself, I was terrified. He did raise me to know how to shoot a gun, and he kept two or three shotguns, a pistol, and a rifle in the house.

"After Ma died, Pa started drinking pretty heavy. If I didn't have supper ready when he got home, he'd slap me around, always swearing at me. He changed from a loving Pa to one that wasn't so loving. Sometimes he'd feel guilty about it. He'd take me to town and buy me some pretty clothes. All and all, the years between when I was 11 and when I was 14 were pretty bad.

"I never knew if Pa was coming home at suppertime or if I'd have to get up in the middle of the night and let him in. We had chains on the doors I fastened every night before I went to bed. I was afraid to leave the house unlocked so he'd have to bang on the door for me to let him in. Once or twice he slapped me around for not getting to the door quick enough. I realized all this was involved in Ma's death. He was grieving over her, so I just more or less took it as my part.

"I matured physically right early. When I was 14 I looked like I was 17 or 18. We lived about five miles out of Newnan, Georgia, about a mile from Sargeant. A little creek ran right behind our house. Sometimes it got out of its banks during a big rain, and the water would lap right up to the door and get mud all over the steps.

"I mention this because when I was 14 years old the creek got out and ran so high it actually got mud on the floor. It was on a

Saturday, and it'd been raining hard two or three days. Pa told me to scrub the floors, get 'em cleaned up because he was having a card game that night. He wanted me to stay up and fix the players drinks and something to eat if they got hungry because sometimes these card games lasted all night. That was the first time I knew Pa was gambling. It was also the first time I knew why he stayed out all night. Sometimes he wouldn't come home for a day or two, so I figured gambling must be the reason.

"It took me till well after midday to get the house and floors cleaned up. I had all the windows and doors opened so it would dry out. After I got the house spotless, I laid down and fell asleep.

"When I opened my eyes several hours later, standing over me was a big, fat, greasy, son-of-a-bitch named Blake Thompson. He was one of Pa's wholesale liquor customers.

"He always had tobacco juice running out of the corners of his mouth, and always wore a new pair of overalls. Of course looking back, he probably wasn't no more than 28 or 29 years old when I was ten or eleven, but he seemed like an old man. He smelled bad even though his overalls always looked new.

"I got to hating him more and more because he would come to our house sometimes two and three times a week. He'd pull on my hair, make remarks about what a pretty girl I was, and how when I growed up he was going to marry me—things like that. It made me want to throw up, not only because he smelled bad, but 'cause he was a pig to my notion. He had a slimy countenance that made me want to be somewhere else any time I saw him coming.

"I jumped up and backed away from him. He said, 'Aw Fanny, don't act so scared of me. I wouldn't hurt you at all. You are the prettiest thing I ever saw and one day I'm gonna marry you,' all the time with snuff dripping out of the corner of his mouth, I could smell liquor heavy on his breath.

"I sidled past Blake, went into the kitchen, and started building a fire in the cookstove because I hadn't prepared anything for Pa's supper. I was glad I was going to have to wait on the poker players that night. I wanted to get away from Blake.

"He followed me into the kitchen trying to feel my behind. I jumped out of the way. Gene, are you sure you are interested in this stuff? This happened long ago and I don't see how it could possibly be of any interest to a young man like you. You ought to be out looking for a young lady."

I replied "I already have a young lady who is beautiful like you must have been." As soon as I realized what I'd said, I turned red and tried to make it alright by saying, "You're still beautiful, but you're older now, Miss Fanny."

She gave me a cute little smile and said, "Okay, if you're sure I am not boring you. Could I get you a glass of tea, or water?"

"No ma'am, I'm fine."

Even though I had decided she was the Fanny Hawk that Uncle Will had told me about, she'd gotten me interested. There were already some loose ends I wanted to know about. She was about the same size as my Julie, and I suspected when she was young she was just as pretty, and that's awfully pretty.

She continued, "I asked him if Pa had sold him something that I could get for him, hoping he would say yeah, and I could get him a jug of whiskey and be rid of him. But as I feared, he was one of the players and had come a little early.

"He sat at the table out of my way while I busied myself getting ready to make biscuits for Pa's supper. He tried to talk to me, and wanted to know where Billy was. I told him Pa left pretty early this morning. I didn't know where he was or when he'd get back.

"Blake said, 'I hope his selection of players is good today because I'm feeling lucky. It's been a week or so since we had a good poker game. I understand Rob Gibson is coming to this game—he's richer than four foot up a bull's ass.'"

I guess I blushed a little when she said that because she stopped and said, "Gene, does my language offend you?"

I said, "No ma'am," but I couldn't help but blush with this pretty little old lady talking like men down at the mule barn when no ladies were present. But I assured her it was alright. I was interested in the story.

"I had heard the name, Rob Gibson, before. His family owned one of the cotton mills in Newnan. I'd hoped and dreamed about somebody like him, coming on their white stallion to take me riding away, and me living happily ever after like the kid in the fairy tales.

"Suddenly the prospect of having to wait on the poker players didn't seem quite so somber, even though I couldn't imagine somebody like Rob Gibson, whom I imagined to be young and handsome, associated with the likes of Blake Thompson.

"He followed around my heels as I started to fix Pa some biscuits and sawmill gravy. As soon as the stove got hot, I put several strips of fatback in the skillet, got out the bread tray, and had all the ingredients ready for the biscuits.

"As the sun began to slip behind the horizon, I pulled Pa's chandelier down over the eating table. He had a spring-loaded chain that would let me pull it down to sit on top of the table. I lit the three Aladdin lamps it held. It was a device he'd made for Ma, and he was really proud of it. It lit up the kitchen almost like daylight.

"Ordinarily we set a regular lamp in the middle of the kitchen table while we ate, but I knew with all of his friends coming to play poker, he was probably going to use the eating table. It was a beautiful table, one of my Ma's favorite pieces of furniture. It was six feet in diameter, and had the highest finish I've ever seen on a piece of furniture. The man who made it must have worked for weeks to make it shine that way. She had several round tablecloths she'd made herself.

"I took the nice tablecloth off and put on one that was faded, expecting most of the players to be slobs like Blake Thompson. Ma had also quilted several covers to go under the tablecloth so when somebody spilled something it wouldn't mar the finish.

"Pa used an old undertaker's surrey to deliver liquor to retailers. He thought that disguised the real nature of the surrey from the law. I think everybody in the community knew what Pa did for a living. Of course, I never mentioned it, and nobody ever mentioned it to me, but I could tell the way folks looked at me, I was not viewed the same as the rest of the girls in the community.

"I knew some of my girlfriends from school, my same age, had been asked by boys to let them come calling. No boy had ever asked me. I don't mean to be bragging, but I was as pretty or prettier than any of them. My figure was well filled out, so there had to be something a little wrong or somebody would have asked to come calling, which they hadn't.

"The surrey had a box under it, where the undertaker normally carried the picks and shovels, that would hold five-gallon jugs. That's where Pa put his liquor after he proofed it. He could haul 50 gallons of liquor there if he put it in five-gallon jugs.

"Just about dark, a young handsome fellow, must've been 26 or 27 years old, knocked on the door. He was clean-cut, wore finely polished shoes, and a Sunday suit. A very handsome figure.

"I invited him in. He was so well-spoken and in the light he took my breath away. On top of being good looking, he had a beautiful voice. He said, 'I'm Rob Gibson, is Mr. Hawk home?'

"I said, 'No, I'm Fanny Hawk. He told me to be expecting company, so come on in, sit, and make yourself at home.' I was ashamed for him to see me alone in the same room with Blake Thompson.

"Blake jumped up and said, 'Now don't be fancying that pretty, young thing because I done told her I was gonna marry her as soon as she gets old enough. I'll tell you she ain't as old as she looks. She's only 14.' I could have killed Blake Thompson because I didn't want Rob Gibson to think I'd have anything to do with him.

"Shortly, three more people arrived on horseback. I looked out the window again just as the biscuits got done. There come Pa's surrey up the driveway.

"Pa had been drinking, but not enough to get to his mean stage. He was still mellow and jolly. As soon as he got in the house, I asked him how many of these folks were gonna eat 'cause if all of them were gonna eat, I didn't have nearly enough bacon.

"He turned to the men and asked how many wanted to eat supper. Every one of them raised their hand. I set the big table as quickly as I could, started making more biscuits, and put more wood in the stove.

"They ran me ragged for about an hour trying to feed them all. I never saw so many hungry people, but I finally got them fed. The only one who said thank you during the whole meal was Rob Gibson. He was a man I'd dream about for months to come and I knew it. I couldn't understand why he was running with the scoundrels who'd assembled that night, with the exception of one other fellow, Ferrell Drummond, who was slightly built and had a limp. He spoke proper, and was a Studebaker dealer in Newnan.

"Rob Gibson and Ferrell Drummond were two people very much out of place with the rest of those folks, at least in my mind. They were big burly men who looked like they worked for a living with their hands. One's name was Bob Townley. He was especially rough, and spoke with a bit of a foreign accent, just enough that I knew he came from outside the area. He had a pistol belt with a big .45 hanging in it. It seemed a bit strange, but it was a strange crowd.

"Another fellow said he was a blacksmith from Newnan. His name was Dan Minnish. He was a big fellow. I remember when I first met Will, I sort of compared him to Dan because they were both about the same size. Maybe Will was a little taller.

"The third fellow was named Emmitt Macky. He swaggered in like he owned the place. He was a loudmouth showoff. He took out a wad of $50 bills and fanned it in front of my eyes. 'Sweety, I probably got more money than all the rest of these people put together. I suspect I'll have all of theirs to go with it soon. You're a cute little thing,' as he reached behind me and pinched my butt.

Once again I guess I blushed a little bit. Fanny suddenly stopped and said, "My goodness, Gene, you better get over that blushing. Folks are gonna make your life miserable if you don't stop turning red every time somebody says something a little bit off color."

"I know it Miss Fanny. I hate it, but can't help it. Please don't stop."

"As soon as I cleaned off the table, Pa invited each of the men to take a seat. He took two new decks of playing cards out of an inside jacket pocket, one blue and one red, and put them on the table.

"He told me to get a spittoon for Blake and ashtrays for the smokers, which was everybody around the table. Pa smoked Prince Albert. He rolled his own cigarets. Dan Minnish rolled his own out of a sack of Bull Durham. Emmitt Macky had ready-rolls. The picture on the package looked like eagle wings, just a set of wings, and they must have been six inches long.

"Rob Gibson smoked something called American Cigarets. Ferrell Drummond had some that looked like he'd made 'em with a home-made roller. At least they were in an unmarked package.

"Pa drank a couple cups of coffee. I knew it had been over an hour since he'd had anything to drink. After eating supper he seemed to be fairly sober.

"He picked the blue deck of cards off the table, tossed the joker out, and made sure the deck was complete. Then he passed it to Emmitt Macky on his right and told him, 'Mix them up while we decide the rules we are going to play by.'

"Emmitt Macky started shuffling the cards as Pa asked the table what they would like to play. Blake Thompson said, 'Let's play the only game there is, five-card stud. Anything else is a girl's game. That's the only real man's game, five-card stud.'

"That started an argument with Macky. He said, 'Don't be stupid, draw poker was invented a long time before stud poker was.'

"Bob Townley laid his gun on the table and said, 'Gentlemen, cut out the fuckin' arguing. We'll play five-card stud, seven-card stud, and five-card draw, which are the true poker games in this world. Let's shut up the shit and decide what we're going to bet. That's the most important part.'

"Emmitt Macky started to speak, then looked down at the gun laying in front of Townley. After a brief pause he said, 'I vote you can bet anything you've got on the table or got in your pockets. No markers; if anybody wants to make a private transaction, such as cashing a check, it is absolutely that, a private transaction. The check goes in the pocket of the man who cashes it and the money goes on the table.'

"With that he reached in his pocket, pulled out the big roll I had seen earlier, which must have been more than $2000, and said, 'Here's my roll. You can win any part of it or all of it. When that's gone I'll get up and leave and won't come till another day.'

"Townley said, 'You stupid son-of-a-bitch, Emmitt, put the fuckin' money back in your pocket. Don't have more than $200 or so on the table; put the rest back in your pocket. What if the law wants to raid this damn game? They'll get every cent on the table and we'll never see a penny of it again. That's just plain damn stupid.'

"Emmitt started up out of his chair, but once again looked at the pistol and thought better of it. He said, 'Wait a minute. I'm not gonna let that pistol run this poker game. Do you know something we don't know? Are you expecting the law to raid this game?'

"Townley said, 'Hell, no, but use your brain man. We're playing in a bootlegger's house. You never know when the law is going to decide to raid him for whiskey. If we're playing poker and this money is on this table, it's illegal as hell. He's gonna take all the money and it'll never be seen again.'

"Macky looked around at the rest of the table; everybody nodded in agreement, so Pa announced, 'You can play all the money you've got. Somebody can cash a check for you if they wish. You can play all you can write a check for if somebody will cash it. It's strictly a personal transaction and it goes no further than the two who do it. Is that agreeable to everybody?' All nodded agreement.

"'I know all you fellows are honorable men, but just to make damn sure this game is on the up and up, and stays that way, the man behind the dealer cuts the cards, the man before the dealer names the game. We'll do it in that order. Any objections?' No one spoke. 'Since this game is in my house, I'm going to see we obey the rule we've agreed to. Now the limit, do I hear any suggestions?'

"Townley said, 'Dollar ante, pot limit.'

"Pa looked around the table and once again asked the question, 'Is that agreeable?'

"By now, Gene, I was really spellbound. I knew nothing about poker, but everything was so precise and everybody was so solemn and sober about it. I began to get a spooky feeling about anything where the rules were this stringent. Money appeared in front of each player. I had never seen so much money."

Suddenly a nearby clap of thunder grabbed Fanny's attention. She jumped up out of the chair as if she'd been struck.

"Excuse me Gene. I've got some peaches I'm drying out back. I need to take them in if it's going to rain. They are almost finished drying, and if they get wet, it'll spoil them. I'll be right back."

I asked if I could help.

"No, no, just keep your seat, I'll be right back."

While she was gone I started thinking. Almost every time Uncle Will told me any part of his life, there was a poker game involved. I knew a deck of cards by simply stopping him and having him describe the cards, the number, and the figures on the cards. She seemingly was about to describe another poker game.

I was 17 years old and I'd never seen a deck of playing cards in my life. Of course I knew I'd lived a rather sheltered life. I had

seen a deck of Rook cards. All they had were different colored numbers. I began to wonder if everybody in the world, except my family, engaged in gambling. Gambling and drinking were forbidden
in my family. We just didn't do it. We didn't talk about it. But
apparently everybody else in the world gambled and drank.

Most of the games I'd heard about were really exciting. In one,
Uncle Will told me about a fellow who got shot right between the
eyes. I was already very much interested in the one Fanny Hawk
seemed about ready to describe. Presently she returned and said,
"Where was I, Gene?"

"Miss Fanny, you were talking about how much money was on
the table, more than you'd ever seen."

"Oh, yeah," she said. "They'd agreed on the rules. Pa suddenly
grabbed the deck and started dealing cards around to the left and
said, 'First jack deals.' He dealt all the way around to Emmitt Macky
who got the jack of spades. Pa picked up all the cards and placed
the deck in front of Macky. Everyone put a dollar in the middle of
the table. They called it the ante.

"Emmitt took the cards and slowly shuffled. The excitement I
felt gave me a tingling sensation right down to the tips of my toes.
I don't know if it was all the money, or if it was seeing the strange
and beautiful pictures on the faces of the cards. I had no idea what
it was, but those men captured my total attention.

"As soon as Macky finished shuffling, he placed the cards in front
of Pa. Pa took the cards, halved the deck, and placed the bottom
of the pile on top.

"Macky picked up the cards and asked Minnish to name the game.

"'Seven card stud.'

"Emmitt pushed his chair back and dealt two cards face down to
each player. Then he put the deck on the table and very deliberately turned the cards face up and tossed one to each player in a
clockwise rotation.

"As soon as Emmitt had dealt a card to himself, he looked over
at Gibson and said, 'ace of spades bets.'

"Gibson bet $5. Thompson also tossed in $5. Pa folded his hand.
Macky did the same. Minnish said, 'I call $5,' as he put a $5 bill in
the pot. So did Townley and Drummond.

"Macky dealt one more card around. I don't remember the cards they got, but at the end of the game, Gibson won close to $100. He raked it in and stacked it up. He had $1s in one pile, $5s in another, $10s in another, and $20s and $50s in another stack.

"It appeared to me at that point he probably had $600 or so in front of him. I stood back away from the table, between Macky and Minnish so Gibson could get a good look at me every time he looked up, and he did quite frequently. Once I thought he winked at me, but I wasn't sure. Anyway, it set my heart aflutter.

"It was probably about 11:30, maybe midnight. The game had gone back and forth, and it appeared nobody was losing a lot of money, and nobody was winning a lot of money. It was beginning to get a little bit boring to me.

"Pa told me, 'Get a gallon of the peach brandy I ran off a couple of weeks ago and give everybody a glass. Maybe that will liven the party up.' Pa started bragging on how wonderful it was.

"'Take a sip. You can taste the fuzz on the peaches.'

"I took some glasses, poured eight to ten ounces in each, and set one to the right of each player.

"About ten minutes later the party livened up considerably. They started talking louder and louder, and the betting seemed to be getting bigger. Every man around the table had consumed eight to ten ounces of 100 proof peach brandy. You could definitely tell it by listening to them.

"Blake Thompson ordered another glass. Then everybody at the table ordered a refill. You could tell their tongues were beginning to get thick. It was taking them longer and longer to look at the cards. I was beginning to get bored again.

"Blake Thompson put two fingers over his lips and shot a stream of snuff toward the cuspidor. It missed the cuspidor and landed on my floor, my freshly mopped floor. I almost said, 'Don't do that any more.' He looked up and saw the scowl on my face. 'Sorry little lady, I'll try to do better next time.'

"There was no way that pig could have known the contempt I held for him in my heart. If he had, he would have got up and left. He laid the deck in front of Gibson. Rob cut the cards. Before he picked them up he said to Pa, 'Name your poison, Billy.'

"Pa said, 'Let's play seven-card stud.' Blake stood up and pushed the chair back so he could reach across the table. He dealt two cards face down to everybody, then sat down and continued to deal face up cards. He flipped the three of hearts. Macky got the four of spades, Minnish, the seven of diamonds, Townley, the six of clubs, Drummond, the jack of diamonds, Gibson, the queen of spades. Thompson dealt himself the deuce of diamonds.

"'Queen of spades is high,' he said, 'your bet Mr. Gibson.' Rob Gibson looked carefully around the table, picked up his two hole cards, studied them for a minute. 'Study long, study wrong,' said Blake in a loud voice."

"Miss Fanny, you know you're telling me about a card game that happened 50 years ago. You're naming what each player got, their names, and where they were sitting. You were 14. How on earth can you remember this much detail from 50 years ago?"

"I was coming to that later on, Gene. It seems I was either cursed or blessed by the Almighty himself. It's more a curse than a blessing. I have what's called a photographic memory. I can look at a page of a book, shut my eyes, and read it to you from memory.

"You may say to me, that's wonderful. But I'm telling you it's more of a curse than a blessing. There are an awful lot of things that happened in my life that would be best forgotten. I don't know how to forget. It is something I just never did learn.

I'd never heard of anything like this. I didn't disbelieve her, but couldn't believe her either. There was a Bible lying on an end table. I picked up the Bible, held it open in front of her, and said, "Would you show me?" She looked at the Bible, I took it away and sat down. She quoted those two pages word for word! I became a believer in photographic memories. I said, "Miss Fanny, please continue."

"Gibson took a $5 and two $1 bills. 'I bet $7, the amount of the pot.' Drummond studied the rest of the table thoroughly, looked at his face-down hole cards twice. Townley was playing with his pistol. He turned it up, looked at it, then laid it down. He finally said, 'Drummond, call or fold.'

"Drummond smiled at him and said, 'I raise, I call his seven, the seven in the pot which makes 14, and my seven to call makes 21, and I raise $21.' That got everybody's attention.

"Townley laid his gun an inch to the right, studied his hole cards, then began to look around the table. By now I was pretty much beginning to catch on to straights, flushes, two of a kind, three of a kind, and a full house. I fairly well understood what beat what because I'd been watching for the better part of three hours.

"Of course with two cards down and only one up, nobody looked that impressive. There was not an ace showing, but you could tell the betting had turned serious. Townley even stood up and pushed his chair back to better see the rest of the table. Once again he studied his hole card, then he called.

"'It'll cost me $28 to see another card, is that right?'

"'That's right,' Blake said.

"'I don't see nothing that powerful,' Townley said. 'I call the $28.'

"Minnish did likewise. Macky called. When it got Pa's turn, he looked at his hole card, then looked at his three of hearts, and back at his hole card. He said, 'That's pretty steep fellows, but I think I'll see another card.' With that, he put in $28. Now it was Blake's turn.

"Blake said, 'Boy that brandy is taking effect now. I don't see nothing that looks like a $21 hand. But I got me a little thing working over here. I'm just gonna call. I call the $21. Now, Mr. Gibson, look what you've started. It'll cost you $14 more to stay in.'

"Looking at me, Rob Gibson said, 'Faint hearts never won fair lady. Count the pot, but let me call first 'cause I want that counted, too. Here's my $14,' he said as he put his money in the pot.

"Townley started back fidgeting with his gun. He said, 'There's seven players and we've all got $21, plus $1 each ante, which makes $22 for each man in the pot. Seven times $22 is the $154 currently in the pot, Mr. Gibson.'

"Rob Gibson said, 'Gentlemen, that is what it is going to cost you folks to see the next card, $154.' He laid three $50s and four $1s on top of the stack. Once again he looked at me, and I know he winked that time. A thrill ran up my spine. God! He was good looking.

"Drummond took a big swig of peach brandy and looked at his hole card, studied everybody else's up card, slid his chair back, then stood up for closer inspection, as if to make certain he hadn't misread anybody's cards. He said, 'I call,' and put his $154 in the pot.

"Now it was Townley's turn. His behavior was almost identical to Drummond's. Finally Emmitt said, 'Goddam, get in or out. Grandma was slow but she was old and blind. Get in or out, one or the other!' Townley picked his pistol up and glared at Emmitt then laid it back down.

"He said, 'You son-of-a-bitch, $154 is a lot of money. I'll put my goddammed money in when I'm ready.'

"The game tightened up just a notch. You could feel the tension. It was no longer a friendly poker game. Most of the men were pretty drunk. Then with great care and deliberation, and without saying a word, Townley counted out $154. Macky followed suit.

"Pa turned his three of hearts over to fold. Blake counted out $154, stacked it in front of him, and picked it up, acting like he was going to throw it in the pot. Then laid it back down and studied his cards some more. Finally, appearing most reluctant, he picked up his money and threw it in the pot and said, 'Cards.'

"Turning up the ten of diamonds Blake said, 'Queen of spades gets the ten of diamonds.' Turning the seven of clubs he said, 'the jack of diamonds gets the seven of clubs.' 'The six of clubs gets the king of clubs, seven of diamonds gets the deuce of hearts, the four of spades gets the nine of hearts. Dealer gets a pair of deuces, deuces check.' 'To the queen ten,' Rob Gibson said, 'queen ten, what is the size of the pot?'

"Bob Townley said, 'There should be $946 in the pot, six of us put in $154 each, and Billy put in $22—there should be $946.'

"Rob Gibson said, 'That's my bet.' He reached inside his jacket pocket, took out a stack of $100 bills that looked new, laid them out in front of his cards, slowly he counted ten $100 bills and threw them in the pot. Then very deliberately, he took out two $20s, a ten, and four $1s, announcing, 'My change is $54.'

"Bob Townley growled, 'Count the goddam pot.'

"Pa stood up and said, 'Gentlemen, gentlemen, please, please, I've been watching the pot. It's correct. I will guarantee the pot, Bob. Now let's be more gentlemanly. We're getting some serious money in this game. How about everybody behaving?'

"Bob Townley said, 'I want the goddammed pot counted *now!*'

"Pa said, 'Okay, Bob.'

"Pa very carefully started stacking the bills in their proper denomination, one on top of the other. When he finished, he asked me to get a pencil and a tablet. I delivered it to the table. They counted the $100s, the $50s, the $20s, the $10s, the $5s, and the $1s and totaled it up. Even though they were all fairly drunk, the pot was correct. There was a total of $1892.

"Blake said, 'Jack, seven, call, raise, or fold.'

"Drummond said, 'Jack, seven, over, too rich for my blood.'

"'Six, king of clubs, fold, call, or raise?'

"'I call,' said Townley, as he counted out his $946.

"'What does the deuce seven do?' he asked Minnish.

"'Deuce seven calls.'

"'Nine, four, call, fold, or raise?'

"'I call,' said Macky.

"Blake once again deliberately counted the money in front of his cards. He picked it up, and started to throw it in the pot when he paused and acted as if he'd changed his mind. Finally and reluctantly, he threw it in and said, 'Pair deuces calls.'

"Once again he started flipping the cards around the table, 'Queen, ten, queen,' he called out as he dealt the queen of diamonds to Rob Gibson.

"'Busted flush,' he said as he tossed Townley the jack of hearts.

"'A pair of sevens,' as he flipped Dan Minnish the seven of spades.

"'A pair of nines to the nine, four, dealer gets the ace of diamonds.'

"'A pair of queens, your bet.'

"Once again, Rob Gibson asked how much was in the pot. Pa had a pencil and a piece of paper. He had multiplied out the figures, and he announced to the table there was $5676 and added, 'Thank God, ain't but $22 of it, mine.'

"That brought a chuckle from Rob Gibson as he said, 'That's my bet.' He counted out 56 $100 bills, two $20s, a $10, a $5, and a $1. He picked it up and tossed it into the pot.

"I caught my breath. That was a fortune laying there on our dining table. I couldn't believe these men so recklessly handled money in that fashion, and I wondered, where did they get it?

"Of course it was my understanding Rob Gibson owned at least one or two cotton mills in Newnan, so I figured he could afford to bet that kind of money. I didn't know much about the other people, but Lord, that was an awful lot of money.

"'Call, raise, or fold,' Blake said to Bob Townley.

"Bob Townley picked his two hole cards up and held them in his hand, passing one in front of the other, back and forth a couple of times. Emmitt Macky said, 'What you trying to do Bob? You can't rub the spots off of them. Call the bet or get out.'

"Bob Townley took a sip of the peach brandy, and picked up his pistol. He pushed his chair back, stood up, reached across the table and put the barrel of the pistol against Emmitt Macky's forehead. He cocked the hammer. When it clicked the only thing you could hear in the kitchen was the ticking of the 8-day clock. I don't think anybody breathed for a full minute. In a low growl, he said, 'Son-of-a-bitch, bat your eyes and I'll blow your fuckin' brains out.' Nobody moved a muscle.

"Just as abruptly, Bob Townley pulled the pistol away, let the hammer fall slowly back in the safe position, and sat down. He took a packet of $100 bills out of his pocket and made the pot right. Everybody breathed easier. Nobody yet said a word.

"'A pair of sevens,' called Blake, weakly.

"'Sevens fold,' said Dan Minnish.

"'A pair of nines,' Blake said to Macky.

"Macky still as white as a ghost, picked up his three other cards and turned them upside down without saying a word.

"'Deuces fold,' Blake said in a subdued voice.

"'Cards to the gamblers,' as he flipped the ten of clubs.

"'Queens and tens bet,' he said as he tossed Bob Townley the king of diamonds.

"Rob looked to have only three or four $100 bills in his stack. Townley looked to have about the same amount of money. Rob said, 'Queens and tens bets $100.'

"'What happened to the nerves of steel? You tried to buy the damn pot and you've run everybody out except me. I call $100, and raise $1000 if you want to see the last card,' Townley said, taking a packet of $100 bills out of his inside coat pocket.'

"Gibson felt around all of his pockets. He said, 'I only have $300. If you'll let me write a check, I'll call the $1000, or I'll have to play all in for $300 and I'll only call $300. You'll have to take out $700.'

"Townley started drumming his fingers on the table, 'We've got a big shot son-of-a-bitch who went broke on one hand. I won't take your damn check. I want your ass out of the game and I got you beat.' Saying that, Townley took $700 out of the pot and put it on his pile and ordered Blake to deal the cards.'

"'Last one down and dirty,' Blake said.

"Gibson said, 'Well, it's nothing but a showdown now. I've got three queens and a pair of tens.'

"Townley said, 'That ain't near enough. Three kings and a pair of jacks, as he turned up a full house, kings full of jacks.'

"Rob Gibson said, 'I have to go home, it's past my bedtime. Gentlemen, if you would excuse me.'

"Drummond said, 'I'm about busted too. Can I tie my horse behind your surrey, we're going the same way?'

"'I'm about tapped out too and I hate to ride my horse back to Newnan. How about me riding along?' Minnish said.

"Rob agreed, then Emmitt Macky made the same request. 'Sure, why not, there's plenty of room in the surrey.'

"Rob Gibson walked around the table and took my hand in his hand. He kissed my hand and said, 'Young lady, I hope to see you again sometime under more pleasant circumstances.' The four men walked out the door leaving three poker players seated at the table.

"No sooner were they gone than Bob Townley reached across, grabbed the deck and said, 'My deal.' Slowly but surely over the course of the next three hours, Townley went broke. At six o'clock in the morning, well after daylight, Bob Townley played all in and went bust just guessing from the pile of money in front of each place. Pa and Blake Thompson each had about the same amount. Between them they must have had maybe $25,000. Townley was so drunk he staggered over to a settee we had in the corner next to the fireplace and passed out. He left his gun on the table.

"Pa and Blake were both pretty drunk. They were arguing whether both should take their money and try another day or whether to continue on with just the two of them butting heads, they called it.

"Finally, Blake went around and sat in Bob Townley's seat. He said, 'Let's play until one of us has all the money.'

"Pa said, 'Suits me.'

"Even though Blake appeared more drunk than Pa, he was slowly winning the money. He would act like he was trying to bluff Pa and bet an outrageous amount on a sorry looking hand. He always had just enough to beat Pa. Pa's pile kept dwindling and his kept growing.

"Finally about 7:30 AM, I didn't think I could stay up another minute. Pa's pile was just about gone. He had an ace, a ten, a jack, and a king. Blake didn't have anything bigger than a ten. They were playing five-card stud. Pa checked after all the cards were down.

"Blake said, 'I'll bet you $1000.'

"Pa picked up his money and started counting it. 'One, two, three, four, five. I ain't got but $500,' he told Blake. 'I'll call $500 of it, take $500 out.'

"Blake looked at me then looked at Pa and said, 'Billy, you can call it all if you will throw her in. Throw her in the pot and you can call the whole $1000.'

"Pa said, 'Blake, I can't bet her, she's my daughter. One day she'll want to do as she pleases even though she is a child now.'

"'Ain't she always done what you told her to, Billy? All you have to do is tell her to come live with me. You just give me your word she belongs to me, that's good enough for me. It don't matter what she wants, she's only a girl anyhow.'

"Pa said, 'You've got it, Blake. Fanny's in the pot, I call. What have you got?'

"Blake turned over a deuce in the hole. 'A pair of deuces,' he said.

"Pa said, 'Shit!' and promptly passed out.

"Blake staggered to his feet. I dodged as he reached out his bear-like arms to grasp me. He said, 'You belong to me now, honey, and you're going home with me.'

"As I darted by him, he fell forward in a big fat ugly heap, passed out cold. Pa was asleep with his head on the table. I scooped their money off the table and put it in a pillow case. I had just become the richest 14-year-old girl in Coweta County or maybe the whole world."

Runaway

I couldn't help but smile as Fanny talked about scooping the money up from the just-terminated poker game and stuffing it in the pillowcase. My mind drifted back to a similar poker game Uncle Will told me about the previous spring, where he did almost exactly the same, except this game had a much more tragic ending. The gods must have decreed these two people meet somewhere during their lifetime.

I guess she noticed the smile on my face. She said, "Do you find this story amusing?"

"No, I find this ironic. You should know about Uncle Will's poker game in Maine."

"Oh yes, I do, I see why you smile."

"I had a pinto named Charger that weighed about 850 pounds. Ma once told me one of the Civil War generals who fought for the South had a horse named Charger. I don't remember which one it was, but that was my pinto's name.

"I went to the barn and saddled him. I took all the clothes I could stuff in another pillowcase. I finished stuffing the pillowcase full of clothes. I closed the tops of them up good and then tied them together. Then I swung them on behind the saddle and headed for Newnan.

"I tied Ol' Charger to the hitching post in front of the biggest dry goods store in Newnan, took my two pillow cases inside, and picked out a nice suitcase, big enough to hold all of the clothes. Then I bought a couple of nice dresses and some fancy underwear.

"I asked the manager if I could use his dressing room. I took all the clothes I'd brought from home, plus the ones I'd just bought, and packed my new suitcase full. There was a secret compartment where I stuffed all the money. I had everything in the suitcase and my new clothes on. I thanked the manager for use of the dressing room and paid my bill. Then I walked to the railroad station with my heavy suitcase.

"I asked the ticket agent when the next train came. He asked, 'Going which way?' I almost said it didn't matter, then, 'North,' and he said there'd be one leaving headed for Carrollton, Bremen, Cedartown, Rome, Chattanooga, within the hour.

"I purchased a ticket to Chattanooga for $8, then sat in the waiting room trying to collect my thoughts. What I hated most about the whole business was leaving Charger. I loved that little pony, but my Pa'd bet an ace-high against a pair of deuces and threw me in the pot. Knowing Pa, he'd have stuck to his word and forced me to live with Blake Thompson. Leaving home forever was a small price to pay to keep Blake from pawing over me.

"I could hardly wait to get out of Newnan. I thought, as drunk as Pa and Blake were, they should stay passed out for a good long time, but I was really happy when I got aboard that train. As it pulled out, I caught sight of an undertaker's surrey out of the corner of my eye. It was Pa and Blake Thompson!

"They tied to the hitching post in front of the railroad station and started in just as the last car cleared the platform. Now I had a real worry. If Pa wired ahead and had the police pull me off the train in Carrollton, I'd shortly be headed back to Newnan to suffer my fate for taking the money. Not only that, he'd surely force me to live with Blake Thompson.

"I sat in the seat and frantically searched for a solution to my problem. If they telegraphed ahead to Carrollton and asked them to search this train, they'd surely find me and put me in jail until Pa and Blake could get there. What could I do?

"Before Ma died, she took a lot of magazines. I'd read in magazines about romantic railroad trips and knew something about railroad trains—dining cars, Pullman compartments, and all—but as far as using this information, I didn't have the faintest notion how.

"As the train went through the countryside and neared Newnan, I got up, passed through the car, went out the door, and stood in the little open compartment between the cars. I thought about jumping off. I'd rather do that and break a leg than to have to go back if they caught me in Carrollton, which they surely would.

"The day coach I was on was next to a Pullman sleeper. As I was standing there pondering my fate, out walked a middle-aged

pullman porter. Very politely he said, 'Good morning, ma'am.' I
said, 'Good morning to you.' I'd never been around blacks in my
life. Ma said the Klan had run 'em all out our neck of the woods 20
years before I was born. He was the first black man I had ever seen.

"A tiny germ of a plan began to take shape in my mind. I asked
him if he took care of more than one car. I had seen black porters'
pictures in the magazines advertising about how comfortable a
sleeper is when traveling across country, as well as what a great
adventure it could be.

"'No, I take care of two cars.'

"I said, 'Which, this one and the next one?'

"'Yes, ma'am.'

"'Are all the compartments full in those two cars?'

"'No, ma'am, I got one empty. It's a little bit early for the folks
to be leaving Florida yet, but after this run they'll all be full.'

"I began to get excited.

"'Could you hide me in that compartment where nobody could
find me if they searched this train?'

"'Well, lord a mercy young lady, why would a pretty young lady
like you wanna hide where nobody couldn't find you?'

"'I didn't say I wanted to, I asked you if it would be possible?'

"'No, ma'am, I don't think it would be possible. If I wanted to
hide you where nobody could find you, there's a hollow compartment over the ceiling where we keeps extra blankets, extra sheets,
stuff like that. If I really wanted to hide you where nobody would
find you, I'd put you up there, let you crawls way back and hide.
Then nobody would find you. But you 'bout as big as anybody could
be and get up there and hide though, I'll tell you that.'

"'I want you to hide me.'

"'No, ma'am, I can't do that.'

"'Why can't you?'

"'Young lady, do you have any idea what these folks here in
Georgia would do to a colored if he touched a white girl, especially a young, white girl as pretty as you is?'

"'I've got to hide,' I pressed him. I knew he was scared, 'before
we get to Carrollton. If you don't hide me I'm gonna tell 'em you
tried to pull my clothes off. If you hide me and get me out when we

get above Cedartown, I'll give you $100. You'll be doing me a great favor if you'll do that. I promise you, you might even save my life.'

"'Ma'am, don't get me mixed up in something like this, please don't do this.'

"'I looked at him, opened my mouth wide and said, 'I'm going to scream you tried to pull my clothes off.'

"'Ma'am, please! You stay right here. Give me two minutes, then you walk in the car. I'll have a blanket hanging across the aisleway of the car. You walk behind the blanket, and I'll boost you up through the trap door. I'll call you when we get above Cedartown. Please ma'am, wait until I call you. Don't make no noise. If you do, you're gonna get me killed.'

"I felt sorry that I did what I did, but that was the only chance I saw to escape from Blake Thompson. I guessed two minutes by counting slowly to 120 and then went into the car. Just as the porter had told me, there was a blanket hanging across the aisle. I hurriedly got behind it. He was standing there with a stepladder under a two-foot trap door.

"I climbed to the top of the ladder. There was room for me to crawl in the attic of the Pullman car. I climbed over some blankets and sheets, and found myself a good comfortable place. Turning around to face the door, I told him I was fixed. He stuck his head up and said, 'Ma'am, please let me tell you when it's time to get out,' then he closed the door. It was very dark.

"Gene, when I saw Papa and Blake Thompson drive into the railroad station just as we pulled out, my heart sank. I knew the train would more than likely stop at Arnco or Sergeant. If he wasn't able to catch up in Arnco or Sergeant, he surely could be in Carrollton before the train stopped there.

"After I was safely hidden in the compartment over the Pullman car, I thought I'd go instantly to sleep, but in the jostling of the train and the excitement, sleep wouldn't come. We hadn't been traveling more than 15 minutes when we started slowing down. It was dark as pitch in the compartment. The train seemed like it had stopped more than a few minutes. I'm guessing it was in Arnco.

"As the train started moving again, I thought I heard some hollering and yelling, which scared me to death, but the train be-

gan to pick up speed and the voice died away. I just knew it was Pa
and Blake outside yelling for the train to stop so they could get
me. I was beginning to wish I'd jumped off and broken my leg.

"I felt trapped. I began to squirm and wiggle my way back to the
very end of the car. There were sheets and blankets there; must
have been dozens of each. I thought they were stacked high enough
so nobody could stick their head up high enough to see me.

"The ride from Arnco to Carrollton was one of the tensest times
of my life. I couldn't know what was in store for me when I got to
Carrollton, but I knew in my bones that Pa and Blake were chasing that train.

"While we were traveling, I eased one of the blankets under me
so I wouldn't bump the ceiling when I had to move to keep from
getting the cramps. Then I pulled a blanket off one of the stacks so
I could cover myself up if it came to be necessary.

"After what seemed like an hour, though it couldn't have been
more than 20 or 30 minutes, the train slowed down for Carrollton.
The minute we stopped I could hear loud voices. I heard somebody yell, 'Don't let any passengers on or off. Keep the doors closed.'
Then there was yelling and cussing right below me.

"I recognized Pa's voice, and Blake's voice, and the porter's voice.
It sounded like I could almost reach out and touch them. There
was a voice I didn't recognize, but I soon came to realize it was the
conductor of the train. He spoke in the most civil voice of all.

"He said, 'Willie, this man Mr. Hawk says his daughter stole the
entire family fortune. His friend here just come along to help him
get her back. She ain't but 14 years old. We know a white girl
bought a ticket in Newnan for Chattanooga, and she ain't in the
coach. Mr. Hawk and Mr. Thompson think somebody has hid her
on this train. Is that possible?'

"'Naw sir, I don't know who'd want to hide nobody on a train.'

"About that time I heard the first voice again, who I now figured to be the conductor, say, 'Mr. Threadgill, how long are you
gonna keep the train here? I've got a schedule I need to make.'

"The voice I assumed to be Mr. Threadgill's answered. He must
have been the sheriff or something. 'We are gonna keep the train
here until we find that gal who stole her Pa's money.'

"'Mr. Hawk, tell me exactly what happened,' Threadgill said.

"Pa started talking, 'Well, we was having ourselves a little card game which I know, Rada, is against the law, but it was just a little private game, you know how those things are. Well it got to be a pretty big game; I lost a whole lot of money. This ain't none of your affair Rada cause this was down in Coweta County. I don't live in Carroll County so it ain't none of your business really.

"'Not only was it the money I had been playing poker with, the little bitch got, I had a trunk where I kept my life savings. She got that, too. The poker game went on pretty late, after the last hand, we went to sleep for a little while, me and Blake here. By God when we woke up she was gone. All the money that belonged to Blake was gone from the poker table. I went to my hiding place and all of my money was gone.'

"Gene, that was a big lie. Every bit of money I took was laying on the poker table. I didn't take a nickel except that, and I figured since I was part of it, it might as well be mine. That's why I took it. Besides, I needed some money if I was going to get away from that place. I didn't want to surrender my virginity to that stinkin' Blake Thompson. What I did may not be right, I'm not trying to justify it, but what they was doing wasn't right either."

"Suddenly there was a loud knock right under me. The man called Rada said, 'What's up there? This railroad car looks taller from the outside. What's up there?'

"'There's storage up there where we keep blankets and sheets.'

"'Is there enough room for a 14-year-old girl to hide?'

"'Yes sir, it would be close, but I suppose a 14-year-old girl could wiggle in there. It'd be a tight fit for a big fellow like you. I suspect a little girl could hide up there alright, if she could get up there.'

"'Mr. Conductor, how many Pullman cars you got on this train?'

"'Seven, Mr. Threadgill.'

"'Are they all made just alike?'

"'Yes they are.'

"'Then all we've got to do is search seven Pullman cars. We might as well begin with his one. How do you get up there, porter?'

"'I've got a ladder right over here, sir.'

"'Is this the only way to get up there?'

"About that time my heart was pounding so hard, I just knew they could hear it standing in the floor below me.

"'Porter, put that ladder up here and hold it. I'm gonna climb up there and see what it looks like up there. Mr. Conductor, does this storage place run all the way from one end of the train to the other or does it stop at the end of each car?'

"'No, it's just the length of each car.'

"About that time they opened the door to the attic. A light from below lit the car all the way to the other end. I was terrified.

"I heard Rada's voice again, 'Now before I go to the trouble to climb this ladder to see if there's a young white 14-year-old girl up there, if I find her up there we're gonna take you right out there to that railroad sign and hang yo black ass. Have you got anything you want to confess afore I go up there and look around?'

"My heart stood still. If the porter answered, I couldn't hear it.

"Threadgill said, 'Hold the ladder steady boys.'

"He stuck his head all the way to the top of the car. I could see him and couldn't understand why he couldn't see me. He asked for a box of kitchen matches, he stood there looking around humming a tune while they brought him the matches. I heard the porter telling him to be careful. That just added to my terror.

"'I don't think these god-damned matches help a bit, I can't see a thing up here. Ed, didn't I see Debbie playing across the street from the station this morning?'

"'Yessir.'

"'Go get her and tell her I'll give her a dollar if she'll crawl around in these cars and see if anybody is up there. We'll start in the car behind. That's the first Pullman, then we'll get this one, then we'll go towards the front. If she's here Mr. Hawk, we'll find her.'

"At that point, I almost started to crawl out. But I was paralyzed with terror, and none of my muscles responded. All I could think about was that greasy Blake Thompson pawing all over me.

"They were gone for a few minutes, they never did close the door. I heard them talking and joking. After a few minutes I heard a little girl's voice, she sounded awful unhappy.

"Rada Threadgill was talking. 'Debbie, I know it's dark and scary in there, but there's a little girl who has run away from home, and she don't know what a bad world this is. If you help find her you'll be doing everybody a big favor. The little girl can't take care of herself in this big bad world, this is her Pa. He was trying to look after her, she's run away from home and that's bad. Now you be a good girl. I'm gonna give you a dollar when you look in all these cars and you've done looked in one. Now go on honey.'

"Rada boosted her up in the door.

"'You go towards the front of the car first, baby, then come back by the door and tell us when you are through with that. Then crawl back to the other end. Look good, honey.'

"'It's dark in here, I'm afraid.'

"She was silent because of the blankets she was crawling over as she explored the front end of the car. Then she came back by the door. 'Pa, there ain't nobody in that end. Let me come down.'

"'Go on, honey, look in the other end of the car.'

"I was lying almost in the car's middle, but at the very end. She went down close to one car wall, made a turn, and then came across me. She felt my leg and moved up, touching every part of my body as she did. She lifted the blanket off my head, I was terrified.

"'Debbie,' I whispered, 'that man down there who claims he's my Pa, he ain't, he's a bad man, and that big one tried to rip my clothes off and see my pee pee. Debbie, they'll kill me if they get me out of the train. You crawl back and please tell them there ain't nobody here. Honey, they'll kill me if you don't.'

"Without saying a word, she crawled on.'

"'Nobody's here, Pa, don't make me go in them other cars.'

"'Honey, you've done two cars, there are only five more to go.'

"Then they were gone. I laid there in terror for another 20 minutes. Finally the train started moving. I uttered a grateful prayer to the Almighty and promptly fell asleep.

"Long before I had slept all I wanted to, I heard his whisper, 'Lady, it's time to come down. Hurry. Hurry!' I snapped wide awake, climbed to the opening, swung down on the ladder, and put a $100 bill in the porter's hand as I headed back for my car. I found my seat, picked up a magazine, and started reading.

"The conductor started through punching tickets, announcing we would be in Rome, Georgia in 30 minutes. While we were in Rome

I checked the timetable and discovered we would be Chattanooga about 5:30 PM, well before dark. That would give me a chance to find a hotel. I needed to make myself up a story that seemed reasonable in the event any of the authorities took notice of a young, unattended girl. I needed to decided what I would tell them.

"I flipped through a magazine and my eye caught an ad for the Beeman Hotel in Chattanooga. I decided I'd tell anybody who inquired first of all, it was none of their business. If that didn't work, I'd say that I was meeting my grandfather at the Beeman. He was to pick me up and take me west to Nashville. I would say I was 19 years old, which was about as old as anybody was going to believe.

"Nobody paid me any attention at the Rome station, so I felt reasonably safe that Pa hadn't sent a telegram to Chattanooga. I decided if anybody asked me my name, it would be Mary Johnson, at least until I got away from Chattanooga.

"There was about an hour of daylight left when we got to Chattanooga. I stepped out on the platform. A porter took my bag, put it on a little cart, and asked me if somebody was waiting for me. I told him, 'No, I need to take a carriage to the Beeman Hotel.' He carried me through the station and put my bag aboard an open carriage with an old man driving. I told him to go to the Beeman Hotel where I was to meet my grandpa.

"He clucked to his horse, I was safely out of the railroad station. I relaxed for the short ride to the Beeman Hotel.

"The desk clerk eyed me suspiciously. I told him that my grandpa was supposed to pick me up tomorrow morning, but we had had a telegram before I left Atlanta, saying it was going to be Saturday, almost a week away, before he picked me up. I would be staying until next Saturday. I gave my name as Mary Johnson.

"A young man in uniform carried my bag up to the second floor of the hotel, unlocked the door, let me in, and handed me the key. I had read enough stories in magazines to know I was supposed to give him a tip but I had no idea how much so I gave him a $1 bill. He seemed very pleased so I made a mental note that $1 was possibly a little too much. I needed to watch what other people did.

"I couldn't believe the luxury for $3 a night. I paid six days rent in advance. I even had my own private, indoor bathroom. I turned the water on and filled a huge tub. One handle got hot water, one handle got cold water. There was soap and towels an inch thick on the shelf. I took one of the most luxurious baths a lady ever had. I felt like a million dollars. 'So this is the way people live in the real world,' I thought as I soaked in luxury in that wonderful warm water I didn't have to heat on a stove. 'This is heaven, how could 24 hours change a life so much?'

"When I finished my bath and got dressed, I went down in to the lobby to see how the rest of the guests behaved. I had to become sophisticated very rapidly if I didn't want to be sent back to Pa and Blake Thompson. I decided I would rather be dead than go back, so I had to learn quickly how to behave as a young lady in an adult world looking after myself.

"I planted myself in front of a settee near the stairway and entrance to the hotel dining room and watched the comings and goings of the men and women. There were far more men than women; there were hardly any women alone.

"I had bought two reasonably fashionable dresses in Newnan, but after noticing what the rest of the women were carrying, my little handbag looked badly out of style. Inquiring at the hotel desk, I asked the clerk if there was a store open at this hour where I could buy a handbag.

"'Yes ma'am, John's Ladies Ready To Wear is open till 9 o'clock and it is only one block east and one block south. You don't even have to cross the street.' Taking my tacky little handbag and pressing it under my arm, I walked the two blocks to John's Ladies Ready To Wear and purchased myself another change of clothes, some more underwear, and a nice handbag. I also stopped by another store to buy some stationery. I thought maybe I ought to write myself a couple of letters from relatives from a distant city in the event I had to show my name was Mary Johnson.

"I went back to the hotel, took my new handbag, which had a nice purse inside it, and put $500 in the purse in various denominated bills. The rest of my money stayed in the secret compartment of my suitcase. By now I was very hungry.

"The waiter was curious whether or not someone was going to join me. I told him I would dine alone and ask him for a few minutes to look at the menu. This gave me an opportunity to observe the behavior of the other guests. The restaurant was half full.'

"I listened intently and watched everything that went on around me so I could adjust my behavior to fit into this kind of world.

"When I finished my meal, I went upstairs and practiced writing with my left hand. I wrote myself a letter from my Aunt Nan Jackson, my father's old-maid sister who was expecting me sometime in late August.

"My newly acquired Aunt Nan Jackson was the headmistress of Tennessee's finest finishing school. Even the Governor's daughter attended her school, as she told me in the letter. She hoped I would take advantage of the opportunity I had from now until the first of the year to enroll in classes of my choice in her finishing school. Of course, she stated in her letter, there would be no tuition charge, which she pointed out would be a savings of over $400. I signed the letter with my left hand, 'Your loving Aunt Nan. Looking forward to seeing you in late August. PS: Tell Billy I was so sorry I couldn't make it to your mother's funeral, but there was no way I could turn loose here.'

"I looked at the letter. It appeared genuine to me and that last touch about mother's funeral seemed to remove all doubt it was a legitimate letter even though Ma had been dead for three years.

"Then with my right hand I wrote myself a letter from my Aunt Jenny, who lived in Baltimore, Maryland. Aunt Jenny insisted that on my way to New York, after I left Aunt Nan's house in Nashville, I should visit with her a few days before I went off on the liner to Europe to begin my studies.

"She, too, mentioned her inability to come to mother's funeral, but her excuse was that Uncle George had recently suffered a spell of gout. He was hardly able to walk and she had to stay and look after him. I dated both letters early July, one the 5th, one the 9th.

"I went to the desk and purchased several three-cent stamps, went back upstairs and put a postage stamp on an envelope and addressed it to Mary Jackson, 1300 Peachtree Street, Atlanta, Georgia. I didn't know if that was a real address for a resident or not, but I didn't figure anybody else who might want some identification would know the difference, either. I addressed one of the

envelopes with my right hand and the other with my left hand and, very carefully, drew the cancellation mark of the post office, one from Baltimore, the other from Nashville.

"I put the letters in an envelope and put the envelopes in my purse. I felt certain if anybody got curious why such a young lady was traveling alone, those letters would be convincing proof I was supposed to be where I was. I worded each of the letters to mention that I had recently celebrated my 19th birthday.

"I had bluffed my way into a room at the Beeman Hotel, but I wanted some better form of identification than these forged letters. I thought it would be helpful to have something more official indicating that I was 19 years old."

"Miss Fanny, I hate to stop you and I want you to continue in just a minute, but I've got to ask you a question. Have you seen Uncle Will since the night he told me he beat the hell out of you and you disappeared?"

"Why do you want to know that, Gene?" she asked.

"Well, I can't figure, unless you've seen him since he claims you left him, how he knew where to look for you. He told me exactly how to get here. The question that comes to mind if you haven't seen him since that time, how did he know how to find you?"

"I did see Will one time about six months after I left. He begged me to come back. Said he would swear off drinking, that he'd never touch another drop if I would just come back. He would marry me, he wanted to settle down, but at that time I was dating a man whom I later married. I just couldn't trust Will. Even though I loved him dearly, I just couldn't trust him. He was too hot tempered and I was pretty sure he was gonna get himself killed. He was a wild one.

"I used to drive around with him on that Harley motorcycle, both of us drunk. He'd get in a poker game, then send me back to the farm for some money. I've dug up that damn stash of money in the middle of the night I don't know how many times to get him another $1000. People around Tallapoosa thought he was made out of money, but I'll get to that later on. I need to tell the story the way it unfolded."

"I want to hear it. He told me who you were with when he first met you and how the first meeting was. The way your story is going, I can't possibly see how you got to be with a carnival man. But I'll shut up and let you tell the story."

"I had to get me some positive identification. People might accept the fact I was 19 years old, but I needed more than two letters. I picked 19 because nobody was going to try to tell a 19-year-old woman what to do.

"In that day and time, most 19-year-old women had been married two or three years, or else they were considered old maids. But I needed some proof I was 19. For the life of me, I couldn't think of anything that would actually prove it, short of a birth certificate. I was not even sure if I was born in Coweta County, Carroll County, or Heard County, Georgia. My own birth certificate was no good anyway for my purposes because I would be only 14 years old.

"While taking breakfast, I realized what I needed was to speak to a lawyer. As soon as I finished, I asked the desk clerk where I could find a good lawyer. Next to me there was a man just registering. When he was asked for identification, he pulled out a document in a red leather case and gave it to the clerk. The clerk opened it and said, 'A passport is about as good an identification as you can get,' while he copied the name on the hotel register.

"That was what I needed, a passport, if that was perfect identification. I didn't know what they were or where you got them, but I bet a lawyer would know. When it came my turn, I asked the clerk if there was a lawyer nearby. He gave me a name and address, wrote them down, along with brief directions on how to get there.

"A short time later I arrived at the address. There was a small reception room with a rather comfortable chair and elegant furnishings. The first thing I thought was, 'This'll be expensive.'

"When the lady behind the desk with a shorthand pad and a typewriter asked if she could help me, I asked her, 'How expensive is an appointment with the lawyer, Mr. Burns?'

"'Just an office call,' she informed me, 'is $6. If he does any serious work for you, he gets $10 an hour, but only while he is working. He doesn't charge unless he was actually working on your case.'

"I then asked her when I might be able to see him. She said, 'He's with a client now. I expect the meeting to last no more than 30 or so minutes. If you would like to wait, you may see him then.'

"I told her I would wait.

"As I sat there, I began formulating the story I planned to tell the lawyer and tried to think of anything that might trip me up if he asked me unexpected questions. I told myself over and over again to think carefully before I answered any questions he might ask and to answer as few questions as I could.

"A short time later the young lady said, 'You can go in and see Mr. Burns now.'

"As I walked in to the room, Mr. Burns got up, came around, and put his hand on the back of a chair in front of his desk. He bowed politely and asked me to have a seat. He went back around the desk and sat in his chair and said, 'What can I do for you?'

"'Mr. Burns, I am new at this sort of thing. I am on my way to New York to spend some time with an aunt of mine, then I am going on to Paris for school. I left the letter at home in Atlanta that told me all the things I would need before I could depart overseas. As I recollect one of the items was a passport. I don't have a passport and I don't know how to get one.'

"He said, 'The first thing you are going to need young lady, is a birth certificate. Do you have that?'

"I said, 'I don't know. My mother died two years ago and she looked after all those things. Pa is a bit careless. He and I have lived alone for the past two years and I don't know even if he knows. If we don't have it or can't find it, can I get another one?'

"He said, 'You are from Atlanta, is that right?'

"'Yes, sir.'

"'Well I am trained in law in the state of Tennessee, of course we are just across the Georgia line; our laws are very similar. We have the Bureau of Vital Statistics here. You call the keeper of the birth and death records in Georgia the Ordinary. We call them a Probate Judge. Each county has one.

"'If there was a doctor present at your birth, then the doctor sent that information to the Ordinary. If you live in Atlanta, it would more than likely be in the Fulton County Courthouse. You would go to the Ordinary's office, tell them your birthday, and ask them to look up your date of birth. You will have to know your parents' and your grandparents' full names.

"'Once you've told them that, they'll find the record of your birth. Very frequently the doctor never bothers to give the child a name. You might be listed as a female child, born to your mother and father. If everything is in order, the Ordinary will prepare a piece of paper stating that you are who you claim to be, and put the seal of his office on that piece of paper. That is your birth certificate.

"'You can go right across the hall, more than likely, to the Clerk of Courts' Office. The Clerk of Courts would ask you to get a photograph, and, in two or three weeks, he would deliver a passport to you, which is good enough identification any where in the world.'

"'Is that the only way you can get a passport?'

"He thought about the question for a minute. 'As far I know it is. Is that a big problem?'

"I said, 'No, I hadn't planned to go back to Atlanta. I guess I'll have to get Pa to do all those things. I don't actually have to be there, do I?'

"'Of course not. Your father can do it all by mail, but it will take a good bit longer that way.'

"I thanked him, and asked if I paid him or the lady out front?

"'Pay her. I hope I've been of some value to you.'

"I assured him he had and left his office, but I was very much troubled. I knew I really needed some positive identification. I had a lot of money. I didn't want to carry it around in the suitcase for the rest of my life. Before I could put it in a bank, folks were going to have to know who I was.

"I went back to the hotel and got a newspaper, hoping something would come to mind that'd help me get a passport showing I was 19 years old. But I didn't really believe that would be easy.

"As I read the paper I looked at each of the ads to see if there was any way I could use the services or products offered to help me get a passport. While thumbing through the paper, I came across the obituaries. For no reason at all, I started reading. The first person in the obituary column was a girl named Judy Collins, who was 19 years old. She'd been thrown from an automobile traveling at high speed, and had died instantly of a broken neck. According to the story, her family had moved from Rome, Georgia, 17 years ago, which would have been when she was two years old. I wondered if the Ordinary in Rome had her in his records. At that moment I made up my mind to go to Rome, Georgia and see.

"I caught a carriage, and asked him to take me to the railroad station. Twenty minutes later I bought a ticket to Rome for the following morning.

"I slept very little that night, thinking of all the things that might happen if anybody in Rome grew suspicious of me or my motives while I was in the courthouse. What on earth would the law do to somebody who stole a dead person's identification? It sent a shutter up my spine, but I needed some identification.

"At 10:30 the next morning, the train pulled into Rome. I took a carriage to the Floyd County Courthouse and went to the Ordinary's office. There was a young man who couldn't have been more than 16 or 17 years old, sitting at a desk. I asked him if he was the Ordinary. 'No, Miss, the Ordinary is my Pa, and he's gone over to the Busy Bee Cafe to get himself a cup of coffee. Can I help you?'

"'I am Judy Collins, I was born in Rome 19 years ago on the 8th day of May, which would be May 8, 1883. Can you look up and see if my birth was recorded or would your Pa have to do that?' He stood up at the desk and stretched up to his full five-foot-five. 'No Miss, I'll be glad to do that. I know as much about this office as Pa does.' He went to a row of shelves behind the desk, pulled out a folder, turned several pages, and holding his hand, he turned and said, 'What was your Ma and Pa's name?'

"I said, 'Ma's name was Alice Robinson Collins, my papa's name was James A. Collins.' I knew that from the surviving parents in the newspaper.

"He said, 'It must be you, your great grandma was Celia Robinson and Zach Robinson?' I nodded. 'On the other side was Lillie Collins and Jeff Collins?' Once again I nodded.

"He said, 'It must be you, I'll make you a copy of it and notarize it for $1—that's what we charge.'

"I said, 'You mean a young fellow like you can do that without your Pa even knowing about it? What's to keep you from taking the money and putting it in your pocket?'

"He bragged, 'I forge Pa's name lots of times for folks, just as long as I collect the money. If Pa thinks I can run the office right, he'll stay over at the coffee house. He's sweet on a waitress over there. He don't know that I know it, but believe me, Miss, he won't care. His seal is here and I can sign his name better than he can.'

"I couldn't believe my good fortune. In less than five minutes I had a notarized copy of a birth certificate. It was so easy. But now my name was no longer Mary Johnson, as I had registered in the hotel in Chattanooga, my name was Judy Collins. My birthday was May 8, 1883, and I had to remember that. I had an official document saying that I was 19 years old.

"I brought my suitcase thinking I might have to spend the night in Rome. Since I had a new name, I couldn't go back to the hotel where I had a week's rent paid, but I had plenty of money. So I went to the railroad station and bought a ticket to Knoxville. The train was leaving in less than 30 minutes, and they assured me I would be in Knoxville well before dark.

"When I got to Knoxville, I took a carriage to the hotel nearest the railroad station which was actually within walking distance. The name of the hotel was the Tennessean. The accommodations were about the same as they were in Chattanooga. I registered under my new name, Judy Collins. As soon as I was in the hotel room, I copied the letters I had been carrying, making sure to change the names in the right places to fit my new identity. I destroyed the other two letters by burning them in the fireplace.

"I went back to the lobby, picked up the evening newspaper, and started looking for advertisements by lawyers. I now had a birth certificate and that seemed to be the most important document on the road to getting a passport.'

"Gene, I know you wonder why I was so frantically trying to get some identification, but it was a man's world back then. It's still a man's world. Women are very much restricted at what they can and can't do, though that sometimes had advantages.

"'A woman was usually safe, especially if she kept good company and stayed away from sleazy joints and that sort of thing. If you appeared to be a woman of means and breeding, nobody bothered you. But I had to have the proper identification to feel safe. I hope you can understand how urgent my quest for a passport was."

"Yes, ma'am."

I looked outside at the lengthening shadows and realized it was getting late.

"Miss Fanny, I have to go, but I truly want to hear the rest of the story, if you'll tell me. May I come back tomorrow?"

She gave me a wistful little smile and said, "Certainly, I don't have any pressing social obligations. I'd love your company."

"There's one other thing I would like to ask you: If I brought Uncle Will, would you see him? Or if he can't come to see you, would you let me take you to the hospital to see him?"

"I'll have to think about that, Gene. I must think on it. I'll think about it tonight, then tomorrow when you come, you'll have my answer."

The Road to Riches

As I drove out of Miss Fanny's front yard and headed back toward Bremen by way of Tallapoosa, my mind kept turning over the predicament of a young woman with no identification, no proof of who she was. When only 14 years old, she'd already suffered the indignity of having a father toss her into a poker pot in the full knowledge that if he lost, he'd force her to live with Blake Thompson. By some bizarre twist of fate, she had now totally captured my imagination. And I was finding it very difficult to not think about her as I bounced along the dirt road leading toward highway Seventy-Eight and my Julie.

Late Saturday afternoon, I wanted to stop by to see Julie, and ask her if we could go out again that night. Just the thought of being alone with her once more pushed me to the very edge of ecstasy. As I drove into her yard, the family's two big red-bone hounds came bouncing out, barking, as if in a fox hunt. A minute later, she emerged from the house looking rather dejected, I thought. I immediately took it to mean bad news for me. She walked over to the passenger side, opened the door, and got in.

"I can't ever see you again."

That wrapped me tighter than a goat's ass.

"Why?" I pleaded.

"I met somebody today I like better," she said.

If she had taken a butcher knife and plunged it in my heart, the pain would have been no greater. I was crushed. I was ashamed and humiliated. How could this beautiful girl say these dreadful words to me after last night?

"I did something last night I never did before," she said, "and I'm not going to do it again until I get married. I met the boy today that I plan to marry. Besides that, you ain't the marrying kind."

I put my head down on the steering wheel trying to think of some rebuttal. I wanted to scream, "I love you, Julie, I love you!" But before I could bring myself to say a single word, she had opened the door and with a little twitch of her butt disappeared into the house.

I started the car and headed for Bremen in the blackest depression I had ever known. In my mind, I turned over and over all of the things she'd said in that brief encounter a thousand times. None of it made any sense to me. I almost ran directly across highway Seventy-Eight when I got back to it, such was my despair. Catching myself, I turned right and drove on to the hospital where I parked and went to room #4.

There were two nurses working with Uncle Will when I walked in. One of them said, "He's taken a terrible relapse. We don't know if we can save him or not. Dr. King is trying the newest sulfa drug on him. He's very weak. We've given him enough morphine to knock out a horse, but he still won't sleep. Every time he shuts his eyes he starts screaming about a terrible person named 'Ebo.'" The nurse was facing away from Uncle Will talking to me. He was weakly motioning with his fingers for me to come to him. Lord, this has been one awful day, I thought.

As I took the chair next to his bed, he whispered in a voice I could hardly hear, "Nephew, I have to confess. Every time I shut my eyes Ol' Ebo is beckoning for me. My life is already as limp as a strand of corn silk. If I go now, my soul'll hang like a spider's ass in the breeze. Get rid of these nurses," he said weakly. "I have a story I have to tell you or my soul will simmer forever. Please, Nephew."

Sitting with one elbow resting on the mattress, and with my head down close to his mouth, I remembered that I had his $23,000 in an old inner-tube in the car parked out front. I hadn't even thought about it since putting it in the tube as I approached Fanny Hawk's house. It was now almost dark, and I was supposed to have the car home and full of gas or else Mama was gonna raise hell.

"Uncle Will, I have to go home. As soon as I get home I have a friend I think I can get to bring me back. I'll spend the night with you if I have to, but now I have to go home. If I don't, Ma will never let me come back to see you." He weakly waved goodbye and said, "Hurry back, Nephew, hurry back."

It was totally dark when I got home, after first stopping at Bud Cole's to fill the car with gasoline. Our barn was across the road from the house. I stopped there, went up in the loft, raked up a pile of hay, and then covered the money-stuffed inner-tube under loose hay so nobody would find it. Then I went to the house and reported to Ma that the tank was full of gas, and I had to go back and see Uncle Will. I told her I'd go and get Harvey Wright to take me. I knew they weren't going to let me have the car.

Ma said, "You sure as hell aren't going to have the car anymore, and I don't even know if I'm going to let you go to the hospital or not. As long as you stick your feet under my table, you're going to do like I say."

I gave Pa a pleading look. He said, "Aw, Ma, let him go. You know how much Will means to him."

"Well, I hope the son-of-a-bitch dies tonight. That way we'll be rid of one parasite."

"Mama, I know how you feel about Uncle Will. You don't have to keep telling me. You've made it clear."

"Sometimes I think he's in league with the devil. He's got some kind of unholy grip on you that's going to take you down the same path of destruction. You'll be lucky if you don't wind up in one of hell's front seats, right alongside him. You'd better listen to your Mama. I'm telling you!"

"I'm going to walk over to Harvey's house and see if I can get him to take me to Bremen. I may not be home before morning."

"You better be here in time to milk the cow. Your Pa took pity-sakes on you and milked her when you weren't back here before dark. But we're leaving early in the morning, and he'll not milk the cow for you then. You get your butt back home and milk that cow the way you're supposed to. That's your chore as long as you stick your feet under my table. Do you hear me young man?"

"I hear you, Ma."

I walked out the back door. It was about a mile to Harvey's house. I was afraid of the dark when I was 6, just as afraid when I was 10, and even though I was now almost 17, I was still afraid. I wished for a dogwood brush-broom to drag behind me and scare off all the lurking spirits as I walked down our country dirt road. When I topped the hill just behind the house, I could see a kerosene lamp glowing from the kitchen window at Harvey's house. Just that feeble light made me a touch braver, but I could still hear them ghosts stepping in every footprint I left, which made me step lively.

At Harvey's house, I asked him if he would carry me to Bremen and then come in the morning and pick me up. Harvey, good friend that he was, said, "I'll be glad to do that, but I don't know if I've got enough gas."

"They've got a gas station that stays open until 11 o'clock in Bremen. I'll buy you a whole tank of gas if you'll take me and come back in the morning to pick me up." I still had $400 of Will's money in my wallet.

Harvey was pleased with my offer.

A short time later, I was back in the hospital room with Uncle Will. There was only one nurse with him when I walked in. She was sitting in the chair holding his hand. He saw me as I walked in and motioned me to the bedside. As I approached, the nurse left the room. I sat down to hear my great uncle's final confession. His voice was weak so I had to listen carefully.

"Nephew, do you remember the morning I walked into Dryden Lumber Company and had my run-in with Preacher Cooper?"

"I sure do, Uncle Will. You embarrassed the hell out of me."

He smiled weakly, "That was not my intention, Nephew. I always took great pleasure in poking a needle in the ass of sanctimonious preachers. I remember when that little son-of-a-bitch was the biggest whorehopper in this part of the country.

"He started whoring around with a streetwalker in Tallapoosa and got himself a good case of clap. Dr. Kirby thought his dick was going to rot off. Back in those days, the treatment for the clap was worse than the clap itself. I would see him every night in Tallapoosa at one of the roadhouses. That was back when they were still mining gold out of the old gold mine. After I heard he had the clap, I didn't see him any more for a good long while. The next thing I know of him, he's a man of God. He's out telling the gospel to everybody who will listen, talking about whorehoppers and whores, and how they take hold on hell.

"I wanted you to know, and this is not what I needed to confess, I was just putting the needle to his ass that morning, letting him know that I remember when he was one of the biggest whorehoppers in this country. I didn't mean to embarrass you."

I remembered that morning very well. Uncle Will drove up in his old bus and came sauntering up across Dryden's yard like he owned the company. As he walked into the office, he said, "Good morning, Nephew." Then he turned to Preacher Cooper and said, "Good morning, Brother Cooper." Just that greeting was designed to piss Preacher Cooper off because Primitive Baptists called each other Brother and Sister, but not outsiders.

Though Preacher Cooper was a man of the cloth, he had the habit of dipping snuff. He kept it in his mouth all the time, and never did rightly learn how to spit. Instead of spitting the way most folks do, puckering up and forcing out a little blob of tobacco juice, he just sort of sprayed it out. 'Cause he did this, he'd coated the whole corner of the office a light chocolate color.

"Will, I'm writing a trip ticket for the boy to deliver some lumber. I'll be with you momentarily."

"Don't pay me no mind, Brother Cooper, I was just in the neighborhood, and I need a little bit of lumber. I got some corn liquor I thought I might be able to trade for it since you hardshells enjoy a nip now and again."

When Uncle Will said that, Preacher Cooper sprayed the trash can and the corner of the office with a mighty explosion of snuff juice.

"Will, this is a business office. We don't carry on such foolishness around here. If that's all you came for, you'd best be on your way."

Uncle Will knew Primitive Baptists didn't believe in drinking strong spirits and he knew for a fact that Preacher Cooper didn't drink anymore. The whole conversation was just to get a rise out of the preacher.

By this time I had backed all the way into the corner of the little office, and was embarrassed to tears. Then Will really stuck his foot in it. He said, "Well, Brother Cooper, I thought you liked liquor, but if you don't like my corn liquor, I know where you can swap it for some hot pussy."

At that, Preacher Cooper sat up quick like he had a pain in his back. He sprayed the trash can in the corner of his office with snuff juice again, and then levitated! He whirled on Will, his face purple with rage, stared for a moment, and then snatched up the telephone.

"Get me the police!" he screamed to the operator.

In a towering rage, he suddenly slammed the phone down in the cradle so hard I thought he'd break it.

"No, Will, I'll throw your ass out myself."

Of course, Uncle Will stood six-feet, six inches tall. It would have pushed Preacher Cooper to reach five feet, so it was a rich sight when he tried to pick Will up by the seat of his pants. Uncle Will simply strolled out of the office, saying, "Brother Cooper, you sure do know how to make a fellow feel unwelcome."

Uncle Will interrupted my reminiscence, tugging at my sleeve. In his low, weak voice, "Nephew, listen carefully. I have to get this burden lifted off my soul. Don't stop me unless you can't hear me.

"Once, when times were real bad, I went up to Tallapoosa and caught a freight train into the Atlanta yards. From there, I caught a train heading north. I was sick of being poor and not having enough to eat, so one day I just up and left for good. When it got dark, I knew the train was already somewhere in Tennessee. I began to see little camp fires alongside the tracks. I was awful hungry, and thought maybe somebody at one of those hobo fires would give me something to eat.

"So I jumped off the train and sprained my ankle. It hurt a lot and began to swell rapidly. I hobbled up to a camp where several hobos squatted around a fire with a can of beans and a can of coffee.

"All I had was an old discarded army sleeping bag and a sore ankle. Even though it was springtime, and I was somewhere near the middle of Tennessee, it still got cold enough at night to freeze the balls off a brass monkey. The swelling in my ankle made me feverish, so I felt all the colder. I pushed in close to the fire. One of the feisty little hobos said, 'Big un', in this part of the country, you don't come scrounging into some other man's fire unless you want your ass whooped. Would you like your ass whooped?'

"You little son-of-a-bitch, I'll pop you in two like a dried corn stalk. No half-pint talks to me like that."

"Due to my size and other considerations, the hobo grudgingly admitted he'd made a mistake. He said he thought he knew me and was just kidding. Of course, when I realized I had somebody who was going to back down a bit, I reached over and got his can of pork and beans, which was just warm enough to start eating. Having no silverware, I just turned the can up and poured a big mouthful. This so infuriated him, he grabbed up a rock as big as a softball and cracked me upside the head.

"I rolled away from the blow, spitting out the beans as that small man crawled on top of me and started pounding me with the rock. I managed to knock the rock out of his hand and stagger to my feet. That's when I realized my ankle was hurt worse than I thought 'cause I couldn't stand it. Falling down from the pain I managed to land on the hobo, momentarily knocking the breath out of him. We wrestled around over the ground in the rough gravel and sand, hitting at each other, clawing, kicking, and scratching. And though he managed an almost death grip on me, I soon flipped him over, pushing his back down into the fire, and then all hell broke loose.

"It's amazing, the strength of a little man when he's thrust onto a bed of hot coals. He managed to scatter the fire over half an acre while trying to get free from the grip he thought he had on me.

"There was a row of plum bushes growing just off the railroad track. Bruised and beaten, my ankle throbbing with pain, I crawled through the bushes to end the fight. I stretched out in my sleeping bag, but sleep wouldn't come. The pain was excruciating.

"About midnight, the swelling seemed to stop, but it was still hurtin' something awful. The hobos were now gathered on the other side of the plum bushes and built a new fire. I crawled through the bushes toward it, and as I got close, I stretched both legs out so's I could examine my ankle by the fire's light.

"All the while, none of the hobos spoke a single word. Rubbing my sore ankle, I finally said, 'I hurt it when I jumped off the train, and when I got down to the first camp fire, I had to whip some smart little son-of-a-bitch's ass, and hurt it even worse. I've been trying to sleep on the other side of these bushes, but the way this thing hurts, sleep won't come. I hope you folks don't mind me sitting here. I mean you no harm.'

"After that, conversation around the camp fire resumed. One of the young hobos spoke first, 'Jim, go ahead and tell us the story you started about that preacher man up in KaneTuck who's got a daughter uglier than a mud fence daubed with green-eye frogs.'

"The word is out around Lexington, a little town about four miles away called Plowshare, that you can get yourself a wife plus a lot of money, if you'll marry the ugliest girl in the world. The story going about those parts is that the preacher, Preacher Nelson they call him, and his wife were out riding in a buggy when his wife was first pregnant with his daughter. It was in the spring, and a sudden thunderstorm came up, as they sometimes do in that part of Kentucky. He started racing the horse, trying to get back to the house before the rain. He was whipping the horse for all he was worth when a bolt of lightning struck the animal atop the head and killed it instantly, slam damn dead.

"'When the horse went down, the shaft of the buggy dug into the ground and flipped it over. Preacher Nelson—he wasn't a preacher at that time, just an ordinary farmer—was okay. He just brushed himself off, as the rain started pouring down. But his poor wife was unable to get up by herself. He tried helping her to her feet, but she couldn't stand up until three months later after she had delivered a baby girl whom the preacher named Josephine.

"As a the result of the near brush with death that killed his horse, and injured his wife, while he came out unscathed, Farmer Nelson decided the Lord was trying to tell him to mend his ways. He felt it was a direct calling to preach the gospel, so he told the brethren in his church he felt he had a summons from the Lord to serve in the ministry, and since he was such an influential farmer and an exceedingly generous contributor to the biggest Methodist church in the town of Plowshare, they ordained him a minister before he'd ever preached a sermon.

"'When his baby daughter was born, his world was complete. He'd made his life right with the Lord. His wife seemed to be recovered, and, at that point, the little girl looked like most little babies. All newborns are ugly, so nothing was thought about her looks till she was about three years old. She just didn't get any prettier, and simply stayed all ugly. But she was a bright girl. There was nothing wrong with her mind. She finished first grade in half a year and graduated from the second grade class about the time she was seven years old. Still, she didn't get any better looking over the years. Of course, the girls didn't seem to pay that fact no mind, but none of the boys wanted to sit close to her or hold her hand. She was so ugly the boys dodged her like a side bar mower.

"'They say when she was a young girl in grade school, she had one of the most wonderful personalities around. But as she grew older she started to develop a personality that matched her looks. She eventually had such a waspish attitude that nobody, not even the girls, wanted to be around her. Finally, she got to where she stayed to herself most of the time.

"'Studies came easy to her. She graduated from high school with honors, or so the story goes. All the time she was writing poetry, beautiful poetry they said, and all of it fantasizing about love. It seemed there was so little love in her life. Her poetry won prizes while she was still in high school, and her Pa, wealthy preacher that he was, sent her to the University of Kentucky, hoping she'd find her a man in college. But she didn't make a single friend while at the university, though she continued to write her poetry and it began to be published in magazines all over the country.

"'It was said her poems were hauntingly beautiful, but with a profound sadness only a broken heart can know. When she graduated at the age of 20, she came back home to sit at her desk in her lonely room and write her beloved poetry. She would go downstairs to eat, but as soon as the meal was done, she'd return upstairs. And there was nothing for her to do, since the Nelson household had plenty of servants. So she pined away her days.

"'This is a part of the story you can believe or not believe,' Jim continued. 'Her father promised a young and ignorant farm boy a section of land, all of the horses, mules, and livestock he needed to make a good farm out of it, plus a new house, if he would just marry the daughter. The only condition was that the boy was not to let her know that Preacher Nelson had anything to do with it. But the ignorant fool started talking about how things were going to be when they moved into the new house Preacher Nelson was building them on a farm he had given him. And he let it slip that he'd been given all this to marry her. She promptly threw him out on his ear, cussed her Pa out for intruding into her life, and went back to her poetry.

"'That taught the preacher a lesson. He was broken hearted. She was the only child they had. He always felt God had visited a terrible shame on him by making her so ugly, but he figured he'd done something to deserve it, so he accepted it as his burden. But he learned not to interfere in her life again directly. He just quietly put out the word that he was not going to make a formal offer to anybody, but whoever married his daughter and made her happy, that fellow would have a very promising future.'

"'I've been there,' Jim said. It was one of the biggest houses I ever saw. I've seen museums, courthouses, and banks bigger, but I never saw a bigger house folks live in. It was white, and there must have been miles of white fences. They had the most beautiful horses I've ever seen. As a matter of fact, I was going to try my luck with that woman. I didn't care how ugly she was. If I could live like that, I could be good to her. I even walked up to the front of the house and started up onto the porch, but my nerves failed me. I just turned around and walked back to the railroad tracks and hopped me a freight. But I always wished I'd gone in there. That was better than a year ago now.'

"The fellow who asked the question in the beginning—whose name was Bill—interrupted Jim at this point, asking him exactly how to get to this farm. Jim laughed a little bit.

"'Why? You want to try your luck with the preacher's daughter?'

"'I might.'

"'If you ride the Great Northern tracks toward Cincinnati and get off at the first stop after Lexington, that'll be Plowshare. The railroad track almost splits the town in half. The folks on the east side of the track are the rich folks, and the poor folks are on the west side of the track. Go to the depot—there's just one road that comes straight in. You walk up that road, it curves around a little bit, but eventually you'll wind up heading almost due west. In about two miles you'll be there.'

"'I wish you had knocked on the door and had a look at her yourself,' Bill said. I'd just like to know for real, somebody who had seen her, how ugly she is. To marry into a family that wealthy, get all of that money, and have that life of ease, she'd have to be powerful ugly or I'd be willing to do it.'

"'I got scared for two or three different reasons. First of all, there was two new Packards in the yard that looked like they had just been drove off the showroom floor. There was a new Harley-Davidson motorcycle with a sidecar. Boy, that was the most streamline looking motorcycle I ever saw. I got to thinking that anybody who could afford to park that much automobile power in their yard just had to be someone to be scared of. I remember how them folks at home who was rich would run up and down the road. One of them killed my Pa's horse, and it hitched to his buggy at the time. So I took off; I guess I was wrong. Then, too, I was thinking about how ugly she was.'

"'Well hell,' said Bill, 'if she's that ugly, you do most of your screwing at night anyway, you can't see what she looks like. If you want some in the daytime, you can put a sack over her head. Why shit, if she's all that ugly, you could put a sack over your own head just in case hers fell off. I sure would have took a peep at her if I'd've got that close.'

"'Well, you're welcome to go on up there and knock on the door. There ain't nobody stopping you. I dare say, ain't nobody married her yet. She's up in her middle 20s now.'

"Finally their talk petered out. I crawled back in my sleeping bag and went off to sleep. I dreamed about what I was going to do the next time I headed north on a freight train. About daybreak, I hobbled back to the railroad tracks and managed to hop the last car of a train heading toward Lexington. All tattered and torn when I left the train in Lexington, I wound up at another hobo camp. It had taken me two days to get to Lexington and my ankle was still very sore, though I could hobble around pretty good. I had every intention of going off to claim the preacher's daughter, but I never mentioned this to the local hobos. 'Cause my clothes were so shabby, and I didn't want to go knock on her door looking that way, I had to find a way to get some better duds. I slept fitfully that night, but at the break of day, I was up and hobbling toward town.

"I limped up Main Street. It was barely 6 o'clock in the morning and there was very little activity. I looked off down one side street and saw a mule barn. There was a big sign across the front of it that read: 'Barr's Mules, Horses, and Other Livestock. We Buy and Sell.' Here was something I knew something about, so I hobbled down to the barn, climbed two steps into a little office, and asked the fellow sitting at a desk if they needed any help. The fellow looked me over from head to toe as if he was judging a horse ready for the dog meat market.

"'You're big enough—what do you know how to do?'

"'I can do any damn thing to a mule or a horse that needs to be done, from shoeing to grooming, to saddling to riding, whatever you need.'

"'What about feeding?'

"'I can do that, too.'

"'I'll pay you $1 a day and let you sleep in the barn.'

"'I'll do it for $2.'

"'Then be on your way, stranger.'

"'On second thought, I'll do it for $1.'

"'I thought so. Go out this door, and ask somebody out there working in the hall how much to feed which mule and get started.'

"'Ain't you even gonna ask me my name?'

"'I don't care what your name is. You're Big Un' as far as I'm concerned, and we pay in cash. I got no need to know your name.'

"There was a fellow about my age in the hall of the barn. I told him I'd just been hired and asked him to show me how they fed the different animals, which the other man obligingly did. During the short tour of the barn, I learned that my young instructor's name was Ben Reeves. He had grown up an orphan and liked working with animals. I also learned that the mule barn didn't belong to the Barr family as the sign said on the front, but was owned by a silent partner, none other than Preacher Nelson. According to Ben, the preacher owned almost every business in town and was a kindly boss, very generous to the people who worked for him.

"Then the subject of Josephine came up. I wanted to know if Ben had ever seen her. The object of the whole masquerade for me was Josephine. Ben had never seen Josephine, but he had talked to a couple of people who had. She was really rather hideous looking according to Ben.

"Ben showed me our quarters, which were really just stables with a wooden floor. All the odors of fresh and ancient manures, mixed there with those of rotting straw and animal liniments, wafted through the walls. But I quickly got used to that. Anyway, I was only going to work there long enough to get some money, buy some decent clothes, and get introduced to the good life as soon as my ankle got well.

"By the time I'd earned enough money to dress suitably, it was late May. I had learned all the details about the estate where the family lived and who was important in their scheme of things. It was time for me to visit the manorhouse of Reverend Nelson.

"I went up the long white walkway to the front door of Preacher Nelson's house and boldly knocked on the door. The birds were singing, the trees still had those pale-green leaves that look so tender before the sun thickens them to a darker green. The lilacs were in full bloom in a flower garden such as I'd never seen in my life. The front and side yards were cut and trimmed in an orderly fashion and looked almost artificial. Overhead, I could hear a blue jay arguing with a mockingbird. Ah, I thought as I knocked on the door, what a beautiful day to meet my true love.

"I stood there expectantly. After a couple of minutes without an answer at the door, I banged louder. Eventually, I heard movement inside. The door opened, and there she stood. I had a strong urge to flee and then another urge to upchuck. My intended bride stood five feet tall. Her eyes were slightly crossed. She could eat corn-on-the-cob through a picket fence, her teeth were so widely spaced. Her complexion looked like cottage cheese, and her greeting matched her appearance."

"'What do you want?' she asked.

"I had made my plans well. I was not going to be turned aside that easily.

"'I came to see the best poetry writer since Elizabeth Browning. Her name is Miss Josephine Nelson.'

"'You've seen her, now goodbye.'

"In my worst hurt tone, I said, 'How could you be so cold to a total stranger? I've never done anything to you. I've read your beautiful poems in Collier's. I once saw one in Harper's. How could you be so cold? You're certainly not like your poetry?'

"'You mean Pa didn't send you?' she said with a slight smile that looked a bit gruesome.

"'Wouldn't know your pop from a sack of salt.' I said, 'I just come from Georgia. My name is Will Cotton. Times are a mite hard, and there isn't much doing down there, so I thought I'd swing by and see the lady who writes such fine poetry on my way north.'

"'That's different. Come in, Mr. Will Cotton.'

"I walked into probably the most elegant room I'd ever seen in my life. Persian rugs covered the floors. Big, comfortable-looking, easy chairs were spaced around in little conversation groups all over the huge room. Three or four Aladdin lamps with spotless globes sat around the room. I knew it would be almost as bright as day when the lights were lit. Such luxury was unimaginable, and my greed was growing by the moment as I gave every article in that room a once-over.

"I noted with wandering eyes that Miss Josephine had a rather trim and neat figure. I thought, if she just had a different face then this would be something else, but then reminded myself that was why I'd come here.

"Josephine invited me to sit. I dropped down in the most luxurious settee I'd ever seen. She picked up a little silver bell from the end table. Almost instantly after it chimed, a servant appeared.

"'Yes ma'am.'

"Josephine asked me if I would like to have a drink. I thought, 'maybe I can drink her pretty,' and ordered bourbon and water. After several minutes, the whiskey began to mellow me. I asked Josephine if she would get some of her poems and read to me. 'In the meantime, if you would, that was awful good bourbon and water—I would like another.'

"She rang the little bell again and ordered me another bourbon and water. She excused herself and presently returned with several magazines and sheets of loose paper. The servant delivered me another drink. I took a man-sized swig, set the glass on the end table at the corner of the settee, turned with all of the poise and culture I could muster as the liquor began to make me a little light-headed, and said, 'May I call you Josie? That name seems to me to fit you so much better.'

"Josephine had grown hard and callous by the treatment she had received at the hands of men, but she couldn't help but melt a little as I spoke of pet names. She felt a little blush.

"'If you like,' she said, still with a bit of acid in her voice.

"Almost instantly she was sorry she hadn't used a softer tone because she could see the hurt in my face.

"'Please forgive me for being so curt. Why, certainly you may call me Josie. I wouldn't mind.'

"'Now, would you read me some of that wonderful poetry?'

"'You choose one, Will. Having read as many of my poems as you have, which do you prefer?'

"Of course, I'd never read any of her poems and had no idea what they were about, but made a lucky guess as to some of them having been published in Collier's and Harper's. I dropped my head as if in deep thought.

"'What is the name of the one where you spoke of spring's beauty?'

"I was hoping with all my might she had written concerning spring, and indeed she had.

"'Oh!' she said, 'you mean *Lilacs*.'

"She began to read a poem of great depth praising the wonderful fragrance of the lilacs and the beauty of spring. As the whiskey did its work, I almost nodded off while she was finishing the poem.

"'Josie, that was lovely. But there was another one that spoke more eloquently of the seasons.'

"'You must mean 'When the Snow Falls on Sugar Loaf.'

"'That's it,' I said, 'that's it.'

"She flipped rapidly through the magazine and came to the poem mentioned and began to read with great emotion. I began to feel a twinge of conscience because the poem was indeed lovely and moving. It spoke of sad hearts and of long, lonely days and nights, and the beauty of the virgin snow, the unspoiled trackless mountain standing majestically in front of the picture window now clothed in its springtime glory, and all that. But I quickly put these feelings of guilt aside while I downed my glass of bourbon and listened to Josephine finish reading 'When the Snow Falls on Sugar Loaf.' She noticed that my glass was once again empty and asked if I would like to have another. Only half thinking how it might look if I had three stiff drinks in the middle of the day, I said, 'Sure, Josie, that would be wonderful if you'll promise to continue to read this magnificent poetry of yours.' She was more than willing.

"The servant brought my third bourbon and water. I drank deeply, then slid about four inches closer to Josephine and let my knee accidentally brush against hers. Her knee did not move.

"I slid closer, my hip touching hers. Once again, she gave no ground. I placed my right arm across her shoulder. Her voice began to break, and she breathed faster while trying to read. Suddenly, she announced it was almost time for dinner and asked if I'd stay and join the family at table. My plan was working more rapidly than I'd expected. I quickly agreed to break bread with them.

"Josephine led the way down a long hallway to a huge dining room with a table that must have been 25 feet long. At a glance, I figured it'd seat 30 people comfortably, maybe more. Presiding at the far end in solitary splendor was her father, Preacher Nelson. She marched me to him, holding my hand, and introduced me.

"'Poppa, could we join you for dinner?'

"The preacher looked thunderstruck because this behavior was totally out of character for Josephine. She was the most disagreeable child a man had ever been cursed with. Even the servants hated her, and suddenly she was the personification of civility.

"'Certainly, Josephine. I would be delighted,' the preacher said as he half-stood. I motioned him back into this seat and took the chair to his right. Josephine sat in the chair to his left.

"'Henceforth, Poppa, you will call me Josie. Will likes that name.'

"'Yes, my dear. Very well.'

"I enjoyed the best meal I'd eaten in my whole life. When it was done, the servants swiftly cleared the table. The preacher ordered a glass of red wine, 'for thy stomach's sake,' and asked me if I would join him. Josephine likewise.

"'Poppa, I asked you to call me Josie,' she said. 'Yes, I will have a glass of wine. Will likes bourbon and water.'

"One eyebrow shot up as Preacher Nelson took me in, a stranger who had in such a short time tamed his hateful daughter. He took two huge Cuban cigars from the tobacco box on the table and offered me one. I accepted; we both smoked as we enjoyed our drinks. Josephine sat staring at me, looking as if she could almost take a bite out of me. Her father couldn't help but notice.

"After Preacher Nelson finished his wine, he asked Josephine whether she would mind if he showed me about the farm.

"'No, Poppa. I asked you please to call me Josie. I'd like to show Will the farm myself. Please just have the surrey brought around.'

"'Why don't you take one of the Packards. It would be more comfortable.'

"'You know I don't know how to drive the cars.'

"'I know how to drive,' I said.

"'Oh you do? Would you rather go in the Packard or would you rather go in the surrey?'

"She stood expectantly as I mulled over the idea.

"'Those are two beautiful cars. I sure would like to give them a whirl. Which one can we take?'

"'Your choice,' said Preacher Nelson with a smile, as I took Josie's hand and headed out the front door. Preacher Nelson stared after us as we walked down the hallway, with a frown on his face as if he were worried about his only daughter and quite uncertain about me or my intentions.

"I walked Josie around to the passenger side, opened the door, gallantly waited until she was comfortably seated, shut the door, then went to the driver's side. I climbed onto the luxurious leather covered seat of the big Packard and looked over the controls. I turned the ignition key to the start position and barely touched the kickstarter as the engine roared to life. Feeling the liquor, I leaned over and whispered into Josie's ear, 'Where to, beautiful?'

"She pointed straight ahead. I shifted the big car into low gear, and let out the clutch. The Packard glided forward as if on a cushion of air. I figured there must be an eight-cylinder engine under the hood, and it would probably run 70 miles an hour. The greed in my heart to own such a machine knew no bounds as I quickly shifted the gears into high along the well-kept country road.

"As we rounded a curve stretching to great distance, fine fences wound along the road as far as the eye could see, with sections of land where cross fences layed the farm into one gigantic, crazy quilt of white fences—an architect's model. Beautiful livestock grazed contentedly over all the farm. After we had gone a couple of miles through the country and still had not run out of fences, I asked, 'Why haven't we met anybody else on this road? We've been traveling for two miles.'

"'It's a private road that belongs to Pa. In about a mile, it will end where the foreman's home is.

"True enough, after about a mile the road began to turn right and made a big loop. At the very end of the loop, sat a mansion comparable almost to the home where Josie lived.

"'That's Poppa's foreman's home. It's his brother Jeb. He looks after all the hired help.'

"There was a farm road that went off down through some tall virgin pine trees.

"'Where does that go?'

"'It's just an old logging road that goes down to Bear Creek. It dead ends, as best I recall. I've walked down there a few times when I was feeling depressed. There used to be a sawmill. There's a huge pile of sawdust as best I remember—should be mostly rotted now.'

"'Can we drive down in the car?'

"'I don't see why not. If we get stuck, all we do is walk to Uncle Jeb's house, and he'll have the hands come and pull us out.'

"I turned off and headed down the logging road. After 600 yards through heavy woods, the road began to narrow. I saw a little clearing off to the left, just big enough to turn around in. The pine thicket had ended, and it was now mostly blackjacks and water oaks. The limbs grew so low to the ground you couldn't see more than 20 yards in any direction. The soft spring breeze wafted through the car. Josie's perfume, along with the nearly eight ounces of bourbon I had consumed, made me light-headed.

"I reached over and pulled Josie close. She turned her face to me and with eager and passionate lips, we embraced. Josie was breathing heavily as I slipped my left hand through her blouse and caressed her soft, supple breast.

"Just as Josie began to relax, a bullwhip cracked close by. We quickly straightened up. I couldn't tell exactly the direction the sound came from. I got out. Approaching from the road she had thought was impassable for the car were six mules pulling a log wagon loaded with virgin long-leaf pines. I quickly cranked the car, backed around, and sped out of the woods ahead of the wagon. We drove almost back to Josie's house before either one of us said anything.

"'Can you read me some more of your lovely poems as we ride along?'

"'Not now, we're almost back to the house. I usually take a nap about this time in the afternoon. If you'll excuse me, I'll do that now. But I do hope you'll stay for supper.'

"'No, I can see right now, Miss Josie, that I am going to fall in love with you if I haven't already. I'd best be moving on. I have no place to stay here anyway.'

"'You can sleep here. I'll speak with father after my nap. You can walk around and do as you please; take a horse and ride over the fields this afternoon, I'll see you at supper.'

"By then we were back in front of the house. Preacher Nelson was sitting in a big swing slowly swaying back and forth. She jumped out of the car with a great deal of animation, went bouncing up the front steps, and yelled at Preacher Nelson as she ran into the house.

"'Poppa, talk to Will. He's going to spend the night with us.'"

Courtship

"When I stepped up on the front veranda, Preacher Nelson invited me to have a seat on the glider off to the right, facing their landscaped front garden. I sat for several minutes. The stillness was not broken except for the squeak of the glider's chains rubbing against each other as the preacher pushed himself to and fro.

"'What's your name?' he finally asked.

"'I'm Will Cotton.' I lied.

"'Where are you from, Will?'

"'I come from south Georgia.'

"'You frighten me young man.'

"I looked preacher Nelson in the eye. 'I don't understand that, sir.'

"'For two reasons. You've made a remarkable difference in my daughter's disposition in these last few hours she's been in your company. You don't appear to me to be a man who's blind or hard of hearing. It's as if you waved some magic wand at my daughter and changed my unfortunate duckling into a graceful swan in a matter of minutes. I've got the feeling the devil himself can't do such a thing, certainly no mortal man. On my rights as her Pa, I ask you straight out, fair and square, what your intentions toward her might be? Anyone who can make my daughter that happy can also make her sad. So I ask you a father's legitimate question. What are your intentions toward my Josephine?'

"Nothing was said for a couple of minutes. I sat there and pondered the question that had been put to me, but before I could answer, he continued.

"'I am a man, you have already discovered, of considerable wealth. I love my daughter, even with her mean and ornery disposition. I also feel obligated to protect her from scoundrels and fortune seekers. I'd like to make you a proposition right now. If your intentions are anything other than marrying her, settling down, and making her a good husband and a good provider, I will pay you $10,000 in United States currency to leave today rather than see you bring shame and hurt her.

"'If you are a fortune seeker, and a man of any decency and honesty, you'll make it a proposition between you and me right now. I'll even throw in that Packard, the best traveling machine that presently exists on this ball of dirt. I'm asking you, Will Cotton, no, I'm begging you, if your intentions are anything other than honorable, take my offer, go with me to the bank right now, and leave this house in peace. If my offer is not generous enough, provided your intentions aren't honorable, then you tell me what you require and I'll do it.'

"I had to think that one over. I wanted all the preacher had, except his daughter. I wanted all the property, and all the money, and I thought I could get it through the daughter."

"'Sir, I feel insulted that my intentions are in question. My intentions are indeed honorable. I love her mind, I love her poetry, I love your daughter. I'll marry her, and I'll treat her right. I'll be asking her soon, and I'll thank you to stay out of it.'

"Of course, that was what Preacher Nelson wanted to hear. But I was afraid he still held a great deal of skepticism in his heart about me. He asked me whether I'd like a tour around the farm. In order to take the old man's money, I had to know where it was. I eagerly joined him for a trip around the farm. We walked down to the barn where there was a young man, dressed, I imagined, as well as a servant for a rich man should dress."

"'Yes, sir?' the servant said.

"'Hitch ol' George to the buggy and bring him around.'

"'Yes, sir,' replied the stable boy.

"Shortly we were headed on a grand tour, pulled by one of the prettiest black stallions, in the most plush buggy I ever laid eyes on. I sank deep in the cushions. The single leaf spring came up in a great loop and went back and fastened on top of the rear axle. The front axle had a similar arrangement, and the ride was like floating on the clouds. Preacher Nelson clucked to the black stallion, and the animal started off in a slow trot. That day I saw more cattle, more cross fences, more watering holes, more corn and cotton, more tobacco, more sorghum cane growing than I would have believed existed in the whole state of Georgia, much less owned by one man.

"While riding over that grand farm, Preacher Nelson told me the story of his life. About how his wife had been struck by lightning, how she had died at the birth of his daughter, how he had accepted it as a sign from God that he was to preach the gospel, and how he had done so. He told me how he had watched what was to be the joy of his life become the hideous looking creature she was now, with a disposition to match, and how in one afternoon he had watched as I changed her disposition back to the sweet child that she had been before discovering her own ugliness. What a great joy it was to imagine that if I married his daughter and produced grandchildren, they would inherit his great wealth through me and Josie.

"As Preacher Nelson and I approached the house, Josie was standing on the veranda with a bourbon and water for me. She ushered me into the living room. As soon as I finished my drink, she asked me if would I like to go upstairs and see my sleeping quarters. We went up to a beautifully appointed bedroom. She showed me the bath, and it, too, spoke of great wealth and luxury. Laid across the bed were some gentlemen's clothes that looked to me like they'd probably fit.

"'Will, I took the liberty of going into town and purchasing you more presentable clothes while you and Pa rode around the farm. I hope you don't mind. When you finish with your bath, try them on. My bedroom is the next room down on the right side of the hall. We'll be having dinner shortly.'

"When I finished bathing, I tried on the clothes. The silk underwear, the silk pants, the white shirt, every piece of clothing fit as if it had been made for me. I finished dressing and strolled downstairs, looking the very elegant bachelor. Preacher Nelson and Josie were already seated at the table.

"After dinner, Josie volunteered to show me to my room, and in ten minutes I was in bed. But soon I opened the door a crack, and peered up and down the hallway. There was only a very small kerosene lamp at the end of the barely lighted hallway. I crept to Josie's bedroom and gently knocked. The door opened instantly. She was expecting me. There was no light in her room. I grabbed her and started backing her to the bed. We fumbled at each other's clothes and whispered in total darkness. I found her and began a night of such mad passion that neither of us slept a wink. Just before daylight I slipped back to my own bedroom, and whispered, 'One day soon, I'll marry you.' Back in my room I fell exhausted into a deep sleep.

"It was well past noon when she knocked. I staggered to the door, and the very sight of her almost made me sick. But I smiled sweetly, embraced her, shut my eyes, and kissed her. This time she pushed me backward to my bed and the mad orgy took on a renewed life. Presently, we heard footsteps in the hall. Without even knocking, the servant walked into my room as we were both groaning in full sexual flight. Without missing a stroke, Josie raised up and said, 'Millie, I'll thank you to stay the hell out of here.'

"'Yessum.'

"Unfortunately, my courage wilted from the interruption, and that was the end of that for the present. I got up and bathed; and Josie returned to her room.

"For the first few days and nights, me and Josie were practically inseparable, but I rapidly grew bored with nothing to do each day but ride around over the countryside in the surrey, which is what Josie liked to do. She, however, was so very happy and, a time or two, mentioned my promise to marry her. I kept pledging my undying love, but said I wanted to wait until the fall to get married.

"One day in late September Josie announced she was pregnant. I acted as if I were very proud of it, proud of the fact that I was going to become a father, but still I told her I was not ready to get married. I went to Preacher Nelson and asked about some responsibilities.

"'Josie and I have talked it over, and we are going to marry in December, but I want some responsibilities in the business. I want to learn about your business, what all is involved. I don't want to just live off my father-in-law.'

"Preacher Nelson grew cold and suspicious. Then I made my startling announcement. Instead of calling him Preacher Nelson, I said, 'Brother Nelson, I think I've been called by the Almighty to preach. I want to join the church, the church where you are the pastor. I have an overwhelming desire to address that congregation.'

"Immediately Preacher Nelson's attitude changed.

"'I would like to join the church and be baptized on Sunday, before the weather gets cold. I think I have a contribution to make to the church. I was wondering if there would be any chance of you letting me preach the sermon Sunday after you baptize me? I just feel the spirit of the Lord moving me, and it is so powerful.'

"Man of God that he was, Preacher Nelson was very sympathetic. So on Sunday morning, I was baptized and, at the same time, he proposed my name to the Board as a candidate for the ministry, asking them to consider ordaining me as a minister, which was still rather unusual since I hadn't any formal religious training. Most of the Methodists in those days didn't really have a set procedure of formal education. Many a Methodist minister simply felt the call of God, and answered by revealing that call to some other member of the church. But I had revealed my calling to my future father-in-law and benefactor.

"All who'd attended the service that day said I'd done a creditable job. I had preached against sins of the flesh, gluttony, and pride, and many of the congregation had gone away from the service thinking that was not the first time I had preached. And indeed it was not. I'd spent many long hours practicing the art of sounding like a preacher, but that's a different story.

"Immediately following the Sunday morning service, Preacher Nelson opened all of his company books. We went to his safe at the bank, and he showed me the deeds to all the different properties he owned, including, much to my surprise, the bank itself. For all practical purposes, he truly owned the whole county.

"On Wednesday, I asked Preacher Nelson if I might conduct the Wednesday night prayer service and speak a few words. Once again, every member of the congregation was moved by my sincerity as I explained my vision for the salvation of the condemned.

"Josie sat in the front pew, puzzled by the man who stole into her bedroom every night without the benefit of marriage, and yet preached so powerful a sermon. But she was so happy that I'd come into her life.

"That Wednesday night, following that eloquent sermon, I once again sneaked into the bedroom with Josie. After we made love, she asked me why we didn't go ahead and get married. She was going to start looking pregnant in another few weeks.

"'Darling, we are already married. Do you think a preacher mumbling some words over us makes us married? Remember the Bible

itself states 'he took unto himself a wife.' There is absolutely nowhere in the scriptures that it says words must be spoken over a
couple for them to be married. Darling, you're my wife. We'll sol-
emnize the occasion to make you feel better on the first day of
December. But until then, I wish things to go on as they are. I will
know that way, darling, that you trust me. Nobody has ever really
trusted me before.'

"Josie thought about that. She'd never really heard any scriptures quoted that mentioned a specific kind of marriage ceremony.
And so she fell asleep in my arms, at peace with the world.

"The next day, I approached Preacher Nelson. 'Brother Nelson,
Josie and I have settled our wedding date. It will be Sunday, the
1st day of December. If you would permit it, I would like to preach
the service that day and then immediately following, we will stand
before the altar and exchange our wedding vows with you officiating.'

"There was absolutely nothing I could have said that would have
been more pleasing to his ears."

'Son, I have been thinking about an appropriate position for you.
You seem to be gifted in almost everything you've done; you learn
very quickly. I think the most fitting job I could arrange for you
would be as president of the bank.'

"I turned red, stammered, and put on one of the greatest acts of
false humility anybody ever saw. 'Brother Nelson, don't you think
you ought to make me vice-president first and let me really learn
it from the ground up. I feel so unworthy to be president.'

"'No, Will. What makes it such a pleasure to name you president of the bank is the humility you've just expressed. Charlie Jetter
is at retirement age. He knows I've been looking for his replace-
ment for a couple of years, and I told him last week that I thought
maybe you were the man. Your modesty removes any doubt I ever
had. You are the man. What I'd like for you to do is to start there
in the morning and move straight into the president's office. You
just sit in at Jetter's secretary's desk and watch every move he makes.
You're a quick learner, Will, and if there is anything you don't
understand about the way he does things, you just ask him.

"'There's a fellow named Sam Timmons who has been there 25 years.
He thinks he's going to be promoted, but Sam just ain't quite got what

it takes. He's a good number two man, but that's all he's ever going to be, just a number two man. But after you take over from Jetter, if you ever get in a bind, he'll be a good man to ask for help. He'll more than likely know what to do. I'll tell you now, Will, I pretty much let my managers manage my businesses. I try my best to use my time to do the will of the Lord. I try to hire good people, then I'll leave them alone.

"'As befits your stature as a bank president, I'll give you that white Packard you love so much. I'll have a bill of sale made out to you, and in the president's office tomorrow. So get in your car and go to work.'

"Times were good. Everybody was doing well in the community, or so the president, Mr. Jetter, told me. He had Miss Agnes, his long-time secretary, bring the files for the different people who had loans outstanding, and the collateral they had. He went through them one by one, showing me the ledger cards with what this fellow owed on this piece of property and where the property was, along with the deed to secure the debt, and all the other legal instruments that a bank needed to forcibly collect a debt in the event the debtor might try to default. Jetter made very clear to me that he tried not to loan money to anybody who wasn't going to try to pay it back.

"'By the way Will, I was at church Sunday and I heard that sermon you preached. It was as good as I have ever heard. I'm glad to know a good Christian fellow like you is going to take my place.'

"As the days went by, I became familiar with all the depositors and all the borrowers of the bank. I went out front and worked behind the teller's cage, cashing checks while the teller was away for lunch. I watched Mr. Jetter make loans; I watched him write deeds in longhand. I saw him put his official seal on them and send them to the courthouse to be recorded.

"About the middle of October, Jetter told Preacher Nelson that I was ready to take over as bank president."

"'He's one of the fastest learners I've ever been around. I think you've made a wonderful choice. Besides being a good Christian, he's got some brains in his head.'

"In less than a month's time, the folks around town started showing me the respect due a bank president.

"On a Monday morning about the middle of November, Preacher Nelson confronted Josie with the fact that he knew I was sneaking

into her bedroom and sleeping with her every night. He pointed
out to her that we were still unwed, even though she had a promised wedding date of December 1st. He asked her whether she
wasn't a bit worried about a man who'd treat her like that in her
daddy's house, didn't that speak about his character?

"Josie flew into a shit fit like her father had not seen since she
met me. He had become accustomed to her gentle, sweet behavior. He thought back on the creature she used to be and how I had
changed her to a gentle child.

"'Pa, I asked him the same thing. I don't like you sticking your
nose in our business, but I am going to tell you what he said to ease
your mind. I asked him the same thing three months ago and he
said, 'Josie, you go to your father, he's an ordained minister and
has been one for years. Ask him to show you where in the Holy
Scriptures it says anything at all about a formal ceremony for marrying people. I was married to you the moment I took you as my wife.
That first night I pushed you backward on your bed and took you
in the Biblical sense, from that moment on, we were man and wife.
That's the only reference the Bible makes to any ceremony whatsoever. You ask your daddy about it, he knows the Bible. It says, 'he
took unto himself a wife,' and that's what I did.'

"Preacher Nelson sat stunned on the bed's edge because he knew it
was the truth. All this broiling, seething anger inside him was for naught,
and I was right. There was nothing in the Holy Scriptures that prescribed any sort of ceremony. It was just as I'd told his daughter.

"'Josie, I've got to tell you. I've been suspicious of Will's motives all the time. But he has been here since spring, and there has
been absolutely not one thing that he's done that I could in any
fashion reprimand. Still I've had this uneasy feeling the whole time.'

"Josie told her father she'd had the same feeling until she questioned him on the delay of the ceremony. She said, 'Pa, he looked
me in the eye and told me, 'Josie, I married you the moment I had
you in a Biblical sense. I knew it and I thought you knew it.'

"'From that moment on, I have never doubted Will's sincerity. I
do think he's working too much at the bank now. Sometimes it's
dark when he gets home. I got suspicious the other day and rode
by, but he was in his office working. I feared I'd see him out courtin'

some pretty young thing, but he was hard at work behind his desk. So, Pa, I've got absolutely no doubts about Will. I don't know how you feel, but there is no doubt in my heart that he is who he says he is, and what he says he is. I know I'm ugly as homemade sin, and I sometimes can't imagine the man loving me, but I truly believe he does.'

"'Are you pregnant?'

"'Yes, Pa, I am.'

"'How long?'

"'I think about two and a half months.'

"'Josie, you know regardless of how rich and powerful we are, if you have a baby five months after you get married, there's going to be some raised eyebrows. Your good name is going to be smudged. It's going to leave a bad taste about your moral character with the community.'

"'No, Pa. Will and I have already talked about that. Will says the vice-president of the bank can look after the bank for a while and about three months before the baby is born, he and I are going to take a trip down to the Caribbean. He has spent some time down there before, he tells me how lovely it is. When we return, we will have a child, and nobody will have counted the days and nobody will know how old it is. He's convinced me there is absolutely nothing to be worried about. I believe him. How about you?'

"'I'm glad we had this talk. Yes, I think we are awful, awful lucky Will came along. But I am real glad we had this conversation.'

"It was Saturday night, the 30th day of November. The next day was the big wedding. All of the dresses and everything had been bought. I had almost taken over complete control of the Sunday services. I did the morning services and Preacher Nelson did the evening services. I always did the Wednesday night prayer meeting. Preacher Nelson was beginning to relax some and really enjoy the liberty his son-in-law-to-be afforded him.

"We had already finished the wedding rehearsal and were having supper when I told them, 'I want to change our plans for tomorrow.'

"A troubled look crept across Preacher Nelson's face, as well as Josie's. I noted the expressions on their faces.

"'I don't think you'll mind the change I'm going to suggest. What I'd like to do is conduct the 11 o'clock service while both of you wait here at the house. I'm not superstitious about much, but I am superstitious about one thing my Ma always told me, 'If you want a good marriage, don't see your bride on your weddin' morn'. Have your wedding in the afternoon, and don't see her that day before the wedding.'

"'I can go to Sunday School and hold church services. As soon as the sermon has ended and we sing the hymn of invitation, I'll dismiss the congregation and make sure it is at 12:05. I want ya'll to drive into the churchyard at that time. I want you to bring the best man, Jimmy Abbott, with you. I want Jimmy to stay in the car with you, Josie, and I want you, Preacher Nelson, to walk in. I am going to walk out of the pulpit, come down and stand in our positions like we have practiced. You walk in beside me and the organist will play *'Here Comes the Bride'* after we've been standing there a couple of minutes. Then I want you, Josie, to come through the back door and march down the aisle. What does that sound like to you? Are ya'll willing to do that? It's really important to me, but if you have any objections, then we'll do something else.' Of course, Josie and Preacher Nelson were ecstatic.

"'You make sure, darling, that in the morning when it is time to get up, you stay in your room until 9:30. I'll be gone to the morning worship service, I don't want to see you until you walk down the aisle to proclaim to the whole world you are my bride.'

"We sat around and had a glass of wine and chatted while I read the Bible until about 9:30. One by one we all went to bed. Shortly after Josie had gone to bed, I crawled in beside her.

"'What about that superstition you have about seeing the bride on the day of the wedding?' Josie asked.

"'I really mean that. I'm going to leave you before midnight and go back to my own bedroom. I won't see you anymore until you come marching down that aisle about eight minutes past 12 o'clock, tomorrow. Good night now, darling. You sleep tight and sweet dreams.'

"I went downstairs and knocked on Preacher Nelson's door.

"'Come in.'

"He was laying in the bed with his nightgown on and with the Holy Bible in his hand. The Bible was turned to the Book of Job.

"'Preacher Nelson, tomorrow is a day of such great promise, why are you reading Job?'

"The preacher placed a bookmark in his Bible, took his half-rimmed glasses off, and laid them on the nightstand.

"'I try always to close out my day with reading a few verses from the Book of Job. It has always been a great mystery to my mind why God loved Job so much, and yet he turned him over almost completely to the devil for any sort of punishment or vile thing the devil wanted to do, except take his life. Will, the Lord has been so good to me, I'm not now, nor ever will be, a man with such faith as Job. Sometimes, I can't help but wonder why the Almighty has been so very kind and generous in all respects to me, and permitted such cruelty to be visited upon Job. I read Job mostly to remind myself that God loved Job a great deal and permitted all of those terrible things to happen to him. So, no matter what happens to me, I must remember, I constantly remind myself, that God loves me, too.'

"'I've never looked at it like that, Preacher Nelson. I won't bother you but a minute, but there are a couple of things I wanted to speak with you about before I officially become your son-in-law. You've already named me president of the bank, for which I am grateful. I've tried to do you a good job. I just want you to know that I appreciate what you have done for me more than you'll ever know. I hope our first child is a boy. I hope you'll live long enough to see your grandson mature. Of course, our first born may be a girl, and that's alright, too, because we expect to have many.

"'I've got a Ma and Pa who are just as poor as church mice who live in the southeast corner of the state of Georgia in a little town called Brunswick. I finally managed to get the neighbors to get Ma on the telephone the day before yesterday, I think it was. They sure are down and out. I wanted to mail them a bank draft for $5000 to pay for the farm they live on, but I ain't quite saved up that much money yet. I'd like to ask your indulgence to let the bank loan me enough money so I can mail them a check next Monday. I'd like to tell them I'm married and, at the same time, tell them to pay off their farm.'

"Preacher Nelson's eyes teared up; two great big tears ran down his cheek. He wiped them off as quickly as he could and tried not to let me see them.

"'Of course you can, Will. You should have come to me before. Not only that, when you mail them a check, mail them enough money to come up and see you. It's not that far. Three hundred miles across Georgia, another 300 here. Send them enough money.

They can catch a train and come up and see us. I would like to meet 'em.'

"Preacher Nelson opened his nightstand and took out his checkbook.

"'What is your father's name, Will?'

"'It's Jeb Cotton.'

"Preacher Nelson wrote, 'Pay to the Order of: Jeb Cotton, Six-Thousand Dollars,' and signed the check. Under 'for' he wrote, 'For having one of the most wonderful sons I have ever known.'

"I read the check and the little notation as big tears rolled down his cheeks. I reached over and hugged my soon to be father-in-law.

"'Will, that is an insignificant amount of money to me. It would do my heart good if you would accept it as a wedding gift from your father-in-law. You've earned it by the job you've done at the bank. I'd like you to give this to your parents as a wedding present from me.'

"'Brother Nelson, you'll never know what this gesture means to me. Of course I accept. There is one other thing I had thought of about the wedding tomorrow. I said I wanted you to be there at five after twelve, but I got to thinking about it. I believe every single person there will stay for the wedding, but I don't know for sure. I won't know until the time comes, but I am going to ask you not to come to the church until ten minutes after the hour. That will give the people time to clear the front yard of the church before you and Josie get there. It's just an afterthought. It's only a matter of three of four minutes, but in the event anybody does decide to leave the church and not stay for the ceremony, that will give them time to clear the grounds before you arrive.

"'I've asked some friends of mine to make sure you can drive right up to the front door. So if you will, just wait until about ten after twelve. As soon as you stop the car, you get out and walk to the church, I'll be waiting in front of the altar for you. Then the best man will bring in little Josie for the wedding. Is that alright with you?'

"'Of course that's alright with me, Will. You're probably right. You would think everybody would stay for the wedding, but if some have somebody coming for Sunday dinner, they might want to leave the church. You can't figure all of them will stay for the ceremony, so I think that is a good idea.'

"'Then, I'll take my leave Brother Nelson, and I'll see you at the church tomorrow between 12:10 and 12:15. There, Josie and I will be joined in holy wedlock by her father. Good night sir, and once again, thank you for the wonderful gesture towards my parents in Brunswick."

"I was awake at 7 o'clock Sunday morning. I took my own good time as I bathed and shaved, being careful not to cut myself for my wedding day. I put on a dark business suit with a bow tie. I turned in front of a full length mirror and liked what I saw.

"The cook asked me what I would like for breakfast. I told her I wanted some of those wonderful flapjacks of hers with some of the light maple syrup they imported from up north. She asked me, on my wedding day, if I wanted something that would stick to my ribs better than that, like some of that thick slab bacon or salty ham they had in such abundance.

"'Sure, that will be nice. Give me some of that good country ham.'

"By the time I finished breakfast it was 8:30. I eased the Packard out of the driveway toward the church.

"As I passed the road that turned off toward the church, I kept on going straight into town. I went to the bank and opened the safe. I took out a rather large briefcase, opened it, examined the contents, and closed it again. I locked the safe and walked out of the bank, placing the briefcase in the trunk of my car, and drove back to the church.

"As was customary, I greeted a few early parishioners on their way to the Sunday School rooms. Then I walked on to the pastor's study. There I set to work on my Sunday morning sermon.

"At precisely 11 o'clock, the choir director lifted his baton, and the choir softly began to hum, '*Pass Me Not, Oh Gentle Savior.*' At the lectern, I prayed a prayer for blessings upon the congregation at the opening of the worship service. When I said 'Amen,' I motioned to the choir to be seated and for the choir director to take a seat. This was a little unusual, because their custom was to sing a couple of songs.

"'I have news for this congregation that breaks my heart. I don't even know where to start to tell you exactly what has happened. As everybody under the sound of my voice knows, I was to be married to Josephine Nelson this afternoon and each and every person here was invited to attend that ceremony. This morning when I arose, I had an overwhelming desire to see my betrothed.

We sleep on the same floor. I cracked the door to my bedroom just in time to see another man enter her bedroom. Being unable to contain myself, I'll admit to this congregation that I had a flare of temper.

"'In my nightgown, I walked down to her bedroom door, and I heard voices. The lock was not even on her door. The door had drifted open almost a quarter of the way. I stuck my head in the door, and to my horror, when I looked in the room my betrothed and her father, the minister of this church, were in the act of copulation, totally oblivious to me or anything surrounding them. I quickly withdrew, went to my room, dressed, and came directly to the church. Needless to say, folks, I am so devastated by what I observed that I am going to leave this community. I ask the Almighty God to forgive them. I leave it up to you folks as to what to do. No man has ever suffered a greater sense of shame, outrage, and injustice than I have this morning. I also ask you folks to pray for me.

"'I am going to leave now, but I am going to ask this congregation to do me a favor. Please sit here, sing hymns, and pray about what to do about this disgrace, because nobody at Preacher Nelson's house knows I saw what I saw. I am going to ask you, the congregation of this church, to sing and pray about it until they come driving up. Then, you folks do what you must do. I hope to see all of you, my friends, at some other happier time and place than here this morning. I bid you farewell.'

"With that, I walked out of the church, got in my big white Packard, and headed north. I drove for a couple of hours at a moderate rate of speed, heading generally to the west. I came to a sign indicating 20 miles to Evansville, Indiana. I headed toward Evansville and eased the accelerator toward the floorboard. I wondered what might be going on at First Baptist Church."

"Nephew, later on, I found a diary that informed me of some of the goings on that day that I couldn't have known at the time. But to make it less complicated, I will tell you the story as if I were there. So don't wonder how I could know. I do know."

About that time, the nurse came in and gave him another shot, along with a couple of pills. She told him he should rest and let me go home for the night. He shook his head, 'No,' and told her he had serious business with me and asked her if she would please leave.

G. B. Balls Takes the Case

"After I was gone, Charlie Jetter, the ex-president of the bank, sat in his pew pondering the revelation he had just heard. He couldn't believe it. Will Cotton was seemingly such a Godly man. How could he tell such an outrageous lie? And for what purpose? He knew he needed to do something, but could not possibly believe Preacher Nelson was guilty of such an insult to the Almighty Himself. Yet the young giant was so convincing. He had worked with Will in the office, and he had seemed sincere. Charlie Jetter was a man mightily torn the hour he sat waiting for things to happen.

"First, he wanted to go to the bank to see if everything was alright, but he no longer had a key. Then he felt he had an obligation to stay until Preacher Nelson arrived and had his say. So, he positioned himself at a window where he would be the first to see the big black Packard when it drove in sight of the church.

"As Josie and Preacher Nelson approached the church with the best man, the first thing they noticed was that the white Packard was not parked in the front yard in Will's usual parking place. But the occasion was so happy they paid little note to it. An avenue had been held open for them to drive up to the front door of the church.

"The car stopped and Preacher Nelson got out. Charlie Jetter approached him.

"'I need to talk to you, Preacher.'

"Josie could tell by the expression on Charlie's face that something was terribly wrong. Within two minutes time, he'd told Preacher Nelson the entire story, watching his face for any trace of guilt. But he only saw anger, not guilt. When Jetter finished telling Preacher Nelson that Will had instructed the congregation to stay in their places and confront him, he said, 'I need to go in and talk to the congregation, but I've got to tell Josie what has happened. If you will, go in to the church and tell them I'll be with them presently.'

"While they had been talking, Josie had slipped under the steering wheel. The preacher went to face his daughter. He leaned down,

129

stuck his head in the window, and asked the best man to please go into the church, explaining that he needed to talk to Josie alone. He then related to Josie the tale Will had told the congregation.

"'Darling, there is no way I might have believed that this would happen, at least not in the last several weeks. I was suspicious of Will at the beginning, but in the last month or so, all of my suspicions had been removed. I have to go into the church now and speak to the congregation, then I'll take you home.'

"With a great screaming sob, Josie started the car and headed toward White Horse Creek. She had never driven the car before. It was a powerful machine, and it rapidly gained speed.

"While the car was still in sight of the church, Josie drove it straight off the road and into the biggest water oak in sight. The huge Packard folded around the water oak like so much putty on a door frame.

"Everybody poured out of the church and in a few short minutes stood at the scene of the wreck. Josie's head had smashed into the engine block as it rose up in protest against the sudden stop. Her head and face were no longer recognizable, and every able bodied man dreaded the job of having to pry her body out of the wreck.

"Jetter led Preacher Nelson away from the gruesome scene.

"'I'll have the logging foreman bring some teams up here. We'll take care of the body. You and I need to go somewhere and have a talk.'

"They got in Jetter's car and headed toward town. Jetter asked Preacher Nelson if he had a key to the bank. They went in and unlocked the safe. There was not a single scrap of paper currency in the safe. It was all in the brief case I had retrieved earlier in the morning. Preacher Nelson asked Jetter whether it would take long to ascertain how much money should be in the safe. The president assured him it should be only a matter of moments if the ledger were correct. There wouldn't be much reason for it not to be, even if I had planned this for months.

"When Charlie Jetter opened the ledger, the hair on his neck stood up. He turned the tellers' balance sheets, and they showed there should have been $160,000 in cash in the bank's vault. Not one bill was there. Wherever I was, I had $160,000 in cash and a practically new eight-cylinder Packard. Preacher Nelson and Charlie Jetter sat in the president's office for a long while without a word passing."

"'Jetter, you are once again president of this bank, if you'll take it. You are also in charge of hiring somebody who will run down that son-of-a-bitch, find him, and bring him back here alive. Knowing now what I didn't know last night, I'll lay you odds, he's not from Brunswick, Georgia. My guess would be he's from somewhere in Alabama or Mississippi. He's certainly not from south Georgia. If he's from Georgia at all, it will be the northern part. I'm not even certain his name is Cotton, but I want you to find somebody who will track him down. I want him brought back here, manacled. Not only will I pay the expenses for the man who brings him back, I'll pay him a $100,000 cash bonus when he brings that bastard in and turns him over to the sheriff. Will you take the job, my friend?'

"'I feel like a dog asking this, Preacher, but I must ask. Is anything he told the congregation true?'

"It was several seconds before Preacher Nelson spoke.

"'Jetter, I would think you would know me better than that, but I realize that under the circumstances, it's a proper question. No it's not true, but I did let something go on in my house that I shouldn't have. I knew they were sleeping together. I went to my daughter and warned her about getting pregnant and what that would do to the family name.'

"'Pa,' she said, 'I was worried about the same thing so I asked Will. Will said, 'Darling, we are married, you go ask your Pa. There is nothing is the Holy Scriptures anywhere that says words have to be said over a couple for them to be married. The only reference to marriage in the Holy Scripture is, 'he took unto himself a wife.'

"'And he's right, Jetter. Whether you know it or not, there is nothing in all of the Holy Scriptures that describes any prescribed ceremony in order that a man and woman be wedded, absolutely nothing. There are descriptions of feasts, and of all night vigils, but there is absolutely nothing in the Holy Scriptures—and I've searched it from end to end.

"'He was smart enough to know that he'd tied my hands when he told her that, and she was satisfied that he meant every word. She considered herself to be married. They were kind enough, however, not to flaunt it. She was pregnant on the order of two to three months, I guess, according to her words. But now she's dead, and he killed her as surely as God makes green apples. I want my hands on that son-of-a-bitch and I will spend my entire fortune to accomplish that purpose.'

"About that time, there was a knock at the bank's front door. It was the logging foreman, who told Jetter they had extracted Josie's body from the car, and that she had been carried to the undertaking establishment across the street. Charlie went back in and informed Preacher Nelson.

"'Jetter, you go tell Undertaker Jobson no fancy waxworks, not to make her pretty. I want her placed in a sealed casket. There will be no photographs, just flowers on top of the casket, and I want the funeral as soon as is practical.

"'When you hire your man to run Will down and bring him back here, I want to meet him. I want to tell him how much I hate that son-of-a-bitch, but also I want him to know I'll not pay one cent for him dead. $100,000 cash—but only if he's alive.' Finally rage gave way to grief and tears poured out.

"The following day they held a closed-casket funeral for Josie, and laid her to rest. After it was over, Preacher Nelson rode back to the bank with Jetter. For a while they discussed the funeral. Despite the scandal, the turnout was somewhat less than either had expected, especially since she was so young, and it was a suicide."

* * *

"Nephew, I want you and God to know that never did I expect such a thing to happen. I never dreamed anything like that would happen."

Uncle Will continued his story;

"Early that morning, Jetter sent a courier to a nearby town to pick up $30,000 in case the depositors had been unnerved by the events of the preceding day and started a run on the bank. He thought $30,000 would be sufficient, but just to be on the safe side, he had also ordered the vice-president to put a wreath on the front door and announce that the bank would not be open until the following morning due to a sudden death in the community. He told all the employees to be at work, but to leave the doors locked. They would be going over the books.

"When the bank opened on Tuesday morning, there were a few people standing outside to withdraw their funds, but very few. Less than $10,000 left the bank. Word of mouth had already spread that Will had more than likely stolen some money from the bank, but not enough to cause it to fail. Generally, the feeling around town was that Brother Nelson was a man of profound sorrow and needed the support of the community. He got it.

"Mr. Jetter personally went over every transaction. Everything seemed to be in order except I had kept more cash in the bank than was necessary. After three days of auditing, he reported to Preacher Nelson that it seemed all I did was steal whatever cash was lying around. Of course, he still had to go over the bond portfolio and match the records against the government bonds owned by the bank.

"In the upper right hand corner of the bank's safe, all the US Treasury Bonds were kept folded together with a rubber band around each separate denomination. Jetter asked the head teller to come into his office. They started the tedious process of determining whether any of the bonds were missing. The president unwrapped the package of each denomination and started reading serial numbers as the head teller checked off the numbers. The first package of $10,000 bonds tallied perfectly. Next was the $50,000 bonds. Once again the president took the rubber band off the folded package and began to read the serial numbers. The package was in order. Then he picked up the $100,000 denominated bonds. The package felt suspiciously thin to Jetter, who then read the first serial number. The teller checked it. The second serial number ended in 32, which was a correct number; the bond was there. The third serial number, however, ended in 31, and it was missing, as were the next four. Some $500,000 worth of bearer bonds were missing. Jetter went to tell Rev. Nelson the bad news. Will Cotton had vanished with $660,000 of his money.

"They sat in Preacher Nelson's kitchen over a glass of wine and cigars long into the night trying to determine what their course of action should be.

"'You tell me—what can we do? It seems we should be able to trace those bonds some way and find him through the bonds. He's surely going to cash them. Can we or can't we? Tell me, what can we do?'

"'Brother Nelson, we have several problems. The first problem is we don't know how smart Will really is. He can go somewhere and set up a false identity. He can open up a bank account and cash bearer bonds at any bank in this country. They will deposit $100,000 to his account the instant he shows one of the bonds. Unless he does something real stupid, like try to con the bank out of something, he is going to be a respected member of the community immediately. I think we've pretty well established Will ain't stupid. I do remember that when I was showing him the assets of the bank, he asked me several questions about bearer bonds—like why were they not made out to anybody. Of course I told him the reason was they were more easily sold overseas. That the general aim of the treasury was to put out freely convertible high denominated securities that would be readily accepted overseas that could easily be sold anywhere in the world at face value with the full backing of the United States Treasury. Will was definitely interested and asked a number of questions along those lines. Since you put him there as my replacement, I had no qualms about answering his questions, so he knows about as much about treasury bonds as I do.

"'Maybe I should circulate a memo to the presidents of all the large banks across the country offering a reward for information when one of our bonds is cashed. Of course, Will is probably going to think of that himself, so he's not going to stay in one spot very long, especially after he cashes one.

"'We don't really know whether he had any weaknesses other than that he loved bourbon. I saw him drunk, but never drunk enough to be out of control. So the problem we are faced with, Brother Nelson, is finding a mustard seed in a hayfield, and that field could have the dimensions of the whole world because he can cash those bonds in London as easily as he can in New York or Chicago. If he decides to go overseas, our chances of finding him are almost nil. What I propose we do is to trace him as far back as we can, and try to find where he came from. I am going to telegraph the Pinkerton Detective Agency and tell them I want the best man they've got for a highly confidential job, and I want him here as rapidly as he can get here.

"'I've heard they've got a young fellow, 30 years old, who is as mean as a rattlesnake. I think he's been with them since he was

18, and has never set out to find someone without bringing him back. I read a story about him in a magazine; I recall his name was G. B. Balls. I'll ask for him by name. If they send him, I'll bring him out to the farm and introduce you. We'll see what happens.'

"Two or three days later a young man walked into Jetter's office.

"'I'm with the Pinkerton Detective Agency. My name is G. B. Balls. You asked for me, and said you had some rather urgent business.'

"Jetter introduced himself to the young man who stood six-two, looked to weigh 210, and was blonde and handsome."

"'Mr. Jetter, are you the man who is going to be paying my salary?'

"'No, Mr. Balls, I'm not. The man who owns this bank will be paying your salary. I'm only the president.'

"'Let me tell you briefly about the man we are looking for. He calls himself Will Cotton. He's approximately six-six and weighs in the neighborhood of 200 pounds. A bit of a bean pole, extremely tall. That alone should be some help in tracking him down.'

"'Has the man committed a crime?' the detective inquired.

"'We have sworn out warrants for embezzlement and outright thievery of undetermined sums of money from the bank. Naturally, we know the amount of money he stole, but we want to leave the wording that way so the depositors won't become anxious.'

"Mr. Balls asked if secrecy on the amount of money stolen extended to him.

"'Of course not,' replied Mr. Jetter, 'Will left here with a half million dollars worth of bearer bonds and $160,000 in cash.'

"Mr. Balls let out a low whistle at the amount of money involved, then was abruptly all business.

"'I work for salary and expenses. The Pinkerton Agency charges $50 a day for my services plus expenses. I put everything I buy on my expense account, from a plug of tobacco to a tin of Prince Albert, whatever I need, whatever I want, or whatever I use goes on the expense account, and they pay me. On average you are looking at a bill of approximately $100 a day for as long as I stay on this case. But one thing I'll grant you, catching Will Cotton'll have my full and undivided attention. Of course, my travel is additional.'

"When Balls finished, Jetter benignly looked at him over his half-rimmed glasses. 'Mr. Balls, if you stay on the case 20 years, you still won't cost us as much as that son-of-a-bitch already has, not counting Preacher Nelson's grief in losing his daughter Josephine. Mr. Balls, you speak only of money. I speak of human misery. Find that bastard. When the bank gets a bill, Pinkerton will get paid.'

"A scowl crossed Balls' face as if he had been reprimanded, which indeed he had. But after thinking it over a moment, he came to the conclusion that maybe he deserved it.

"'Understood, Mr. Jetter. Now, how did Will Cotton get introduced to Josephine?'

"'That's the hell of it,' Jetter said. 'He just walked up on the front porch one day and knocked on the door, as if he had fallen from the sky. She was immediately taken with him. No search was ever made into his background, and really, as far as I know, no questions were ever asked. He volunteered he was from Brunswick, Georgia, but we've concluded he made such a show of being from Brunswick he probably isn't. Because of his accent, we suspect he was either from Georgia, Alabama, or Mississippi, possibly even the northern part of Florida. But all that is guesswork by amateurs, you're the professional.'

"'Well, one thing's sure,' replied Balls, 'He had to come from somewhere. First, I'll trace him back as far as I can, and if that doesn't work, then I'll turn around and start the chase. I consider myself on your payroll at this moment. Would you have lunch with me?'

"'No, but I would like for you to go meet the man who is paying you. I have the authority to hire you, but I would like for you to talk to him. It's about a five-minute drive. I'll take you out there now, if you'll go.'

"The entire trip was made in silence. When they drove into the front yard of the great house, Balls let out another little whistle in appreciation of the magnificence of the country home. Jetter led him to the kitchen where Preacher Nelson sat staring out of the window with vacant eyes. When Preacher Nelson turned to meet Mr. Balls, the young man was struck by how ancient and haggard the preacher looked. He had two days growth of beard, and his clothes were unkempt and dirty. He was much surprised that such a pathetic creature was master of so magnificent a plantation. The preacher was no more than 58 years old but looked 75, at least in Balls' eyes. The preacher studied Balls from asshole to appetite.

"'So you're the man that's gonna catch Will Cotton, are ya?'

"'I've never failed yet, Reverend.'

"'Did Charlie Jetter tell you about my reward?'

"'No sir,' Balls replied. 'The only discussion of money was about my fee, which is going to average about $100 a day, including expenses. It could be a little more or a little less; that's a ballpark figure depending on how much traveling I have to do. But you're going to pay for everything I do till I catch him.'

"'In addition to that young man, I'll pay you $100,000 the moment you turn him over to our sheriff—alive. I won't pay you an extra nickel for him dead. I want to see the son-of-a-bitch die, and I'm willing to pay an additional $100,000 for that privilege.'

"'Now wait a minute. All I was told about was the theft of money, and they're not going to execute a man no matter how much money he steals. Is there something I don't know?'

"'Did you not tell him about the suicide, Charlie?'

"Preacher Nelson suggested they go in to the living room. They poured three glasses of wine.

"'Young man, let me tell you my Josephine's story.'

"For the next three hours he recounted the story of Josephine and me, from time to time bursting into uncontrollable sobs. Other times, his jaw was set firmly, as if he himself intended to trip the gallows, and then the story was finished, right up to Josie's funeral.

"'Preacher, under any other circumstances I'd tell you to go to hell and hire a bounty hunter who didn't give a damn what he does. But considering what you've just told me, I'll be delighted to turn him over to the sheriff, and what he does with the bastard is no business of mine. I'd like to get started. Would you take me back to Plowshare, Mr. Jetter?'

"When they returned to the bank, the Pinkerton man said to Jetter, 'I don't know where I can get a car, but I'd like to scout around town before I leave. I came by train, and I'll leave by train, but I'd like to see if I can track Will Cotton before he showed up at the farm.'

"'Take my car and when you are done with it, leave it in front of the depot. I'll have it picked up. Mr. Balls, as a matter of my own curiosity, what does the G. B. stand for?'

"'Gordon Bacchus—my father was a winemaker. He came from the old country; the God of wine was Bacchus.'

"'I had an idea that maybe it stood for something else. Good day, Mr. Balls.'

"Balls drove around looking at what appeared to be a very prosperous town with a population he imagined would be 6000 to 10,000. He kept thinking about a man in that small of a town being wealthy enough that $660,000 wouldn't weaken the bank. He began to roll numbers around in his head, wishing he could guess how much Preacher Nelson must be worth.

"As he wandered through town, Brother Nelson's name was not to be seen on any buildings, but he guessed quite correctly that the Preacher must own a fair number of them. He pulled up in front of the mule barn. In the office of the mule barn, a clerk sat before an enormous ledger, the traditional green bill on his half-cap, and stared over his half-rimmed glasses."

"'Ain't that Charlie Jetter's car you're driving, stranger?'

"Balls couldn't help but smile at the abrupt, gruff greeting."

"'Yes it is; how'd you know?'

"'Everybody in town knows the bank president's car, at least the old president's car. If you ask around town, the new president, who was going to marry Preacher Nelson's daughter, done up and toted half the bank off. Can't say I rightly blame him though. Courtin' that ugly daughter deserves a reward. Of course, it's a damn pity she ran into that tree. Some say it was suicide. I say she musta just been madder than hell and didn't know how to drive. I don't believe it was suicide. Everybody in town know'd she couldn't drive no car. I'd dread to be that son-of-a-bitch if they ever get him back. They are gonna stomp a mudhole in his ass as big as Lake Jackson.'

"'He's the reason I'm here. I'm trying to piece together how he got here. Nobody seems to know anything about him except one morning he walked up on the front porch at the Preacher's home.'

"'Hell, I know how he got here. The son-of-a-bitch used to work here. He hoboed a freight, that's how he got in here.'

"Balls' sudden interest did not escape his informant's notice.

"'How do you know?'

"'Hell, when he come here, I was the stable boy. I was in charge of getting all the horses the clerk ordered. The clerk left here, and they moved me up.'

"'Then you didn't hire Will to work here?'

"'No, but I saw him just as soon as he came into the barn. As a matter of fact, the clerk at that time told him to come and find me, he would room with me. He asked me, didn't I want to know his name. I told him I didn't give a damn what his name was, I was going to call him Big Un'. I do remember one thing about him, he was limping. He said something about jumping off a moving freight train and sprained his ankle or something like that, I don't remember. But he was a good worker. He done what we told him to do. Then one day he disappeared.'

"'Do you have any idea how long he worked here? We know when he showed up at the farm, do you have any idea when he started work here or how long he stayed?'

"'It was cool weather; as a matter of fact it was cold weather. I'm guessing that it was a better part of six weeks because he limped a long while. You could tell his ankle was sore. I felt sorry for him, but he kept going.'

"'So you would guess he showed up here in March, is that right?' Balls asked.

"'I'd say that's a good guess.'

"'You say you were his roommate. Did you ever talk to him about where he lived, where he'd been, why he was here, or things like that?

"'No, he didn't do a lot of talking. He did do a lot of reading.'

"'What kind of reading?'

"'Well, he always had magazines. As a matter of fact, there's some magazines in the room he had about Al Capone, gangsters, detective stories, all that kind of stuff. Believe it or not, he had a Bible. I kidded him one time about it. I asked him if he had thought about starting preaching, because all the time he was reading the Bible. He just looked at me sort of funny and said, 'Well that's one way to make a living;' it just passed off like that.'

"'You never once remember him remarking about being from Georgia, Alabama, or Mississippi?'

"'No, anytime I'd ever bring up something like that, he'd just say he had done a fair amount of hoboing in his time, and it was good way to get across the country for a poor man. But he did make the remark he didn't plan to stay poor, so I'm guessing he come here with some kind of mischief in mind. But the last thing on earth I would have thought of is the stunt he pulled. I didn't think there was nobody in the world for no amount of money, could have stood to look at Josephine Nelson long enough to marry her. She was one ugly woman. She had a beautiful body, but, boy, she had a face that would make a freight train take a dirt road.'

"'Who owns this mule barn?' Balls asked.

"'The same fellow who owns damn near everything else in town, Preacher Nelson.'

"'Did Will have any bad habits that you know of?'

"'Like what?'

"'Gambling, drinking, whoring?'

"'When he first moved in here, he asked where he could get some liquor and I told him. He kept some whiskey in our room all the time, but I never saw him too drunk. He would always take a few drinks with some water, go to bed, read a while, and then blow out the lamp. Naw, he was actually a pretty nice fellow, I thought.'"

* * *

"While the Pinkerton was jawing around, poking into my past, I was approaching downtown Evansville, Indiana, which was one of the largest towns I had ever been in, at least with any money in my pocket.

"I drove around town and spotted the best looking hotel I could find. I went to the front desk and asked for a room, told the clerk to bring in the trunk off the back of the white Packard out front, then park it and bring me the key. The clerk handed me my room key and told me the bellboys would be along shortly with my trunk.

"As an afterthought, I asked the desk clerk where in Evansville I could get a Lexington, Kentucky newspaper. The clerk told me he'd check, and if he could find one, would send it up.

"I went to the room, kicked my shoes off, and stretched out across the bed. I began to think about what might be happening back in Plowshare, Kentucky.

"I was dreaming of the vast wealth I now possessed, without the liability of that ugly bride I was supposed to marry three days ago. Now that I had plenty of money, I could marry anybody I chose. But I couldn't help having a twinge of conscience. Josie had been really wonderful to me; I couldn't help but feel depressed.

"My thoughts were interrupted by a knock at the door. Two young men in uniform, one on either handle of my trunk asked where they should put it.

"'Just put it over near the bathroom door,' I said, noticing a folded newspaper lying atop of the trunk.

"As the boys set the trunk down, I reached for the newspaper and handed each a $5 bill, which caused their eyes to pop out. Bowing deeply, the boys scampered out of the room with the request if I needed anything else, call for Jim and Eddie. They closed the door as I unfolded the *Lexington News*.

"I had almost finished scanning the front page when I noticed down in the lower right hand corner, a small headline that read, 'A Chain of Bizarre Events in Plowshare.'

"'As we go to press,' the article started, 'all of the details are not known for certain, but from our early, sketchy reports, we have been able to establish the following: The recently hired president of the only bank in Plowshare, Kentucky, announced to the full membership of a local church, where he was part-time minister, that he had observed his betrothed and her father in the act of copulation only hours before they were to be married in the very church from which he spoke.

"'All of this was unknown to his future father-in-law and the bride-to-be. They were informed of the accusations when they arrived at the church. The daughter, who reportedly had never driven a car before, in a fit of rage, drove the car a half-mile down the road at full speed and crashed into a tree, killing herself and totally demolishing the car.

"'It has been determined at press time that the name of the bank's president, most likely an alias, is Will Cotton. Cotton is approximately 6 foot 6 inches tall, weighs around 200 pounds, is a flashy dresser. It is thought that he absconded with at least $160,000, possibly more. The vice-president of the bank has assured the depositors that the bank is very strong, is in no danger of failing from that small loss, and has announced that funds may be withdrawn at any time.

"'So far there has been very little panic at the bank. The former president of the bank, while talking to this reporter, stated: "The owner of the bank, who is also the father of the dead woman, has

authorized me to spend whatever is necessary to bring this criminal, this embezzler, back to Plowshare. No cost will be spared."

"'A $10,000 reward for information on the whereabouts of a
white Packard touring car, with a single spare tire mounted on the
back, and a seaman's trunk buckled behind the spare tire, was immediately announced. The car had been a gift to Cotton as a wedding present from his future father-in-law.

"'Reverend Nelson, the father of the dead woman, was in seclu-
sion, grieving the death of his daughter and refused an interview.

"My room was at the front of the hotel. I immediately went to
the window; the Packard had been moved. Though I had been
congratulating myself on how cool I had been during the whole
episode, almost instantly, I found myself in a state of panic. I could
imagine a thousand things going wrong.

"Why did the bitch have to kill herself? That'd only infuriate
her father, and with his money, there's no telling what the man
would do. How stupid of me to drive the car 200 miles.

"I started stomping the floor aimlessly with my right foot. 'How
could anybody be that stupid?'

"Suddenly, a knock at the door interrupted my self-flagellation.
A shock of terror I hadn't felt since I tumbled into the muddy waters
of Indian Creek during a raging thunderstorm shook me. Did I dare
answer the knock at the door—did I dare not answer the knock?

"Two minutes earlier I had been as cool as steam in an icehouse.
Now I felt the perspiration bead up on my back and trace my
muscles, streaming toward the small of my back.

"Who could be knocking at this door?

"I didn't even have a gun.

"How stupid, stupid, stupid!

"I found my voice and yelled, 'Just a minute,' and holding back
my panic I opened the door.

"There, with the keys to the white Packard, stood one of the
boys who had brought my trunk up to the room. I took a deep breath
and very carefully, and cautiously, in a low voice not to give away
the sheer terror that I felt said, 'Where did you park it, lad?'

"'I parked it around back, sir. I backed it up into the space next
to the road at the far end of the parking lot. You can pull out on

Essex Street, turn right, and you'll be on Main Street. Mister, that sure is some fine automobile.'

"'Yes it is. Are you Eddie or are you Jimmy?"

"'I'm Jimmy, sir.'

"'Where's Eddie?'

"'Oh, he's toting somebody's bag upstairs.'

"'Do you work as a team most of the time?'

"'Sometimes. I like Eddie. We get along good. There aren't many jobs around here that folks as young as we are can get. Sometimes, the tips are good like yours, sometimes, we make as much as our Pas. Of course, sometimes, when there ain't nobody in the hotel, we don't make nothing. We get along; we're just sixteen.'

"I was frantically searching for the kind of questions I needed to ask this young man to decide if it was safe for me to drive the car. Lexington was no more than five minutes away by telegraph if anybody read the newspaper story I had just read."

"'The newspaper you boys brought me,' I asked, 'where did you get it?'

"'Down at the rail depot. They've got a newsstand down there with newspapers from all over the country, that come in nearly every day.'

"'Do they get many newspapers from Lexington and places like that?'

"'They come from all over, but when I went to get the one from Lexington, the man at the newsstand said they didn't get a regular paper from Lexington. One of the railroad passengers had gotten off the train from back east and laid it on his counter as he walked by. He never ordinarily has it; he just looked at the headlines, handed it to me and said no charge.'

"There was no way Jimmy could possibly know the comfort the words he had just spoken gave me. But if anybody in the world understood the fickleness of lady fate, it was me. I had registered as Will W. Cotton, Jr.

"There was one thing I knew, they had no pictures of me, but my height made folks notice me. If one passenger bought a newspaper from Lexington, so could another. I had to get out of that hotel, now! And I also had to get rid of that car.

"I felt a powerful thirst for a drink of bourbon. It would calm my nerves, so I could think and not do something stupid that would land me back in Plowshare.

"'Jimmy, do you know where a fellow could get a bottle of good Canadian whiskey. There's got to be some good whiskey around here somewhere.'

"'Oh, you can buy it, but it's expensive.'

"'How much?'

"'Five dollars a pint.'

"I reached in to my pocket and gave Jimmy a $10 bill.

"'You can keep the change if you're back here in ten minutes.'

"Jimmy said, 'Yes, sir,' and was gone.

"I sat down on the bed. My mind was racing. It jumped from Josie, to Preacher Nelson, to Charlie Jetter. I couldn't get the picture of Josie wrapped around the big tree out of my head. I wondered how she managed to get the car in gear. I didn't think she'd driven a car in her life. Did she do it because of heartbreak, in fury? Not only did she get herself killed, she killed my child.

"God, what a mess. But I'm alive, and I'm rich. At the time, nephew, that was all that really mattered to me.

"In less than five minutes, Jimmy returned with a pint bottle of Canadian whiskey. I turned it up and drank half of it in one gulp. Jimmy made the observation, 'Mister, you are thirsty, aren't you?'

"'What time is it, lad?'

"Jimmy went to the window, pressed his nose against the pane, and looked off to the left in the distance at some kind of public building.

"'It's 4 o'clock.'"

Finishing School

Uncle Will's voice suddenly trailed off and fell into the even rhythmic breathing of sleep. Earlier that night I'd told Harvey Wright that if I didn't come out to meet him the next morning, I'd be sleeping in the waiting room where there was a settee long enough for me to stretch out on.

As soon as Uncle Will was asleep, I went to the settee and promptly fell asleep. The next thing I knew, it was 6 AM, and Harvey was kicking me on the foot. I got up, stretched, and checking back at Room 4, found Uncle Will still asleep.

On the way home, I confided to Harvey that Uncle Will was furnishing my expenses, and as soon as I got the milking done, I hoped he could take me to Muscadine Junction in Alabama for an appointment I had with a lady. I asked him if he would do that. Harvey was a couple of years older than I was, and his Mama had died when he was a youngster. He only had his Pa at home, and Pa never seemed to give him any kind of orders, but just let him come and go as he pleased. I thought that was a wonderful arrangement. So I asked Harvey how much he thought it would be worth to take me over to Muscadine Junction. He allowed that $5 would be plenty. When I told him he might have to stay all day, he said make it $7.50; if he had to stay all day, that would be fine with him. Since I had almost $400 of Uncle Will's money, it certainly didn't bother me any to have to pay. Besides that, I was mostly doing it for Uncle Will. When Harvey dropped me off at the house, I told him to give me an hour. I'd milk the cows, do the chores, wash up, and then I'd be ready to leave.

When I walked in, Mama, Rodger and Neeley, and Pa were sitting at the table.

"Well, did the son-of-a-bitch die?"

"No, Ma. Much to your sorrow, he's still living. Looks like maybe he might survive for a while."

I said that more to exasperate her than from any real conviction he was going to get well.

"I believe you think more of that cheating, conniving, son-of-a-bitch than you do your own Mama."

"I don't want to fuss this morning, Ma. Where did you put the milkbucket? I need to get the cows milked 'cause I'm going back to Muscadine in a little bit."

"Oh? You don't want to go on our trip?"

"Ma, you already told me I can't go. No, I don't want to go."

"We're thinking about going to Atlanta to Grant Park and see the Cyclorama. Wouldn't you like to see the Cyclorama? You never have seen it."

"Ma, I've got promises I made. You said I couldn't go, I accepted I couldn't go. I got promises I made, so please, what did you do with the milkbucket?"

"It's on the porch with water already in it. Clean off the cow sack."

"Why do you tell me that every time I milk? I don't want to drink cowshit any more than you do."

I went out the door thinking to myself, how is it that I always manage to get into a cuss fight with Ma every time I see her? I thought folks always loved their mothers. You're supposed to love your mother. I felt guilty because I didn't love mine; I didn't even like her very much. Especially when she was in a mood like this morning's.

While I was straining the milk, washing the bucket, and cleaning up the breakfast dishes, they all jumped in the car and left. Ten minutes later, Harvey drove up to take me to Muscadine Junction. Since we had to go to Bremen anyway, I asked him to take me by the hospital to make sure Uncle Will was okay. When I got there, it looked like he'd perked up a little. He motioned me over to his bed; his voice was stronger.

"Nephew, I didn't near get done last night, I need to talk to you. Today's Sunday, you don't have to work, you need to stay here. Let's get it over with."

"Naw, Uncle Will, some of your kin will be coming by to see you today, I know they will. We won't be able to finish the job. Besides that, I'm supposed to go back and see Fanny Hawk today."

"Nephew, you never did tell me how much money there was."

I told him, "$23,500." I hadn't even thought about it. When his life seemed threatened, it just slipped my mind. I reached in my wallet and pulled out all but two $20 bills of my expense money and gave it to him. "Here's $340. I'm going to spend the rest of it. I took $400 out. The jars were just like you told me they would be, but you've got a whole lot more than you said. Were you drunk when you hid it?"

"I could have been, Nephew. I sure didn't think there was that much money there."

"What did you do with the rest of it?"

"I got it hid where nobody can find it. I'll get it for you anytime you want it, just as long as you let me have some of it for expenses. Ma raises hell every time I want to borrow the car, and I have to buy more gas."

"Nephew, you're a good boy. Not many people would do what you're doing for me. Why did you tell me you found more? You could have had the extra money. You didn't have to tell me how much there was. I'd have been happy if you'd said there was $7000 or $8000. I ain't got many kin like that."

"You're not going to be wanting to get out of the hospital Monday anyway. They won't let you out, will they?"

"I 'spect not, lad."

"Well, I'm going to call on Miss Fanny. I'll see you tonight at visiting hours."

All the way over to Muscadine Junction, Harvey and I chatted about our work at General Shoe. How he was thinking about applying for a job at Western Electric; they paid good. He'd heard through a friend that they were looking for some help with a high school education. We both had that. Or at least we had diplomas saying we'd had high school educations; I don't really know how much we knew.

The subject got around to Julie about the time we passed the road to her house. I couldn't bring myself to tell Harvey about that ecstatic night in the back seat. But I did tell him she'd dumped me for absolutely no reason I could figure, and had said she never wanted to see me again. Harvey was very sympathetic. He mentioned what a pretty girl she was and how he'd often thought of asking her out himself, but hadn't because he'd seen us eating our sack lunches together under the shade tree at the plant. He thought she was sweet on me, so he'd never asked her.

"Well, you can ask her now. She's not going to have anything else to do with me. And I really don't understand it."

Harvey allowed as to how understanding women was a pretty hard thing to do. I remember him saying, when we were in the fourth, fifth, or sixth grade, how he used to think about girls as soft boys. But they ain't, there's a lot more to them than that. I wanted to tell Harvey just how much more there was to them than that, but I just couldn't.

About a mile from Fanny Hawk's house, Harvey said, "I know somebody who lives about three miles down the road. He worked for General Shoe before you started, then got himself a better job. I think I'll go over and talk to him. I'll come back to get you at about 3 o'clock?"

"Miss Fanny, before you start your story again I need to tell you I had to know you were alive. I'm very fond of my Great Uncle Will, but I know he's been a liar and a cheat all of his life. This past spring when he started telling me the story of his life, I thought that the story was complete. Then he asked me to run an errand, to do a favor for him. And when I went to do that favor, I ran into a man who had some very unsettling speculation about you for me. He opined that you might have been murdered by Uncle Will.

"I wasn't going to do anything for him unless I could find out he didn't murder you. You see this past spring he told me a lot of things about you. I sort of got to liking you, even though I never met you. The kindly little things you did, how you didn't care what people said or thought about you, how you could dip a turd out of the punch bowl and pretend it was a Baby Ruth. I just began to like you from the things he told me about you. Then when this fellow said the thinking around Tallapoosa was that he'd murdered you, I had to know. So when you told me you drove his Harley-Davidson, that you knew about his buried money, and you even knew something about the metal box hidden with the glass fruit jars, I just had to know more about you and him. I had to hear your side.

"I told him this morning how much money I'd found buried under the fireplace, and he couldn't believe it. He said he might have been drunk when he buried it, but he didn't think so. Then he wanted to know why I told him that there was all of $23,500.

"It is such a thrill to think about you as a 14-year-old girl in Knoxville. You know, I'm 17. That's three years older than you were when you ran away from home, and I ain't never been past Atlanta. This weekend was the first time I've ever been out of the state of Georgia. I ain't never been 50 miles away from home, and I'm 17 going on 18.

"Yesterday you told me about Judy Collins being killed in Chattanooga and how she'd moved from Rome with her family when she was two. How'd you figure out that you could go to Rome and get her birth certificate? That's wonderful, but I'd never have thought of anything like that. I've been thinking about it ever since I left."

"Gene, you flatter me. If you'll remember, I also told you that I went to see a lawyer the day before. He told me how those things work. I was frantic. I knew that, if for some reason the authorities picked me up and started pressuring me, they'd find out where I was from. They'd go there and get Pa's side of the story. Pa would tell them I was a runaway, and I would wind up spending the rest of my life with that hateful Blake Thompson.

"It was Mama who told me, 'If it's do or die, do!' I think I know exactly what that means. I was under such terrible fear that I'd somehow be caught, be carried back, and forced to live with that pig, that I had to think of a way I could be on my own without living in fear all my life.

"The trip from Carrollton to Chattanooga was one of the most anxious times of my life. Even more than when Pa didn't come home the night after Mama died. Those were long hours I spent wondering where he was and what had happened to him. Sometimes when he came home drunk, he slapped me around. I couldn't live like a whipped puppy. I guess that's why, when I met Will, he thought me such a free spirit. 'Cause I can't live in fear, can't live all my life dreading what's next. When I puzzled that out, I knew from that moment on I could look after myself. That I didn't have to be dependent on any person alive. That's also why I left Will. I simply wasn't going to sit around worrying over what he was going to do to me next time. No matter how much you love somebody, you can't let them lord it over you. I did love him dearly, and I'm not so certain that I don't love him now.

"You know the last thing you asked before you left last night, if I would see Will again? I told you I'd give you my answer today. But I'm not ready; I can't say yet, though I did think about it an awful lot. You say Will's old and beat up, and near dead. Is he going to survive whatever's wrong with him this time?"

"I don't know. When I left him to come here yesterday, he was in good spirits. When I got back last night, the people at the hospital acted like he was just about dead. The nurse told me they were giving him the newest and most powerful sulfa drug they had. Miss Fanny, he's got an awful lot on his mind. Last night he whispered some tales that made the hair on the back of my neck stand up—stories he'd never told me before, and I thought he'd told me everything. There is much more to Uncle Will than I ever knew.

"Miss Fanny, I want you to know one thing. When I come to see you now, it ain't got nothing to do with Uncle Will. It seems like you've had a very exciting life and I only know little bits and pieces of it. I'd like to know more about you, but it ain't got nothing to do with Uncle Will.

"Grandma used to tell me fascinating stories about her early life, but nothing like what you've told me. You can't imagine how exciting it is to know somebody who's danced with the Devil. In your story last night, you'd just gotten to Knoxville and were looking for a lawyer. Could you tell me more about that?"

"While I was looking for a lawyer's ad in the newspaper, I ran across one for a girls' finishing school. According to a little map in the ad, the finishing school didn't look like it was more than seven or eight blocks from where I was. I decided that maybe I'd let the passport business rest for a while because, if I settled down and people got to know me, and I told them where I was from and where I was going, pretty soon they'd know me and I'd have some witnesses to my character. What I needed more than anything else then, it seemed to me, was some credibility.

"According to the ad, school started the next week. The first semester, which ran all the way to Christmas, board, tuition, and everything was only $275. My trip from Newnan had made me realize how badly I needed to know more about things. So, I decided I'd postpone seeing a lawyer, and would instead visit the headmistress of the girls' finishing school the very next morning, and that's what I did.

"The headmistress' name was Mary Claire. She was a widow I would guess to be about 40. She was a kind and gentle woman; I liked her immediately. She asked me a great many questions about how I came to be in Knoxville. Of course, I had to fabricate a story as to why a 19-year-old girl, born in Rome, grown in Atlanta, wanted to go to her school. She seemed pretty well satisfied with my answers.

"The one thing that troubled her was that I'd told her in the beginning I was on my way to Baltimore to a finishing school. She was concerned whether my father would like it that I'd decided I'd rather study in Knoxville. I assured her that I loved Knoxville, and that it would be alright with my Pa. I told her I'd get a letter from him if it was a big concern of hers. She decided that I knew Pa better than she did, so she wouldn't make it an issue.

"I told her I'd be back the following morning with the money for the first semester's tuition and asked her if I could move into the dormitory at that time. She said I could, but that I might have to eat with her for a few days because not all of the staff had yet been assembled. Though the opening of the school was still a week away, I could certainly move in and settle down.

"Miss Mary told me I'd have a roommate as soon as school started. Her name would be Nell Miller, from a fine old family in Memphis. 'But,' she said, 'I need to tell you now, Nell is not up to the Miller name, or at least her conduct is not. The family's unable to control her and she's being sent here as punishment. I hate to put you in a room with such a girl, but you do seem rather level-headed to me. And if it becomes a problem, you just let me know privately. But I'm hoping you'll be a good influence on Nell.'

"Nell was an angry young woman. She told me in no uncertain terms that she was there against her will, there was nothing she could do about it, but she sure as hell didn't have to like it. The first two or three days, she was rather disagreeable, but after classes started and we got busy, she settled down, and I began to like her. We had long conversations at night.

"It developed over the first month of our rooming together that her chief problem was her boyfriend, who didn't come up to the standards of the Millers of Memphis. She was madly in love with the boy and had allowed him to seduce her when she was only 16. She decided it had been an occasion of such profound ecstasy that she was now perfectly willing to swap her entire life for one more encounter. Her vivid descriptions of her consuming passion raised some feelings in me that I hadn't known existed. Maybe it was my age, but I began to understand how she could be so bitter at being arbitrarily snatched from such bliss.

"But she was 19 now. That had been all of three years ago, still the memory was fresh in her mind. I was curious how the Millers had managed to keep them separated for three years. Nell said they hadn't, but that she'd been kept on such a tight rein that only by telling monumental lies had she been able to be alone with him, and this only on four different occasions in the entire three years. She allowed as to how she had lied enough to send two preachers to hell just to accomplish those get togethers, but that the moments of bliss they'd enjoyed had made it worth all the trouble.

"Just before she left Memphis, she had discovered her lover was engaged to marry another girl and had already given that girl a ring. The family's reason for sending her to school actually no longer existed, but there was no use in telling them that because they wouldn't have believed it anyway. Nell just decided to make the best of her finishing school adventure. We grew very fond of each other. She shared all of her deepest secrets and feelings with me—I was really ashamed I couldn't be more forthcoming with her. I dared not let anybody know my history. Even though I was very much tempted at times to get it off my chest, and though I thought she would be a perfect person to share it with, I resisted that temptation.

"Nell was almost like a mother and big sister all rolled into one. She was sophisticated, she knew how the upper layers of society functioned, and she was worldly wise. I insistently questioned her about hypothetical situations I might find myself in. I asked about the appropriate thing to do, what's polite, what's genteel, and what's ladylike. Not only did I drink in what the school taught me, but I learned first-hand all the fancy rules of etiquette used by the wealthy folk living in the upper fringes of society.

"One morning, just before Thanksgiving, Miss Mary called me into her office and asked me if there were any troubles I'd like to talk to her about. Quite frankly, I was surprised at such a question and I said, 'Certainly not. What makes you ask?'

"'It has come to my attention that you have not received any mail since you have been here. That is very unusual. I just want to know whether there's a problem, and can I do anything to help you?'

"I assured her there was no problem. But she still looked unsatisfied. I stood before her desk thinking about the situation for a minute. To relieve any suspicions that things weren't right in my life, I needed to resolve her concerns right now. So I said, 'Miss Mary, my father is a proud man. He's done well in business, but he can't read and write. That's the reason I had sufficient money to take care of myself until I visit him at Christmastime.'

"She said, 'I want you to know, I was not prying, I was just concerned, you understand that?'

"'Yes, ma'am, I do, and I appreciate your concern. But in this case, it's unwarranted and it's a very sensitive issue with my father. If you ever, by any chance meet him, please, don't let him know that you know his secret.'

"'Of course not, dear, I wouldn't dream of it. You run along, and I'm glad I called you in.'

"I started out the door and remembered that Nell had asked me to go home with her to Memphis at Christmastime. I had indicated to her that I would. That was going to arouse Miss Mary's concerns—if I went to Memphis instead of Atlanta at Christmastime, and didn't get to see my Pa. So, I turned and said, 'Miss Mary, I'd like a special favor from you if you would.'

"'Yes, what would that be?'

"'I would like to visit my Pa at Christmas, but Nell invited me to go home with her over the holidays, and I'm thinking seriously I'd like to do that.'

"Miss Mary raised one eyebrow. 'You know, Judy, the trouble that got her here. You don't want to go to Memphis and get yourself into the same kind of trouble, do you?'

"'No, ma'am. I won't do that. And besides, Nell tells me the boy who caused all that trouble is engaged to somebody else; she no longer cares for him. I'm just going to visit her family because if I go to Atlanta, there won't be anybody but Pa and me, and if I visit with him on Thanksgiving, that will be sufficient. All I need is one extra day at Thanksgiving. Let me come back to school on Tuesday instead of Monday; I can get a train ticket Wednesday night to Atlanta, stay three days with Pa, and be back here Tuesday morning.'

"'I'm going to let you do that, but I hope you will seriously consider whether you really want to go home with Nell over the Christmas holidays. I would hate for somebody at the school to be blamed for getting her into more trouble. She's a girl who's going to get into more trouble.'

"I was offended that she'd make such a dire prediction about the girl I had come to admire and whose company I really enjoyed. Of course, I had no business in Atlanta, but I did want to get away from the school and try out some of the charming little things they had taught us, as well as exercise a little bit of freedom. I was beginning to feel cramped at the school. So I bought a ticket to Atlanta and left on the Wednesday night before Thanksgiving.

"I'd been cooped up so long, I felt like splurging, so I bought a compartment on the Pullman car and traveled in luxury. I arrived in Atlanta the next morning at 8 o'clock, took a carriage, and registered at a nearby hotel. I rented another carriage and took in the sights of Atlanta. Later, I had the carriage drive me by 1300 Peachtree Street; it was a beautiful residence that I would have been proud of. If I ran into anybody who knew about Atlanta and gave them that address, they were going to know I lived in a rather exclusive residential area.

"It was a lot of fun, but I had a loneliness that I couldn't shake. Mama was dead. Pa had betrayed me. I was truly alone in the world. It became a sad holiday. Sometime during my stay in Atlanta, I made up my mind that I'd go home with Nell regardless of what Miss Mary wanted. I needed the companionship and the love. That's what was missing from my life.

"Each day I was in Atlanta, I mailed a letter from my fictitious aunt who had moved from Baltimore to Atlanta, and from my fictitious aunt who had moved from Nashville to Atlanta. So, that took care of my two aunts whose letters I carried. Those letters would have bona fide United States Post Office postmarks on them when I received them after I got back to the girls' school.

"I returned to the school as scheduled, and sometime the following week I told Nell that I would be happy to accompany her to Memphis for Christmas.

"On the last day of the first semester, which was over on the twentieth of December, we had a little party. From there, we went directly to the railroad station and took the train to Memphis.

"It was a warm day when we arrived. Nell's family lived in a house that was unbelievable in it's size and beauty. I was given a bedroom next to Nell's bigger than most houses in Coweta County. All of her family were charming people. They took me in as if I were one of their own. Her father, Jeff, told me that Jeff was short for Jefferson, which I suspected anyway.

"Nell's mother's name was Christine. She was a lovely lady in her late 30s or early 40s, and so elegant in her speech. I immediately fell in love not only with the luxury in which Nell lived, but with her family as well.

"There was a party scheduled somewhere every night. I met so many eligible young bachelors, all of them very charming, that I couldn't keep up with their names. But the family, especially Nell, kept telling me that I hadn't seen anything yet until Jeff Davis Cannon got home. He was a first cousin, once removed, who was away studying engineering at the Virginia Military Academy. They had a photograph of him. He was a handsome young man of 22. The minute I met him in person, my knees turned to jelly. I fell madly in love with him.

"His family lived about eight blocks from Nell's. He brought me home from a party on the night before Christmas. The weather had turned much colder. The Millers invited him in, and he had a couple of drinks. The Millers excused themselves and went to bed after advising us not to stay up too long.

"After they had gone to bed, Nell got out her father's jug of brandy, and insisted I take a drink. I did, and no sooner had it settled in my stomach than it's warm glow found it's way through every capillary of my body. I felt beautiful. I felt as if I were glowing from head to toe with a radiance my prince charming, Jefferson

Davis Cannon, would find irresistible. When I was offered a second cup of this nectar of the gods, I drank that, too. The next thing I knew, I was in my bedroom with Jefferson Davis Cannon taking my blouse off and caressing my breasts, and somewhere in that pink, glowing, warm, misty haze, I lost my virginity in an explosion this earth has not seen the likes of before or since."

As she finished that sentence she looked over her glasses at me, and I'm sure I was a brilliant red.

"Gene, I embarrass you."

"No, ma'am, I know about such things," I stammered.

"Miss Fanny, I hate to leave now, but I see Harvey driving up. Can I come back? I want to hear the rest of the story. You haven't even got to where you met Uncle Will yet. May I come back another day?"

"Any day, Gene, I'll be glad to have you. Maybe next time I'll have you an answer about me and Will."

I walked out of the house giddy from the feeling she'd aroused in me.

Will the Banker

As Harvey and I made our way back to Bremen, I told him about Miss Fanny embarrassing me with her story about losing her virginity. He tried to make out like he wasn't embarrassed, but I think he was. Even though he was two years older than me, he was still bashful around girls. He was red-headed, freckle-faced, and very fair-skinned, and his face had turned redder than a fox's ass at pokeberry time.

As I told him the story, I could see the lobes of his ears turning scarlet, I started kidding him about his embarrassment. He said it wasn't embarrassment at all, just his "courage" trying to rise while I was talking about that kind of stuff.

Folks don't usually have a friend as good as Harvey, so I didn't press him too much. I asked him if he would run me back by the hospital in Bremen so I could see if Uncle Will was okay before I went home.

Even though I knew nothing of such things, it seemed to me Uncle Will was hanging by a very thin thread, I had absolutely no faith that by just listening to his confession, I could ease his pathway into the afterlife. Still I had to do what he asked me simply because Uncle Will seemed to live in such terror of crossing into the great beyond.

In all my life I'd never heard of anybody that old fearing to cross over. I'd even asked Dad about it one time. He said Will had lived a terrible life. But even to Dad, it seemed that Uncle Will was old enough he should have put his house in order by now. He too allowed as he'd never seen anybody that frantic about joining the innumerable caravan. So I felt an obligation to do what Uncle Will asked of me, over and above the ordinary sense of obligation.

When we got to the hospital he was alone in his room and appeared to be a bit stronger. I asked him how he felt. He allowed as to how he thought he was some better. He said, "Nephew, maybe I'm going to live this time, but let me tell you, it was a close call. Are you here to hear me finish my confession?"

I told him, "not yet. It's just a little after mid-afternoon. I have to go home, milk the cow, and do all the evening chores, but I'll be back during visiting hours." He said he'd try to get a nap and looked forward to seeing me then. As I started away he called, "Nephew, you need to come on back. Every time I close my eyes, Ol' Ebo is standing there, so I know I ain't out of the woods yet. Please be coming back during visiting hours." I promised him I would.

Harvey carried me home and promised to pick me up about 6:30. He told me he'd read a magazine in the hospital waiting room while I visited Uncle Will.

Just as I arrived back at his room, the nurse finished giving Uncle Will his medicine for the night. She told me not to let him get too excited, then left. Uncle Will picked up his story exactly where he'd left off—talking to the bellhop.

"I asked him what time he got off work, Jimmy told me the last train going east arrived at 8 o'clock, and the last train going west arrived at 9 o'clock. If nobody checked into the hotel from the 9 o'clock train going west, Jimmy'd go home.

"'Ain't you got no trains that run north and south here, Jimmy?'

"'Not here. If you want to go north, you've first got to head west to St. Louis or back east to Cincinnati. Our railroad tracks around here run east and west. Why would a fellow like you, whose got that big automobile, want to get on a train? I'd go to California if I had that machine.'

"'Oh, I didn't mean I want to ride a train, Jimmy. It just seems odd you didn't say anything about the trains running north and south, only east and west, but if that's the way they run around here, that's the way they run.'

"I realized I was making small talk with the kid simply because I didn't want to be alone. But by now, the whiskey had taken it's effect and my nerves had settled down.

"'Do me a favor, Jimmy. Before you leave for the night, come by and knock on my door. If I answer the door, I may have another errand for you. In any event, I'll give you a dollar if you'll just come by and knock on the door before you leave. Now be gone with ya.'

"'Thanks, mister,' Jimmy said as he scampered off.

"I finished off the pint bottle, then lay down on the bed to try to collect my wits and decide what I needed to do. It was going to be dark soon, I had to do something with that car and do it quickly.

"Since it was going to be cool, I went to my trunk and picked out a black topcoat. Then I went down through the lobby and out into a breezy early December afternoon. The temperature must have been in the low forties. The traffic was fairly heavy, with a general mixture of mules with coal carts, horses pulling milkwagons, and Model-Ts scampering around with their horns sounding like sick goats.

"When I got to the corner, I turned left and spotted the Packard backed into the end parking slot, exactly the way Jimmy had described. I walked along even with it and wondered how I was going to get rid of it.

"The December breeze had by now washed enough of the alcohol from my brain that I remembered I'd left my briefcase with all of the money in the hotel room. I quickly retraced my steps, but when I unlocked the door and went in, everything was just as I left it.

"I dug around in the trunk for the money belt that I'd bought. Most of the money was in large bills and easily fit into the belt, along with the five $100,000 bearer bonds. I stuffed $1000 in $10s and $20s inside the pocket of my topcoat, picked up the newspaper, went down to the lobby, and back again to the car. What could I do with the car?

"No answer would come to mind. Walking to the next intersection, I turned left, and could see the depot a few blocks down, and headed straight for it. Going through the passenger terminal, I found a timetable: 'St. Louis to Chicago—Train leaving at 8 o'clock.' I approached the ticket agent.

"'Could I get a Pullman sleeper to Chicago tonight?' I asked.

"'If you've got $88 you can,' he answered.

"I paid the $88, took the ticket, and asked the ticket agent if the train usually left on time.

"'Exactly.'

"As I returned to the hotel, I saw two police officers standing almost directly in front of the door, talking to each other. That made my ass suck wind. I had an idea if I ever went back to Plowshare, Kentucky, my life wouldn't be worth two cents, and I had no intention of letting that happen.

"One of the policemen looked up and seemed to notice that I was just standing there watching them. That really put a shine on my nose. I decided to face the opposition boldly, and so as calmly as I could, I strolled up the sidewalk within inches of them, then turned into the hotel and went to my room to collect my wits and make some decision about that damn Packard.

"I felt I could just leave it sitting on the lot, but when I disappeared from the hotel, somebody would eventually grow suspicious of the car. Sooner or later they'd find those boys. I couldn't just go to Chicago and leave the car in the parking lot. I'd bet the last nickel in my money belt they had a professional chasing me right now who'd sure enough find it.

"I simply had to dispose of that white Packard.

"As darkness descended, the streetlamps began to wink on, and I could see the town wasn't going to be very well-lighted. About 6:30, I slipped out of the hotel and into the parking lot, taking only my money belt, the clothes on my back, and a change of underwear.

"I had an hour-and-a-half to get rid of the car. So I drove around in a tight circle near the hotel and the railroad station. Automobile headlights in those days weren't much better than kerosene lamps; the weak light from the headlamps didn't even show against the street lamps.

"I thought of taking a length of hose, siphoning the gas tank empty, and tossing a match. But I didn't know if the gas would puddle up, soak into the ground, or blow up. If I burned the car on the streets of Evansville, it was certainly going to cause a great deal of commotion I would like to avoid.

"By now it was 7 o'clock, and I still had an hour before the train. I'd made up my mind to burn the car, but how?

"I pulled into a Standard station and ordered the attendant to fill it up. They didn't yet have electric pumps, so he had to raise the gasoline up by hand into a glass jug which had the gallons marked up its side.

"The attendant filled the glass jug full as I sat impatiently drumming my knuckles against the steering wheel. Ten gallons ran into the tank. The attendant pumped the bowl full of gasoline again. It only took two-and-a-half gallons to finish the fillup. Noticing they had several metal five-gallon containers for kerosene or gasoline stacked in front of the station, I asked the attendant to fill up two of these emergency cans.

"I gave the attendant a $10 bill and drove off. Of course, for a gas station attendant to get a tip was an unusual event, and it later proved not to have been very wise since it would make the young man remember me—not hardly what you want when you're on the run. I had the young man put the two cans between the back seat and the front seat in the leg space.

"I had selected a site 500 yards from the railroad station, and now opening the compartment where the emergency crank was stored, I took out the two tow ropes that were standard equipment for automobiles in those days. They were approximately 20 feet long and 3/4 -inch in diameter, and made of jute.

"I took the tops off each of the gas cans and soaked them 20-foot ropes in gasoline. Setting one of the emergency cans against each door, I now cut a shorter length of rope, maybe 6 feet long, and put one end of the rope in each can. I took the other 20-foot rope and stuck one end in one of the cans. Then I laid the emergency hand crank across the rope to make sure it didn't come out. I then placed my King James Bible on top of the rope on the other can to make sure it stayed in place. Opening the left back door, I pulled the rope through and slammed it on the rope to prevent it from moving. Then I tied the two ends of the rope together and looped it all around behind the spare tire. Now I put half of my handkerchief in the gas tank, leaving half of it laying across the gas-saturated rope. Then playing out the full length of rope to its end about 30 feet away, I lit a match and hustled away.

"By now it was almost 8 o'clock. The train was already boarding when I got there. Just as I reached my compartment, an explosion shook the station. A much more violent explosion than I had expected.

"Twelve minutes later, at exactly 8 o'clock, as predicted by the ticket agent, the train pulled out of the station. As we cleared the platform, I looked off to the left and saw a huge building on fire, in a place very near, it seemed, to where I'd left the Packard. I went off to the dining car to see if anybody there knew what exactly was on fire.

"There was an elderly man at one of the dining tables. I asked him if he was dining alone.

"'No, my daughter will be along shortly, but I'll be most happy to have you join us if you would like.'

"Pointing out the window at the huge glow in the sky, I asked if he had any idea what was on fire even before I asked his name.

"'Yes,' the stranger replied, "I think it's a cotton warehouse where 10,000 bales of cotton must be stored. The banks of the Ohio River are lined with warehouses, I can't think of anything else down there that would make that big a blaze. It has to be one of them big cotton warehouses. If so, it's going to be burning for days.'

"'Excuse me for not introducing myself,' I said. 'I'm Jessie Robinson, from Brunswick, Georgia.'

"The old man said, 'I'm Bill Taylor. My home is here in Evansville. My daughter and I are going to Chicago to meet the man she is supposed to marry, and I damn well don't like it. He should come here. I don't like the way this new generation conducts its affairs. A young lady should be chaperoned everywhere she goes until she is betrothed. She sure as hell has no business running off to a city like Chicago while her man sits on his ass up there waiting for her.'

"He went on, 'Excuse me, Mr. Robinson, I got a bit carried away. I'm an old-fashioned man who believes ladies should behave like ladies, and gentlemen should behave like gentlemen. It sticks in my craw that my daughter is chasing all the way to Chicago for some son-of-a-bitch I don't much like anyway. But excuse me for burdening you with my problems. It's none of your concern.'

"At that moment, one of the most lovely women that I, alias Jessie Robinson, had ever seen came in and sat beside her father. The older man introduced her.

"'This is my daughter, Kathy, Mr. Robinson.'

"I stood up, bowed low, and said, 'Ma'am, I don't think I've ever met anyone so beautiful. Excuse me if I stare.'

Kathy blushed a brilliant red, which made her that much lovelier.

"'Thank you, sir.'

"I couldn't keep my eyes off the beauty who sat before me. Her hair was shoulder-length, as black as coal, as silky as shiny satin. She had a tiny nose and full red lips with turned-up corners that gave her a constant, secretive smile. It made me feel faint just to think about holding that exquisite work of art in my arms. It seemed her personality matched her good looks. She appeared totally at ease with me, and our chitchat as I told some tall tale was punctuated by her tantalizing giggle.

"Dinner was beginning to be served, and as the train made a long slow turn, I could see Evansville and the conflagration at the cotton warehouse disappear from view. The hectic past few hours slowly faded from my memory as if they had never happened.

"We had a delightful repast. As soon as we were finished, Kathy's father excused himself, complaining of a headache. I asked Kathy if she would join me for a drink. Much to my surprise she agreed, but first she went to check whether her father was okay. Soon enough she knocked on my compartment door. I quickly admitted her.

"I had already let down a table between the two facing seats and had readied a bucket of ice, some water, and two glasses. Kathy slid into the seat opposite me as I closed and locked the door.

"Kathy then began to explain why she'd agreed to join me. First, she liked a nightcap before she went to bed, but there was a more compelling reason. Her fiancé in Chicago was heavily in debt to some underworld figures, and I seemed to her a man of worldly experience who might know what could be done to extract him safely from the mobsters' clutches.

"As she told me why she'd come to my compartment—not at all the purpose I had in mind—my countenance gradually took on a less pleasant hue. I stopped her.

"'Miss Kathy, I'd do anything in the world for you, or for me and you, but this young fellow you're involved with has more problems than any young fellow ought to have. He may well prove more pain than pleasure and only a nitwit would tie up with someone like that.'

"'No, no, Jesse, you don't understand. If he could just get free of these gamblers, these crime lords, he's sworn he'll never touch another drop of whiskey and never turn another deck of cards. I believe him.'

"'The greater fool.'

"'What do you mean?'

"'I've never figured out who's the greater fool, the drunk swearing he'll never take another drink, or the one who believes him.'

"She reached for the lock on the door, but I pulled her back. I reached across the slender let-down table, and embraced her across it, planting a passionate kiss on those bountiful lips. She relaxed, and my hand began to wander toward the front of her blouse, then down inside. She stiffened and sat back in her chair.

"'No, I'm not that kind of girl, Jesse. The whiskey hit me hard, but I see you do not intend to help me. I'll leave now, if you please.'

"I made no move to stop her. She stood up, reached for the lock on the door, turned to say something. But before she could, I offered, 'What if I prove to you that he isn't going to stop drinking, and isn't going to stop gambling, what about you and me then?'

"'How are you going to do that?'

"'You'll have to agree not to marry him, not to live with him for at least three months. If you do, I'll help you—and if what I say about him proves right, then I want you to be my woman. If what you think proves right, then you've lost nothing and, in fact, you've been helped.'

"' But how will I know that you're proving he won't change? It's no problem not to marry him for three months, but I must hear how you are going to prove he isn't going to change.'

"'Do you know how much he owes the gamblers?'

"'Somewhere around $20,000, no more than $25,000 at most.'

"'What does he do for a living?'

"'He's a stockbroker.'

"'How much money does he make?'

"'In a good year, he will make $10,000 to $25,000.'

"'Alright, I'll tell you how I'll prove it to you. I will loan him the money to pay off his indebtedness plus $5000 for living expenses, a total of $30,000. I'll give him ten years to pay me back at 2% interest. That should never strain him and should enable you to live like a queen on his salary.' Since I stole the money and had plenty of it, I could afford it. God, Nephew, she was gorgeous.

"'I predict he'll take you out to celebrate his good fortune by getting drunk and gamble away the loan before he ever pays off his debts.'

"'If he does that, I'm yours if you want me.'

"'Do you have hotel reservations in Chicago?'

"'We're registered at the Ingram Hotel, about six blocks from the railroad station.'

"'As soon as I get to Chicago, I'll open a bank account. I should have the cash available in no more than two or three days. I have some bonds I'll have to cash, but in the meantime, how are you going to approach your fiancé? How are you going to tell him you have another man who is willing to loan him that much money?'

"'I can just tell him I met a very wealthy man on the train who is willing to lend money to people of good character for small interest. That is true, isn't it? He'll be so happy to get the money, I don't think it's going to be a big question in his mind. I think he'll just be grateful.'

"'So once I have the cash in hand, we'll meet for supper. I will have the proper paperwork drawn for him to sign. Something else, when we have supper together, I want you to bring your father along so that your fiance' will know that you and your father met me together on the train. I don't want him to say later on that thinking about what you promised me made him get drunk and lose the loan, because I also predict that will be his excuse.'

"'My, my, Jesse Robinson, if he is such a scoundrel, how on earth could you make such startling predictions without being one yourself?'"

"'Remember, I was in the banking business for several years. You learn a lot about people in the banking business.'

"The next morning, when we arrived in Chicago, I headed for the Ingram Hotel. It was more than nice, it was elegant. When I laid my briefcase on the polished marble counter, the desk clerk arched an eyebrow and inquired, 'Sir, is this all your luggage?'

"'At the present moment it is. I suffered an accident back in Indiana and lost my luggage, but will shortly acquire some more. If that's a problem for you, I'll be glad to leave a cash deposit at the desk.'

"The clerk blushed as if he'd been caught with his hand in the till, and stammered, 'No sir, that won't be necessary,' instantly judging me a man of means.

"I then asked the clerk for writing paper. At the top of the memo pad he offered I wrote my room number noting the advertising where the hotel boasted about rooms being connected by telephones. I also wrote, 'As soon as you're settled, call me, give me your room number, and let's make arrangements when to meet.'

"Ten minutes after I'd gone to my room, Kathy called and told me she and her father had a suite on the seventh floor, Room 704, and asked me to please call her as soon as I had made the financial arrangements.

"I sat on the bed for several minutes, trying to decide whether I wanted to keep all my money in the money belt or put it under the mattress in the hotel room. I finally opened the money belt and took out one of the bearer bonds. I stared at it for a long time before putting it in my hip pocket along with $300 in cash and then left the hotel.

"A few minutes and four blocks later I arrived at the Continental Bank and asked to see the president. The receptionist asked my name.

"'I'm Jesse Robinson, an investor.'

"The receptionist walked through a half-glass door with *Private* stroked in gold letters across the middle of the glass. She returned a minute later and said,

"'Mr. Logan is busy right now, could you see anybody else in the bank?'

"I was a little bit peeved. I placed the bearer bond for $100,000 on her desk and said, 'I intended to open an account with you folks, but apparently you don't want my business.'

"Making sure she could read the numbers across the bearer bond she said, 'One moment, sir,' and disappeared through the same door. One second later, an early middle-aged, prematurely graying man emerged and said, 'I'm Logan, will you please come in.'

"I followed Logan into a plush office.

"'I hope you'll excuse my boldness, but I'm not accustomed to doing business with second and third-level management. When I talk business, I like to speak with the boss.'

"'I understand that. I didn't get your name.'

"'My name is Jesse Robinson, I'm an investor. I've been in Chicago one day and I've already found an investment for about $30,000. I'm not sure just when I will require the cash, but wanted to make sure there was no problem with opening an account with this.'

"I handed him the bearer bond. Logan gave it a cursory glance while rubbing his hands over the high quality paper that told him it was the real thing. He laid it on the desk.

"'Not at all. Let me present you to our executive vice-president, who will open your account. I'd do it myself, but I don't really know all the paperwork involved. Will that be alright, Mr. Robinson?'

"'It certainly will,' I replied, as Mr. Logan ushered me through a side door. Apparently Mr. Logan liked to have his executives close at hand. He introduced John Davis, executive vice-president of the Continental Bank.

"'John, would you please open Mr. Robinson's account? He wants to do it with this bearer bond. Everything seems in order to me, and welcome to Continental Bank, Mr. Robinson. We hope to have a long, profitable relationship.'

"As John Davis pulled out the papers to open the account, I kept a close eye on him to see whether he recorded the serial number of the bond and whether he showed any extra curiosity. He did copy the serial number of the bond, but seemed to take no particular notice that he was opening an account of that size with a bearer bond. Perhaps it was a frequent occurrence in big city banks.

"While I was watching John Davis filling out the paper, I began to wish I had destroyed the bond ledger at the Plowshare Bank. I now strongly suspected that those serial numbers would soon come into the hands of many bankers.

"I was lost in my own thoughts when John Davis announced the paperwork had been taken care of. He handed me a book of checks, gave me a receipt with my account number, my balance, and asked whether there was anything else he could do for me. I thought for a moment.

"'Yes there is. I have an ex-business associate who lost a great deal of money as a result of his carelessness. He has blamed me for this, even to the point of harassing me with detectives. As a matter of fact, he might presently have a Pinkerton man, or somebody masquerading as a Pinkerton man, following me.'

"'What I'd like you to do if there are inquiries from any quarter is let me know about them. I have nothing to hide, but a time or two he has gotten me into some embarrassing situations. I would greatly appreciate a call. This is my room number at the Ingram. I plan to be there for several days, possibly weeks. I am trying to buy a piece of property on the lake. If I find a suitable piece of property, only then will I be moving. Good day sir,' As I stood up to leave, John Davis jumped up, beat me to the door, and let me out.

"'By the way, this fellow following me knows the serial numbers of several bearer bonds I possess. That's the way he manages to sound semilegitimate. He also may very well be carrying a Pinkerton ID. If you have any queries with regard to me or the bearer bond I've just deposited, I'd appreciate it if you'd let me know.'

"'We certainly will.'

"'One other thought, I might leave with you. He is going to tell you my name is Will Cotton, Jr., when in fact it is not. That's another trick he's developed to make his story more believable, to tell people I am using an alias.' As I crossed the lobby of the huge bank building and descended into the noonday traffic of Chicago, I felt I had pulled the fangs from whomever might be chasing me.

"After I returned, Kathy called and told me about the lunch with her fiancé that she and her father had just been partaking in the Ingram hotel's dining room. As soon as the meal was finished, Kathy's father had excused himself on the grounds that he needed a nap. He was hoping that his prospective son-in-law, Harold Nail, would take it as a sign that he didn't like him very much. But Harold was too busy courting Kathy to take any notice of her father.

"Harold Nail was tall and blonde. One couldn't miss his Swedish ancestry. He was just a tiny bit overweight, and had a sweaty handshake and darting eyes. It put one on notice almost instantly: 'Here's a man to beware of.'

"As soon as the old man was out of earshot, Harold began his oration, 'Sweetie, I'm so sorry about the letter I wrote you. It was so frantic, so stupid to write that way because you certainly couldn't do anything about it. But I've got myself into a real pickle. The mob has given me two weeks to pay up and the juice is 10% a week.'

"Kathy could not help but compare this sweating, frantic, overweight man to the tall, elegant, slender, Jesse, who seemed so cool, deliberate, and solid. His frantic effort to impress her with the importance of her help in extricating him from his dilemma was beginning to wear thin.

"'I met a man on the train willing to lend you the money you need to get out of debt. Father and I met him one evening at dinner. Maybe I shouldn't have, and I hope you won't be offended, but I told him all about how you'd gotten in with gamblers and how you might have a drinking problem. I'm sorry Harold, but I had to tell him this because he appeared to be a very wealthy man.

"'He said that due to the fact you are a stockbroker and make $25,000 a year, he might be willing to make the loan. If you pay them this week, how much money do you owe them?'

"'The juice is figured up on Friday. If I pay them before Friday, $30,000 will pay me up in full. I owed them $25,000, but last week $2500 in juice was added. This week it'll be another $2500, which makes an even $30,000. That's on the condition I have the money before Friday. That will square me up.'

"Kathy began to wonder what she'd seen in this fellow when she first fell madly in love two summers ago. She had matured since. But she had promised to marry him and was not going to admit she was wrong this easily.

"'Let me speak to my friend from the train and see if he's willing to go a little more with his loan.'

"'Okay, Sweetie, would you ask him for $35,000? Two percent is a wonderful interest rate, especially if he's willing to stretch it out 10 years. We can live very comfortably while I pay him back."

"Harold had to get back to work. A major client was going to call on him in less than 30 minutes. He reached down and gave her a swat across the lips that could have possibly have passed for a kiss, patted her on the shoulder, and walked out.

"Kathy was stung by his abrupt departure. She sat at the table a good while before she got up, returned to her room, and placed a call.

"I answered the phone; she said, 'I'm so glad you're in. May I come to your room?'

"'I'd be delighted.'

"Five minutes later she knocked on the door. I already had drinks on the coffee table in front of the settee.

"She sat down on the settee a good three feet away from me, picked up her Haig & Haig, and looked over the top of the glass at me. 'It's worse than I thought. It's going to take $35,000 to bail Harold out. Will you let him have that much?'

"'What the hell, Kathy. For you, what's another $5000? Certainly I'll loan him the $35,000.'

"'Can you do it before Friday?'

"'That will be fine. Tonight, or this afternoon, as far as that goes, but I need to get some legal papers drawn up if he wants it that quickly.'

"'I think you're wrong about what Harold is going to do. But the sooner I know, the better it will be for me. I keep bargains I make.

I'd like to call him at his office and arrange for us to meet tonight and finish the deal. The sooner I know, the better I'll like it.'

"'Why don't you use my phone and call now. It's 3 PM. I should be able to get a stenographer to draw up a couple of papers between now and, shall we say, 6 o'clock? If you like, call now, and we'll make it dinner here at the hotel. I'll give him a check tonight.'

"'Alright, I'll tell him.'

"She turned to me white as a ghost, smiling sickly, and said, 'He called me stupid. He said, 'Stupid, the people I deal with don't like checks. I've got to have cash. Can you supply that much cash tonight?'

"'Sure, see you at dinner.'

"Kathy finished her drink and stood up to leave.

"'Kathy I just want you to remember our deal. That's what's important to me. That $35,000 is not nearly as important as your promise that you're my girl if my predictions are correct.'

"'Harold and I will see you here at 6 PM,' she said as she closed the door.

"I found a public stenographer's office and had the necessary papers drawn. Then I went to one of Chicago's finest department stores and purchased the fanciest tuxedo, white shirt, and black tie in the house, plus a pair of black boots with such a high sheen you could see yourself in it. I didn't want to be outshone by a two-bit gambler.

"When I answered the knock at 6 o'clock, Kathy stood holding hands with Harold Nail.

"My heart pounded at the sight of her beautiful face. For some ungodly reason, I saw Josie Nelson's face. I shook my head to wash that image from my mind, but I was shaken.

"I had the loan papers on the desk. Harold Nail signed the documents without even reading them. I went to the phone and called the desk to have them send a notary public to my room. Shortly the notary arrived and witnessed the promissory note for Harold's $35,000 at 2% interest.

"As soon as the deal was done, Nail said, 'Darling, let's go out on the town for the rest of the evening,' taking Kathy by the hand.

He pulled her to a standing position and turned to me, 'Thank you very much, Mr. Robinson. I will have your first monthly payment in your hands by the first of the month.'

"With that they walked out the door, leaving me furious.

"I suspect, Nephew, I would have felt a greater urgency had I known at the time that G. B. Balls had made some very good guesses about my direction of travel. Balls had arrived in Evansville less than five hours after I left.

"As Balls settled comfortably into his Pullman compartment headed for Evansville, he read the story in the morning paper that had so frightened me. A plan to capture me was beginning to take shape in Balls' mind. I had broken no federal law, so the postal authorities would not place my picture at the post office, even though, in the eyes of Josephine's father, I had committed cold-blooded murder. As to law, I had done no such a thing. All Balls could do was put reward posters in every sheriff's office and every police office in the country. But he would have to do so at Pinkerton's expense. That was rather insignificant compared to the riches stored in my money belt.

"As his train pulled out of the station in Lexington, Balls noticed for the first time that Christmas lights and candles were up in the windows of the houses all along the railroad tracks. He just couldn't get into the Christmas spirit with me, that son-of-a-bitch, loose out there. He was a man of a single mind—to bring me back to Plowshare.

"G. B. had had a busy day. He rang for the Pullman porter and asked him to fix his bed, not knowing he was less than 200 miles from me as I bought a railroad ticket in Evansville, destination Chicago, by way of St. Louis."

Remorseless

"Nephew, I suppose you must wonder how I know so much about the thoughts and actions of Mr. G. B. Balls. Just take it as an article of faith that I do know these things, for a fact, about the man. Maybe I need to tell you how, in mitigation of my behavior in this whole sorry episode. Maybe the Almighty himself will take into consideration some of the circumstances. I was arrogant in those days. Showed a total indifference to the pain and suffering I caused my family, or the Nelsons, or the Balls of the world—until now it has come my turn.

"When you judge me, Nephew, and I know you will—you're shaking your head but as time goes on, you'll judge me—when you do, try to take everything into consideration. I lived the high life, but I've paid a great price. So when you judge me, remember all the darkness.

"When G. B. Balls arrived, the warehouse was still burning furiously and could be seen for miles around. The pumper boats on the Ohio River were wetting down the nearby buildings to keep them from going up in smoke.

"Balls decided it wasn't worth the effort trying to determine anything about the disaster until the following morning. He went to the hotel for a good night's sleep.

"He thought about sending a telegram to his Chicago office, but didn't even know what Will looked like, except he was tall. Pinkerton people didn't harass innocent people, and, besides that, he had a yen to arrest the son-of-a-bitch himself.

"The next morning, Balls went to the warehouse, which was still smoldering, and examined the remains of an automobile. Besides the obvious bits and pieces of the fenders and bumpers, there was some cheap metal that looked like it might once have been a fuel can—the kind people strapped on their autos when they didn't know how far away the next gas station was. There were two of those close to the car.

"As a detective, he couldn't find anything else on the scene that interested him—except those two carcasses, the remains of the two fuel cans that appeared to have exploded themselves.

"Balls hurried back to the hotel to see whether he could find the young bellboy who had told him of the tall man driving a Packard. Shortly, he saw Jimmy struggling up the sidewalk with a heavy trunk on a steel-wheeled cart that looked to have been borrowed from the railroad. When he was ready to bring it up the steps, Balls picked up one end, told Jimmy he'd help him, and asked where Eddie was.

"Eddie's mother had some things for him to do before he came to work. Mainly shoveling a ton of coal down the basement chute, so's he could fire up the furnace, but he'll be along shortly.

"Balls helped Jimmy carry the heavy trunk all the way to the second floor. They placed it in the room that had recently been rented to me.

"'Jimmy, you can have my half the tip. All I want you to do is try to remember something about Will Cotton's car. You said you drove it.'

"'Yes sir, I did.'

"'Did you happen to look in the back seat when you moved the car?'

"'Yes sir, Mr. Balls. Like I said, when you get to drive a fancy car like that, you like to know everything about it.'

"'Was there anything on the floorboard of the car you wouldn't ordinarily expect to be there?'

"'No sir, it was just like it had come from the factory. The only thing on the floorboard was the little box where the tow rope and the crank comes, that's all.'

"'Jimmy, that's interesting. One of the back doors was blown all the way across the street in the fire. I went down this morning, and the other back door was all the way down against the warehouse. There was some remains of what looked like extra fuel cans. Since the doors were blown to the outside, I thought there might have been a couple of cans sitting there in the foot space.'

"'No sir, there was nothing in the foot space except what was supposed be there. No fuel cans.'

"'I'm certain there were two fuel cans inside the car when it exploded. The doors blew out. Where do you suppose he'd have gotten the cans if they weren't in the car when he got here?'

"'Oh, there's a Standard Gas Station just three blocks west of here on the corner. They sell gas cans all the time, it would be easy.'

"'Like I said Jimmy, you collect my tip for me. You've been very helpful.'

"It was a rather brisk morning. Balls, rather than hire a surrey, decided to walk the few blocks from the hotel. Stacked neatly in front of the station were perhaps 25 or 30 gas cans very similar to what he thought the exploded cans would look like.

"He walked into the station. A young man seated at a desk asked, 'Can I help you?'

"Balls extended his hand and a business card identifying him as a Pinkerton agent. The young man looked duly impressed and said, 'I'm L. B. Pecker.'

"In spite of himself, a small smile crossed Balls' face, but the younger man didn't seem to notice as Balls quickly inquired whether L. B. worked every day at the station. L. B. informed Balls that indeed he did.

"'Sometime late afternoon or early evening yesterday, there was a tall man who came in, in a white automobile, and purchased two of those cans, I believe. Am I correct?'

"'Indeed you are, sir.'

"'That man, I believe, is a fugitive from justice. Did he give you a name?'

"'No sir.'

"'What kind of car was he driving? Did you notice?'

"'I sure did; it was a Packard. It was white, and it was beautiful.'

"'Can you describe the man for me?'

"'He was tall. Maybe 6 foot 5 or 6 inches, slender.'

"'No, I mean can you give me a physical description of his features?'

"'Oh, I can do better than that.' L. B. took a pencil and quickly sketched an exact likeness of Will Cotton.

"'That is what he looked like.'

"Balls was astonished. He handed the kid a $10 bill, put a note in his expense book, and walked back to the hotel. He could not believe anybody was capable of reconstructing a human face from memory after so brief an encounter. He'd found a daffodil in a pile of cowshit. The thought occurred that there was one sure way of checking out the young man's memory. He hurried to the hotel, found his friend Jimmy, and asked whether he had time to do an errand for him.

"'Sure, what is it?'

"'Jimmy, I want you to go to the service station you sent me to, the Standard station; the young man on duty is named L. B. Pecker. I want you to ask him to draw you the face of the man who just questioned him about the driver of the white Packard. If the drawing looks like me, you give him $10. If it doesn't look like me, don't give him anything and come back. Here's $10 for you and $10 for him,' as he made a notation in his expense account book.

"'I'll stay here in the lobby of the hotel. Get back as quickly as you can; it's important.'

"About 20 minutes later, Jimmy was back in the hotel grinning from ear to ear and showed Balls an exact likeness of himself. Looking at the drawing was like looking in a mirror. He handed Jimmy $10 more, and went off directly to the railroad station where his baggage had now arrived. Paying for the baggage, he purchased a ticket to Chicago. He got a Pullman compartment on the same train that I had left on just 24 hours earlier.

"Balls was feeling pretty good as the train pulled out of Evansville. He had an exact likeness of his quarry. He felt quite sure that I, his quarry, had not the faintest idea that this was so. Cotton always went to an awful lot of trouble to be sure nobody photographed him. But drawing, for identification purposes, was just as good as a photograph.

"Ball's ego was no greater, and perhaps no less, than that of any 30-year-old man's at the top of his profession. He took great pride at having begun to grow famous all over the country. Magazine articles were appearing. But he was also a practical man. He realized that people in his profession weren't permitted many mistakes, and a fall from such heights as he had attained usually meant great pain. So he needed to plan very carefully. He knew the man he was chasing was not foolish—perhaps a bit overconfident, but not foolish.

"Balls ran through the different uses he might make of knowing what Will Cotton looked like. With one telegram and a printer's shop, he could have Will's picture in every police department and sheriff's department in the whole country in a matter of days.

"He wondered whether he wouldn't be a bit foolish to advertise that he knew what Will Cotton looked like because, sooner or later, Cotton was going to see any poster put out by Pinkerton, and it would make him just that much more cautious. Then, too, there was the consideration that Cotton had become Ball's own private quarry, and he sure didn't want to share him with any other Pinkerton operative.

"Balls folded the likeness of Will Cotton four times until it was small enough to fit neatly into his wallet and rang for the pullman porter to prepare his compartment for sleep. As the porter answered the call, Balls asked if he might find him a good bottle of whiskey, something of which he rarely partook.

"The porter gave him a cold stare, 'We ain't got no whiskey on this train.'

"'I know we ain't got no whiskey on this train, but I'd bet my left nut you got whiskey on this train. How much does it cost?'

"The porter felt fairly safe in selling Mr. Balls a bottle of whiskey.

"'It'll cost you $15 a pint.'

"'That's ridiculous, I've never paid over $5 for a pint of whiskey in my life.'

"A sheepish grin formed on the porter's face, 'I just wanted to see how thirsty you are. I'll be back in a minute.'

"Shortly, the porter returned with a pint of Haig & Haig.

"'Bring me a bowl of ice and a pitcher of water,' he said, handing the porter a $10 bill. 'Keep the change.'

"Shortly after the porter brought the ice, Balls sat down, drank half the pint straight out of the bottle, and chased it with a swallow of ice water. He sat on his Pullman bed while the burst of alcohol took effect, producing that marvelous rush only those willing to drink deeply of the nectar of the gods ever feel.

"As Balls came out of Union station, he pulled his topcoat up tightly against the icy blast coming across Lake Michigan that December morning. The sky was mostly overcast, and an occasional pellet of sleet chipped at his face as he headed north to the Ingall hotel, very near the Ingram where I lay wide awake with a monstrous headache from my own overindulgence after Kathy's departure with her gambler last evening. My teeth itched, my hair hurt, and my mouth tasted like swamp rats swimmin' in a sewer.

"Unable to stand the pain any longer, I got up, washed my face, and stared at the bloodshot eyes in the mirror. I picked up the telephone and ordered a bottle of aspirin and a bowl of ice. I paced the floor nervously, cursing my stupidity at getting so drunk as to leave myself in such a condition.

"The bellhop delivered the aspirin and ice. I swallowed a handful of the pills and chased them with ice water and a good belt of Haig & Haig. Then I lay down again, hoping the little drummer boy would shortly vacate my head. The aspirin and booze both took effect about 7 AM as I was falling asleep.

"Balls too was getting comfortable in his room. He picked up the telephone and asked the operator to connect him with the telegraph office. He dictated a telegram to one Mr. Jetter, President of the Plowshare Bank in Plowshare, Kentucky.

"'Arrived in Chicago AM Thursday, December the 6th. STOP Suspect my quarry here. STOP'

"Balls then did something he had never done before in his working life. He wrote, 'If you have not heard from me in seven days, please advise my St. Louis office. STOP.'

"He paused for a couple of minutes, so long in fact that the operator on the other end asked,

"'Is that all? We need a signature.'

"'Sign it, G. B. Balls.'

"He placed the earpiece in its cradle and stood looking at the instrument for a couple of more minutes. The longer he was in pursuit of Will Cotton, the more he was astounded by the swindle Cotton had pulled off in the brief period of six months, and the more he respected his cunning. He couldn't help but wonder if this son-of-a-bitch could outsmart him. But Balls was not the kind of man to think very long that anybody was his equal, let alone his superior.

"He ordered a newspaper and went through it page by page hoping something would catch his eye, point him in the right direction. Balls knew his sixth sense for puzzle-solving was what had made him successful.

"The ads in the paper were mostly for Christmas gifts. One item caught his eye—Continental Bank was offering 2-1/4% interest on savings accounts. It gave a little table showing that after four years, $100 would be worth $110, and listed the various offices of the Continental Bank.

"Balls cut the ad out of the paper, stuffed it in his pocket, and went downstairs. He asked one of the bellhops to look at the addresses and tell him which was closest to the hotel.

"'The Eighteenth Street Branch is about four and a half blocks from here.'

"He circled two other branches that were within 20 blocks of the hotel. Balls got directions to the Eighteenth Street Branch and started walking. Approaching the same receptionist I had spoken to the day before, he asked to see the president of the bank.

"In the same fashion as the day before, she excused herself, went into the president's office, returned and repeated to Balls the same thing she had said to me the preceding day: 'Mr. Logan is unavailable at the moment. Would you speak to executive vice-president Davis?' Balls readily agreed.

"She introduced him to John Davis, vice-president.

"'How can I help?'

"Balls produced a drawing and laid it on the desk in front of Davis.

"'Have you ever seen this man before?'

"The likeness of the previous day's customer was startling. John Davis tried not to show any emotion, realized he could not tell whether he'd been successful, but had enough composure to say in a normal voice,

"'Why do you need to know that?'

"'I have a warrant for his arrest. I'm G. B. Balls with the Pinkerton Detective Agency; my home office is in St. Louis. Over the years I've become pretty good at reading the reactions of people, and right now I'd bet my front seat in Hell that you've seen this man in the last 24 hours. I might point out to you, Mr. Davis, that aiding and abetting a criminal is a serious offense under the law.'

"By now, John Davis was thoroughly pissed off.

"'Mr. Balls, intimidation is not the way to get help from me. I frankly don't give a damn who you work for or where you are going, I've never seen that man before, and you, sir, can go straight to hell.'

"He regretted saying that instantly, but it seemed to work because Balls stood up and appeared about to leave his office, then paused a minute and said, 'Mr. Davis, maybe I got this conversation off on the wrong foot. I need your help.'

"'I would like to be a good citizen, but this man told me there would be a man masquerading as a Pinkerton agent who was an unhappy former business partner. I'll give you five minutes to convince me you truly are a Pinkerton agent, and maybe we can get off to a better start.'

"Balls sat down, laid his credentials on the table one by one, his Missouri driver's license, his detective's ID, a checkbook with his name imprinted on the checks, a gold Hamilton railroad watch with his initials engraved in the face cover of the watch. In addition, he gave Davis a list of five serial numbers, one of which was the bond Continental had cashed the day before.

"'Besides that, we have long distance telephone service between here and St. Louis. Let me give you the Pinkerton Detective Agency telephone number and you see if you can get a call through. I will pay the charges.'

"'No, you have to yell too loud on those long distance telephone calls. I don't like to unless I've got to. You've convinced me you are a Pinkerton detective. You do have the serial number of a bearer bond deposited here. Of course, the fact that he cashed a bearer bond, of which you have a serial number, in itself doesn't mean anything, but I am going to give you the address he gave us because you have convinced me you're a Pinkerton man; you can settle this matter between yourselves. I'll help you find him. He's staying in room 302 at the Ingram hotel. It's about five blocks from here. Or at least that's the address he gave us.'

"'Thank you very much, Mr. Davis.'

"Balls started to walk out the door, then turned and said, 'What happens to that $100,000 he has deposited with you if he never shows up to claim it?'

"'There are laws governing such matters, laws covering almost any eventuality,' replied Davis.

"'What if we prove in a court of law that money belongs to the Bank of Plowshare, Kentucky?'

"'Then sir, we would be subject to a federal court order to transfer those funds to the rightful owner, but it's a rather lengthy process. We try to protect our depositors. You would need a lawyer for such matters; you don't need me.'

"Balls thanked Mr. Davis and walked out of his office, across the lobby, and down to the street. Before he had ever gotten to the street, Mr. Davis picked up his telephone and asked the operator to connect him with the Ingram hotel. When the hotel switchboard operator came on, he asked for room 302.

"'Mr. Robinson?'

"'Yes, this is Jesse Robinson.'

"'The Pinkerton man you predicted to be here just left my office. I gave him your hotel room and number. I felt that he was telling the truth when he said he was a Pinkerton man. I hate to go counter to your requests, but at the same time he was very convincing. But I decided, to make all things even, I would call you and tell you that he knows your room number. Whatever measures you take are your concern. And, oh yes, Mr. Robinson, he has an exact pencil-drawn likeness of you. If you think he doesn't know what you look like, you are wrong.'

"'What does he look like?' I asked.

"'I'd say he's six-one or-two, a very muscular build, 210 to 220, young, maybe 32, somewhere in that neighborhood. If he's somebody you are thinking about doing physical battle with, he'll be a handful.'

"'Thank you, Mr. Davis. He can be over here in eight to ten minutes. I need to make arrangements to meet him. Good day, sir, and once again, thanks.'

"As I put the earpiece back on the hook, I pulled out my Hamilton pocket watch, popped the face cover, noted the time. 'I have a maximum of ten minutes before the Pinkerton man gets here.' I took the watch out again checked the second hand as I walked three flights of stairs to the front desk. Exactly 50 seconds had elapsed when I reached the counter.

"I pulled one of the desk clerks aside. 'I am Jesse Robinson. I'm registered in room 302. Would you look and see whether the room directly across the hall from me is occupied? I haven't seen anybody go or come.'

"The clerk checked the registry and told me it was not.

"'I have a friend coming down from Canada, and he'll be arriving here late tonight. I'd like to pay for that room for one night, and, if it's suitable to him, he'll sign the register in the morning.

I'll just pay you cash now, and he can pay me back when he arrives. I'd like to go up and look at the room now; then I'll bring the key back down so he can pick it up later tonight when he arrives. Would that be agreeable?'

"'It certainly would. And in what name will the room be, sir?'

"'Norman Miller is the name. He's the president of a mining company in Canada. We have some business. He will be alone, so I can go ahead and register for him.'

"In two minutes, Norman Miller was registered in the room directly across the hall from mine.

"It had taken five minutes, so I now had only three to five minutes before Balls arrived. There was a half-glass door with the word *Stairs* on the glass just to the left of a bank of elevators. I decided I would stand in the stairwell behind the door to see whether I could identify Mr. Balls when he arrived, and whether he said anything to the desk clerk or just headed straight to my room.

"I didn't have to wait long. A good-looking man came through the front door alone. John Davis had given me an excellent description of G. B. Balls. Balls walked right on past the desk straight to the bank of elevators.

"I raced up three flights of stairs. The door at each floor was situated so I could see the elevator when it opened. I stood back in the shadows just a bit and watched G. B. Balls get out of the elevator and turn toward 302. Balls knocked on the door.

"When there was no answer, he tried to turn the door knob and, much to my surprise, the door opened. I didn't remember whether I'd locked it when I left the room. Balls opened the door a couple of inches, then quickly closed it, and once again knocked lively. When there was no answer, he stood back with one hand rubbing his chin, contemplating the knob. Suddenly making up his mind, he took a pistol from a shoulder holster, then opened the door very cautiously and almost jumped into the room. The door closed behind him.

"I took out my watch and popped the face cover. It had been 17 minutes since I had placed the earpiece on it's hanger in the room Balls was now exploring. Shortly he reappeared. I waited until he was in the elevator and the doors closed, then went racing downstairs. Once again I stood behind the half-glass door and watched him emerge from the elevator, walk toward the front door, and leave. When he did not turn around, but walked across the street, I came out of the stairwell, went to the front door, and watched him turn right. He went all the way to the corner and then turned left. I followed.

"When I reached the corner, I paused a moment before stepping around it just in time to see Balls crossing the street two blocks away. He continued away and was soon lost among the buildings. I crossed the street, made a left turn and, at a very rapid pace, was quickly at the corner where he had disappeared.

"I poked my head around the corner just in time to see Balls enter the Ingall hotel. Now I knew as much about G. B. Balls as he did about me. At least I knew where he was staying and what he looked like. That put us on a more even footing.

"Of a sudden, I had an overwhelming desire for the company of Kathy. It was almost 20 hours since I had seen or talked to her. As I stood there trying to decide what to do about Balls, it started snowing. Huge wet flakes were coming down in quantities I had never seen before. It was only a matter of minutes before everything above street level was covered in snow. It came down so fast I could barely see ten yards ahead as I headed back to the Ingram.

"When I got back, I noticed the desk clerk to whom I was supposed to return the key to 303 was no longer on duty. Not waiting for the elevator, I climbed the three flights of stairs and went into 302. I looked around to see whether I could tell if Balls had been there, but could not on quick inspection. I came out, locked the door, and opened the door to room 303. Picking up the telephone, I asked the operator to ring suite 704.

"Kathy answered the phone, and as soon as she heard my voice, asked where I had been because she had been trying to call me since noon. Between great sobs, she told me the sorry story of last night's events. It had turned out exactly as I'd predicted. Her fiancé had taken Kathy to a speak-easy, at least that's what it appeared to be when they first went in. But there were some secret passageways they were then taken through, and pretty soon they'd found themselves in a fabulous restaurant with many well-dressed people.

"They ate dinner but before dinner was over, her fiancé was pretty drunk. They were then led through still more secret passages and secret doors, and came at last to a huge gaming room. Her fiancé had immediately parked himself at the roulette wheel and lost the entire $35,000. She raised such a ruckus, the management forcibly ejected her, though they did send her back to the hotel in a limousine at 5 o'clock in the morning. She had no idea where her fiancé was now, but was convinced he ought to be taking meals in hell. 'I belong to you, Jesse Robinson, if you still want me.'

"A wave of raw desire rushed through me. I wanted her more than anything in the world, but I had a more urgent problem at the moment. My mind was racing for some excuse, something I could tell her that sounded reasonable for not hurrying straight to her room, or permitting her to rush to mine after such wonderful news. Then I remembered an ad I'd seen in the newspaper that solved my problem.

"'Darling, in yesterday's paper I saw an ad for a freighter leaving tomorrow afternoon at 3:00 PM for Buffalo that has a honeymoon suite. It's the last passage before the winter freeze-up. I have a meeting with a business associate at the Navy pier that I'll have to make in about an hour. But let's get married tomorrow at noon and take the Buffalo freighter tomorrow night. Have you ever been on a ship before?' I asked.

"'No, but it sounds wonderful to me, darling.'

"'I won't call you back tonight, sweetie, but I will wake you in the morning. We'll get married about noon and board the ship at about 3 o'clock. We'll take the voyage to Buffalo and then go on to Niagara Falls to round out our honeymoon. Does that please the lady?'

"'Jesse, you've made me happier than any ol' thing.'

"'I'll talk to you in the morning, honey.'

"Now I had to make up my mind what to do about the Pinkerton man, and what to do greatly depended on what Balls did next. I tried to decide the best way to settle this thing once and for all. The man has a perfect likeness of me. I didn't like that, but what to do? I would have to confront him face-to-face. Would bribery work? I was a man of great wealth. I could offer him $100,000. Would that work? These thoughts tumbled through my mind as I sat there totally preoccupied with G. B. Balls.

"I had no weapon, but I had watched Balls draw his gun before he entered the room earlier in the day. So I called room service, identified myself as Mr. Miller, and asked them to deliver the biggest steak they had to room 303.

"About 20 minutes later there was a knock on the door. I opened the door, stuck a $5 bill out in the lighted hallway, telling the delivery boy I had been having an eye problem for which the doctor had advised me to stay out of strong light. Of course, all the delivery boy saw was the $5 tip.

"'Thanks, Mr. Miller,' he said, and was gone as I pulled the cart inside the room.

"I let the door stand open just enough to see my meal while I watched room 302 to make certain it didn't have a visitor until I finished.

"Even though it did not offer a clear view, the vertical shaft of light coming through the door was adequate. When I took the cover off of the room service cart, I found the biggest T-bone steak I'd ever seen, along with pan-fried potatoes, hot rolls, blackberry cobbler, and a pot of hot coffee. And the customary silverware included a steak knife with a stiff, sharp 6-inch blade. I took my time eating and enjoyed the meal immensely, all the while watching the door across the hall. When I finished, I wiped the knife and spoon clean, put them in my pocket, and closed the door without locking it.

"Then I went across the hall into room 302. The light switch controlling the overhead chandelier was one of the newest spring-loaded, push switches on the market. Its cover was held in place by screws above and below the switch. The spoon fit neatly into the slot of the screw, and I quickly took the screws out and the face plate off. I removed the plunger that rotated the toggle switch, first pushing it one last time to return the room to darkness. Then, in the dark, I located the screw holes and reattached the screws to the face plate.

"Now with my stomach full, all I had to do was wait for my guest. I pulled the most comfortable chair in the room up just outside the swinging arc of the door, and sat down. I felt it could be a long wait.

"After several minutes, I very quietly slipped my shoes off in the event I had to stand up. My stocking feet would be much less likely to make noise than the highly polished boots I wore. As I sat in the darkness, I realized I had no plan, nothing actually, other than a steak knife and a spoon.

"I tried to visualize what I would do were I in Balls' position. The first thing I would do would be to open the door, slide sideways into the room, quickly close the door again, and hit the light switch. I didn't have long to contemplate my own actions for soon there was a knock on the door. Every fiber in my body stiffened. I stood up almost as if I were spring-loaded. Fully alert, with the knife in my right hand, I watched in fascination as G. B. Balls did precisely what I imagined I would have done in the same circumstance.

"Balls backed away from the switch one step. When he did, I wrapped my arms around him bringing the knife in just below the sternum, a little to the left, and shoved the blade in hard. There was one low grunt and a gush of blood swept over my hand. The warm, sticky, blood momentarily sickened me. I let the body slide gently to the floor, cursing the darkness. Balls would not ever see again, but neither could I see right now.

"I took several steps backward to the coffee table in front of the settee. There was a table lamp; with my left hand I fumbled until I found the switch. I quickly inspected my hands and clothes. My right sleeve was saturated with blood. I turned to look at my handiwork and saw Balls crumpled in a wad and lying in a great pool of blood. Enough time had elapsed that the blood had already started to congeal. There would be barely enough room for me to open the door and leave the hotel room without stepping in the blood.

"I went to the sink, took off my shirt, and washed my hands thoroughly. Then I took Balls' arm and rolled him over so I could get at his pockets and stay out of the blood at his feet. I found the drawing the banker told me about. Then I took every scrap of paper that was on the body, plus all his money, and the Hamilton Railroad watch, which was a copy of my own.

"The only other clothes I had were the fancy evening wear I had worn the night before. I quickly dressed in those, leaving off the tie which I thought would look out of place. I shouldn't draw too much attention so long as I didn't wear the tie. I fashioned a 'Do Not Disturb' sign out of a sheet of hotel stationery and hung it on the outside doorknob. Then I locked the room from the inside and left the key at a 45 degree angle in the lock. Raising the window, I climbed out on the fire escape. Going around to the front of the hotel, I watched carefully to see whether anybody had observed me. Then I entered the lobby, went to the elevator, rode to the third floor, and entered room 303.

"As soon as I got into the room, I turned the light on and repeated the switch-rigging I had done in 302. I replaced the switch cover, turning the light out before I did so, and I went down the fire escape, vanishing into the night.

"Walking several blocks let the cold night air clear my head. I passed another plush hotel, and needing some place to think, I went in, paid $25 cash, and registered as Harold Nail.

"As soon as I got in the room, I laid all of Ball's things out on the bed. In the watch face cover, the inscription read, *To G. B. with Love, Nancy*. It suddenly struck me that there was no gun. He must have had a gun when he went into that room, but if he did, I couldn't understand how I'd missed it. I had searched him thoroughly, and I hadn't heard a gun drop to the floor. I looked at his room key. Maybe he'd left it in his room. Did I dare go to Balls' hotel?

"I picked up the telephone and told the operator I would like to be connected to room 704 in the Ingram hotel. Kathy answered. 'Kathy, darling,' I said into the mouthpiece as soon as I heard her voice on the other end.

"'Jesse, darling, you said you wouldn't call me until the morning.'

"'The man I was supposed to meet from Canada has not arrived yet,' I lied to her. 'Besides that, darling, the bridal suite has been sold, we can't cross the lake. When does your father plan to return home?'

"'Oh, he left in a rage on the 6 o'clock train earlier this evening after I told him our plans. But Pa is not feeling well; he's a sick man. Once we're married, it'll be okay. I've already told the hotel I'm checking out in the morning at 9 o'clock.'

"'That's okay. At this moment, my plans are a little bit up in the air, but if you don't hear from me before 9 o'clock, there will be a carriage in front of the hotel. You take it; the driver will know where to take you. He'll bring you to me. I wish I could be more specific than that, but I really need to make this business appointment. I need to wait at least until the morning to see if he arrives. Never fear, darling. If I can, I'll come with the carriage. If I can't, the carriage will bring you to me. I'll see you sometime tomorrow. Good night, darling.'

"Then I went to the toilet, ripping the identity papers of Balls as well as the likeness of me to shreds, and flushed them away. It was 10:45, and the holiday parties were starting up. There was still a fair amount of traffic on the street below.

"I felt an overpowering urge to know more about Balls. The room key was for number 202, the Ingall hotel, I could be there in five minutes. As I walked into the Ingall , a smiling night clerk stood up as I approached the counter, 'Yes sir, may I help you?' the clerk said.

"'Do you have a vacant room?'

"'We certainly do, sir. Do you have any baggage, sir?'

"'No my baggage was left at the railroad station, but I will leave an adequate deposit to assure you I am not going to leave with the hotel's linen.'

"'I'm sorry, sir,' stammered the clerk, 'I didn't mean....'

"'Never mind. It's been a long day.'

"As the clerk was looking over the selection of rooms available, I said to him, 'I have an unholy fear of elevators. If I could, I 'd like one of the lower floors so I'll be able to walk up and down easily.'

The night clerk looked over his glasses and said, 'A big fellow like you fears an elevator?'

"'Well, it's not the elevator I fear. I'm just always afraid the operator will be asleep when I need to go down. If I'm seven or eight floors up, that can be a problem.'

"'Oh, I see what you mean. But, sir, our elevator operators are on duty 24 hours a day. We do have a room available on the second floor. Here you are sir, room 206. That will be $25.'

"I paid him and walked up the stairwell. As I came to room 202 going to 206, I stopped. After hesitating a moment, I took G. B. Balls's key out of my pocket, unlocked the door, and stepped inside.

"The instant the door opened, the light came on in the room. As I pushed the door behind me, I was looking into the barrel of a Colt .45.

"'Greetings, Will Cotton, I've been expecting you. I'm G. B. Balls of the Pinkerton Agency.'

"I could feel my heart jumping out of my throat, but I calmly said, 'What a remarkable recovery, Mr. Balls. The last time I saw you, you were laying in a puddle of your own blood, quite cold. What a remarkable, remarkable recovery.'

"'So that's what you did to my pimp. The one thing I regret giving him along with my ID and other papers was that perfect likeness of you. By God, it is a perfect likeness, Mr. Cotton. That kid had an uncanny memory. Would you like to know who drew that picture? It was the kid you bought the gas cans from in Evansville. Quite an artist, wouldn't you say?'

"'I want to tell you now, it was almost me you murdered back at your hotel. When I saw the masterful, patient plan you worked back in Plowshare, Kentucky, I knew I was not dealing with a fool. I hope you realize now, neither are you.'

"I had to acknowledge, to my own dismay, that I had never expected to cross this bridge.

"'Mr. Balls, let me ask you one question. What made you so sure, so absolutely certain, I would come here that you were willing to sit in that chair facing the door all this time?'

"'Oh, Mr. Cotton, that's simple. I knew you'd know a Pinkerton detective'd carry a gun. And when you searched the body you thought to be G. B. Balls, you didn't find the gun. I knew—as thorough and careful as you are and as recklessly you live—you'd want to know why a Pinkerton detective didn't have a gun. That's the only reason for giving the poor bloke a key to my room. It cost me two bucks on the expense account to get one made, but, of course, I put it on Mr. Jetter's tab. There will be one key on the expense account, two dollars, and being the banker he is, he'll want to know what the key was for and I will tell him it was the key that unlocked the cage that I placed Will Cotton in. Of course, I used that same key to relock the cage. That's $2 Mr. Jetter won't argue about.'

"I relaxed a bit, hoping Balls would do the same. 'Mr. Balls, it's obvious you don't intend to shoot me at this moment. As a matter of fact, I doubt whether you would shoot me if I walked out of here, it was such child's play to catch me. But you have to admit, a lot of luck was involved.'

"Balls was immediately upset by my statement. 'I'll have you know, Will Cotton, luck is never a factor in the detective's mind. I outsmarted you. I caught you, and I'm going to take you back to Plowshare. I have been promised a $100,000 bonus, over and above my salary with the Pinkerton Agency, and I'd like you to know,

Will Cotton, it was my plan that brought us together here tonight and not one, no not one, modicum of luck was involved.'

"'Have it your way, but you seem to be a reasonable man. If the $100,000 is important to you, maybe you and I could discuss money. I go my way and you go your way, both of us still very rich men. I am a man of considerable means.'

"'But you stole yours, Cotton.'

"'I never have carried any money to the bank and have them ask me where I got it.'

"'Let me tell you this, Will Cotton, G. B. Balls can neither be bought nor sold. I do the work I do because I like the work. Money is rather inconsequential to me at this point in my life. But I realize that one day I'll grow old and my skills will fade and the only thing to take the place of those skills is money. I can buy those skills if I have enough money, but I'm a young man and there's plenty of time.

"'I'm already famous, and you're going to make me even more famous, especially when they put my pimp's picture on the front page of the paper, along with the gruesome puddle of blood you just described. The people will be paying $100 just for my autograph while you rot in jail, Will Cotton. Actually I suspect you won't spend a lot of time in jail when I get you back to Plowshare. They'll find some legal means of hanging you. But once I get you back, that's no concern of mine.'

"'I'm talking about a lot of money, Mr. Balls, an *awful lot* of money. I will give you three times the $100,000 he's going to pay you.'

"'I am not in the least interested in your proposal, Will Cotton.' Holding up a set of handcuffs, he said, 'Let's get on with it. Give me your hands.'

"I held both hands up in front of him, palms facing up, and said, 'I'll let you handcuff me to you, but you'll not handcuff both my hands together. You'll have to kill me first.

"'You can handcuff my right hand to your left hand since you are right-handed, and we'll walk out of the hotel together side by side, but you are not going to handcuff me to a piece of furniture and let the building catch fire. Let's go on to jail tonight and get it over with. But you handcuff me to you; that's the only way I'll go.'

"Balls shrugged, 'Why not.' As he reached out to take my hand, I said, 'Put it on your left hand first.' Balls shrugged, snapped the handcuff on his own wrist. He had to take his finger off the trigger momentarily to push the handcuffs together. The instant I heard the first click, I took both hands and grabbed the dangling hand-cuff and snatched it as hard as I could, taking the skin off G. B. Balls wrist and the upper part of his hand as he howled in pain.

"In the process, he dropped the gun. Reaching down to retrieve it, his face met my knee coming up at ferocious velocity. His head snapped back as he tumbled over backwards with the handcuffs still dangling from his arm as I retrieved the gun.

"Balls lay semiconscious on his back. I quickly looked around the room. Balls had had a steak the same as I had, and it looked as if the cutlery had come from the same kitchen. I took the steak knife, still greasy, and shoved it deep into Mr. Ball's heart as he lay dazed.

"'You sure are a hard son-of-a-bitch to kill, Mr. Balls, but I think this ought to do it.' As the blood pumped out of Ball's chest, he let out a small sigh.

"Going through Balls' steamer trunk, I found a shoulder holster for the gun I still had in my hand. I put it on under my coat; it was a very nice fit. Somehow that .45 gave me a warm, powerful feel-ing. I also found enough identification papers for 14 detectives, but they all had G. B. Balls name, with a little blank space for a photograph to fit inside a cellophane holder. While I was rum-maging through the personal effects of the dead man on the floor, I began to wonder who the fellow was I'd killed earlier in the night. But I satisfied myself that this was the real G. B. Balls. He per-fectly fitted the description John Davis had given me, plus the monumental arrogance of the man. I was sure I would no longer be bothered by G. B. Balls.

"Nephew, when the deed was done, I threw Balls' greatcoat open. In its inside pocket was a black book, a half-inch thick, finely crafted, with a leather cover. I fished it out and opened it up. It was a diary. On the first page it said, 'Diary of G. B. Balls. If lost, a reward of $500 will be paid by the Pinkerton Detective Agency, St. Louis Office.

"'Dear Diary: There is no shortage of work for a good detective in this crime-ridden society, so I now begin case #59. This AM delivered to my hotel room was a telegram that read as follows: To: G. B. Balls

"'Dear G. B.: Congratulations on successful completion of your Case #58. It is requested you proceed to Plowshare, Kentucky, a small town of approximately 8000 people just outside of Louisville. There, you will go to the Plowshare Bank and receive, from the president of that bank, all information necessary for you to begin Case #59.

"'Dear Diary: I had an interesting conversation with one Will Jetter about a most dangerous scoundrel.'

"Nephew, this was truly intriguing reading. But I had too many loose ends to tie up, so I put the diary in my coat pocket.

"Then I locked the door to room 202, leaving the key at a 45 degree angle, I opened the window, and went down the fire escape. I looked through the lobby window, and while the night clerk who had registered me a few minutes earlier had his back turned, I went in again and headed straight to room 206. Taking a piece of paper, I wrote 'Do Not Disturb' and put it on the doorknob of room 202. Then I went back to room 206, put the key on the night stand, descended the fire escape, and went back to my hotel to read a diary."

When Uncle Will stopped for just a minute, I said, "Good Lord, Uncle Will, I don't see how you have lived with yourself all these years with stuff like this on your mind. If I'd had any idea you wanted to confess things like this to me, I don't know if I would have listened to you or not. It scares the willies out of me just to hear you tell these tales."

"Well, Nephew, you didn't think I wanted to confess to you about singing too loud in Sunday School did you?"

"No sir, I guess I didn't, but I can see very well why you needed to confess to somebody, though I still think it ain't me."

At about that time, the nurse came in with a handful of pills and told me visiting hours were over. I promised Uncle Will I would see him tomorrow night at 7 o'clock, and mentioning I expected to visit Fanny Hawk the following day, I asked whether he'd like to send her a message.

"Yes, tell her to come to see me. I still love her."

The Riverboat

I got to Miss Fanny's about noon. That was as soon as I could make it, and I had no idea she would ask me to dine with her.

"Miss Fanny, I saw Uncle Will last night. He wants you to come see him so he can tell you he still loves you."

"I'll think on it," she said.

"I think I embarrassed you the last time, which I didn't mean to do. When you're 17 years old, a lot of things are embarrassing that we older folk take in stride. Men use phrases among men that they don't use around women and vice-versa. We pretend so much that the faces we present to the rest of the world usually aren't much like those we present privately to our friends.

"I've known people who, when telling about their most exquisite sexual experiences, manage to make them sound as exciting as slopping hogs. I knew when I watched your ears turn bright red yesterday that I had your attention. But enough of that.

"I was so wildly in love with Jefferson Davis Cannon, and he with me, that we didn't get out of each other's sight for the rest of the holidays. As a matter of fact, much against his parents' will we were married New Year's Eve, and I accompanied him back to Virginia as his bride. The next three months were a deliriously happy time of my life. But as spring approached our romance faded.

"Jeff grew totally disagreeable, and even quit sleeping with me. I suspected that whatever his problem was, it would pass, so I tried to carry on with my daily activities and let him do as he pleased. Still he became more and more morose. Then he stopped coming home at night. He would go two or three nights without showing up. Then he would drop by for some clean clothes that I'd washed and ironed. I still refused to pry into his world. It seemed he had shut me out. This went on for the better part of April into May. One afternoon, I decided I'd pack my suitcase.

"I went in, opened the secret compartment of the suitcase, and there was most of the money I'd had almost a year. I finished pack-

192

ing everything I wanted to take away from that place in that one suitcase. Suddenly, I had a real strong urge to get my old name back. I didn't want to be Mrs. Jeff Davis Cannon any more. I wanted to be Fanny Hawk.

"By the time I finished packing, I'd made up my mind I would go to the train station the next morning and buy a ticket. The only decision I had to make was my destination. I no longer feared not having the proper identification, or that somebody will force me do something I don't want to do.

"Just as I finished my preparations for leaving, Jeff came in. He sat down at the dining room table and said, 'Judy, I need to talk to you. I made a terrible mistake when I married you. I'd had a flirtation with a girl here before I went home, and hadn't seen her until about six weeks ago. But once I did, everything started up again, and now she's pregnant. I need to divorce you so I can do what's right by her.'

"I sat there and listened to this little boy's confession. That's what he was, a little boy. He hadn't grown up. Believe it or not, I couldn't feel any anger toward him. He was trapped in a man's body doomed forever to behave like a child wanting to be punished. I thought the predicament he was in was enough punishment. And I felt no hurt, and no malice.

"At that moment, sitting at the table, speaking with my new husband, who was telling me he had just knocked up another girl, I felt as free as an eagle soaring 10,000 feet high. I didn't feel hurt; I didn't feel bitter. I felt free. I knew I could take care of myself, and I hoped that child, my husband, sitting across the table from me, could take care of himself. But I doubted it, and I had great sympathy for him.

"'Tomorrow at noon you bring her here,' I said. 'I'll be gone, and you'll never see me again. Good luck.'

"'I can't do this to you. It's a terrible thing. Judy, do something!'

"That's the only moment I got upset. I wanted to scream out, 'Jeff my name is Fanny, call me Fanny, Fanny Hawk!' But I didn't. Instead, I asked him what he thought I should do.

"'Scream at me, throw things, show me what a terrible person I am. Please don't just walk away.'

"'Jeff, you've made your decision. Now live with it. Tomorrow at noon I'll be gone.'

"I still had plenty of time to walk to the depot, where I checked the timetable for departing trains. The first was leaving at 9:45 the next morning, headed west to St. Louis. I bought a ticket for a Pullman compartment and returned home. Jeff was already gone.

"The next morning I was up early. I fixed breakfast, washed the dishes, grabbed my bag, and went back to the railroad station in time to catch the train to St. Louis. When I finally sat down in my compartment, I think that was the most free I've ever felt.

"The Pullman porter stuck his head in and said, 'Can I get you anything, Miss?' I said, 'Yes, I would like you to bring me a magazine, preferably a detective magazine. And please call me Fanny.'

"St. Louis was a very busy city. I arrived there early in the morning, rented a carriage, and went down to the river to watch the paddlewheel steamers.

"I ordered the carriage to take me to a good hotel. Later I decided I'd take a ride on the river down to New Orleans. At that time I was only a little over 15 years old, but I was a wise 15 years old. I had already been married, but not divorced. I left that up to my husband. It didn't really matter, I thought, because I was married as Judy Collins. That was never my name and never really me.

"Sometimes even now I remember my frantic search to get a passport for identification. Just to have a piece of paper that said I was somebody was such an important thing to me. Over the years I've come to believe maybe that was because after Ma died, Daddy treated me like I didn't count.

"But that morning in St. Louis, I was free as a bird, and I was somebody. I was Fanny Hawk. I could take care of myself, and I was 15 years old going on 20. I was all grown up, in charge of my life. I had just lost a boy husband, and that was alright with me.

"I began to check my suitcase to see what I needed for a trip downriver. By noon I had visited half the fashionable shops in St. Louis and purchased many new outfits. I would now surely fit in with the wealthy crowd who traveled the river on the sternwheelers, who won and lost their fortunes at the gaming tables as they leisurely floated down to New Orleans.

"Two days later, I booked passage on the Memphis Queen to New Orleans and set out on my high adventure. As I sat in my cabin, and we began the journey south, I spent a few minutes taking personal stock of the previous year.

"When I left Daddy's house that frantic morning, I had stuffed $23,500 in a pillow case. I still had over $21,000 of that money, and had lived very well for a year. At that rate there was enough money to last me 10 more years, which at 15 seemed like an eternity. It had been an exciting year. I learned much about how the world works, and now considered myself rather sophisticated.

"I'd packed a lot of living into that one year, even during the last two months with Jefferson, which had been a time for reflection, of trying to understand how two people live with each other. I was amazed as a jumped rabbit that they can be so peaceable together, but when something happens, and things change, they're no longer so wonderful and it's not really anybody's fault. What have I got to lose? I'm free. I'm somebody, and life is grand.

"I walked out on the steamer's deck and watched the sights of the Mississippi slide by. Even though it was 10 o'clock in the morning, a steward was offering a tray of drinks. Disdaining the coffee and the tea, I took a brandy. I remembered with a smile how the last brandy I took had cost my virginity. Well, at least there wasn't any danger of that happening this time.

"After circling the deck a couple of times, I walked into the gaming room with all it's roulette wheels, and blackjack and poker tables. There were a couple of interesting looking fellows playing blackjack for $5 a hand. I stopped momentarily to observe the game. The dealer looked up and said, 'We don't permit unescorted ladies in the gaming room, ma'am. You will have to leave or else come in the company of a man.'

"Here was a threat to my newly found freedom. I turned, looked around the room, and saw no females present. Momentarily, a blind fury washed over me at the unfairness of the rule. I decided then and there to test it, and so I pulled up a stool and said, 'I have money, deal me a hand.'

"The dealer shuffled the cards. I noticed he had a nervous tick. He took the cards, holding them in the middle and fanned them.

From the angle he held them, I could read every card as they fanned by. I knew where every card in the deck was.

"He dealt by me. With a faint smile curling his lips and a go-to-hell expression on his face. I sat on my stool and stewed until the hand was finished, trying to think of what to do. He gathered the cards up, turned them face up, and put them at the bottom of the deck. He was about to throw the first card to the man sitting on my right. I stopped him and said, 'The sign behind you says, Gamblers Must Have Cash. No Tokens, Checks, Only United States Currency. I am a gambler, I have United States Currency.'

"He paused while I made my little speech, then once again dealt the two men by me a blackjack hand. While they played out their hand, I tried to figure out a solution to my problem. This curtailed my freedom terribly. Suddenly I remembered the .38 snub-nosed colt that Jeff had given me when we first moved to Virginia. Though I'd always thought it was rather unnecessary, I'd carried the pistol since, and I knew how to use it.

"As he poised ready to deal the third hand around me, I set my handbag on the counter, reached in, and took out the snub-nosed .38. I pointed it at his crotch and said, 'You deal by me this time, buster, and I'm gonna shoot your dick off.' Immediately, cards began to appear at my spot. I suddenly became a gambler—not a woman, not a lady, not a girl—a gambler. I know this may sound like Will, but just remember he didn't teach me everything I know.

"I sat there for 30 minutes neither winning nor losing, but knowing very well what my next hand would be. He continued nervously fanning the cards. If I had been willing to sit out the bad hands, knowing when the good ones were coming up, I could beat the house handily. But to me just the freedom to play was important.

"Some 45 minutes later, I grew rather bored by the game, knowing what everybody had, so I strolled out on deck and took another brandy from the first passing steward. I felt rather pleased with myself. About three in the afternoon, I decided to nap so I could better enjoy the gaming room that night.

"About 6 PM there was a knock on my door. A young man informed me that the captain would like to see me on the bridge. I told him I'd be along as soon as I freshened up. He said, 'No ma'am,

I'll wait outside while you freshen up. He asked me to escort you to the bridge. May I?'

"'Certainly, I'll be just a couple of minutes.'

"When we arrived on the bridge, there was a little glassed-in enclosure off from the wheel where the captain sat. The young sailor opened the door, and the captain said, 'Hello, Miss Hawk. That was quite a show you put on in the gaming room. But I need to inform you that those rules were made for your benefit. It's my job as captain of this vessel to enforce all the rules aboard this vessel.

"'Miss Hawk, I am sort of the riverboat equivalent of God. What I say is the absolute, irrevocable, law. The rules aboard this vessel are my laws, and they say that unescorted women are not allowed in the gaming room. Now that applies to you, Miss Hawk. I hope you won't distress any of the dealers by trying to go back into the gaming room unescorted. I'd like you to make that promise now.'

"'Captain, how many states do you pass through or by on your journey to the sea?'

"'First, Miss Hawk, I need a promise that you will not disrupt the gaming room during the rest of this voyage. Then, I'll discuss the geography of our trip.'

"'Looking at your map, I counted nine states we passed through on the way to the Gulf of Mexico. Captain, how many of those states issue you a license or permit?'

"'All of them.'

"'How many of them have laws on their books about gambling?'

"'All of them.'

"'What do those laws say about gambling?'

"'It's forbidden.'

"'That's exactly what I thought. And you're running in the middle of the river, a no-man's land where you play God for those who put themselves under your care. You make rules that fit only men. But I have money and my urge to gamble is just as strong as theirs. I say you have absolutely no right, first of all, to permit gambling on this boat and, second, if you make a goddammed issue of it, I'll file a lawsuit against the steamboat companies to totally outlaw gambling because you literally, by weaving in and out, pass through each of these states where gambling is prohibited.

"'Now, Captain, my freedom is very important to me. When I walk into your goddammed gaming room, stop at a table, and put my money on that table, I become a gambler, a player if you will. All the signs all over that room are addressed to the player or the gambler. The moment I put my money on the table, I cease being a woman or a man; I'm a player. Goddammit, your dealers'd better play with me.'

"'Now look, Miss Hawk, what you say is true, but it's traditional that no captain on this river permits unescorted ladies in the gaming room.'

"'Good, Captain, then you will go down in history as a great man who ended this ridiculous tradition.'

"With that, Gene, I left the captain's quarters, returned to my room, and soon went to supper. Later on that evening, I had a very enjoyable time and left the gaming room $1088 richer than when I arrived. Altogether, I had a wonderful trip to New Orleans.

"The funny thing about it, everywhere I went, men jumped up and offered me a chair. Wherever I went on the deck, people noticed me. I enjoyed it, and, believe it or not, the sign over the gaming room that said *No Unescorted Ladies Permitted* suddenly was gone. Gene, in all modesty, I was very beautiful at that time of my life. I learned very soon to use my good looks. Remember, Gene, I said I used my beauty, not my body. I was not a tramp."

"I know, Miss Fanny. Uncle Will told me that you were a lady."

"Gene, I had a yen for family. I even thought about the time I had with Jeff Cannon. I was at odds with myself and really looked forward to being into something exciting again. Briefly, I even considered opening up a private club, and starting a poker game. None of this made any real sense though.

"I had loved my steamboat trip south, so on the spur of the moment, I decided to board another paddlewheel and head back north. The next day I checked my money out of the bank, hid it in my secret compartment again, and bought a ticket to Vicksburg."

I interrupted Miss Fanny to tell her I'd promised Uncle Will I'd run some errands for him before the stores closed. I asked her whether I could talk to her soon.

"Any time, Gene, you are always welcome."

"I'm going to try and make it Saturday if I can, depending on how Uncle Will is. Have you ever thought about whether you want to see him again or not? I don't even know how you folks met."

"I'm coming to that one day, Gene; as of now I can't answer your question."

"Bye, Miss Fanny, I hope to see you Saturday."

Headed Back South

I hurried back to the hospital in Bremen, where Uncle Will insisted on continuing his story.

"I had many things that needed doing. Even though reading Balls' diary was a fascinating business, it would have to wait until another time. I placed it in my topcoat pocket, left the hotel, and caught a taxi to the railroad station.

"I bought a compartment ticket to St. Louis on the train that was leaving that evening at 6 PM. Once there, I went to a livery stable and asked the cost of a carriage for the day, one big enough to haul two steamer trunks as well as two people.

"When the driver said the price would be $25, I took a $50 bill, tore it in half, and gave him half of it. I told him I'd give him the other half when he delivered me to the railroad station 5:30 that afternoon. He protested he didn't have any money to buy his horse a bag of oats at noon, that I ought to at least give him $1 for that. I gave him $2.

"I was going at a frantic pace, thinking of the two bodies that would have to be discovered soon. Not until late afternoon, I hoped, but I wanted to be as far away as possible when that happened.

"I promised to have a carriage in front of Kathy's hotel at 9 o'clock. I certainly wanted her away from there just in case the body was discovered two floors below her. She would know it was my room if she happened to know the room number.

"I needed to go to the Continental Bank and withdraw my money; I sure wasn't going to leave $100,000 in the bank when all I had to do was walk in and write a check for that amount of money.

"I told the carriage driver to meet Kathy at the Ingram at 9 o'clock, to drive around a few minutes, and then pick me up at the Continental Bank at 10 o'clock. When he was gone, I hired another carriage to take me to the bank so I'd be there when it opened.

"When I arrived at the Continental Bank, it was a quarter to nine. Just across the street was a men's clothing store. I needed to be rid of the evening clothes I had on. I could see people scurrying around inside. I knocked on the glass asking to come in. They pointed to a sign that said, 'Open at 9:30.' I kept beating on the glass until finally an older man came to the door. He was very ill-tempered. 'Friend, we don't open until 9:30.' He glanced down at the $100 bill I was holding in my hand and stopped talking.

"'Mister, there're a couple more of those for you. I need some clothes, and I need them now. I need to change into them and use your facilities. Is that possible?'

"'Why, certainly sir. You come on back to my office.'

"I purchased a conservative business suit, with a jacket large enough that no one could detect any bulge from the shoulder holster I was wearing. I also bought a topcoat. When I was properly dressed, I thanked the owner and gave him a $100 tip for the inconvenience. I also gave him an extra $10 to dispose of the clothes I'd been wearing, as I had no further need of them. I hated evening wear anyway.

"I went across the street to the Continental Bank, went up to the tellers' window, and presented a check for $100,000. I told the teller I would like to close my account.

"'I'll have to let Mr. Davis clear this. I'll be back in a moment.'

"Presently, Mr. Davis appeared, 'Well Mr. Robinson, I see you and Mr. Balls settled your differences.'

"'That's true, we had a meeting, I explained to him I was tired of being harassed. I didn't need the grief. As a matter of fact, just to settle the whole matter, I offered to pay him $20,000. That's what some of this money is going for.'

"'Mr. Robinson, do you have any idea how dangerous it is to carry this kind of money on your person? Chicago is a dangerous city.'

"'Mr. Davis, I don't expect to be in Chicago very much longer. To tell you the truth, I've had my fill of it. I came from a warmer climate, the snow we had last night helped me decide this is no place for me, especially in the wintertime. Could I please my have my money in the largest bills available?'

"'That will be $1000 bills, Mr. Robinson.' Davis nodded to the teller; shortly, the teller was back and counted out one hundred $1000 bills.

"Nephew, that was my first experience with $1000 bills.

"As I watched the counting process my mind drifted back to a few years before when I was child. A thousand dollars was an unheard of sum of money. Here I had a handful of $1000 bills.

"I put the money inside my coat pocket, and came out of the bank just as my carriage and Kathy drove up. I told Kathy I wanted her to shop for anything she wanted. We were headed for St. Louis by train. At that point, I was thinking about taking a riverboat from St. Louis to New Orleans for our honeymoon.

"While Kathy was looking at clothes, I was inspecting steamer trunks. I asked the clerk for one with a false bottom. He showed one with a two-inch space at the bottom covered with a heavy fabric. It certainly gave the appearance of being a solid bottom, but you could fold slats back and expose a two-inch space underneath. I purchased the trunk, then slipped Balls' diary into the false bottom. I purchased Kathy a steamer trunk exactly like mine, except hers was covered with white leather, while mine was brown.

"As she made her purchases, the clerks, under her supervision, packed her trunk. When she was finished in each store, her steamer trunk was transported to the back of the carriage. We went to the men's department and did the same thing for me. They altered the clothes I bought as I bought them. Except for lunch, we spent most of the day buying our honeymoon clothes.

"Since we expected to eat dinner on the train headed for St. Louis, we shopped until almost departure time. I didn't want Kathy to hear any idle gossip or street news in the event the bodies had been found. I was going to feel much better once we boarded a train headed south.

"After dinner that evening, our marriage was consummated in our railroad compartment.

"Nephew, Pullman compartments were not designed as a honeymoon suite for a man who stands 6 foot 6. Of course that was not to say the trip was not delightful, but it would have been a lot more so if the bed had been a foot longer.

"When we arrived in St. Louis we took a carriage from the station to the best hotel close to the riverfront. As I checked in, I was not prepared for the headline of the newspaper on the desk.

"'*World Famous Detective Found Dead in Chicago Hotel*' it said in 4-inch letters.

"Kathy supervised the unloading of the luggage while I registered. Then I steered her quickly upstairs to our room. As soon as we got into the room, Kathy said she was going to take an hour's bath to get the coal dust from the train ride off. She would be grateful if I gave her first chance at the bathroom, which suited me. I told her I was going downstairs to stretch my legs after being on the train overnight. I walked to the lobby, bought a newspaper, and started reading.

"The story started, 'the police are not giving out much information concerning the murder of G. B. Balls, world famous detective, who according to the Pinkerton's home office, was working on his 59th case. He had solved 58 consecutive cases considered by the Pinkerton Detective Agency to be their toughest. Mr. Balls enjoyed a reputation for his detective work never before equaled.

"'The police did release some brief details about the case on which Mr. Balls was working. He was chasing a suspect believed guilty of bilking a bank in Kentucky of over a half a million dollars. The police theorize Mr. Balls lured his suspect to his room, where somehow he managed to overpower and kill Mr. Balls.

"'There was one very puzzling aspect to Mr. Balls' death. He had a single ring from a police handcuff on his left hand that appeared to have been violently snatched away, peeling the skin off of his wrist and hand. The big mystery, as far as the police are concerned, is how did that handcuff get on Mr. Balls' left hand when he was in his own room? The police feel they won't know until Mr. Balls' assailant is captured, if he chooses to tell what happened.

"'The superintendent of Pinkerton's detectives, Mr. T. D. Bronski, was interviewed by this reporter. Superintendent Bronski stated that the entire resources of the Pinkerton Agency would be at the disposal of a detective he would name shortly to replace Mr. Balls. Bronski had not decided at press time who this would be, but did allow that no other Pinkerton agent was equal in stature to Balls. If the new detective proves successful, his reputation will be made.

"'When this reporter asked Mr. Bronski whether they had heard at all from Balls while he was working on this case, Superintendent Bronski said the only message was a telegram Balls sent. That telegram simply informed the client that Balls felt he was very close to apprehending his suspect.

"'Mr. Bronski requested that this story mention Pinkerton's offer of a reward for the recovery of Mr. Balls' diary, or other information leading to the killer's capture.

"'It was known by all close to Mr. Balls that he kept a diary recording everything he did. Superintendent Bronski felt the diary might be important to the Pinkerton effort to apprehend Balls' killer.

"'In another downtown Chicago hotel at about the same time, a second man was discovered murdered in almost the exact fashion as Mr. Balls. Each victim had been murdered with identical steak knives. It would appear the two cases may be somehow related.'

"After reading that, I went to the riverfront to see whether we could get a boat out of St. Louis the next morning. I needed to put more distance between us and Chicago. I thought that if I got on a riverboat and headed south, that would at least cut off Kathy's access to newspapers. I truly loved her, and wanted to make her happy. I sure didn't want her to suffer the slightest suspicion that I might be the fugitive they were hunting.

"The boat was to shove off at 8 o'clock the next morning. I went back to the hotel to tell her. Kathy was not altogether happy about moving so quickly. She wanted to spend more time in St. Louis. I argued the cold weather was going to sweep across the area soon. I hated cold weather and would be a lot happier in New Orleans. She didn't fuss a lot, but said she hoped we could settle down and stay in one place for a while when we got to New Orleans. I assured her we would.

"Nephew, I didn't sleep very well that night and it wasn't from a guilty conscience, though it should have been. It was worrying about how I was going to keep her from seeing newspapers on our way south. Never having been on a riverboat, I didn't know whether they stopped every day and picked up newspapers, but I suspected they would. I thought the further we got away from Chicago, the less likely she'd see a newspaper with any stories about Balls' death.

"The worrisome thought I had was her picking up a newspaper and reading that the suspect in Balls' death was using the alias of

Jesse Robinson, along with the fact Robinson was 6 foot 6. I felt I could convince her that Jesse Robinson was a common enough name, but she was going to have to be awfully gullible to believe that Jesse Robinson, the killer, also just happened to be the same height I was. That was going to be more difficult; the easiest way to avoid it was not to let her see any newspapers.

"I was up early the next morning preparing to get our luggage taken to the boat; the first thing I did was to go down to the lobby for a newspaper. Once again Balls' murder was on the front page.

"The headlines said, 'Super Sleuth's Murder Spurs Massive Manhunt. In a press release last night Pinkerton Detective Superintendent T. D. Bronski released this description of the suspect in the murder of G. B. Balls. His name is thought to be Will Cotton. He stands 6 foot 6 inches tall. He speaks with a southern accent. It is believed by people who have met the suspect that he grew up in North Florida, Georgia, Alabama, or South Carolina. The fugitive allegedly stole $660,000 from a bank in Plowshare, Kentucky.

"'The superintendent speculated they were dealing with a brilliant criminal by the apparent ease with which he accomplished the bank theft. This reporter heard from reliable sources that the police are questioning John Davis, vice president of the Eighteenth Street Branch of the Continental Bank. It is not certain what information Mr. Davis may have, but it is thought that he opened a checking account for the suspect in Mr. Balls' death.

"'No one at police headquarters would confirm or deny this. A police honor guard escorted Mr. Ball's remains to the railroad station to begin their final journey home to Dallas, Texas. This is one of the most complex cases this reporter has ever followed.'

"Nephew, when I read they were questioning John Davis of Continental Bank, I knew the next newspaper would give my name, or at least my alias, and I did not dare let Kathy see that newspaper. Fortunately, there wouldn't be another newspaper until we were on the riverboat. I couldn't remember its schedule, but wherever we stopped next would be farther away from Chicago than we were that morning.

"We got on the boat without Kathy paying any attention to newspapers. She was too busy enjoying the sights. When we went

aboard, the first thing I noticed was a gaming room filled with all
sorts of fancy ways to take your money.

"The sternwheeler pushed off right on schedule, and I breathed
a great sigh of relief. Kathy and I had the biggest stateroom on the
boat. We spent most of the trip in the gaming room. She loved to
play blackjack and spent hours betting $5 a hand. She never won
or lost more than $30 at a sitting.

"The first morning out of St. Louis, they brought aboard several
Little Rock, Arkansas newspapers. I got one while Kathy was still
asleep. There was nothing about Balls' murder on the front page.
Page four had the story I'd read the previous day in the St. Louis
newspaper. As I suspected, the farther we got away from Chicago,
the less important the death of one detective was going to be. Still
I couldn't relax. I couldn't run the risk that Kathy would find a
newspaper and read it, especially after their interview with John
Davis. We managed to get to New Orleans without Kathy ever
seeing a newspaper. I began to breath a lot easier.

"On Sunday, Kathy ordered breakfast in bed, along with a newspaper and a jug of coffee. She said we'd been cut off from the real
world and she'd like to know what's going on. I had some uneasy
moments, but told her that would be great. Since New Orleans
was so far from Chicago, I felt what was important in Chicago probably wouldn't be so important in New Orleans. But the headline
was about G. B. Balls, 'The greatest detective who ever lived' as
The *New Orleans Picayune* called him, being murdered by some
master criminal. Kathy couldn't eat for reading the story. All I could
do was sit in bed, pick at my breakfast, and sweat while she read.
Occasionally, she'd give me a sidewise glance while I was trying to
read another part of the paper, but I couldn't keep my eyes off her.

"Finally, she put the paper down and said, 'Jesse, the suspect
they describe in this newspaper story of the murdered detective
seems like you. You didn't murder somebody in Chicago and not
tell me about it did you, sweetie?'

"Taking a cue from her light treatment of the question, I said,
'Oh, darling, I don't remember, I was so madly in love with you.
Maybe I killed ten men and have no recollection of it. So it's mur-
der you find so interesting, is it? I was wondering what subject was

so totally absorbing that you couldn't pay any attention to your husband of less than a week. Pass me that part when you finish it; maybe I can learn more about things that interest you.'

"At the bottom of page she was reading it said, 'continued on page 14.' While she looked for page 14, I read almost precisely the same stuff I'd read in the three previous newspaper accounts.

"Suddenly she sucked her breath in and said, 'Oh, my God, Jesse! The man they think killed Balls is named Jesse Robinson. He's the same height as you, and had an account at the Continental Bank, Eighteenth Street. That's where we picked you up. My God!'

"She looked at me with pleading eyes. I asked her to let me see the newspaper. In the newspaper was the story told by John Davis. He gave an account of our conversation, an account of his conversation with Balls, and the fact that he had called me and told me Balls was coming to see me.

"She jumped out of bed and shouted, 'Jesse, how could you?' I knew there were some mysterious things going on. You kept calling me and telling me this or that. Jesse, it must have been you. The description is too much like you. Who would pick 'Jesse Robinson' out of the air as an alias if it were not Will Cotton? Where did you get so much money? Did you steal all this money from the bank in Plowshare?'

"She fired question after question at me. Finally, I said, 'Kathy! Kathy! I love you. Darling, stop! This is all complete rubbish. I married you, I love you, but I want you to listen to me. That person was not me. It is a strange set of circumstances, but you're just going to have to take that on faith.

"'I'll tell you what I'll do, darling. We'll go back to Chicago, see Mr. Davis, and that will prove to you that I'm not the Jesse Robinson they're looking for. We'll leave by the next boat north. I don't for one minute want you to worry your pretty head about such things as this, and that's the only way you're ever going to be satisfied. I can't have this come between us. I'll go right now and arrange for us to head back north.'

"I got out of bed and started putting my clothes on. She let me get almost dressed, then said, 'Jesse, I believe you, I believe you. Get back in bed.'

"It took her that long to decide she believed I wasn't guilty. I sulked for the rest of the day, acting gravely wounded that she would so much as entertain the idea that I could possibly kill somebody.

"It wasn't a good time in my life. The palms of my hands itched; I'd wake up in a cold sweat. And I'm going to tell you now, while I'm thinking about it, don't ever kill anybody unless they're about to kill you. Sometimes, I think it'd be better to let them kill you.

"It's a terrible thing to tote around on your conscience, that kind of burden. But I still was not yet through. The awful temper that God saw fittin' to give me knew no bounds when I got mad.

"I told Kathy I was homesick for where they grow cotton, and I'd heard that Brownsville, Texas was the best cotton-growing territory in the whole world. I wanted to go to Brownsville and buy a gin. I was homesick for the smell of fresh, white lint.

"I remember when I was a kid we'd pick cotton, fill the cottonhouse four-feet deep, get in and jump around and climb up to the roof and jump off into the cotton. It was a wonderful time in my life. I was homesick alright, but more than that. Well, we'd always had to pay the gin man for ginning. He got more money for an hour's work than we got for growing the cotton all summer. I wanted to be that man now. I wanted to make all that money.

"Nephew, I made such a persuasive argument that I thought Kathy had forgotten about Chicago. So we boarded a train the next day and headed for Brownsville, Texas by way of Houston and Corpus Christi.

"When we got to Brownsville, we took a room in a hotel. The first thing I did was find the newspaper office and see what the current story was about G. B. Balls. They let me see the last three issues of the Brownsville Daily News. Not a single line about Balls. I breathed a sigh of relief.

"Kathy and I took our time picking out a place to live. By now it was mid-January, and the weather was wonderful in Brownsville. As warm as it was in January, I guessed it would be awful hot in the summertime, so we looked only at houses along the shore of the Gulf of Mexico. We found a beautiful 15-room mansion for sale for $55,000. Even in those days, that was a good buy for what we were getting. I bought the house, but because I was afraid the bankers might possibly have the numbers of the bearer bonds, and I didn't want to shit in my own new nest, I paid cash for it.

"This is where I expected to spend the rest of my life, and I was not going to start off by putting one of those bonds in the bank. Even though that was the beauty of the bonds—they were designed so that whoever had possession of them could use them—the word might go out that one of them had been cashed. I didn't want to risk that. Besides, after giving Harold Nail $35,000, I still had over $100,000 of the original money from the Plowshare Bank, as well as the $100,000 I'd gotten from cashing the first bearer bond.

"When we were settled in our mansion, I hired Kathy a gardener and a maid. The house we bought had plenty of outbuildings. We kept discovering things for weeks after we moved into it. For instance, there was a three-bedroom apartment over the garage. The previous owner had built it especially for his chauffeur.

"I bought myself a brand new Model-T Runabout—the fanciest one they had, with ising-glass curtains and the usual complement of accessories, such as tow ropes, cranks, and two spare tires. I drove the Model-T home and taught Kathy how to drive it. She was a quick learner, and shortly could drive it as well as I could, though she couldn't crank it in those days before electric starters.

"Kathy turned out to have a knack for gardening. She started planting flowers and shrubs all over the place. Pretty soon she had the whole place planted in citrus trees and other sorts of tropical trees that had fancy names I couldn't remember.

"Somehow, I knew, Nephew, that Kathy still believed I was the murderer of G. B. Balls. Of course, I knew I was, but it still hurt me that she thought I was, even after I told her I'd go back and meet Mr. Davis in Chicago. So our relationship never enjoyed the warmth and enthusiasm again that it had at the outset. I still loved her, but slowly I came to resent that she couldn't love me enough to believe me. She never said so overtly. It was just a trace of sand on the sheets, so subtle I didn't dare bring the subject up and accuse her of still thinking I was Balls' assailant.

"I spent most of my time searching for exactly the kind of business I wanted to be in. I'd already made a substantial deposit at the local bank and was on a first name basis with the president. And

I'd discovered a gin more modern than anything I'd seen back in Georgia. It was huge, having 10 stations. The owner said each station would suck the seed cotton off a wagon in three minutes flat.

"It had the newest screw-type presses, which had the capacity to bag, bale, and tie 10 bales of cotton at a time. According to the owner, it was the newest machine out. It used the exhaust from the vacuum system to blow the lint cotton into the baling presses.

"The top of the presses were two pieces that slid back to open the cavity where the lint was blown in. Once the bagging and ties were put into place by the baler, the two top pieces of the press slid together. When the bale was properly compressed, the top of the press slid back enough for the baler to crimp the ties. One baler could load and unload all 10 presses.

"The labor savings were enormous. I was completely fascinated by the gin. The gins here in Georgia, even now, handle only two bales at a time. The manager's office was high up in the gin building, where he could watch the whole gin and every working part, even the presses. There was a slow-moving belt outside of the two rows of five presses. All the baler had to do to get the cotton out to the dock was to roll it onto the belt, and it would be conveyed directly onto the dock and into the wagon that had brought it.

"The man who owned the gin was John Swim. When I was talking to him, it was spring, a long way from the ginning season. They were lubricating, changing, checking for worn parts, and replacing belts that drove the machinery. Once the ginning season started, the gin would be running almost nonstop 16–18 hours a day. They didn't want any breakdowns.

"Mr. Swim was an elderly man. He had two boys who were bitter disappointments. He'd wanted them to follow him into the ginning business. He also had presses to crush the oil from the cottonseeds. He swapped cottonseed meal and hulls to the farmers for the cottonseeds, and took the cottonseed oil as his profit. That was a lucrative part of the business. It also made damn sure the poor farmers stayed poor. He got more for the oil than the meal and the hulls were worth.

"His boys liked the shrimping business. He bought them each a shrimp boat so they could be shrimp boat captains; they rarely ever came around to see him. As we sat in his office discussing such such matters, I told him I'd always wanted to own a gin, but had never seen one back home as impressive as this. I was very much impressed with his operation, so I asked him if he would like to have a partner.

"The old man sat there and thought about it for several minutes, not saying a word. He'd look at me occasionally, then turn to gaze out the window, then back at me. Finally he said, 'Son, if you own a goose, you have a goose. If you own half a goose, you got a feed bill. No, I don't want a partner. I'm getting old, my family don't care nothing about this kind of business. I'll sell it to you for $200,000. If you pay me $100,000, I'll finance the balance at 4% interest.'

"I told him that, if I bought it, I'd pay cash. I'd been spending money pretty rapidly fixing the house the way Kathy wanted it and buying automobiles, so I was down to about $40,000 cash. To pay for the gin I needed to cash two bearer bonds. Of course, once I bought the gin there'd be enough income that I shouldn't ever have to cash the other two. I told Swim I'd think about it seriously, and asked him whether $10,000 in earnest money would hold the deal while I turned some assets I had into money. He said that'd be fine with him.

"One of the things Kathy used to keep herself busy with when she was not landscaping, working with Lola, or playing with their children, was reading *True Romance* magazines. Almost every week, there was a different magazine in the house. Our marriage continued to be uneasy, in a melancholy way, yet satisfying.

"I told her I was taking a business trip. The more I thought about going to any bank in the United States and cashing those bearer bonds, the more frightening the proposition became. I felt it in my bones, Nephew, that somebody was going to be watching me once I walked out of a bank if I cashed those bonds in the United States.

"I cursed the day I had murdered G. B. Balls. I had $400,000 of bearer bonds, and I was afraid to cash them."

Cashing In

"I had decided I would go back to New Orleans. There were several major banks, as well as a great port. If things got tight I could always flee the country.

"I left Kathy $10,000 in the checking account and took the remaining $30,000 I had left, along with the bonds. I told Kathy I was planning to buy the gin, but first I was going to New Orleans to see another just like it and find out whether it was really worth what I was being asked to pay. Plus, I was going to have to borrow some money, and I had some business connections in New Orleans who might help.

"A couple of times I thought she was going to ask me a question, but then she seemed to decide against it. She finally said, 'When are you going?' I told her I had the train tickets, and was leaving the next morning. I'd be back as soon as I could, but it might take up to a month to look after the business I had. If I was going to be longer, I'd write her a letter.

"When I was ready to leave I stooped down to kiss her, but she only managed a peck. I didn't make an issue of it, told her I'd miss her, and left without another word being said.

"It was a three-day train trip to New Orleans. I left on a Thursday, so I'd be ready to do business on Monday. I arrived late Sunday afternoon, took a carriage, and rode through the streets of downtown New Orleans. I passed by an enormous bank building with a sign, 'Bank of Commerce, New Orleans, Louisiana.'

"While circling the area, we passed a hotel two blocks east and two blocks south of the bank. I went in and registered at the Magnolia Hotel under the name of James Roberts. The next morning at 9 o'clock, I went to the Bank of Commerce and opened a checking account in the name of James Roberts.

"The teller was a rather striking young woman; I started up a conversation with her while she was filling out the paperwork. Her name was Nellie Miller. She was single, 21 years old, and available. I had a date with her before I left the bank, and was to call at 8 o'clock. We were to have supper and see a stage play.

"During dinner I worked many questions about the employees of the bank into our conversation. As a matter of fact, I asked so many questions, that I began to sense a reluctance from her to answer some of them. In an effort to put her mind at ease, I told her I was a very wealthy man looking for a bank in which to deposit a great deal of money. I had asked her for a date because she was beautiful, but there was no reason not to mix a little business with pleasure. I wanted to know about some of the employees at the bank because of the large amount of money I planned to deposit. I needed to take due care that there wasn't a light-fingered vice-president who'd make off with the bank's funds, leaving the bank to fold as a result. With that, her reluctance to answer my questions immediately vanished.

"'What I am trying to do, Nellie, is to find out whether the bank has any weaknesses. The biggest scoundrel in the world can be the most charming individual you ever met. But, usually, if such a scoundrel is around, there are whispers and rumors. That is really what I am looking for, somebody in the higher echelons of management having bad habits, like drinking too much, gambling too much, that sort of thing.'

"'Well you know, James, I am not high enough in management to tell you some of the things you want to know. I know there is sort of standing joke in the bank about Mr. Erickson, the son-in-law of the president, spending too much time in Calavaras County. I think it is an oblique reference to Mark Twain's story about the Calavaras County frog jumping contest, where one of the contestants fed his opponent's frog some buckshot. But I'm not even certain of that. Mr. Erickson is the only person in the bank I've ever heard any such remarks about.'

"When I carried Nellie home that night, I told her I'd like to see her again sometime. She mentioned she'd love to go to a prayer meeting with me on Wednesday night. They always had supper at the prayer meeting, so it wouldn't cost us anything for dinner. I said I had some business to attend to, but if it was at all possible, I'd let her know sometime during banking hours on Wednesday.

"I decided even while thinking about Kathy that I'd need to give Nellie a good night kiss, or at least see if she was agreeable to such things. I took her in my arms and she returned my kiss most fervently. I decided at that moment I needed to see moreof her, but first I needed to cash my bearer bonds. She could prove to be a very interesting young lady. Back in those days, nephew, it was usually four or five dates before a nice girl would let you kiss her. Even then you had to pretend you had matrimony in mind.

"I could hardly wait to check into the background of Mr. C. P. Erickson, son-in-law of the president and vice-president of the Bank of Commerce of New Orleans. I found out from Nellie that he frequented a downtown athletic club called the Forty-Fourth Street Yacht Club, which could mean anything. The next morning at 11 o'clock, I presented myself at the club door, which stated, "Members Only." I was admitted into a little foyer by a formally dressed man even at that hour. He used very formal language and informed me that since I was not a member, I would have to speak to the manager before I could be admitted to the dining room. The manager presently entered the foyer and inquired whether I was a guest of a member who had not announced my arrival. I told him no, that I didn't know any club members, but was interested in joining, having heard it was the most exclusive club in New Orleans.

"He immediately informed me that membership in the Forty-Fourth Street Yacht Club was by invitation only. I asked him to supply a list of members who might invite me to join. He said, 'Certainly not, sir, and I'll be most happy if you'll leave now. The manager of the club is not allowed to pry into private affairs of members, and if the members wish me to do something, they would so inform me. Good day, sir.'

"I reached in my pocket and pulled out five $100 bills that I had placed there just for such an occasion and fanned them out. 'Don't you know somebody who's in a difficult financial position and might be willing to put my name before the house committee as a candidate for membership.' He opened the outside door with a nod and invited me inside. 'One of our most active members, especially at bringing new members into the club, is named C. P. Erickson,' he said as he reached and slid the $500 out of my hand.

"'How can I get in touch with him?'

"'He works at the Bank of Commerce. The main branch.'

"'I don't really want to go to the place where he works. Isn't there some other place I could meet him.'

"'I am not allowed to give out our members home addresses, but I'll tell you what I will do for five hundred dollars, and this is all you get. You write him a note and I'll give it to him.'

"'Let me have a pen and paper to write such a note.'

"'Certainly.'

"I wrote, 'Dear Mr. Erickson, I am a new depositor at your bank. I am fascinated by the Forty-Fourth Street Yacht Club and would like to speak with you about becoming a member, as well as the fitness of your bank to handle large sums of money. I am currently staying in room 324 at the Magnolia Hotel.'

"I folded the note and gave it to the manager, not really knowing what to expect. But I guessed the best thing for me to do was to wait for something to happen and look forward to Wednesday night prayer meeting.

"I went back to the hotel and had a drink. Feeling sleepy, I went to my room for a nap and was awakened by a knock on the door at about 6 PM. It was a bellboy telling me that there was a gentleman waiting for me in the dining room. He guided me to a table near a window and introduced me to Mr. C. P. Erickson, who had a touch of gray hair at the temples that made him look distinguished.

"'Mr. Roberts, I received your note when I went to the Forty-Fourth Street Yacht Club for lunch. What can I do for you, sir? You spoke of depositing large sums of money. How may I help?'

"'Of course, Mr. Erickson, you're a banker and realize that we who've managed to acquire a great deal of wealth like to protect it. I just wanted a high official of the bank to sit down with me privately, away from the bank, to discuss its stability. Once, for a brief time, I myself was a bank president, and I grew rather bored with the job. But I do know something of the laws governing banks. And how to determine whether a bank is stable.'

"'Mr. Roberts, this bank has been in business for 70 years. My wife's grandfather started it, and my wife's father is president. There is no more sound institution in the whole United States. We're very conservative, and invest only in gilt-edge corporations. All our commercial loans are highly collateralized.

"'The manager of the Forty-Fourth Street Club said you have interest in becoming a member. The initiation fee is $3000, and the monthly dues are $100. If you're still interested and you make those substantial deposits of which you speak, I would be most happy, sir, to consider placing your name before the house committee to become a member. However, if you are in a greater hurry than that, since I can see that you are a man of means, all this other stuff is just a formality. For, shall we say $2000, I would place your name before the committee this very night, and it will certainly be acted on within the week. I will need a brief resumé telling me something about yourself.'

"After I gave him a fictitious resumé, I told him I enjoyed a hand of poker and a drink of bourbon now and again. Occasionally, I enjoyed the company of young ladies, if they were young enough and beautiful enough, especially when my wife was not around. I threw all of those things in just to make sure he understood that I was a man of the world. I pulled out the checkbook that they had given me at his bank when I opened the account and started to write a check. He stopped me.

"'Mr. Roberts, if it's all the same to you, I would rather have cash. I would not like my father-in-law to know that I had charged one of our depositors a fee for presenting his name to the Yacht Club. Would you mind?'

"I closed the check book and stuck it in my jacket pocket, took out my wallet, counted out twenty $100 bills, and placed them on the table, 'I expect to be in your club this week.'

"'You shall, Mr. Roberts, you shall. In the meantime, you may go as my guest now. I'll introduce you to some of the members.'

"C. P. Erickson escorted me through the Forty-Fourth Street Yacht Club. It was a plush affair. There was a smoking room, a card room for bridge and other card games, a domino room, a dining room, and then another huge room. In the middle was a poker table that must have been eight feet in diameter. I would guess at least 15 people could be comfortably seated around the table. The money tray extended all the way around.

"Erickson explained that this was the poker table. There was a $2000 take-out game, pot limit, dollar ante. In most of the games they played, each player got two cards down and the rest of the hand was thrown face up in the middle. Some of the games were played with three cards down and the rest in the middle. The games had such names as 'grab 'em,' 'hold 'em,' 'pistol Pete,' 'big pistol,' and 'fire across.' As he described the workings of each game, his eyes lit up like he was having a spiritual experience.

"Nephew, if I had been bettin' at that moment where the $2000 I had just given Mr. Erickson would be spent, my guess would be on that table. He said, 'There is a poker game here every night. The first 14 people who claim a seat get to play. Usually the seats have been claimed by 8:30. The game starts promptly at 9 o'clock and ends promptly at 2 AM, house rules. There is absolutely no credit extended to anybody. Unless one of the players is willing to cash a check, no checks are cashed by the house for anyone in the game. This is the best poker game in New Orleans,' he said with a shine in his eyes that told me this man was a gambler.

"'I suppose this is for members only.'

"'Yes, yes, of course.'

"'Too bad, I'm in a strange town with very little to do; it's a damn pity I can't play with you folks.'

"'I submitted your name to the house committee when you came in. If the game is not full tonight, I will check it out with the other players. If it's okay with them, you'd be more than welcome to sit in. As a matter of fact, I'd plan to sit in. And if you don't, you can certainly stand and watch the game, maybe learn something.'

"The tour was over. We strolled through the dining room. There were many people eating, but absolutely no women, or at least none I could see. I asked Erickson about that. He said, 'Oh, there are no women allowed.' As far as he knew, there had never been a woman in the building. It made some of their wives furious, and he allowed as how his own wife was among that number.

"The game was full that night. I stood around for a little while and watched. There appeared to be a fair amount of excitement and considerable sums of money involved. I would suspect that $20–30,000 changed hands during the hour I watched. Nobody appeared inclined to leave the game, so I told Mr. Erickson that I was returning to the hotel for the night, and to let me know once I had been approved.

"The next evening, Mr. Erickson came to my hotel and informed me that I had been approved for membership. All I had to do was pay the dues, and I would officially become a member. He asked if I would like to walk over to the club with him. We had a very interesting evening, playing cards until the club closed at 2 o'clock. I wound up about $3000 ahead, and hadn't had to cheat any. I decided, sitting there that night, that this would be a very easy place to make a living.

"Nephew, gambling will get you into a lot of trouble, and I'm gonna advise you to avoid that activity. Gambling gets in some folk's blood and they can't leave it alone. Those people can't win. Oh, they'll win one time, but they'll come back the next time and give it all back and more. Nephew, I'm telling you from my heart, gambling is a terrible vice. I hope you don't ever get into it.

"I went to the Bank of Commerce the next morning to deposit my winnings and to see Miss Nellie Miller again. I told her I was awfully sorry, but business had kept me away from prayer meeting on Wednesday night. I promised her that I would go the next Wednesday without fail. She said she understood and made a firm date for the following Wednesday.

"I played poker every other night at the Forty-Fourth Street Yacht Club. Every night I was there, Erickson was there. For a married man, he kept late hours. He never left before the game was over at 2 o'clock. During five poker sessions, I cashed three $2000 checks for Erickson and agreed to hold them until the end of the month, when he got paid. I now had an inside man at the bank.

"The following Wednesday night I went to see Nellie, and we rode off to the Wednesday night prayer meeting service. The preacher was a hell-fire and brimstone man. He was giving folks hell for doing damn near everything I enjoyed doing. Of course, I was more bored than anything, but I pretended to enjoy the service like some of Nellie's friends.

"I ordered a closed surrey to take us to the church and back. The driver waited for us until the service was over, I told him to take us the long way home. As soon as we got in the surrey, I pulled the curtains and wrapped my arms around Miss Nellie. Maybe all heated up by the preacher, she returned my kisses as passionately as she had on the first date, and it was not long until we were naked on the floor of the surrey. Nephew, that was one of the more pleasurable surrey rides I ever had.

"When we arrived at Nellie's place, I walked her to the door, and told her I'd like to see her again, soon. She said, 'Let me know.'

"On Friday night, I decided I'd go down to the Yacht Club and see whether I needed to cash another check for my vice president friend. When the game started, Mr. Erickson was already pretty drunk. He kept mumbling something about how he and his wife were having a bit of trouble, and made some rather disparaging remarks about his wife, the daughter of his boss. I changed the subject to more immediate topics, such as what kind of crazy game are we going to play this time?

"By 10:30, I had already cashed two checks for Mr. Erickson for $3000 each and guessed I was roughly up $4–5000 above those checks. He was much too drunk to be playing poker when I won a particularly big hand about midnight, and started talking about me owning him and asking me to cash a $10,000 check. I could tell from the glances about the table that the other players considered this a risky venture for me, but pretended not to notice the obvious and cashed his $10,000 check.

"When the game broke up at 2 AM, counting those I'd previously cashed, I was holding checks on Mr. Erickson for the sum total of $33,000. Mr. Erickson staggered off, and one of the younger players, Timothy by name, asked if he could speak with me.

"'Mr. Roberts, you seem to be a man who is worldly-wise, and the fact that Mr. Erickson kept his drunkenly bragging all night about being the vice president of the Bank of Commerce as well as the son-in-law of the President doesn't make his checks good. If I were you, I wouldn't try and cash those checks.

"'You see, Mr. Roberts, C. P. has a problem with gambling. We who are playing the game sort of try to keep things evened out. The money is collectible. You can take those checks into the president's office and you'll get your money. But you're going to

put a terrible strain on a family that's already strained to the breaking point. There are several of us who enjoy the game who are
deeply indebted to the bank of Commerce.

"'It's sort of an unwritten understanding that we will look after
C. P. I suppose you have not been advised of the gentleman's understanding about that matter. If you would, Mr. Roberts, please
give the regulars playing there a chance to meet and discuss this
situation before you go to the bank and demand payment on those
checks. Would you do that for us?'

"'What you're telling me, Timothy, is that you folks who owe
the bank lots of money are a baby-sitting service for C. P.'

"Well, I guess you could call it that, Mr. Roberts. We like to
look at it in another fashion. We're just saving the president of
the bank a certain embarrassment that his daughter picked such a
bad poker player, one who can't stay away from the game. Arrangements can be made to take care of your checks. We just need a
little time to do it.'

"'Well, as you said at the beginning, Timothy, I am a man of
some experience in these things and I really didn't think I would
go down, present these checks, and they would pay me off in $100
bills. As a matter of fact, I expected to have to take my money as
he wins it back at some later period of time.'

"'To us, Mr. Roberts, right now, you're a stranger. We don't want
to impose on your good nature by letting this go on, but if you'll
just give us until Wednesday evening to discuss it among ourselves,
we'll come up with some satisfactory solution for getting you your
money. You obviously don't owe the Bank of Commerce anything.
So there is nothing in it for you.' I told Timothy that I would raise
no ruckus before we talked again. We parted company.

"On Saturday afternoon, I called on Nellie at her home. I asked
her if we could go somewhere and register as man and wife, or if
she could spend the night with me in my hotel. She said no. Her
parents wouldn't stand for her staying away all night. But she would
go to my hotel with me if I'd bring her home by midnight. We did
the same thing on Sunday afternoon and evening.

"On Monday morning when the bank opened, I went in and
asked the receptionist for C. P. Erickson. After a lengthy wait, I

was ushered into his office. He appeared a bit sheepish, very anxious and fidgety.

"'Mr. Roberts, I know what you're here for,' were his first words.

"'I doubt that you do. But I have a very delicate problem that I think you can help me with. In exchange for your help, I'm prepared to pay you handsomely.'

"'Now, Mr. Roberts, if you expect me to make you a big loan on some bogus collateral, you're talking to the wrong man.'

"'Oh, no, nothing like that. I want you to help me with a problem I have through no fault of my own.

"'About two months ago, this fellow I met in a poker game got pretty heavily in debt. He thought I was a man of great wealth. What gave him that idea, I haven't the faintest notion. But he came to me with four US Treasury Bearer Bonds and offered to discount those bonds rather steeply on condition that I would hold them at least a couple of months before cashing them. It's been four or five months now, and whatever the problem was with the bonds, of which I have no knowledge, it certainly should have resolved itself by this time. What I need for you to do is to look in your files and see if there is any information about the bonds that I need to know. Any private correspondence between other banks, anything that flags these particular bearer bonds as special.'

"'Do you have the numbers with you now?'

"'Yes, I do. They are written on this paper.'

"'If you'll excuse me one moment, Mr. Roberts, I'll be right back.'

"He walked out of the room and was not gone more than five minutes. He sat back down in his chair a ghostly white. 'Mr. Roberts, how did you say you came by those bonds?'

"'I bought them from a man who said his name was Jesse Robinson. As I told you, at a rather steep discount.'

"'There is a $25,000 reward for any bank officer who provides the Pinkerton Detective Agency with any information about the person cashing those bonds. Mr. Roberts, it is my opinion that you are Jesse Robinson masquerading as James Roberts. The $25,000 reward won't get my check back, but it'll get a big chunk of it back.

"'I didn't come here to quibble about such things, I came here to enlist your aid and as I said earlier, to pay you handsomely for it.

Do you have the authority, the ability, and does the bank have enough funds, to purchase those bearer bonds?'

"'Of course we do, we keep over a million dollars in our safe at all times. But saying we can and saying we will are entirely two different things.'

"'When you left the room a few minutes ago, where did you go?'

"'I went over to the bond ledger. We have a special ledger where all communications about bonds are entered. I just looked under bearer bonds and there were the numbers you gave me, with a long-hand note about the offer I just described written by the numbers.'

"'Who wrote the numbers and the message in the bond ledger?'

"'I would guess it was the president's secretary; it looks like her handwriting.'

"'Something caused her to write that note in the bond ledger. Do you know what that might have been?'

"'It would have had to have been a telegram or a letter. Knowing the Pinkerton Agency, I would guess they'd send a telegram. They wanted to make it as important as they could.'

"'Does the bank have a filing system for telegrams?'

"'Believe me, Mr. Roberts, or Mr. Robinson, whatever your name, we have a filing system for everything.'

"'If it came in the form of a telegram, and that telegram is filed, could you find it or would you have the authority to look into it?'

"'Of course I would have the authority. Nobody here would dare stop me. Well, maybe I don't have the authority, but nobody here has the nerve to stop me from going anywhere I choose to go.'

"'Could you, without raising any suspicions toward yourself, check the telegram file and see if you can find the telegram that informed you about those bonds?'

"'I could, but I don't have any good reason to do so.'

"'Suppose I hand this $3000 check you wrote me Thursday night across the desk. Would that make it worth your while?'

"'That indeed would make it worth my while.'

"'If I sit here and wait, could you do that now?'

"'I told you, I can do any damn thing I choose in this bank. Nobody has the nerve to stop me except the president, and he's not even in town this week.'

"'If you find such a telegram, can you let me see it?'

"'I certainly could if I chose to do that, but I don't have any reason at all to do that.'

"'Well, for the sake of argument, let's say I were to take this $3000 check of yours and hand it across the desk, would that give you a reason to want to do that?'

"'You have a couple of $10,000 checks that would make me want to do it a lot quicker.'

"'Now come, come, Mr. Erickson, $10,000 for walking across the bank lobby. I haven't run out of requests yet. Let's be reasonable.'

"'I'll be back in a minute.'

"Nephew, while he was gone from the office, I sat there and thought about what a fantastic stroke of good fortune I had in choosing Mr. Erickson to be my foil.

"He returned shortly.

"'It was a telegram, and here it is.'

"I'd long since memorized the numbers on the bearer bonds. In them, one of the eights looked almost like a zero because the writer hadn't closed the loop at the top, but those were the correct numbers. As I looked across the desk at Erickson, he seemed like a schoolboy wanting to show off for the prettiest girl in the class. I thought he'd to do what I wanted him to do just to show me he could. He wasn't afraid of a murderer, wasn't afraid of his father-in-law. Just for the pure thrill of it, I believe he'd have done everything I asked him from that point on without any reward.

"'Mr. Erickson, do you suppose there would be any other copy of this telegram in the bank?'

"'There would be no reason for any other copy to be in the bank.'

"'Was there any other information in the note regarding the reward other than what you told me?'

"'Oh, yeah, it said Robinson was thought to be an alias for Will Cotton. They didn't mention James Roberts. He was the number one suspect in the murder of the greatest Pinkerton detective in modern times. Mr. Roberts, or Mr. Cotton, or Mr. Robinson, do you have a single piece of paper with your name on it?'

"'Of course, I do, I have plenty of identification. And it is perfectly ridiculous for you to think that I am Jesse Robinson. You don't want to make that accusation. You might discover that would be a very foolish mistake simply because it's not so. Of all things you don't want, you don't want to be made to look like a damn fool. That's what will happen if you make any such accusation.

"'I bought the bonds with legal tender, and all I want to do is convert them back into legal tender. I think I can do that with your help, and I am prepared to make it worth your while. But I, like any other person who enters into a business proposition, wants to get all out of the transaction that is possible. You, Mr. Erickson, are in somewhat of a financial bind. The $25,000 the Pinkerton Agency is offering is not going to get you out of a bind. After the $6000 I just gave you, I still have $27,000 of your checks. So, Pinkerton's reward wouldn't even pay off the checks I'm holding, not to speak of what others around town are holding.

"'I have another request of you, and I suspect that you're going to want some small token of payment for that favor.'

"'Let me guess, Mr. Roberts, you want me to destroy this telegram, and if you do, and I agree, that's gonna cost you one of those $10,000 checks.'

"'Oh no, I wouldn't ask you to do that, I want you to put the telegram back exactly where you got it. But before you do, may I walk around your desk and look at it?

"'This telegram was written in pencil. Have you noticed?'

"'All telegrams are written in pencil. The operator doesn't have time to dip his quill in ink; he has to write rapidly.'

"'Right. So, any #2 lead pencil will match the color, but it'll take a real artist to do what needs to be done.

"'Are you familiar with bearer bonds?'

"'Nothing more than they're to be cashed at face value and anyone who brings one in collects its accrued interest. The interest accrues from the date of issue until the date of surrender. That's about all I know about them.'

"'Look at the numbers on these bonds. There are 13 digits. Of course, all those numbers mean something to the Treasury Department, but the only numbers that count, once you look at the series and the denomination of the bond, are the last six digits read from left to right. All those numbers are the same on these bonds, and if you'll look to the right the succeeding numbers are the same. Only the very last number is different from your list.

"'In the bond department, the first thing they will do is get out their treasury catalog. They'll make sure from the catalog that the dates these numbers were issued coincide, that all of the numbers on the certificate are correct according to the treasury catalog, then simply by the feel of the paper, they'll determine whether it is a United States Government Bond.

"'The people in your bond department are very skilled. What I want you to do is to change the numbers on the telegram.

"'If you will notice, the person who wrote this telegram was very careless with the ones and the sevens. As a matter of fact, the cap on the seven is not sloped quiet as much as it is on the one, and it's a little longer. That makes it very easy to change those numbers. Now, for the numbers on the ledger. I have not seen those numbers. Those numbers must be made to correspond with any numbers that we change here. My request to you is to let me compare the telegram and the numbers on the bond ledger and see whether we can alter them both to match without being detected. By the way, are the numbers in the ledger written with pen or pencil?'

"'I didn't really notice, but I believe it was pencil.'

"'Would it arouse suspicion in any fashion if you brought me to the room where the bond ledger is? Are there other people working there?'

"'Well, Mr. Roberts, as you might guess, we do a whole lot of business in bonds, but I'm not familiar with that department. There are several employees in that department. I have people who come here from time to time for many reasons, and it certainly would not seem strange, especially in view of our extended conference, if I carried you over and let you look at the bond ledger.'

"'Mr. Erickson, what would happen if I suddenly took a pencil and started writing in that bond ledger?'

"'Why do it in the bond department? Why not bring the ledger over here to the privacy of my office?'

"'You mean you can do that?'

"'I told you, Mr. Roberts, nobody in this bank would dare stop me. Watch this.'

"He half opened the door and said, 'Nancy, would you bring me the bond ledger for a minute, I want to check something.'

"Shortly she returned with a ledger, 'Will that be all, sir?'

"'For the moment, yes.'

"Once again, I walked around and stood behind him. He laid the bond ledger open, then placed the telegram above it. There were the four matching numbers for the bonds I carried in my money belt. 'Now, Mr. Erickson, we come to the nut-cuttin'.'

"'For five minutes, how much would you charge me to let me have a pencil and alter those numbers?'

"'The rest of my checks.'

"'Mr. Erickson, let's be more reasonable. I've been in your office less than fifteen minutes. You've already earned $6000, and you haven't exposed yourself to any possible criminal prosecution. You let me alter the numbers, then you replace the telegram in the proper file, replace the bond ledger back in it's proper place, and take me over to the bond department and tell them that they should cash my bonds.

"'Each of those bonds has accumulated roughly $4000 in interest. As you noticed, I brought a briefcase. You stay in the bond department until they've done their calculations and cashed the bonds. Then we come back in here. I will give you the interest, which will be almost $16,000, plus your checks. You can go to the poker game Wednesday night with a pocket full of cash and me holding no checks on you. You'll have a hell of a time.'

"'I'll do it on one condition. You change the numbers. I'll replace the ledger and the telegram while you're still here in the office. I'll tell the bond department that you're going to be in tomorrow to cash four bonds for $100,000 dollars each. I want to make sure we have $416,000 in $100 or $1000 bills here in the bank when you come in. We can certainly do that by tomorrow.'

"Erickson walked to the door, called his secretary, and told her to return the ledger to the bond department. When she was back at her desk, he went to the file room, and replaced the telegram.

"Nephew, the reason I wanted to make the changes myself is that I didn't want Erickson to know what the new numbers were. I didn't believe he could remember the numbers. I suggested I was going to change ones into sevens. In fact what I did was to change ones into sixes by erasing the caps from the ones and drawing a circle at the bottom. I looked at the job closely when I finished, and would not have been able to tell what I'd done had I not known.

"I figured that as soon as Mr. Erickson collected his reward from me he would forward those numbers by telegram to the Pinkerton Detective Agency and collect the $25,000 reward from them. By that time, I expected to be long gone. But he'd list the bond numbers, changing all of the sevens to ones thinking that that's what I'd done without even going over to the bond department and checking the bonds themselves, which were probably kept under lock and key. That would be more trouble than he'd be willing to go to.

"When the Pinkerton detective got the numbers he wired and they didn't match, maybe they wouldn't even bother to check out the tip. If they did check the tip when they got the telegram, they would immediately realize the numbers had been altered and that Erickson was in on some kind of conspiracy. How else could the real bonds and the recorded numbers not match. It certainly would leave Mr. Erickson with a lot of explaining to do when the Pinkerton folks showed up. If they didn't have an office in New Orleans, it could possibly give me an extra day.

"'Mr. Erickson, everything's agreed to, is that correct?'

"'Yes it is, Mr. Roberts, and we'll have your funds here in the morning at 9 o'clock. After the money has been counted, if you will just step into my office and give me my checks back, and my $16,000, you can go wherever you came from and thank you sir. I'll be glad to be done with this business.'

"When I left the bank I walked by Miss Nellie's teller's cage and asked whether I could see her that evening. She said she'd be delighted and could hardly wait. I walked out the front door, went directly across the street, and then into the corner building, which happened to be a cafe. I ordered a cup of coffee from a table where I could watch the front door of the Bank of Commerce.

"In less than five minutes, Mr. Erickson came out of the bank, crossed the street, turned left, and went through a door over which hung a sign saying, 'Telegraph Office.' He was in the office maybe five minutes, then emerged, and walked back into the bank. As soon as he'd had time to get to his office, I went to the telegraph office. There was only a single operator sitting behind a desk.

"As I walked in he said, 'Good morning, sir, could I help you?'

"'Maybe. A man left here about three or four minutes ago. I suspect he sent a telegram. I am with the Pinkerton Detective Agency and we're working on a smuggling case. We think the man who just telegraphed is involved in our case. I need to know what was in the telegram he just sent.'

"'Mr., I don't give a damn what you need. That telegram is the private business of the person who sent it. And part of my job is to make sure it stays that way. Besides that, it's against the law for me to tell you. I could lose my license.'

"Holding a $100 bill in my hand, which I guessed to be more than he made in a month, I waited until he glanced down and saw it. I then asked him if he would let me go through his trashcan for that $100 bill. He thought about it a minute and said, 'I don't think there is anything illegal about that.'

"Smiling, he took his foot and pushed the trash basket under the barroom-type door that led into his cubby hole. The first piece of paper I picked up said, 'To the Pinkerton Detective Agency's Main Office, St. Louis, Missouri: Dear Sir, Regarding the bearer bonds mentioned in your telegram to this institution. Stop. The bonds have been presented at this bank for cashing. Stop. The bonds are numbered as follows:'

"I looked at the numbers. He had, in fact, done exactly what I thought he would. He changed all of the ones in the serial numbers to sevens rather than sixes. The numbers he had transmitted to the Pinkerton Detective Agency were wrong numbers. If they investigated, he indeed would have some explaining to do why the bank's handwritten recorded numbers were not the numbers he wired the Pinkerton Agency.

"'The man who has possession of the bonds is presently registered at the Magnolia Hotel, room 326, in New Orleans, Louisiana. Stop. My name is C. P. Erickson, Vice President, the Bank of Commerce, New Orleans, Louisiana. Stop.'

"I put the crumpled up piece of paper back in the trash can and slid it back toward the operator, who was staring intently at me.

"'Sounds to me like the man is trying to catch a thief, not help a bunch of smugglers. What does it sound like to you, Mr. Pinkerton man?'

"'I have discovered, young man, that many times things are not what they seem. Thank you and good day.'

"Walking back to the Magnolia Hotel, I passed the Crepe Myrtle Hotel. I decided that maybe if the Pinkerton Agency acted quickly, I might need another place to stay that night. I registered at the Crepe Myrtle Hotel. They put me in room 205.

"I sat down in an easy chair beside the bed and tried to sort through exactly where I stood. If the Pinkerton Agency acted on the telegram as soon as they received it, they'd more than likely telegraph their office in New Orleans. But as I sat there, the thought occurred that when they discovered the numbers didn't match the bonds they were looking for, they'd wire back to confirm the numbers, or would they telegraph their office to send somebody to look at the actual bonds. If they did that, they'd find the bank didn't have the bonds. All they had were the altered numbers.

"I went back to the Magnolia Hotel and checked out. I told them to send my bags to the railway station immediately. I would call for them there. I gave the bellman a $10 tip to ensure that they would move rapidly. I took only a briefcase out of my luggage as I walked back to the Hotel Crepe Myrtle.

"On the way I decided to stop by the telegraph office again before I went to my new hotel. The same operator was on duty. By then it was between 3 and 4 o'clock, and I suspected all the Pinkerton offices would be closed in the central time zone in another two hours or less."

The Journey Home

"'Well that didn't take long,' the young telegraph operator said.

"'No. Now I know you zealously guard your private communications young man, but I need some further information, and I'm willing to pay for it. What you don't know is just as important as what you do know, so I'd like to buy the truth—$100 worth.

"'Have you had any further communication with the Pinkerton Detective Agency in St. Louis since I left?'

"'You know what mister? You are the easiest man to make money off of I ever saw. You pay me two months salary to answer that question. I haven't received a telegraph message from anybody since you left. Boy, that's easy. What else do you want to know?'

"Before I could answer, the telegraph key started clattering. He snatched a pencil and pad and began to write furiously. I stood in amazement. That was the first time I'd ever watched a telegraph operator at work. I couldn't believe how quickly he constructed a message on the pad. Then he took the key, made a few rapid strokes, and started reading the message. He looked at me, and I knew instantly the message was of great interest to me.

"As he sat there looking at me trying to phrase his next statement to help him make up his mind the way it should be made up, I reached in my pocket and pulled out a couple of $100 bills so he could see them.

"'This is a reply from Pinkerton to C. P. Erickson.'

"'How much?'

"'If you want to read this, mister, it's gonna cost you $500, and before you read it, no matter whether you like or don't like it, the telegram will have to be delivered. I'm not going to let you just buy the telegram and walk out of here for $500. The price to read it is $500. You ain't got enough money to buy it.'

"Nephew, I've played a lot of poker, and I thought he was bluffing. But I was in a pickle. Just for the hell of it,' I said, 'I'll give you two.'

230

"'No sir.'

"I turned as if to walk out. 'Okay, you can read it for two.' I gave him two $100 bills. The telegram read, 'To Mr. C. P. Erickson, Bank of Credit, New Orleans, Louisiana. Dear Sir: The numbers you have sent us are not the numbers on our inquiry. STOP. We have checked with other banks we sent telegrams. Their numbers are correct. STOP. This raises the question of whether or not the numbers were misread by the telegraph operator. STOP. The correct numbers are in sequence, 260117131, 30, 29, 28, 27; would you please check your records. STOP. Since we are working with a capital murder case, an answer is most urgently requested. STOP. T. D. Bronski, Superintendent of Detectives, Pinkerton Agency, St. Louis, Missouri.'

"I handed the telegram back to the operator. Standing there, I knew the bank had already closed for the day. I didn't think the operator would deliver the telegram after the bank was closed. I couldn't be sure of any of this, and needed as much time for my escape as I could get.

"'Let me make you an offer. Now you can earn the rest of the $500 you wanted.'

"'By doing what?'

"I handed him a piece of paper with the same numbers Erickson had sent before.

"'You use these numbers instead of the ones you wrote and give me the old telegram in the trash.'

"He reached in the trash can and handed me the earlier telegram. I unwadded the paper. It was the same one I'd seen earlier in the day. I said, 'How about it?'

"'I don't know, this could get me in a world of trouble.'

"'This day you have already made half a year's salary. You are going to deliver the telegram; the error in the numbers could be you misread or miswrote the message. There could be all sorts of reasons the numbers wouldn't be right.

"'All that's going to happen is C. P. Erickson is going to look at the numbers, and know they are the same ones he sent them before. Then he's going to send them another telegram saying the numbers they sent are the numbers he sent. Somebody in St. Louis has made an error. Then they are going to resend the numbers, and everything will be okay. It will just be a day later.'

"He erased the four rows of numbers, took my piece of paper, and copied the numbers very carefully. He handed the telegram to me along with my numbers so I could compare them. I handed him the $300 and asked him when the telegram would be delivered?

"'It will be delivered immediately to the mail box at the bank. Somebody will still be inside balancing the books. It's possible Mr. Erickson would get an answer out today, but it would be highly unlikely. If he did it would probably be after the Pinkerton Agency closed.' His best guess was I had bought a day's delay.

"I went back to the corner cafe and watched the bank to see if anybody picked up the telegram after it was delivered. I watched for the better part of an hour while I drank coffee. It appeared nobody was going to take the telegram into the bank that day.

"I went directly to the railroad station, opened my big suitcase, and put a change of clothes along with G. B. Balls' pistol in the smallest bag I had. I asked the ticket agent if I could store my bags until the train left the following day, and bought a ticket to Dallas in the event I was seen leaving the station.

"By the time I was finished, it was approaching 6 PM. I couldn't decide whether I wanted to go to the poker game and see Mr. Erickson squirm a little bit about his perfidy, or whether I wanted to spend my last night in New Orleans with Miss Nellie Miller. 'What the hell, why not both?'

"I called on Miss Miller and told her I had a late appointment at 9 o'clock, and invited her to my hotel until that time. She readily agreed. I later dropped Nellie off at home and went directly to the Forty-Fourth Street Club.

"The poker game was already in progress, and all the seats were filled. There were 14 players, and I was the only kibitzer. As the night wore on, Mr. Erickson got more and more antsy. To relieve his anxiety, I asked if anybody expected to leave before closing time; if not, I was going back to my hotel. Nobody said anything. 'Good night gentlemen. See you next time.'

"The next morning at 9 o'clock I was in the Bank of Commerce requesting to see Mr. C. P. Erickson. His secretary announced my presence. My eye caught the corner of a yellow piece of paper, which had to be a telegram, as he stuffed it inside his coat pocket.

"'Come in, Mr. Roberts. I suppose you're here to cash the bearer bonds. You know Mr. Roberts, we have discussed these bonds on several occasions, but I've never seen them.' I laid the four sheets of fine linen paper in front of him. He picked them up and felt each one in turn.

"'You know, there's hardly any mistake in that fine government paper, eh, Mr. Roberts, Robinson, Cotton? Well, let's go over and get your money.'

"We went to the bond department where he introduced Mr. Kelly. 'These are the bonds I told you about. Would you see what you can do about cashing them for Mr. Roberts? He's a friend of mine.'

"Mr. Kelly took out a jeweler's loupe and examined the paper with great care. After a couple or three minutes, he looked up at me a bit sheepishly and said, "Excuse me, Mr. Roberts, but we are about to give $416,000 for these four bonds. I need to make sure what we are getting is worth it, if you don't mind.'

"Not at all sir. Take any amount of time. I'm pleased to see how thorough you are. I was once the president of a bank, not as big as this, but in the whole time I was president, I never saw a transaction with a bearer bond. Of course, it was a small community.'

"It took Mr. Kelly the better part of 30 minutes to decide they were genuine bonds. Since they were indeed negotiable, he signed a draft ordering the teller to pay me $416,000, which was immediately counted in front of me. I put it in my briefcase. We went back to C. P. Erickson's office for his payoff.

"The teller had packaged the $100 bills in $10,000 packages. I handed him one package of $100 bills, broke the band on the second package and counted out 60 of the $100 bills. I put the remainder in my briefcase, took his checks out of my wallet, laid them on the desk, and said, 'As far as I know Mr. Erickson, that completes our transaction. I'll be on my way now.'

"I started for the door. Mr. Erickson said, 'Mr. Roberts would you tarry with me a moment? I always believe in giving a fellow a sporting chance, gambler that I am, so I am going to tell you something you don't know that may give you another day to live.

"'Mr. Roberts, Mr. Robinson, Mr. Cotton, don't you ever think, as they close in on you, that I treated you unfairly. There probably is a Pinkerton man at your hotel now, trying to persuade the local police to let him arrest you under their commission. But I must confess, Mr. Roberts, I don't like a smart-ass, and you are about the smartest ass I ever ran across. But I like to see even a smart-ass get an even break.'

"While he sat there gloating, I couldn't decide whether I wanted to puncture his balloon now or let the Pinkerton people do it once they discovered all those crazy numbers, and tried to make sense out of the bonds and how the bank's numbers came to be wrong.

"'Mr. Erickson, since it's confession time between us girls, I have a little one to make, too. When you reconstructed the numbers on the bearer bonds, I suspect you changed the numbers back from sevens to ones and you shouldn't have. You should have changed the sixes to ones to have the right serial numbers.

"'I suggest you spend the time until the Pinkertons arrive figuring out what you're going to say about how the numbers you sent them weren't the right ones, but yet you knew the bonds had been stolen. Even if you change the telegram, and change the bond ledger, to the right numbers, how are you going to explain sending them the wrong numbers? It'll be interesting to hear your story, Mr. Erickson, but I don't have time. Good day, sir.'

"I walked by Nellie's teller window and told her goodbye. I also told her that if I was ever back in New Orleans, I'd look her up. As I left, she said, 'I hope you'll come back soon.'

"I went back to my hotel to await my train's departure. As I reached the first corner, I looked across the street. There was a man who reminded me very much of G. B. Balls—the same bowler hat, the same tailored clothes. I turned to my right to look at the corner of the next block, and there was another man dressed just like him reading a newspaper. My first thought was 'two Pinkerton detectives.' Somehow Erickson's message did get through, and Pinkerton had moved.

"I then walked several blocks, all the time staying alert for anybody who might be following me, taking a very roundabout route to my hotel. If anybody was following me, they were very good.

"When I got to the hotel, it was only about 11 AM and I had nothing to do until train time that evening. I poured about three fingers of whiskey to relieve the tension from the morning encounter with Mr. Erickson and from my fear that I might have seen a couple of Pinkerton detectives. After the second good drink, I was mellowed out, and the tension drained away even as I began to feel the warm glow initiated by the booze.

"I checked the false bottom of my bag to make sure I hadn't lost Balls' gun and diary that I had taken from my steamer trunk before leaving home. I didn't dare leave that. Though I didn't think Kathy would search my stuff, I didn't want to take any chances that she would grow bored and see whether she could discover more of her husband's secrets while I was away. And I decided that now would be a good time to read Balls' diary, since I had never been able to find an opportunity earlier.

"First I looked at the entry that must have been made only minutes before I killed him, and then I thumbed back through his days. He was a very careful and meticulous man, and apparently used a new diary for every case because this one closed out Case #58 and began Case #59 in the first paragraph.

"Mr. Balls gave a most detailed picture of his chase after me, and seemed to write down nearly everything he did. It was almost like reading a novel. I was most anxious to discover how he'd happened to stumble across my trail.

"It didn't take long. I flipped to a page entitled 'Evansville, Indiana.' He wrote about how Eddie and Jimmy, the bellboys, told him about the artistic skills of L. B. Pecker, the man who sold me the gas cans to blow up the Packard. That's how he got a drawing of my likeness. The kid was an excellent artist. That explains that, but it also means, loner that he was, Mr. Balls was probably the only person except John Davis who ever saw that drawing.

"John Davis was more than likely no artist, so there was nobody but the kid in Evansville who knew what I looked like. I wonder whether any new detective would be tracing Balls' footsteps, or would they only concentrate on what happened in Chicago? They certainly didn't have his diary as a guide; I had that. It seemed to me the Pinkertons would need much good fortune ever to trace

Mr. Balls' footsteps and run across L. B. Pecker in Evansville. These were my thoughts as I drifted off into an alcoholic stupor.

"Late in the afternoon a shaft of sunlight brought me to consciousness. I had an evil taste in my mouth and felt a little bit hung over. I got up and brushed my teeth before taking a couple of fingers of Haig & Haig. I went to close the drapes, but glanced down to the street, and was startled again to see the man who reminded me of G. B. Balls sitting in a doorway, across the street and directly below me, reading a newspaper.

"For several minutes I stood away from the window, in a spot where I was certain he couldn't see me, but where I could still view the man I thought to be a Pinkerton agent. He occasionally glanced up at the building. It was obvious he was watching for somebody.

"I went out of the room and down the hallway all the way to the back of the hotel. There was another similarly dressed man standing around talking to a carriage-for-hire operator. A wave of panic momentarily flooded through me.

"I went back to the room feeling certain the Pinkerton Detective Agency had a man watching both the front and the rear entrances of the hotel. Though they couldn't possibly know I had train tickets leaving New Orleans that night, I had to think of a way to lose them. Though I imagined I'd lost them when I left the bank, obviously I had not.

"So I went to the back of the hotel. The carriage and the Pinkerton man were still there. I took my bag and briefcase, went to the rear of the hotel, crossed the street to where the agent was still conversing with the carriage driver, and asked him whether the carriage was available for rent. They looked at each other in a quizzical fashion. The man I thought to be an agent gave a slight nod, and the carriage driver immediately said, 'Yes sir.'

"I suspect they thought I hadn't noticed their behavior. I got into the carriage and said, 'Canal Street, please.' The carriage was closed, with the driver sitting out front. The side doors were loose-hanging curtains of ising glass. I looked out the back window as we made a left at the first corner.

"The Pinkerton agent had run across the street and was frantically waving at the man sitting at the front of the hotel. I gathered it was his responsibility to follow me in the event I headed toward the back of the hotel, I was now reasonably certain the Pinkertons thought I was unaware of their presence.

"I stuck my head out of the window and asked the driver to please hurry. He clucked to the horse, which started a slow canter that wasn't fast enough at all to suit me. Holding on to the door jamb, I slung myself around and sat alongside the driver with G. B. Balls' pistol in my hand. I ordered him to hand me the harness lines and jump. I raised the gun up to the level of his eyes as he reached to hand me the lines. I took them in one hand then brought the pistol down and shot a hole in the floorboard. The driver levitated at the same instant the horse did. It was a wild run through the streets of New Orleans.

"For several minutes I gave the terrified horse her head. She must have established some sort of record for speed. When we got to Canal Street, we turned and headed toward the river.

"At that time Canal Street actually ended at a pier, but there was a little road just before the pier that veered off and went right down to the river bank. I was whipping the horse every step of the way.

"About 20 feet before we got to the river, I picked up my suitcase and tossed it off, grabbed my briefcase in the other hand, jumped off, and shot the pistol. The horse, in terror, plunged right into the river, carriage and all. Picking up my suitcase, I walked back up to Canal Street, and went one block west. There I hailed another carriage and asked to be taken to the railroad station.

"I had the carriage stop a good two blocks before it reached the station so that I could see whether anybody appeared to be a Pinkerton. There was nothing that raised my suspicions in the waiting room or along the dock; I couldn't believe they had covered the hotel, but not the railroad station. Maybe they had used all their men covering the piers.

"My Pullman compartment was several cars toward the back of the train from the actual waiting room area, and I walked back and entered my compartment. It was on the station side, so I could keep an eye up and down the platform as far as I could see. I had $400,000 cash on me, but I felt trapped. So I sat at the window and swept my eyes continuously across the platform until the train started to move.

"As my car passed the waiting room, I saw my Pinkerton man stand up in the ticket agent's office and race to the doorway. He was running alongside the last pullman car, and swung aboard just as the track bent the other way. I lost sight of him, but would have bet the whole $400,000 he worked for Pinkerton.

"He had come out of the ticket agent's office, so that meant he knew where I was. Now I had to wonder why they hadn't tried to arrest me, instead of letting me get in the carriage. I wondered why, if he had been sitting in the ticket agent's office, he didn't arrest me as I boarded the train. Maybe they weren't sure I was the man. Maybe they had already interviewed Erickson, and he'd passed along my story that I'd bought the bonds from Jesse Robinson. It didn't make a whole lot of sense that they didn't try to arrest me.

"At length, it occurred to me, the reason they hadn't tried to arrest me on the street was simple. They were planning to kill me, just as I had killed one of their friends.

"It was rapidly growing dark. Every time the tracks bent to the right I could see the sparks flying from the engine. The people had put my baggage in my car; I went through it to see whether there was anything that would indicate where I was going. I put on some clean clothes and stuffed all the money I could in my money belt, which I estimated to be about $100,000. I put the rest in my small suitcase, along with Balls' diary and the gun. Then I tried to see whether there was anything else that would give them a clue where I was going.

"I estimated we'd been traveling 40 minutes. It was now pitch dark, no moon. The train began to slow, I guessed for Reserve, Louisiana. I stuck my head out and looked both ways; there was nobody in view. I went to the front door of the car, popped it open, and jumped.

"I landed on soft, spongy, almost marshy soil. As I stood in the darkness and watched the train pass out of sight, I was struck by the grim reality that the Pinkertons really wanted me, but hadn't the least idea where I was until now. Since the bonds were now cashed, I began to feel free and easy for the first time in many months. I wouldn't have to expose myself again.

"It had been a full seven months since I had killed G. B. Balls, and though I had almost stopped worrying about it, obviously I could never do it again. Mr. Pinkerton's memory was just too long.

"Nephew, ever since I left Plowshare, Kentucky, I'd lived a life of luxury. It is awful easy to get used to that kind of life. As I stood there in the darkness trying to think what I could do, I remembered how I'd gotten to Plowshare; how I hoboed a freight train. I'd never run across a hobo with a suitcase before.

"In the distance I could see a kerosene lamp burning in the window of a farmhouse. The going was rough because there was no moonlight that night. I kept stumbling and falling. I was awfully afraid of snakes, and had heard some horrendous tales about the snakes that grow in Louisiana. In the darkness, I walked right into a creek, falling face forward and thoroughly soaking my clothes. The creek was a little less than waist deep. When I got out, I carefully made my way through the blackness up onto a little knoll, sat down on my suitcase, and let my clothes dry in the August air. Even though it was a warm night, I grew chill while drying out.

"Sitting there on the suitcase, shaking from the cold, I realized that even though I had $400,000 plus at that particular moment, I couldn't buy anything. It was no more useful than driftwood. I'd killed two men in order to keep it, and possibly caused the death of a young woman, a very unhappy young woman, to obtain it.

"I was full of guilt and remorse, and almost wished I could call my life back and undo what I had done for the past year and a half. As I sat on that little knoll shivering, an echo of an old Baptist preacher spouting hell-fire and brimstone about murderers, thieves, and whorehoppers whispered through the air. My god, how can people do those awful things, I thought? I'd broken almost every commandment the preacher had orated about.

"But I was young, strong, healthy, and I had $400,000, and that made all those things I'd done alright. I was on my way to Brownsville to pay for a gin that would make me a very wealthy man. I had a beautiful wife, I called the president of the Brownsville Bank by his first name, and so I decided, while sitting there shivering and shaking, that it was worth having done those deeds to be an important man in this very large world. It was years before I remembered those terrible deeds again.

At about that moment, a full moon broke the horizon. It's amazing how much light a full moon gives off. I sat there and watched it crawl up among the stars. After the near pitch black, I could now see pretty well. But even though the moon gave quite a bit of light, it didn't give any heat, and I was still cold.

"I opened the suitcase. Very little water had gotten on the clothes or the money, so I changed clothes right out in the wide open spaces, and pretty soon was warm again.

"Walking toward a light, I found myself slipping and sliding into some mudholes left behind when the creek overflowed its banks. My freshly changed clothes got dirty again rather quickly, but since my plan was now to masquerade as a hobo, it didn't matter.

"When I reached the house, I went straight to the barn, got in the feed room, found a couple of old croker sacks, and put one inside the other. All I had left was a pistol, G. B. Balls' diary, and the money which I then transferred into the croker sack. Now I looked, and felt, much like all the hobos I'd ever seen. Then I made my way back to the railroad tracks.

"Once there, I found myself a clump of alder bushes to hide behind, near the start of a slight grade. I thought a freight train might slow down enough here to climb aboard. I didn't have long to wait. A freight train was coming through, and when it had almost passed, I jumped out of the bushes and clambered up into one of the cars.

"No sooner was I inside than a voice out of the darkness snarled, 'Go find your own goddammed car. This one's taken.' My first thought was to pull my pistol and start shooting in his general direction, but I decided I'd try to get along with whoever it was. I said, 'Buddy, I'm too winded right now to get off. The train is picking up speed. I'll get out and give you the car as soon as it slows down again. Is that alright?'

"'That's alright, but you remember whose goddammed car it is.'

"Gradually my eyes began to adjust to the darkness. I could make out a figure in one corner of the boxcar, laying on what looked like a bunch of feedsacks. To make conversation I asked him where he came from. He said he was from Savannah, and his name was Bill Alexander. By the time we were half way to Baton Rouge, I knew all about Bill. He'd had quite a bit of experience traveling through Louisiana and Texas as a hobo. His knowledge, I thought, might be very helpful to me.

"While we were talking I snuggled down and got comfortable. There was a covering of some kind of straw on the car's floor. My two croker sacks full of money, if I slipped the diary and pistol over to one side, made a pretty good pillow. I almost drifted off to sleep.

"I answered all the questions Bill asked me in a fashion designed not to give out much good information. The thought occurred to me, 'he's nosy as hell for a hobo,' because hobos usually have sense enough not to ask too many damn questions, but I couldn't see him and thought maybe he was new at the trade.

"To keep the pistol from working around inside the sack and getting under my head, I eased it out and buried it under the straw, almost against the wall of the car. We rode on through the night listening to that lonesome sound of the steam locomotive.

"Eventually the train began easing to a crawl. I remembered my promise to get off, and said 'Bill, I promised you I'd give you your car back when the train slowed down, so I'll jump here and see if I can find another car.' When I said that I heard the click of a safety.

"Bill growled in a low voice, 'You ain't going no goddammed place, Jesse Robinson.'

"My heart jumped into my throat! How in the hell could this man suspect me of anything. It was incredible! Then he started explaining. 'F. G. Goodman is going to be awfully proud of himself, Jesse Robinson. When you jumped off the other train, the agent following you didn't know exactly where you'd done it. But Mr. Goodman felt sure you'd do exactly what you did. He ordered us to open the doors on both sides of a couple of cars close to the cab, close all the rest of them, and open one near the back. He predicted that was the car you would crawl into. I've got to hand it to him, I thought it was an idiotic plan myself. Goddamn, he's smart.'

"'I don't know what you're talking about mister. My name is not Jesse Robinson, and I don't know nor have I ever heard that name.'

"As the train bent to the right up ahead, I could see lights to the left. For that time of night it had to be a big city like Baton Rouge; the train would more'n likely stop there. I couldn't imagine it going all the way through with that many cars. I had to get out of this pickle fast if I was going to get out. I strongly suspected he didn't have any help in Baton Rouge in the middle of the night. If he did, he'd have to wake them up. So I thought it wouldn't hurt to try to talk him out of his silly idea that I was Jesse Robinson. 'What did this Jesse Robinson do to, who'd you say, F. G. Goodman?'

"'He's the man assigned by Superintendent Bronski of the Pinkerton Agency to run down and catch the murderer of G. B. Balls and his stool pigeon. You, mister Jesse Robinson, killed them—you know that as well as I do. I never thought the Pinkertons might ever have another detective as good as G. B. Balls. My hat's off to F. G. Goodman. He must be as good as Balls, Mr. Robinson.

"'Every Pinkerton detective in the whole United States wants to see your ass hung. We are going to try and get together a large crowd to witness that event. I am just honored they trusted me enough to send me on this mission. By God, I've got you.'

"'Now that you've got me, what're you going to do with me, Bill?'

"'If I'm not mistaken we're coming into Baton Rouge. There are going to be two Pinkerton detectives to meet us in Baton Rouge just on the off chance Mr. Goodman was correct. I'd say we're not more than ten minutes away.'

"The train began curving around to the left. Up ahead I could see what looked like the superstructure of a bridge. I said, 'By God, Bill, I believe you're right. I believe I see a bridge. That must be the Mississippi coming up.'

"From my position on the floor, I could see the river cutting across my field of view. We're almost on the Mississippi River. Bill got to his feet and grabbed the handle of the door with his left hand. While holding the gun in his right hand, he swung around to get a better look at the river, which we were now directly above. Then he remembered he had a prisoner.

"As he turned to check me, the bullet from G. B. Balls' gun caught him in the right temple. The kick from the lead toppled him out of the car. He hit the rail of the bridge and was gone into the night, down into the almighty Mississippi, just a boy.

"As soon as we got on level ground the train began to slow. Once again I jumped out into the night."

Headed Home

"Apparently we had crossed the Mississippi south of Baton Rouge. After jumping from the train, I lay in the bushes along the track for a few minutes, then got up and followed the track toward the city. Near a mile ahead, the train stopped, and two men jumped up and into the car I had just vacated. A short time later they came back out scratching their heads.

"I'd really pissed Mr. Pinkerton off. I knew I had to abandon the train and figure out another way to get back to Brownsville. I could buy a car, but the trip was almost impossible by car. I was beginning to think Pinkerton was using every man they had to chase me.

"Coming to a dirt road, I crossed the track and headed south. After a couple of hours, I began at last to see the rosy glow of dawn breaking to the east. Off in the distance I spotted a farmhouse that looked well kept. By the time I reached the house the sun was at least an hour high, and it was beginning to grow warm.

"An old farmer with a straw hat was leaning up against the well curb. Tied to a stake out away from the well was one of the most vicious looking bulldogs I ever saw. The farmer had a crockery jug he had just taken from his lips, 'Stranger, would you like a drink of my homemade squeezings?'

"My feet were sore, I was tired, and the mid-August sun had been bearing down on me for the better part of an hour. Since that was all he offered, I said, 'Sure would, mister.' I took a big slug of homemade liquor. Then I pulled up a pretty good sassafras sapling trying to get my breath. I finally caught it and said, 'God, how do you stand it?' He said, 'Son, you have to know how to drink it.'

"He poured a gourd half full of water and handed it to me. 'Here drink this.' The water tasted nearly as bad as the liquor. I almost gagged as it went down. With tears in my eyes I said, 'My God, is that supposed to help?'

"'No. Now you have to kiss my bulldog's ass. That'll take the taste out of your mouth.'

"He'd had his little joke about the taste of Louisiana water and his corn squeezings; I liked him almost instantly. I stuck out my hand and said, 'I'm Jim Parrish.'

"'I'm L. D. Claburne,' he said, 'my friends call me Tiny. What can I do for you? Looks like you've been run hard and put up wet.'

"'Well you might say I have. I'm lookin' for a way to get to El Paso, Texas as fast as I can. I'm afraid of trains. I've tried to overcome it, but I can't.'

"L. D. stood there for a few minutes scratching his head. 'There's a young fellow down at Whitecastle who fools around with these dang airplanes. He's got some Flying Jennies. He's even got a plane they claim was made to train airplane pilots; it's got two seats. I don't know nothing about airplanes, but I suppose if I was in the kind of fizz you are to get somewhere, I'd go down and talk to him. His name is Bob Stogner. He's a daredevil kind of fellow, got a partner in the business by the name of Rodger Miles.

"'If you ask me, they're both damn fools. If God meant for you to fly, he'd a give you a set of wings. If you ever see me flying, you'll hear the flutter of angel feathers, I'll tell you that right now. But in the hurry you seem to be in, that's what I would try.'

"'How far is it to Whitecastle?'

"'Oh, it's the better part of ten miles I'd guess.'

"'Could I get you to take me to Whitecastle to meet those fellows. I'd be willing to pay you handsomely.'

"'I've got to deliver some corn squeezings pretty near there. I'll let you ride along with me for, say, $10?'

"We went out to his barn; there was a good-looking two-horse surrey in a shed on one side of the barn and a fairly new Cadillac on the other side. He started calling the horses. Of course, I was so anxious to get away, I didn't care how we left, but I asked him why he didn't use the car if he was going to deliver some liquor. Wouldn't it be faster?

"'It would be faster, but it would also attract more attention. People still hadn't got used to them shiny cars runnin' up and down the road. They always wondered what a fellow was doing off 10–15 miles away from home. My Maw and Paw both lived to be 75 years old. They lived and died right here on this farm and I'll bet you neither one of them was ever more than 10 miles away from here. I like to drive the Cadillac, but not when I'm on business.'

"I helped him hitch up two bay mares to the surrey. The surrey had rubber tires and big leaf springs. It probably rode better than the Cadillac. We chatted as we went along the road. I was curious, since he was so careful about not attracting attention to his bootlegging, why he told me all this stuff, a total stranger.

"'I saw you walking for the better part of an hour. There ain't no lawman gonna walk that far when he don't have to. Besides you just don't look like no lawman, and I trust my judgment about such things. God knows I've met enough of 'em in my day. I've got no idea who you are, James Parrish, got no idea what you do, but I'd bet my front seat in hell you ain't no lawman.'

"It was close to dinnertime when we got to a pasture where Bob Stogner and Rodger Miles had their little venture with airplanes. Nephew, I guess it was the first time I'd ever saw an airplane. I couldn't ever remember seeing one, funny lookin' things they was.

"They had several different varieties. Some of them were just canvas stretched over what looked like a wooden frame, with great big propellers sticking out the front. One had a wing on top and a wing on the bottom. Rodger showed me a Thomas Morse S-4. He said they was making the things to train pilots, and told me it had an 80-horsepower engine in it. It would fly at a top speed of 100 miles per hour, and it'd fly 250 miles without a fill-up carrying two full-grown men.

"Before I said goodbye to L. D. Claburne, I asked Miles if he would be willing to fly a passenger to El Paso. I made sure L. D. Claburne heard me request a trip to El Paso. I paid him and thanked him as much as I could for taking time to bring me to Whitecastle. I really liked L. D. Maybe it was because he was a lawbreaker like me, only I doubt if he'd ever murdered anybody.

Bob Stogner was in his late 50s or early 60s; you couldn't tell. He was freckle-faced, red-headed, half-bald. His face looked like it had been carved out of a bar of Octagon soap. Miles, his partner, was a little bit younger. He still had some hair. He was the mechanical genius. He kept the old airplane flying, while Bob was the daredevil who constantly tested Miles' ingenuity to make tougher and stronger engines.

"After L. D. Claburne left, I asked Bob what he would charge to fly me to El Paso. He said, 'Call me Uncle Bob, everybody does.' When he said that, Miles spoke up, 'Call me Daddy, everybody calls me Daddy.' So I guessed that everybody who drives airplanes liked nicknames. 'Okay Uncle Bob, tell me what you're gonna charge to take me to El Paso.'

"'Did you ever ride in an airplane before, young man?'

"'No, I never did. I ain't even sure I've ever saw one before.'

"'Why do you particularly want to ride in an airplane? It might be quicker to go by train or automobile.'

"'Trains scare the shit out of me.'

"'Well, if trains scare you that much, this damn airplane will give you a heart attack. Come on, I'll give you a spin around, let's see.'

"He put me up in the front seat of the thing; he got in the back. Daddy come out and twisted the propeller after they said some words between them. When the engine came to life, it made a racket like you ain't never heard. First thing I knowed we was bouncing across the pasture. In a minute or two we left the ground.

"I've rode in the finest cars they make, motorcycles, surreys, you name it. It was even smoother than a boat. I looked around. Daddy, and the old barn the planes were parked by, wasn't much bigger than a frying size chicken to look at him. I guessed you could see 100 miles in every direction. We just kept going higher, until suddenly it felt like we just rolled over the edge of the world. The engine started roaring and we headed straight down for the ground.

"I thought he was going to fly the blooming thing square into the ground. Then he leveled off and started back up. Now I felt like I was growed to the seat, and my heart was coming through my ass. Then we rolled off the edge of the world again and my belly stayed right there while the rest of me went on that long plunge toward the ground. I think he was just trying to give me a heart attack. He swooped, turned right, left, up, and down.

"When we finally landed I was pissed off with him for showing off. He did scare the shit out of me, but I wanted to get out of that part of the country. I was still no more than 25–30 miles from Baton Rouge; I had an idea the town was full of Pinkerton detectives looking for Jesse Robinson.

"Uncle Bob and Daddy insisted I go with them to eat dinner. We got in a Model-T roadster, went bumping across to a farmhouse sitting back in some live oaks. Uncle Bob's wife, Susie, had dinner on the table, a fine meal of fresh corn, string beans, and okra. It had been so long since I'd had that kind of food that I ate so much I couldn't hardly tote it when I stood up.

"We chatted about the trip to El Paso while we had dinner. As a matter of curiosity, I asked Uncle Bob how long they'd been fooling with airplanes. He said six or seven years. He had farmed most all of his life and had done pretty well with it, but he wanted to get into something that would be more interesting than farming.

"Rodger, or Daddy, as everybody called him, was his nephew. He had been tinkering around with old engines ever since he was a little boy. First it was steam, then these gas-burning engines like they got so many of now. He's even had some experience on diesels. If it'll run, Daddy can make one or fix one.

"'I personally wouldn't get in a damn airplane if he didn't check out the working parts first. An awful lot of people get killed in these airplanes, but it's usually cause some cable breaks, the motor locks up, the propeller breaks, something like that. But if you've got a good man who'll look after that kind of stuff, they're just as safe as the arms of your Ma.'

"Uncle Bob winked at Susie and said, 'Everything else I used to enjoy doing so much has sort of slowed down, but I can get up in that airplane, cut di-dos just like the plane is part of me. I know how the great eagles must feel as they swoop down on the rabbit running across the field.'

"'How long did it take to learn to fly, Uncle Bob?'

"'Oh hell, I went up by myself after five minutes of instructions by the fellow who taught me. Back then they didn't have no two seat airplanes.'

"'How long do you think it'd take you to teach me to fly?'

"'Well, if you ain't cold stupid, I can teach you where you won't kill yourself in 30 minutes. There's really not that much to it. You've got a stick, two pedals, and a throttle. You control speed with the throttle, direction with the stick and pedals. Long as you don't stall out when you're taking off, it's hard to screw up.'

"'What would you sell me that airplane for, that...what did you call it, an S-4?'

"'Oh, I'd have to have $3000. That's a fine machine.'

"'Can you teach me to fly before dark?'

"'I told you if you ain't cold stupid I can teach you to fly in 30 minutes. I don't know how long it would take Daddy, but you need somebody who knows about engines to go along with you if you plan on flying from here to El Paso. There is a hell of a lot of things that could wrong with that engine. If you don't know more about engines than I do, you are gonna be up shit creek when it goes.'

"'I've always been rather fond of engines myself, and I know quite a bit about them. I, too, worked on steam engines in sawmills. I know how they work, at least in automobiles. How much difference is there in the way they work in airplanes?'

"Daddy broke in, 'An engine is an engine. If you know something about one, you'll know something about all of them. All you need to make a gasoline engine work is fire and fuel at the same time, and she'll run. That's just a basic rule.'

"'Well, gentlemen, let's go give me a flying lesson. Daddy, while we're riding over to the plane, tell me any tricks you know about engines that I ought to know if I'm going to fly one by myself.'

"By now we were back at the airplane. He stood up on the step and told me to get in the back seat. 'That thing poking up out of the floorboard is called a stick. Those two pedals in the floor control the rudder back on the tail. When you push the stick in this direction, you mash this pedal, then push the stick in that direction, you push the other one.'

"He went through it for about three or four minutes. 'This airplane was designed to train pilots. It has identical controls in the front seat, as you noticed a while ago. I want you to get in the front seat and watch what the controls are doing while we are moving, every time I move something back here, it's gonna move up there. All I want you do the first time is to just watch, mainly taking off and landing, which are the dangerous parts. Once you get that down, flying in a straight line is easy, there ain't a lot to it. Getting off the ground and getting back on the ground safe is the hard part.'

"I climbed up in the front seat and watched the controls move as he flew the airplane. He beat on the side of the airplane to get my attention and motioned for me to take the controls. Nephew, I did; it was just like he said—as easy as pie.

"I flew around for 15 or 20 minutes then pointed to the ground, pushed the stick forward, and we started down. I felt it when he took the controls. I let go; he brought us into a soft, easy landing. We got out and talked it over. 'Are you ready to fly it by yourself now, Jim?' I told him I thought I was.

"I took the airplane off, flew one circle around the field, then came back and landed. It was rougher than his landing, but it wasn't too bad. I thought I could do better so I went right back around and I did it again.

"Uncle Bob and Daddy both complimented me on how quickly I learned. Uncle Bob assured me I'd get better every time I took the airplane up. I asked him, 'What about places to land?' 'When you get ready to land, pick out a good spot—find a road that's straight and close to some houses. You'll need somebody to take you to get gas and oil. Since you're going solo, you can put four 5-gallon cans in the back seat; you'll have one free stop where you won't have to go for gas.

"'This airplane is going to burn about ten gallons an hour depending on how wide open you've got the throttle. It holds 25 gallons. So you've got 2-1/2 hours of flying time, if you've got a tail wind you're going to cover more territory than if you've got a headwind.'

"At that point I made up my mind. 'Folks, I'm gonna buy your airplane. You want $3000 for the airplane. I want four cans full of gasoline. But first I need to get some fresh clothes and a suitcase. Everything I've got is in this croker sack and it looks like hell. I'd hate to be flying around in a plane with all my belongings in a croker sack. If you'll take me to town and let me make a few purchases, then let me spend the rest of the afternoon learning more about how to fly and talking about engines, I'd like to take off early in the morning. How much money would you charge for all that?'

"Uncle Bob said, 'The $3000 you are gonna pay us for the airplane ought to cover that if that's all you want. I'll run you into town now.' We went to Whitecastle. I bought myself a couple of changes of clothes, and a pretty nice suitcase. After I made my purchases, I put all the stuff from my croker sack in my suitcase.

"We went back to Uncle Bob's pasture and I spent the rest of the day practicing flying the airplane. I got to where I felt pretty safe in it well before sundown. I actually made my last landing after the sun went down; it was sort of twilight, but the landing was smooth as silk. In less than a day I had become an airplane pilot.

"We had a good supper. Then I took a hot bath in that stinking Louisiana water, and smelled nearly as bad when I got out as I had when I got in. But at least I felt clean. We ate supper and then chatted until bedtime.

"Next morning, bright and early, Daddy was back for another day with Uncle Bob. They stood in the pasture and waved as I took off to the west away from the sun. Uncle Bob gave me a map; he had made some notes showing things to look for on the way so I could identify my route. Uncle Bob gave me some instructions on how to read a pocket compass and warned me it was best to follow roads. There are some places across Texas where I could run out of gas and still be 200 miles away from any place to buy more. He warned me again to make sure, once I left the eastern rim of Texas, to follow roads or I might wind up walking to El Paso.

"I checked my watch when I left Whitecastle, headed away from the sun. The airplane was running awful sweet. I quickly got up to what I estimated to be 2000 feet above the ground, put the throttle about half wide open, which is the position Daddy said I would get the best fuel efficiency. I should be flying about 60 miles an hour.

"I kept the plane headed in that direction till I'd gone one hour. Looking down, I could see a little place that according to Uncle Bob's map, was Eagan, Louisiana. Flying felt wonderful, an instant love affair for me. Every once in a while I'd wiggle the stick off to the left and go into a little dive just to practice my flying skills, then I'd go off to the right, always keeping in mind that I needed to be as good a pilot as possible to get free of the Pinkertons.

"I took off from Lake Charles at 20 minutes past 10 o'clock. It's important you know what time it is when you're flying. Uncle Bob had reminded me just as I took off, 'When they run out of gas, they ain't going much farther.'

"A little less than two hours later I landed at Beaumont, Texas. I was met by a swarm of people. Airplanes were so unusual, they held a fascination for people I couldn't believe. They'd hardly been known to me just four days earlier, but now I'm being met by throngs everywhere I land.

"I realized that with all these people coming to meet me everywhere I landed, there was no way I could fly this thing into Brownsville. If the Pinkertons ever found out I had an airplane, they'd be asking in all directions and eventually they'd plot my path. No matter how round about my way to Brownsville, they'd eventually figure out where I was. I had to take a train to go safely on into Brownsville. But where to hook up with a train?

"The Pinkertons would certainly cover both the Houston and Dallas railroad stations. If I flew till dark, I could probably make San Antonio. I'd feel pretty safe getting a train from San Antonio and then heading south by way of Laredo into Brownsville.

"I ate in Beaumont, and when I left it was 1 PM. At 3 o'clock I landed at a place called Humble, Texas, filled up with gas, then pushed on west. At a little after 5 o'clock I landed at Brenham, Texas, and realized I was not making as much time as I thought I should. When I took on gas in Brenham, I decided I didn't want to be caught after dark in that plane.

"There was a railroad track running through Brenham. When I asked some of the local people where the track was headed, they said it went to Austin. I was now about 100 miles from Austin, something like an hour's flight. When I took off from Brenham, I decided I'd land outside Austin and catch a train south from there.

"I flew along the railroad tracks 700 or so feet in the air, since I sure didn't want to miss Austin. It was now almost 7 o'clock, the sun was sinking low in the west, and I couldn't see any sign of a city. I began to feel a bit apprehensive.

"A little bit after seven, I spotted a tiny village, set the plane down, and taxied out into a field within sight of some buildings. Once again, people came flocking out to the airplane. I told the folks the plane had a broken oil line, and that I had to go off to a bigger town to get the parts I needed to fix it. I asked if there was anybody who could take me in to Austin. I'd be glad to pay.

"A farmer said that if I was ready to go now, he'd take me. He drove me into Austin, where I asked directions to a boarding house. Once there, I paid a week's rent, which cost $8, and asked the farmer if he'd keep an eye on my plane until I got back in a couple of days. He assured me he would, I paid him, and he left.

"The next morning I explored Austin. It was about a 5-minute walk from the boarding house to the railroad station, where I checked the timetable. There was a train leaving for Brownsville, by the way of San Antonio and Laredo, at 10 PM that night set to arrive in Brownsville at 10 PM the following evening. I wanted to buy a ticket, but didn't dare since I'd been spooked by too many coincidences in which Pinkerton men turned up unexpectedly. So I went back to the boarding house to figure out how to get a railroad ticket without buying it myself.

"While returning I decided to continue my walking tour of Austin. Soon I was at a mule barn called, *Owens Mule Barn—We Buy, Sell, And Trade the Best Mules in Texas.* There was a bench in front of the barn where several old codgers sat whittling with their pocket knives, chewing tobacco, and telling tales.

"One fellow looked to be 20 years younger than anybody else; he was doing most of the talking. He sounded like he might be about half drunk. After several minutes listening to him, he suddenly got up and staggered down the street.

"I said to one of the old men on my left, 'He had an early start didn't he?'

"'Yeah, that's Roy Tillman's boy. He can't put the bottle down. It's ruined him. He lives from one drink to the next. It's a damn pity, too. He comes from a fine family.'

"I said, 'I'm sorry to hear that,' as I got up to follow him. I waited until he turned up an alley out of sight of the men sitting in front of the mule barn. As I approached him, I said, 'Mister Tillman.'

"How do you know my name?"

"It doesn't matter. I've got a job I'd like you to do for me. I'm willing to pay you well.'

"Without as much as 'howdy' or 'go to hell' he said, 'How much?'

"'I'll pay you $100 if you'll do me a favor.'

"'What favor?'

"'I want you to go to the railroad station and buy me three railroad tickets. I want a Pullman compartment. I want one ticket going to El Paso, one ticket going to Brownsville, and one ticket going to Dallas. The name of the person going to Brownsville is Ezra Moon; the person going to El Paso is William Tillman; and the man going to Dallas is John Stogner. I have it written here.'

"I took two $100 bills and tore them in half, handing him two halves. 'What did you do that for?'

"'I'm going to stay right here while you go buy me one railroad ticket. The one to Dallas is going to cost $80, here's your $100 bill. You are going to make three separate trips to the railroad station before you earn your money. Instead of giving you $100 I'm going to give you $200, but you can't spend those two half-hundred dollar bills unless you've got the other half. So when the job is done I will give you the other two halves.'

"In less than an hour I had the three railroad tickets in three different names, to three different destinations, and there was one very happy drunk in Austin, Texas. I figured with that much money, he'd be so drunk the next several days, nobody'd be able to get any intelligent information out of him. But as insurance, I'd purchased a bottle of good whiskey and stayed with him until he passed out. I reminded him to put the money in his shoe before he passed out so nobody'd rob him. I wanted him to stay drunk for several days.

"I waited until just before 10 o'clock that night to go to the railroad station. Walking all around it, I didn't see a single person who remotely resembled a Pinkerton agent, and certainly nobody who paid the slightest attention to me.

"Reassured, I got in my Pullman berth, locked the door, and settled down for a good night's rest. It was around midnight the next night when I got home. Kathy actually seemed glad to see me, and our romance began to blossom again. It was almost like old times.

"On the way down, I had seen several trainloads of cotton. Evidently it grew ready to pick earlier in Texas than in Georgia, and they shipped it from Texas by the trainloads instead of wagonloads. I had no idea how much cotton was in a traincar of cotton, but I was anxious to get in the ginning business. Early the next morning I headed out to see the gin I was shortly going to own."

Showdown

"At the crack of dawn the next morning I was up. I left Kathy peacefully sleeping in our bed. God, she was beautiful. I would have awakened her if I hadn't had far more urgent matters to attend to that morning.

"I went directly to the gin at Mr. Swim's office, where I told him I had the cash and was ready to pay him for the gin. I had already counted out the $190,000 and had it in a paper sack, and set it on his desk.

"He said, 'Let's go to the bank. I'll make you a deed for the gin, and I need to deposit this money. It's a lot to be carrying around.' I assured him it was safe as long as nobody knew he had it.

"On the way to the bank we discussed the transition. He said he had twelve employees he would sure like to be kept on the job. He felt a certain obligation to his employees. I assured him I had no intention of firing anybody as long as they did their jobs.

"His secretary didn't look to be anymore than 23 or 24 years old and was as pretty as a speckled puppy. Her name was Molly Akin. She'd been with him since she was 17 and knew as much or more about the operation of the gin as he did. She knew who the best workers were, who you could depend on and who you couldn't. Swim said if I would take her into my confidence, she'd help me run the gin and it would certainly make money.

"The reason Molly knew so much about the ginning business was that she'd grown up there. Her mother had been Swim's secretary before Molly took over the job when she died. She'd been raised by a widower.

"'She's always been a bit prim and proper around me, but you're a much younger man and she may loosen up a bit. I'll stay with you, advise you, and show you all I know about profitably operating a gin here in south Texas, or I'll go now, whatever you wish. This ginning business is like almost any other—you've got some good customers and you've got some bad customers. You've got some customers who'll want you to give them their cotton before they've paid their ginning fees.

"'We have some general rules under which we operate. One of the things I urge you to do is, keep control of the cotton after you've ginned it. Unless you've thoroughly checked out and established that your customers are creditworthy, make sure you always collect your ginning fees before you release the cotton and seed. Of course that's good business, and I expect you know as much about good business as I do. It doesn't matter how much money you make; if you don't collect it, you are no better off.'

"I couldn't believe how busy the gin was during ginning season. The season usually lasted two and a half months. It was just getting into the first couple of weeks when I bought in, and I worked from sunup till sundown on the books, forcing myself to learn every aspect of the operation. There was one part I really enjoyed; running the presses where we actually compressed the cotton into 500 pound bales.

"When the press was wide open, it held a thousand cubic feet. There was 20 tons of pressure per square inch, and when it was finished, it'd been compacted to 3 x 4 x 5 feet. The top lid on each of the presses was operated by compressed air. There was a trigger mechanism mounted on a pivot at the end of each press. You pushed a lever to the left, it opened the lid, pushed it to the right, it closed the lid, and both the opening and closing were announced by a swish of compressed air.

"I really liked running the presses myself. It gave me a feeling of great power when I felt the building shaking with all the saws and machinery running, and could have 1000 cubic feet of cotton pressed down to just 60 cubic feet by pressing a couple of levers. I could hear the groan of the hydraulics as they closed the press, and I watched the dropping, the bagging and ties, while the sides of the press retracted under the lid and the compressed air whooshed as the lid parted when the ram kicked the finished bale, bagged and tied, onto the floor.

"Once or twice during the day, I would go down and relieve the baler for 20 or 30 minutes just to feel the rumbling of all that power under my feet. I was master of it all.

"The weeks flew by. I was so interested in the gin I even began to go down on Sunday and help oil the moving parts and finish up all the other maintenance work so we'd be ready to gin Monday morning. Kathy began to resent all the time I was spending at the gin, and began to busy herself more and more in her magazines.

"She took out subscriptions to such magazines as *Real Detective*, *True Detective*, *Super Detective*, *True Romances*, and *Modern Romances*. The house was full of magazines. I couldn't understand a girl as bright as Kathy spending all her time on that garbage.

"One night Kathy laid beside my plate a *True Detective* magazine with a picture of G. B. Balls on the front cover. The title of the story was, 'Who Murdered G. B. Balls?' I looked down at the magazine, and then at Kathy. She stared at me in a way she never had before. When I sat down, she stood up.

"'When you have read this, Jesse Robinson, I want you to explain it to me.' She went to the bedroom.

"I opened the magazine to the lead story. It began, 'This reporter has been fascinated by the story of G. B. Balls for the better part of eight months. It is the story of how the most famous detective of modern times managed to get himself murdered, plus some speculation about who and where that murderer might be.

"'The story begins on a spring morning at the plantation of Brother Harmon, a minister in Plowshare, Kentucky. One morning in April a handsome giant of a man knocked on the door of Preacher Harmon's country mansion. The knock was answered by his daughter, Josie Harmon. In reality her name was Josephine, but the tall handsome stranger suggested he would like to call her Josie. Thus began one of the most bizarre tales in modern crime.

"'It was love at first sight for Josie Harmon; Will Cotton did everything he could to make Josie think the feeling was mutual. Will Cotton stayed in the Harmon household from some time in April until the first day of December.

"'In a personal interview with Reverend Harmon by this reporter, Preacher Harmon admitted he knew Will sneaked into Josie's room at night and that they had slept together. He had even spoken to his daughter about the possibility of getting pregnant and disgracing the family name.'

"The story in the magazine laid out all the details from Josie to Balls' murder ending with a personal note to the reader.

"'I intend to follow this case until it is ultimately solved, and hope you will watch for it in future issues of *True Detective*. Mr. T. D. Bronski assures me that the entire resources of the Pinkerton Detective Agency are available to F. G. Goodman in his relentless search to solve this baffling mystery, and I feel confident this case will be solved.'

"When I finished reading the story I went upstairs to the bedroom. Kathy had locked herself in the room. I started beating on the door. There was no response; I could hear her softly crying. I kept banging on the door, begging her to open it, and reminding her that I'd agreed to go back to Chicago to see John Davis and let him see me back when this business first started. It seemed her sobs just grew louder when I said that.

"After several minutes I gave up, went back downstairs, and re-read the story. I had to admit the reporter was very thorough. If all the stories in *True Detective* and these other magazines were as vivid and colorful as this one, I could see why Kathy enjoyed them. Of course I didn't much enjoy reading that particular one.

"Sometime before I finished reading it the second time, Kathy came downstairs, her face puffy and red from crying. She sat down across the table from me with fire in her eyes.

"'Jesse, I want you to leave. I want you to deed me the house, the gin, the car—no, I'll give you the car, take it with you—the bank account, and I want you to leave or else I'll go to the police in Brownsville and swear you're the Jesse Robinson referred to in that detective story.'

"'Kathy, I promised you I'd go back to Chicago with you. We'll see John Davis and he'll put your mind at rest. Why do you have this god-awful obsession that I'm a murderer?'

"'Jesse, the man was found murdered in your hotel room. You did not spend the night in the hotel room. I tried to call that room. When did you check out of the hotel?'

"'I never checked out of the hotel Kathy, I told you then I never checked out of the hotel. I had a business appointment on the lake, remember? It was a little thing; I'd paid a week's rent in advance, and my time was not up. Why should I bother to check out of the hotel? I was eager to get married to you. We were headed south.'

"'But Jesse, why were you so eager?'

"'I liked Chicago fine, but I hated the cold weather. Remember, it snowed that night. I hated the weather. Kathy, dammit, I've never seen you like this. I offered to go back and face John Davis. You said, no, you believed me. There is nothing in that detective magazine you didn't already know, absolutely nothing.'

"'Yes there is, Jesse Robinson. I didn't know that one of the murdered people was found in *your* room.'

"It went back and forth all night. She would cry, I would almost have her convinced that I was not the Jesse Robinson in the story, then she would remember some other detail. It was a nightmarish fight. I never had supper. I never even took off my clothes that night. It came time to go back to the gin, so I said we'd finish the conversation in the evening. We'd work out whatever was necessary to satisfy her I was not G. B. Balls' killer.

"When I got to work that morning, everybody had already begun work; the gin was humming along fine. I had a couch in a little anteroom back behind my office. I told Molly I was going to take a nap, to wake me by noon. I fell into an exhausted sleep.

"At noon Molly awakened me as I had asked, and along about 4 o'clock in the afternoon, when I caught up with my paperwork, I went down to the baling floor and relieved the baler. I told him to go across the street to the boarding house and see whether they still had something to eat; I'd relieve him for 30 or 40 minutes.

"I was toward the back of the building, about to load the last press on the line, when I looked up. There stood a man I knew intuitively was a Pinkerton detective. I was at the foot of the press, and he was standing dead center of the lid.

"'Jesse Robinson, I presume. I am F. G. Goodman of the Pinkerton Detective Agency. I've come to arrest you.'

"Nephew, I already had the bagging and ties in place. I was about to start the baling process, but the cotton had not yet entered the press. Without moving another muscle in my body, I rotated my right toe around and hit the pivot switch to open the lid of the press. In one motion, F. G. Goodman disappeared into the press.

Now I rotated my foot to the right and pushed the 'close' switch. I pulled an overhead cord to open the duct so the cotton could fill the press. I heard a muffled scream as the presses came together making a bale of cotton with Mr. F. G. Goodman as it's core.

"When I opened the press, I kicked the cotton bale and rolled it over twice. There was absolutely no visible evidence it was anything other than an ordinary bale of cotton, except for a barely detectable pink haze on one side of the bale. The compressed air must have coagulated his blood when Mr. Goodman's body burst as the 20-ton-per-square-inch ram made another bale of cotton. I rolled the bale over onto the conveyer belt and watched it disappear toward the dock.

"I continued running the bale presses until the workman returned. He asked me if Mr. Goodman had found me. I told him, no, I didn't know any Mr. Goodman. He said, 'Well, when I started out, he was over behind the wall there. He asked me if I knew where Mr. Robinson was. I pointed back in this direction, and he headed back this way. That's strange.'

"'Well, he obviously knows where to find me. If he can find me once, then he can find me again.'

"I couldn't get Kathy off my mind, and told Molly I was going home for the day, that I hadn't slept too well last night. When I walked into the house, Kathy was sitting at the dining table. On one side of my plate was G. B. Balls' diary; on the other, his pistol.

"'Now, Jesse Robinson, alias Will Cotton, I'm going to do something for you that you never did for the poor souls you murdered. I'm going to give you a fighting chance. Here's paper and pen. You write me a deed to the gin, to the bank account, and to the house, and make it out in the name of Kathy Taylor, my maiden name. Then you get out of this house and out of my life. If you do those things, I'll wait until morning to turn you in to the Pinkertons.'

"Such a towering rage flew over me that I grabbed the pistol, aimed it between her eyes, and pulled the trigger; it clicked. I pulled it again and again and again. The bitch had emptied the gun of ammunition.

"'The hired man's in the dining room with a twelve gage shotgun. All I've got to do is scream, and he'll walk out and blow you

half in two. Jesse Robinson, you do what I tell you or I won't give
you till morning to get out of Brownsville. Remember this, Jesse,
wherever you go, you're going to be hounded because I'm going to
give them a good description of you, and it serves you right. I just
wish I had a photograph. One last thing before you walk out that
door, I wouldn't give you this chance if I weren't carrying your
child, you son-of-a-bitch.'

"I picked up the pistol and the diary, walked off, and got into
the Model-T without uttering a word, knowing I was leaving the
only home I'd ever owned.

"I was furious, and tried to think what I could do. I thought of
waiting until after dark, slipping back in, and killing the bitch, but
I was sure, as many detective stories as she'd read, she had a letter
stashed away in that house, or maybe she'd given one to the maid,
so I felt I'd best use the time she'd promised to get as far away from
Brownsville as I could."

Flight

Just as Uncle Will finished telling me how Kathy'd ordered him out of the house, the nurse came in. "Mr. Will, you've exerted yourself enough. It's about ten minutes till visiting hours are over; I do believe you've talked long enough. You're still a very sick man."

I'd been to the hospital so much the nurse knew me by first name. "Gene, you're gonna have to run along now. You can come back and see him tomorrow night."

I was in a state of shock as I left the hospital. I couldn't believe Uncle Will would've tried to kill that sweet, pretty woman he loved so much. I decided this whole business of listening to his confession, even though I loved Uncle Will, was surely gonna make me sick. I never knew what to expect, and had very little faith that all this truth-telling was going to do anybody any good. I wouldn't want even God to know I'd done some of the things he did.

Before going back the next day, I made up my mind I was gonna talk to my ol' Pa about how I didn't understand this confession and repenting business. I wasn't sure you could repent and confess sins like he told me; I'd never dreamed of folks doing things like that. And even though it was a heavy burden for me to tote, I could tell by looking at Uncle Will he was about spent, and it was going to break his heart if I didn't hear out all his tales. Still it was hard.

When I got home, the light was still on, and Ma was sitting up fretting. One of our cows was giving birth, and was having a hard time. Pa was down behind the barn trying to help. Ma wanted to know what in hell had taken me so long getting home when visiting hours ended at 9 PM. I should have been back in 15 minutes.

"Ma, I didn't drive fast 'cause I thought ya'll would be in bed."

"Well young man, your Pa needs you. Get down there and help him. He's probably gonna lose that cow and we won't have enough milk. We'll right likely starve to death."

I changed out of my good clothes and went down to the barn. Pa had an old lantern for light. The cow was doing her best to

261

calve. It looked like a big un'. Already his head and two front feet were out, but it looked like a perfectly normal birth the best I could see by the old kerosene lantern. I asked Pa, "Is everything alright?"

"Yeah, I just wanted to make sure."

"Has the cow had any trouble?"

"No, no trouble at all."

"Well Ma said we was gonna lose the cow because she was having great trouble giving birth to the calf and wanted me to come help you."

"Aw, you know how excitable your Ma is. She's always looking at the dreary side of everything. You're nearly 18 years old; looks like you'd be used to that by now. She's always exaggerated the worse part of everything. I don't see why you let her get under your skin the way she does. You know how she is."

"Sometimes I can't help it. I wanted to talk to you about some things anyway. I'm glad there ain't nothing wrong. If a man does something really bad, does he have to confess it before the good Lord will forgive him?"

"That's what the Bible says, son."

"What if they've done something really, really bad? I mean like kill more than one person, try to kill people they love. Can they get forgiven for that?

"I suppose so, son. The Bible says if you ask the Lord to forgive you, He will—if you'll repent of those sins. I guess it don't matter how bad your sin is, if you confess it, then the Lord has got the power to forgive you. Sometimes that don't hardly seem right. Some folks are so low-down mean, it looks like they ought to burn in hell for a little while, but that ain't what the Book says. The Book says if they confess, and repent, the Lord will forgive them. I guess the Lord is some how bigger than all our understanding."

"Well ain't there no rules about who to confess to? It looks like there ought to be a preacher or somebody."

"Naw son, the way I read the Bible, it says every tongue will confess. It just says confess and repent. I think it's somewhere in Ecclesiastes. 'The first man knew him not perfectly, neither shall the last one find him out.' I think that means God's beyond our understanding. That's what it means to me, anyway."

About that time the old cow groaned, and the calf slid out over its shoulders. Pa looked at it and said, "About one more good push like that, Daisy, and you'll be all done with this."

He turned his attention back to me. "Your Uncle Will must be telling you some pretty awful stuff. I don't have any idea what, but if you want to listen to him, it's alright. I guess as far as the Bible is concerned, it don't make any difference who he confesses to.

"Will's hinted to me from time to time about some of the things he did. But he never just come right out and confess anything terrible, exceptin' he let me know he'd killed some folks. But what he's telling you may be good for you, son. I'd go ahead and listen if he wants to tell his sins because at least he's gonna show you what not to do. Will's pretty near harmless now. As a matter of fact, with that bad asthma of his, I'm surprised he's lasted this long.

"You go there and listen to what he's got to say 'cause at least you might give him some peace in his last days. Exceptin' he may get over this. They're making new medicines all the time now, and I've been hearing on the radio how they've got a right nigh miracle drug called penicillin, though I don't think nobody but the Army has it. So Will may last on a bit longer. You're doing right to listen like he asked you. I don't know why he picked you, save but he's always been sort of partial to you.

"You remember he made me mad one night, taking you out in the dark you was so afeared of, helping you bring in that stovewood. I guess that's why you think so much of him. Of course, he's done other things for you, I know. He let you ride that old Harley-Davidson motorcycle, and that was a lot of fun. So, you go ahead and listen to his story—you might make his last days easier."

About that time the old cow gave another mighty push and out popped the rest of the calf. She jumped up and started licking the birth sack off him; in three or four minutes, he had staggered to his feet, found her udder, and hunched down to suck. Pa said, "Son, he'll be alright, I'll see you in the morning."

I went to bed so I could go to that hateful General Shoe factory and see my Julie at lunch time. I was thinking seriously about quitting the job. I could hardly stand seeing that pretty little thing now that she wouldn't even speak to me. It was torture.

But that night I was right back up to the Bremen Hospital again, and Uncle Will continued his story.

"I was in total panic, couldn't decide what to do," Will began. "Then I remembered there were some shrimp boats around a dock down at the mouth of the Rio Grande. I headed there.

"I parked the car well away from the docks and walked the re-maining distance out on a long pier. There was a shrimper casting off, and I still had my money belt with approximately $140,000 on, though I didn't know for sure how much. My wallet had twelve $100 bills, and I still had the suitcase with one change of clothes, and Balls' diary and pistol. The shrimper's crew had just tossed off the last line when I jumped aboard the boat. The captain came over and encouraged me to jump back to shore. 'It's going to be a long swim if you stay aboard this boat,' he said.

"'Captain, I need to leave Brownsville and I am in a hurry. I am willing to pay you a good price if you'll take me to Corpus Christi.'

"'What would you call a good price, sir?'

"'I don't know, you tell me.'

"'I'll take you to Corpus Christi for $500.'

"'When will we be there?'

"'We should be there by midday tomorrow if the winds are good. For $600 I'll guarantee we will be there by noon tomorrow; I've got a 60-horse diesel on this boat.'

"'You've got your $600.'

"I took my wallet out and gave him $300. "I'll pay the balance when we arrive in Corpus Christi.'

"I hadn't seen anyone, Pinkerton or not, showing the slightest interest in somebody jumping onto this little ol' shrimp boat just as it pulled way from the pier. I had no intention of sleeping that night, 'cause I had no desire to have my throat slit. So I lay down in the middle of the ship with my suitcase for a pillow, though my best insurance was nobody knew how much money I had.

"I was up and around the deck the next morning at dawn's whitenin'. The captain told me if his instruments were right, we'd be in Corpus Christi before 8 AM, which pleased me very much.

"The moment the boat was alongside the pier in Corpus Christi, I jumped off, walked a good distance inland, and hired the first carriage I could find, telling the driver I wanted to go downtown. While riding along, I noticed a sign on one of the side streets that said, 'Harley-Davidson Motorcycles—Authorized Sales & Service.' I asked the driver to take me there.

"In the showroom was the wickedest looking motorcycle with a sidecar I'd seen in all my life. As I walked around it, admiring the powerful vehicle, a salesman came up, and I asked, 'How much for that lovely machine?'

"'$1795,' was his reply.

"'Make the bill of sale out to Roddy Miles,' I told him, 'and I'll be on my way.'

"Besides the sidecar, the Harley had a rack behind the seat where you could set a suitcase, plus a smaller rack that held two 3-gallon reserve gas tanks. I might have been able to go a 1000 miles with all that gasoline afore having to fill up.

"After the bill of sale was done, I pulled out of the showroom on the Harley and asked the first guy I saw the way north. He pointed in the direction I was going. A short time later I came to a general merchandise store with a gas pump out front where I filled up the two spare cans. There was a cantankerous old gent who pumped gas for me. He asked me where I was going. I told him north. He said, 'How fer?'

"'I don't know. I may just try to find the end of that road. Do you know where it goes?'

"'Naw, I don't rightly know, I know it goes to Victoria. My wife had an uncle once who lived in Victoria. When he died, she had me to load our stuff up on a one-horse wagon and we went up there to claim her fortune. The only trouble was there wasn't no fortune when we got there. He was a lying old son-of-a-bitch. He'd get drunk, come down here and tell her wild tales about him owning a big department store up in Victoria. We got there three days later and they had done buried him in a pauper's grave. He wasn't nothing but a common ordinary drunk.

"'Young fella, if you're going to Victoria I hope you got a gun.'

"I had Balls' gun, but I told him I didn't have one.

"'I got a good shotgun I'll sell you for a $100 and I'll throw in the handmade leather case. If you're goin' to Victoria, you'll find out them damn Mexicans done took over the town. They'll slit your tongue and run your leg through it fer $10.'

"I asked him why on earth would they want to do a thing like that. He said, 'Just for pure damn meanness, pure damn meanness.'

"I didn't intend to stay in Victoria or nowhere else for long. I just wanted to get away from Corpus Christi to a place where the Pinkertons wouldn't find me. Having a shotgun didn't seem like a bad idea, so I went inside and looked at his gun. It was a sleek thing, a double-barrel twelve-gage shotgun. I bought it and four boxes of shells, along with some crackers, cheese, and potted meat.

"Pulling out of Corpus Christi, I headed north toward Victoria. The roads were a shade sandy, but I could run 45 to 50 miles an hour on the Harley, like floating on air. When I got to Victoria, I was a bit disappointed since I didn't see anybody or anything that looked of any least interest whatsoever. So I just kept going until, at about 6 o'clock in the evening, I came to a place called Bryan. I decided to find a boarding house and spend the night, staying clear of hotels and railroad cars—it seemed like every time I got near one of 'em, a Pinkerton detective showed up.

"At the boarding house, I paid a week's room and board, and sat down to their supper. There were three or four other people who didn't say much to each other. Nobody seemed particularly ill-at-ease, but nobody did any talking. One fellow I judged to be as tall as I was asked me where I was from. I told him that I lived the past several years of my life in North Carolina, but I was originally from Georgia, hoping my speech wouldn't raise any suspicions.

"There are some people who can listen to you talk a bit and then tell you where you came from, where you stayed, and how long. I've met people with an uncanny knowledge of accents who could almost tell you the town you came from in any state.

"Anyway, the other boarder's question sent a little shiver of fear down my back. The fellow looked at me like he didn't believe what I was saying, but he didn't say anything. I didn't want to attract too much attention to myself, but sometimes saying nothing attracts more attention than talking a little. To show him that I was friendly I asked him if he knew where a fellow might buy a bottle. He was very helpful, told me exactly where I could get anything I wanted to drink. I thanked him, finished my meal, and left the table as quickly as I could.

"On the way to the liquor store, I passed a drugstore. For no reason at all I went in, there in front of me was a rack of magazines. There must have been four or five copies of *True Detective* that had the story of G. B. Balls' murder, the one Kathy had let me read. I picked it up and flipped through the pages. I put it down and looked around for a newspaper. Not seeing one, I asked the clerk if there was a daily newspaper in Bryan. He said there wasn't, but they got a paper once a week from Austin. They usually got the Sunday paper on Monday, and it was usually sold out Tuesday or Wednesday. They wouldn't have another until next Monday.

"I went on to the liquor store, got myself a bottle, and took it back to the boarding house, where I poured myself a couple of pretty stiff drinks. It was too early for bed, so I went into the living room to find something to read. There was a community living room where everybody congregated to read or to sit and talk. There were three or four easy chairs and a couple of settees scattered around. A table between the two settees had a bunch of books and magazines. On the very top was another damn copy of *True Detective*. One of the men was reading another copy of the issue with the story of G. B. Balls' murder. I picked up the one laying on the table, settled in alongside him, and remarked that this must be a very popular magazine since they had two copies in one boarding house.

"'This is my own copy. I've been taking it for years. That one belongs to the boarding house. I've been reading detectives since I was just a kid. Are you a fan of detective magazines?'

"'No,' I told him, 'not particularly. I read 'em every once in a while.'

"'Well, if you're going to start reading them, this *True Detective* has the best stories in it and the best writers. Everything they put in the *True Detective* is true. Some of these others make up stories. But if you read it in *True Detective*, it's the truth.

"'Here's the story of how G. B. Balls got himself killed. There has been eight or ten stories in *True Detective* magazine about that one detective. He was plenty smart. The fellow who killed him has also got to be one smart son-of-a-bitch. But you better believe the Pinkertons will catch him. There are too many of them.

"'I read the other day where no single city in the whole United States had as many policemen working for them as the Pinkerton Detective Agency. Do you know there ain't no one man gonna manage to stay hid with that many people looking for him? Especially a big tall son-of-a-bitch like he is.'

"'You've read some of Balls' other cases?'

"'I've read every detective story that's been in this magazine for years. I'd guess there's been ten or twelve stories in *True Detective* where Balls solved the case. He was a hell of a detective.'

"'What do you suppose happened in this particular case?'

"'I'm an amateur. I don't know anything about detective work, I just like to read the stories. But I think Balls sent that first fellow who got killed. You know the one that was killed in room 302 in the Ingram Hotel? Oh! Have you read the story?'

"'No, I haven't read the story,' I lied.

"'Well, two people got killed. A fellow, the same size as Balls, one of Balls' stool pigeons. He got killed in room 302 in the Ingram Hotel in Chicago. All of this happened in Chicago, you know. What I think happened, Balls called Jesse Robinson. It don't say so here in the story, but I think he called Jesse Robinson and told him he wanted to come over and talk to him and see if they could work out a deal, maybe divide the money up.

"'I think Balls wanted to see if Jesse Robinson would try to bribe him. You see the banker knew—oh, you haven't read the story. Anyway there was a banker, it's a long story and I won't take up much of your time, but this banker met both of the men and talked to both of them. Both of them knew about the other.

"'I think Balls called him and told him he was coming over, that he wanted to make a deal, and they would split that money Jesse Robinson stole from that bank in Kentucky. Then Balls sent the other fellow, a stool pigeon, over thinking just what happened would happen, Robinson would kill the man he thought was Balls.

"'Then the plan went haywire. I'm thinking Balls got a little too smart for his britches. He let his stool-pigeon have a key to his hotel room. Mind you the story don't say this, but I think he let his stool pigeon have a key with the hotel name and room number on it. Robinson got there before Balls thought he would. Somehow Robinson got the drop on Balls and killed him. If I was a betting man, I'd bet you right now they'll catch Robinson, or whoever he is, and they'll hang him before six months is up. Because he's got them Pinkerton folks madder than hell.'

"'Is it okay if I take this magazine to my room?'

"'Sure, that's what they got them for. You read it and tomorrow night we'll talk about the story. See ya around.'

"I got back to my room and read that magazine from cover to cover before I fell asleep. During the night I dreamed about Balls, and about F. G. Goodman being squeezed in that press till he exploded like a bomb. I saw that bale of cotton go rolling by on the conveyor belt with it's tiny pink spot. I wondered if Goodman would be missed, if they'd try to find him, if anybody'd ever opened that bale of cotton. All night I dreamed of this, and for the first time I dreamed about poor Josie being wrapped around that tree.

"I woke up at 4 AM and finished off the bottle, which knocked me out until 10 the next morning, when it was too late to get any breakfast. Even though I'd paid a week's rent, I decided I better be moving on, so I got on my Harley and headed out.

"All morning long, I rode north. I felt depressed. My life was coming unraveled, and my depression was just that much deeper as a result of the conversation I'd had the night before. That fellow'd been so damn sure I'd be caught and dead in six months. I was beginning to feel pressed from all sides. Every two or three hours I'd come to a little town. I'd look to see if they had a drugstore, and if they did, I'd go in and see if they had any magazines. Every one of them had magazines; and every one of them had *True Detective*. God was I glad they didn't have a picture of me.

"Just before sundown, I made it into Texarkana, Texas, where I found an out-of-the-way boarding house and paid a week's room and board. Once again I found a copy of *True Detective* and started flipping through it. Suddenly I noticed somebody staring intently at me. A little red-headed, freckle-faced kid. He said, 'Mr., you gonna buy that magazine?'

"'I don't know, why?'

"'Well there is a damn good story about G. B. Balls in there. He was one hell of a detective.'

"'Never heard of him.'

"'You must not read many detective magazines.'

"'No, can't rightly say I ever did.'

"'Well that's Balls' picture right there on the front of the magazine. He captured 58 criminals, but the 59th got him. There is something strange. I don't know what it is, but this is the first story I ever read in *True Detective* magazine that hasn't been solved. I've got a feeling they wrote this story hoping somebody would know this fellow, Jesse Robinson, and turn him in. I wouldn't be a bit surprised if the Pinkertons didn't put this fellow up to writing it unfinished to get people looking for Jesse Robinson. The only thing I don't understand is why they didn't put his picture in there, unless they ain't got none. Jesse Robinson'd better hope they ain't.'

"The kid reached down and picked up an October copy of *Super Detective*, took it to the counter, paid for it, and waved to me as he walked out the door. I bought the copy of *True Detective* magazine. I passed a bar on the way back to the boarding house and went in for a shot of straight bourbon. Then I bought a whole bottle, went back to my room, got drunk, and passed out.

"Sometime during the night I heard that low muffled scream of F. G. Goodman as his body exploded. I sat up in bed in a cold sweat with a god-awful headache. I'd bought a quart of whiskey. I had to finish drinking the rest of it before I could get back to sleep.

"Along about 10 o'clock the next morning, I decided I'd stretch my legs, walk around town, and try to get rid of the hangover. Eventually, I wandered by the same drugstore where I'd been the night before. Near the front door was a stack of newspapers with the headline, 'Brownsville Businessman Murder Suspect.' I picked up a copy and carried it to a corner table. The waitress was there immediately; I ordered a cup of coffee. She noticed the headline and acted as if she had already read the story. Her comment as she departed with my order was, 'You never can tell, can you?'

"I suppose she meant you don't expect a businessman to be a murderer. I couldn't wait to get into the story.

"'One of the most bizarre stories of modern times,' it began, 'A young housewife walked into the Pinkerton Detective Agency in Brownsville yesterday morning and informed the detective in charge that her husband was the murderer of their ace detective, G. B. Balls. He had fled the night before. She said she'd like to give a description and hoped they brought him to justice for the terrible crimes he'd committed.

"'At first the detective was very skeptical of the lady's story, until she began to answer questions about events that happened in Chicago over ten months earlier. She was able to answer all the questions posed by the Pinkerton agents to their satisfaction, indicating she had very probably been in Chicago with the suspect, whom she later married, at the time of G. B. Balls' murder.

"'The Pinkertons are convinced that Jesse Robinson, alias Will Cotton, is the murderer of both G. B. Balls, and one of his stool pigeons. They now believe he also murdered a Pinkerton detective who was trying to apprehend him while Robinson was posing as a hobo by throwing the agent from a train as it crossed the Mississippi River near Baton Rouge.

"'Robinson is also a suspect in the disappearance of another Pinkerton detective, F. G. Goodman. Neither the detective, who disappeared near Baton Rouge, nor Goodman's body has been found, but foul play is suspected because Goodman disappeared the same day Jesse Robinson left Brownsville.

"'It is admitted by the Brownsville Pinkerton office that they have no actual proof Jesse Robinson is responsible for foul play in connection with Goodman, but Robinson has turned out to be such a slippery, unpredictable criminal, they are willing to believe so. The Pinkertons are calling reinforcements to Brownsville, hoping to piece together his actions the afternoon Goodman disappeared.

"'Detective Goodman is officially listed as missing, although many fear he, too, may have been murdered. The Pinkerton Agency has been overwhelmed with tips from people who saw this six-foot-six giant exiting Brownsville by various avenues. One witness swore he saw him jump on a boat as it left the Brownsville pier a short time before dark.

"'The Pinkerton Agency discounts that witness because they believe Jesse Robinson is too cautious to do anything on the spur of the moment. Careful planning has kept him at least one step ahead of the Pinkertons since he murdered G. B. Balls.

"'The Pinkerton Agency refused to confirm that one major piece of the puzzle still missing is the diary they believe G. B. Balls had with him when he was killed. Kathy Robinson admitted to reading that diary, but no longer has it in her possession. Her fugitive husband may have taken it with him once she told him she was going to turn him in.

"'Mrs. Robinson gave the best physical description the Pinkertons have ever had for Jesse Robinson. He stands 6-ft 6-in. tall and weighs 190 pounds, which gives him a rather slender appearance; he has clean-cut features. Many women believe he is handsome. He has light brown hair, is clean-shaven, and a neat dresser.

"'At press time, the Associated Press, the Pinkerton Agency, and all the Brownsville hotels are expecting an influx of reporters, detectives, and even gawking spectators for what may shape up as the biggest manhunt in the history of this southeastern Texas town.

"'Anybody with any information that might lead to the capture of Jesse Robinson, alias Will Cotton, is urged to get in touch with local authorities. Special telegraph lines will transmit reports to the Pinkertons in Brownsville almost instantly.

"'The local agent for the Pinkertons stated the manhunt will be directed from the Pinkertons home office in St. Louis, Missouri. This reporter has a feeling that Jesse Robinson, alias Will Cotton, will shortly be run to ground.'

"I was startled when I raised my head. The waitress was standing there staring at me. I'd been so engrossed in the paper I hadn't noticed her approach. She smiled sweetly and asked, 'Refill, sir?' I shoved my cup toward her and quickly folded the paper as she said, 'That story sounds like he's a slippery son-of-a-gun doesn't it? I don't see how a fellow that big could hide, do you?'

"I answered sheepishly, 'No, he'd sure stand out in a crowd.' She couldn't possibly know how much I felt I stood out in a crowd. I felt trapped. Kathy had given them a perfect description.

"I immediately thought about growing a beard as a disguise. Since not too many young men grew beards, I didn't know whether that was a good idea or not. I decided maybe I ought to hang around Texarkana a few days, read the newspaper, and follow the manhunt, at least to see if there were any new developments. This was only the third, fourth, or fifth day since I'd left Brownsville. I'd lost count and so didn't know for sure.

"I decided it was best for me to stay away from everybody. I felt exposed. I felt that everybody was looking at me. It was a terrible feeling, Nephew, a terrible feeling.

"About mid-afternoon I fell asleep reading crime stories and started dreaming. I dreamed I was a great bird flying around, high over the earth. Suddenly the earth started smoking and split open. I was sucked down into the huge crevice that opened below me and then the walls closed up again, trapping me.

"As the edges of the abyss pulled back together, my body felt crushed, and I was suffocating. I screamed in horror, and awoke shaking. At least, I thought I had been screaming, and could almost still hear the echo in the room. I wondered if anybody else had heard me, and had no desire to go to sleep again.

"Later I went down for supper. There were eight other boarders around the table. Nobody paid me any particular attention, and nobody mentioned noises coming from my room, so I supposed I was wrong about the screaming. But I felt so exposed, almost as if everybody there knew who I was, and knew what I had done.

"I didn't sleep a whole lot that night. My mind drifted back to Josie and how truly sweet she was, even though horrendously ugly. She surely hadn't deserved to be treated the way I treated her. Chicago then drifted in. I knew I could have run from G. B. Balls. I didn't really have to kill him or his associate. If I hadn't done that, I wouldn't have had to kill the fellow in Baton Rouge. And none of it would have happened if it hadn't been for my greed.

"It's amazing how greed itself causes you to break every commandment. Even though it's been close to 40 years since all this happened, that night, lying in bed, unable to sleep, I dreamed about Ma and Pa—what they'd think if they knowed what I done. It was just about more than I could bear. I walked the floor all night, afraid to go to sleep, afraid I'd start that infernal dreaming again.

"It must have been close to daylight when I finally fell asleep. I slept till nearly 10 o'clock. Breakfast had already been served at the boarding house. Again I couldn't get nothing to eat, I went back to the drugstore. Not having shaved the night before, my beard was already popping out; I was amazed. It was salt and pepper, I thought maybe it would make me look a good deal older. Maybe I really ought to grow a beard. Examining the hair at my temples, here too I could see a sprinkling of gray hairs.

"I picked up another newspaper: 'Balls' Murderer Escapes on a Motorcycle with a Sidecar.' Pure fear stabbed my chest as I sat down and started to read even before the waitress got to my table.

"'A Harley-Davidson dealer in Corpus Christi says he sold a motorcycle with a sidecar to a person who perfectly fits the description Kathy Robinson gave the Pinkerton Detective Agency of her husband, Jesse Robinson. All citizens are urged to look out for a man six-feet six-inches tall in his early 30s, clean-shaven, and riding a Harley-Davidson motorcycle with a sidecar.'

"I looked around the drugstore. There were 15 or 20 people there, and it looked like every one of them was staring directly at me. It appeared the Pinkertons were trying to raise the interest of everybody in the whole country to help them catch me.

"I needed to get farther away from Brownsville. Even though I'd spent almost three days traveling, I was still on the border of Texas. I had to get away from Texarkana too. I went by a dry goods store, bought myself a sleeping bag with a couple of extra blankets, a skillet, some pots and pans, enough personal items to stay clean, and another small canvas suitcase, put them all on the Harley, and pulled out from Texarkana.

"In those days there weren't many maps worth anything. If you went more'n 50 miles, you had to get another map, and they were totally unreliable. Basically, you just got on a road in the direction you wanted to go, and headed off. So I went off on a road headed east and rode for two or three hours with my camping equipment. I felt like I needed to go into the woods somewhere up in the mountains and stay away from civilization for a while.

"I wound up in a little place called Waldo, Arkansas. There were two general stores; both had gas pumps. I asked about newspapers; they didn't get any big city papers in Waldo, only the *Magnolia Arkansas Gazette*, which was printed once a week. One of the oldtimers said, 'If you want to go to bed with nothing on your mind, just read the *Magnolia Arkansas Gazette* and you'll sleep well.'

"This was the kind of backwoods place I was looking for. There were plenty of woods nearby, so I pulled off on an old logging trail just outside of town and headed up into the hills.

"I found a swift-running trout steam and built a lean-to on its banks. I had a dry place to stay if it came a storm. I was fishing before 3 o'clock in the afternoon; in less than 15 minutes I'd caught a mess of fish. I fried them in my new pan and breathed the fresh Arkansas air. By dark I had cleaned up all my camping equipment, and was snuggled down in my sleeping bag. Listening to the gurgling of the trout steam, I had a better night's rest than for months.

"The next morning, I picked up my shotgun and went for a walk. I thought I might shoot a squirrel or a rabbit, and hadn't gone 200 yards before I jumped a cottontail and dropped him. Returning to my lean-to, I washed the rabbit in the creek, ran a spit through him, and put him on to barbecue, though I'd had breakfast no more than two hours earlier. I realized I needed to stay in the woods at least three weeks to get a good growth of beard, and decided I might as well get in practice cooking for myself. I thought I had plenty of rations to last me as long as I wanted to stay in the woods.

"After three or four days, I got bored around my little camp. In the afternoons late I'd crank up the Harley, go out to the main road, and ride up and down. One day I even ventured into Magnolia, where there were a couple of drugstores. I looked at the magazine racks in both and both had copies of *True Detective* with Balls' picture on the front. I had gotten to where I was sick of seeing that picture, and was sure everybody around was staring at me, knowing that I was the one who had done that terrible deed.

"I spent a lot of time waiting in the Arkansas woods for my beard to grow. I kept thinking of the four people I had killed so far, all because of my greed. My wanting something and not being willing to work for it. Nephew, I wonder when it comes my time to stand before the Almighty to be judged, no matter how much I prayed or how many times I confessed, I wonder if each murder was a separate sin. Anyway, I don't really think killing in self-defense is murder. Even though my life wasn't in immediate danger, anyone of those four people could've put it in danger at any moment. So, in effect, my killings were all self-defense. I know this may sound like I'm trying to get out of my responsibilities, but I'm not. I'm just more or less explaining to you my state of mind.

"I was pretty sure nobody had a photograph of me. But let me tell you how far-fetched my wandering mind got. You remember when Balls told me about the artist in Evansville, Indiana? Well I even thought about going back to find that boy and kill him. He was the only fellow alive I knew for sure could put a face on Jesse Robinson. I became obsessed with going back to Evansville, finding L. B. Pecker, and blowing his brains out.

"If the reporter who wrote the story about Balls was as thorough as the story led you to believe, wouldn't he try to backtrack and find those boys at the Evansville hotel? And wouldn't he find L. B. Pecker? That would mean I'd have to kill the reporter too.

"I was already feeling bad enough about the people I had killed and worrying about the description they had out on me and my motorcycle. I needed to get rid of that motorcycle. I wasn't sure I was done killing. All of this started when I heard them hobos telling about a rich man who had an ugly daughter.

"When I was in the drugstore, there was a stack of newspapers lying there. It had been four or five days since I'd seen one. The headlines read, 'Gruesome Discovery in Bale of Cotton.' I grabbed the newspaper with trembling hands: 'Ace Pinkerton detective's body discovered crushed in a bale of cotton on the docks of Jesse Robinson's cotton gin in Brownsville, Texas.'

"'This tale of murder grows more bizarre as the days go by. A search party of Pinkerton detectives and Brownsville authorities were about ready to give up the search for the body of F. G. Goodman when one of the detectives noticed a pink stain on the open side of a bale of cotton. When he took his knife and cut into the cotton, the stain got redder as it got deeper.

"'They cut the bagging and ties off of the cotton, began pulling the cotton loose, and there inside were the crushed remains of F. G. Goodman. When the bale was finally pulled apart, the remains were spread out before us as an unrecognizable mass of flesh, hair, skin, and bones. Such a gruesome sight this reporter has never before seen. One veteran detective cried like a baby, saying, 'My God. Hell can't burn hot enough for the scoundrel who did this.'

"'The finding of F. G. Goodman's body only strengthens the Pinkerton Agency's resolve to capture Jesse Robinson and bring him to justice. It also strengthens their belief that a fourth person believed killed by Jesse Robinson may be floating somewhere in the Mississippi River, if it's not already out to sea.

"'In Brownsville this morning, T. D. Bronski, Superintendent of Detectives, affirms the Pinkerton Agency will turn heaven and earth upside down to find the butcher who perpetrated these un-speakable crimes. The last reported sighting of someone believed to be Jesse Robinson, alias Will Cotton, was seen headed north out of Corpus Christi. A storekeeper who remembered a man very much fitting Jesse Robinson's description was questioned by the Pinkerton Agency in Corpus Christi. He stated the suspect was at that time going to Victoria, Texas.'

"I breathed a little sigh of relief that I had turned east before I got out of Texas. At least from what the paper stated, they'd be searching for me farther north. I must be momentarily safe here in Arkansas.

"I bought the newspaper, and some more magazines, and went back to my camp, afeared that every human I met knew who I was and what I had done."

S. S. Sorrell

"When I got back, I was so shaken by the events in Magnolia I decided to break camp. I put all my equipment in the sidecar and headed east. I needed to get farther away from Brownsville. I rode all day long through Arkansas, finally coming to a tiny town called McMilan Corner. It was so small there wasn't even a drugstore, but there was a general merchandise store that sold magazines.

"I went in, and much to my relief, did not see one *True Detective*, one *Super Detective*, or even a newspaper lying around. I thought, 'Thank God! I'm so far back in the sticks now they have to pump in sunshine. Surely they've never heard of G. B. Balls.' The man at the cash register eyed me over from head to toe. I was beginning to look rather woolly, with my beard now about three or four inches long. I kept it trimmed, trying to present a neat appearance so's not to attract any more attention than necessary.

"'You are not from these parts are you, son?'

"'No, sir, I'm from Georgia. I'm just passing through on my way home. I've been up in Oregon for the past summer.'

"He looked out the window, didn't see how I was traveling. I had parked the motorcycle at the corner of the store. I didn't want to be associated with a motorcycle and sidecar no more than I had to be, but it was a bit self-defeating since he'd asked he how I was traveling anyway. I told him I had a motorcycle at the corner of the building. I didn't mention the sidecar and hopefully he wouldn't see it before I got out of there.

"I bought some supplies I needed, and asked a few questions about my way home, though I had no intentions of going on to Georgia. I wanted to camp out a while longer and let this G. B. Balls thing die down. I asked him how far I was from the Mississippi River.

"'Not more than ten miles son.'

"I took the road east, but it ended rather abruptly. There was a road that turned north and another that turned south. The sign pointing south said, 'Leland, Mississippi.' The sign pointing north

278

said, 'Arkansas City,' and by the side of it, 'Ferry.' I took that to mean there must not be a ferry at Leland. I had no intentions of crossing the Mississippi River, but still I headed north toward Arkansas City. Shortly I was traveling through some rather dense hardwood trees.

"I pulled off onto an old logging road and followed it right to the end. The road came out overlooking the Mississippi, which must have been a good mile wide at that point. I'd estimate the bank was some 20 feet above the water. I sat down for a while, cogitated my predicament, then got back on the motorcycle, and started looking around for a place to build my camp.

"Riding back for about a half a mile, I soon found another logging road that turned off to the right. I went up that road, and shortly was on the banks of a little creek. By the time I'd found where I wanted to camp, it was dark, too dark to build a lean-to. So hoping it wouldn't rain, I crawled into my sleeping bag.

"The next morning I was up before the rooster. First I built myself a lean-to and then explored my surroundings. The forest was rather lush and I couldn't see where they'd cut many trees. I wondered why the logging roads were in such good shape, with no evidence that any lumber'd been cut out.

"I drove up and down the main road to see how close anybody lived. From the place I'd picked to camp, it was at least two miles to the first sign of any human dwelling. Tucked way back in woods the way I was, I felt relatively safe—after all, the nearest town didn't have any *True Detective* magazines or any newspapers with headlines screaming about the search for Jesse Robinson.

"The lazy days of late autumn and early winter seemed to melt together. I'd spend my days reading, and I went through Balls' diary from cover to cover several times. With every reading I discovered more and more about his thinking. It seemed to me he was one of the most thorough, meticulous people who'd ever lived; he had the uncanny knack of thinking of everything.

"I suppose I'd have been terrified had I known that somebody as bright and thorough as he was chasing me when I was in Chicago. I realized with each reading that I was alive more as a result of dumb, blind luck than of any brilliance of mine.

"Whenever he finished his diary each day, Balls had a habit of writing a little paragraph summarizing the action he expected his opponent, me, to take. It was uncanny, generally speaking, how accurate his foresight had been. He'd even predicted I would get the best of his stool pigeon. In reading his diary, I learned for the first time the man's name had been Jim Tarpley.

"I settled into a rather predictable routine, simply doing nothing but killing time and hoping the Balls' investigation would die down. Occasionally, I'd hear a hunter's shotgun, but I had absolutely no contact with people for a period of time I suspected was close to two weeks. Every morning I'd get up and build a fire, cook some fish, or kill a rabbit or squirrel, and then barbecue it or perhaps eat some of the canned goods I had bought.

"After I'd read everything I had two or three times, I grew bored. So I began to crank up the Harley, drive down the logging road to the bluff above the Mississippi, and sit for long periods of time thinking about how I'd gotten in the pickle I was in, how I would change it if I ever got away, and more and more longing to go back home. I wanted to go back near my family, buy a little farm, and escape the life I'd fallen into. I had enough money that it should be no problem as long as I lived. So I began to envision a little place on the Tallapoosa River with a house tucked close to the riverbank where I could go and spend the rest of my days. I'd grow a little cotton, a little corn, feed myself, and maybe find a good woman and settle down. No more of this wild stuff I'd been through.

"So a great feeling of homesickness and melancholy descended on me, as well as a deep depression. I was restless at night, and my dreams were of all the people I had murdered. Ol' Ebo was visiting me regularly.

"The last time I'd read Balls' diary, I decided to burn it. The book had held a fascination for me. I'd read and enjoyed every word he wrote. His brilliant and cunning mind was so well expressed the hair'd stand up on the back of my neck as I read some of the passages he wrote about me, especially the uncannily accurate understanding of my personality he'd developed in the short time he chased me. So I laid it on the ground, turned up a couple of pages, and struck a match. But I couldn't put the match to the paper.

"I also couldn't afford to leave the diary laying around the lean-to. If a hunter found it along with the newspapers, they'd know right off the camper was Jesse Robinson. The money belt in which I carried my money had a broad pocket in the back of it, so I un-buckled it for the first time since I left Brownsville and counted the money. There was $138,000 total. While I had the money belt off, I shoved the diary in the duck-bill canvasback, then put it back on to see whether it felt comfortable. It was so pliable I couldn't even tell the book was there.

"The next morning I decided to ride up to Arkansas City to see whether there were any newspapers, and maybe to check out the ferry. If there were still stories about Balls, I might decide to get on the ferry and go on east to get still farther away from Brownsville.

"Arkansas City was a tiny village with only a general store and a blacksmith shop. There was a post office in the general store. I went down and looked at the ferry. It was just a barge with a couple of men who poled it across the Mississippi. It probably would have hauled two cars, maybe two wagons.

"I found no newspapers and saw very few people. So I decided I'd spend one more week camping out, then I'd go back to civiliza-tion with a nice beard, find some decent-sized town, buy some styl-ish new clothes, and begin my journey east. I'd also get rid of the motorcycle and buy myself a car.

"When I got back to my campsite I knew immediately that some-thing or somebody had been there. I started looking for things out of place, and went through the magazines and newspapers I had collected. But everything seemed to be the way I'd left it.

"I busied myself making a fire. Then deciding to eat, I sliced a few strips off of a slab of bacon. When I went to unwrap the bacon, the newspaper didn't seem as tightly wrapped as I remembered. The feeling persisted that my camp had been invaded by some-thing or somebody. If it had been a wild animal, it would not have just loosened the paper, but have eaten or dragged off the bacon.

"Going back through my things, it hit me. I had bought three *True Detective* magazines, but now there were only two. Somebody had stolen the one with the story of G. B. Balls. Why on earth would they do that?

"I put out the campfire as soon as it got dark, climbed into my sleeping bag, and lay there very quietly listening to the sounds of the night. I could hear the owls on the banks of the river, their nerve rattling screech, and occasionally a hoot owl. I could hear the grunting of an old boar possum as he made love to his lady friend, but I didn't hear anything out of place.

"The weather was cold enough that no insects were singing. The more intently I listened, the longer I lay awake, and the more agitated I became. Finally, I struck a match to see what time it was. Well after midnight—and I wasn't a bit sleepy. So I made up my mind I'd move camp come the next morning. I knew somebody'd been here, and that they were interested enough to steal a magazine. What else were they interested in? Could it possibly be the Pinkertons? That thought set my heart to racing, but eventually I fell into a troubled sleep.

"The open side of my lean-to faced the southeast where the morning sun usually awoke me. I was jerked awake by the smell of pine pitch smoke, and opened my eyes to see a tall fellow with overalls building a lightwood fire while keeping both eyes on me. He had my shotgun in his hand.

"'Morning, Jesse Robinson,' he said as soon as he realized my eyes were open. I tried as stealthfully as I could to push one arm under the pallet and find my pistol. Before my hand had moved two inches, he held up Ball's pistol and said, 'Is this what you're looking for, Jesse?' Then I realized I hadn't looked under my pillow for Ball's pistol the night before. Damn, Will, this ain't the way you stay alive.

"'What makes you think I'm Jesse Robinson? That name isn't familiar to me.'

"'Oh, you just like detective stories about Jesse Robinson, is that right? How 'bout G. B. Balls, does he strike a familiar chord in your memory?'

"I was frantically searching for some way out of this trap, and had to find out who this young fellow was. I judged him to be close to my own age. He wore overalls and was well-spoken. I couldn't imagine him being a Pinkerton detective. Yet I couldn't imagine any other reason he'd be asking the questions he's asking.

"'I'm Roddy Miles, and I've got a bill of sale for that motorcycle if you'll let me show it to you.'

"'What I want you to do, Jesse Robinson, is very carefully, get out of the sleeping bag and at all times keep your hands where I can see them. This twelve-gage shotgun is going to leave an awful bloody hole in you if I have to use it this close.'

"'What makes you think I'm Jesse Robinson?'

"'Well for one thing, you've got a slab of bacon wrapped up in a newspaper which says Jesse Robinson is riding on a new Harley-Davidson with a sidecar. That one you just rode around on yesterday shows less than a thousand miles on the odometer. If you bought it in Corpus Christi, Texas, like the paper said, you could well be here with that amount of miles on it. You don't see too many six-foot-six men riding new Harley Davidsons with sidecars who look like they might have grown a beard to conceal their identity.

"'I got several other reasons that make me think you're Jesse Robinson, no matter what name you're traveling under. I want you to get up and cook us some of that bacon and some of them eggs. I'll have breakfast with you before I take you over to the Pinkertons.'

"'Oh, I thought maybe you was a Pinkerton.' The instant I said that I could have cut my tongue out.

"'To my notion that statement proves you're Jesse Robinson. Now we can get down to the nut cuttin'. I might as well introduce myself since we're gonna be dining together and probably'll spend some time together. My name is S. S. Sorrell, and I'm in charge of you! Let me tell you how we're gonna be. After you fix my breakfast, I'm gonna eat with that twelve-gage shotgun in my lap. Then I'm gonna get in the sidecar of that motorcycle, and you're gonna drive me to Greenville. There's a Pinkerton Agency there, and I'm gonna turn you over to them folks and collect that $25,000 reward.'

"'Suppose I offered you more'n that $25,000 reward to let me go.'

"'Well, Jesse, how much more?'

"'Suppose I made it $50,000?'

"'Have you got $50,000 here?'

"'Of course not! What kind of damn fool do you think I am? I got less than $1000 in my wallet for traveling money. There's no way I'd carry that kind of money. But I can get it in less than a day's drive on the Harley. You can go with me, but I'm gonna want some kind of assurance you're not gonna let me pay you $50,000 and then still try to turn me in to the Pinkertons and get another $25,000. What kind of assurances can I get that you won't take my $50,000 and then still try to turn me in and get their $25,000?'

"'Well, now, Jesse, I can see how that could be a problem in your mind, but you just have to take my word of honor as a gentleman that I wouldn't do such a thing as that.'

"'Here's your eggs and bacon.'

"As we sat there and ate breakfast my mind was racing, trying to think of some way I could get away from this fellow. I thought about jumping on the Harley, but before I could ever hit the crank he'd blow me half in two with the shotgun. It had been a long time since I had been in a predicament that seemed so totally hopeless. If he crawled into the sidecar and stuck that gun in my face and said, 'Drive,' I couldn't think of any way I could escape.

"A fine how-to-do. Here I'd defeated the most ingenious detective employed by the Pinkerton Agency, and now this Arkansas peckerwood hillbilly had me, and I couldn't think of any way to get away from him.

"'Well, Jesse, let's don't think about it any longer. Let's clean out the sidecar on the motorcycle, get rid of those newspapers, toss the rest of those canned goods you've got in there. You're not gonna need 'em. We'll be in Greenville before you get hungry again. I'm gonna get in the sidecar, I'm gonna lay the pistol on the seat, and I'm gonna keep this shotgun aimed right at your head while you drive us to Greenville. The way I want to go is up to Arkansas City, take the ferry across, then go south to Greenville.'

"Dreading to get on the motorcycle, I lagged back.

"'Can't we talk this over?'

"'Well, you don't seem to be in any bargaining mood. I'd be glad to take $50,000 and let you go. I'll give you my word of honor I won't turn you in to the Pinkertons, but you don't seem willing.'

"'You have to admit, Mr. Sorrells, that somebody who wakes you with a shotgun in your face might leave something to be desired as far as absolutely trusting what they told you. Don't you agree?'

"'Very well put, Mr. Robinson, but I'm all you've got. If you don't trust me, who can you trust? You already said the Pinkertons were gonna have you dead in three or four months, and I'm bettin' after all the mischief you've raised in their lives, they're certainly going to want you dead. You see I'm neutral on that subject. I don't care if you are dead or alive if I can make a few dollars off it. I'd a whole heap rather have $50,000 than $25,000. On my word of honor, if you'll give me $50,000 I'll take it, otherwise, it's time to go.'

"I put my leg over the motorcycle seat and sat down. The motorcycle was still headed toward the Mississippi River. 'As one last favor, Mr. Sorrell, could I ride out to the end of the road and look at the Mississippi River one more time? I got a bit of pleasure out of sittin' on the bank and watchin' things go by. I'd just like to go out there and sit for just a few minutes. We've still got plenty of time to get to Greenville before dark.'

"He thought about it for a minute, 'Okay, ride on out. It won't hurt nothin'. Your days are short anyway.'

"I pushed down the kick start, the Harley purred to life. I twisted the throttle a quarter turn, put it in gear, and eased off. I went up through the gears to about 30 miles an hour, I estimated we were about three quarters of a mile from the river. Already I had a hatred for that son-of-a-bitch sittin' in the sidecar seat that couldn't be contained. I gradually twisted the throttle until the Harley hit 60 down the logging road, then 70. He was waving one hand and holding the gun on me with the other, as I continued to roll the throttle forward against the stop. I saw the terror in his eyes.

"Now we were no more than 100 yards from the Mississippi, and the old Harley was running flat out. There was just a tiny upgrade as we got to the bank. I glanced down at the speedometer; it was sittin' on 80 miles an hour. The next instant we were airborne.

"Nephew, things happened so fast I ain't sure I got it right, but I have firmly imprinted in my mind we'd probably traveled 100 feet or so and were still 10 feet above the water.

"I looked over to the right where Sorrells had climbed up on the windshield, and appeared about to jump. I've never seen such a terrified expression on a human's face. At that moment I pushed clear of the machine, twisting my head back just in time to see him jump forward. He landed a belly-buster in the Mississippi. The instant he landed, the motorcycle hit him full force in the back and snapped him like a twig—I'm sure it must have killed him instantly. A second later my own head hit something, and that's the last I remember."

Uncle Will didn't speak for a long time. I reached over and felt his face. It was fiery hot. I ran and got the nurse. She started slapping his face and yelling for help. Another nurse came running in with a hypodermic needle. She appeared to plunge the needle directly into his heart and ordered me out of the room.

Will Resurrected

"Miss Fanny, I know you ain't expecting me. Uncle Will is really bad. Last night they run me out of the hospital, and Dr. King don't think he's gonna live. I know I've no right to expect you to ever see him again, but I wanted to see if I couldn't get you two together before he dies.

"I asked my Pa about it last night. Pa says it ain't none of my business. But still, Uncle Will would like to see you so bad. I hope you'll decide to see him."

"Gene, I'm still not ready to make any promises about seeing Will. I've forgiven him, but I don't know if I ever want to see him again. Maybe it'll help you understand if I tell you more of our story. Where was I?

"I'd decided I would get on a riverboat and go to Greenville, Mississippi, where the weather was like I was used to at home. So I took my money and got on a steamer. You don't go upstream as fast as downstream on a riverboat, and slow was fine with me.

"Believe it or not, when I got on the boat, The Memphis Queen, there was no sign over the gaming room saying 'No Ladies,' I played blackjack for four solid hours.

"There was a couple of young men who tried to get me drunk and take me to their cabin, which was somewhat of an annoyance, but I managed to put them off without any harsh words being passed and enjoyed my night of gambling. I wound up $1200 ahead. It's downright astounding how money don't seem so much at all when it's passed across the gambling table. It is almost as if you treat it like play money.

"The second night, I had the same luck. When I got off the Memphis Queen in Greenville, I was $3000 richer. I wound up with $25,000 stuffed in the lining of my suitcase.

"Greenville didn't have but two hotels; I chose the biggest and fanciest. I took a monthly rate on the room, which was $37, counting maid service.

"I started looking around for something to invest my money in so I could make a living. I never again wanted to be dependent on a man, only to sit, cook, wash, and iron for him, have him come home, and be lord of the house.

"I ate three meals a day in the hotel. Hardly did a meal pass somebody didn't invite me to come and sit at their table. In the beginning I refused, but it left me powerful lonely, so when people extended me invitations to sit at their tables, I decided I would. I'd turned so many people down previously, it was two or three days before anybody invited me.

"About the third day after I'd decided I would accept invitations, a rather distinguished looking gentleman I guessed to be in his early fifties invited me to join his table. His name was Rosco Harris, a plantation owner who lived just outside Greenville, and he'd recently lost his wife.

"He was 55, and had made quite a bit of money as a cotton farmer. He was a lonely man, but wasn't looking for female companionship, just companionship. He was straightening up his affairs, selling his properties around Greenville, and planning to go to New York City, where his children had all moved. He had disposed of all his properties except his home, which he described in very loving and eloquent terms as 'our house,' as if his wife were still alive.

"Over the course of the meal, I shared with him the idea that I was looking to get into some line of work where I would never be dependent on a man, something I could make a living at. He asked if I had ever thought of becoming a farmer. It was an old and honorable profession; with the right type of management, there could be some money made farming.

"I told him I was widowed, my husband had left me some money, but I was afraid I was far short of the amount it would take to become a farmer.

"'Of course I don't know what you call a lot of money or a little money. You seem to live rather well, but I have a section of land and a grand house I am only asking $20,000 for. Three years ago it would have been worth probably $50,000–60,000, but land prices are depressed now, and I am anxious to move on to New York and get settled near my children.'

"That immediately piqued my interest. So I asked him why, if the house was all that grand, was he in residence at the hotel?

"Oh, I'm having it painted inside and out to make it attractive to a prospective buyer.'

"I told Rosco I would like to go see the place. He said, 'I'll be glad to show you, but I'd like to wait till the end of the week when they've finished painting.'

"He told me where the house was and we made an appointment to go early the following Friday morning. I went to a lawyer and told him I was planning to look at a piece of property that belonged to Rosco Harris. The lawyer assured me the transfer of real estate was very common and any good lawyer could check the title at the County Hall of Records. He certainly doubted there would be any problem whatever with any property owned by Rosco Harris.

"I was so thrilled at the prospect of becoming a plantation owner, I couldn't wait until Friday. I hired a carriage, gave the driver the address, and asked him to drive me by the place. I was not going inside the house. I would wait until Mr. Harris showed me the house, but I could not wait to see whether the setting and house itself were pleasing.

"You can't believe how impressed I was. It was a huge two-story mansion that had six columns across the front. There was a porch extending all the way around. At the upstairs level the porch had beautiful white rails that also ran all the way around the house. It was love at first sight, if that is possible for a house.

"I couldn't understand how 600 acres of land with a house could possibly be bought for $20,000; I could hardly wait until Friday to see the inside.

"By now it was along in November. The rainy season had started. It would rain a couple of days, then a cold front would move through, then it would be pretty a couple of days. On Friday, Mr. Harris took me to see the house. It must have had some type of central heating system 'cause when we went through the front door into a large foyer, it was just as warm as your mother-in-law's heart. The smell of fresh paint was heavy in the air.

"I turned left to see a huge parlor. I looked to the right, a somewhat smaller library. There were double-pocket doors for both.

Swinging French doors directly ahead opened into a spacious hallway, where the ceiling extended all the way to the roof. Rails extended along a balcony on either side of the hallway that ended in
about seven steps then split up and curled back, feeding into each
side of the balcony.

"I raced upstairs. There were four bedrooms, all spacious, all with
private baths and closets bigger than my Pa's bedroom. Though I
liked the outside of the house, the inside was ten times better.
Downstairs was a spacious dining room adjoined to an enormous
kitchen. On the opposite side were servants quarters for a live-in
cook and her husband, Dave Cooley and his wife Nancy.

"I knew absolutely nothing about running a cotton farm. I'd have
still paid him the $20,000. But I'd become sufficiently worldly wise
that I was gonna take the best deal offered.

"I told Mr. Harris it sounded like a wonderful opportunity to get
somebody to run the farm, and I would certainly do it. I loved the
place. 'When can we close the deal?'

"'If you'll meet me at my lawyer's office in the morning, we'll
make the deal final or we can use your lawyer if you have one.'

"I confessed to him I'd hired a lawyer and had him check the
title on the property. 'He said the title was good, so if you will give
me the deed I'll have my lawyer to draw up a new one.'

"I considered the whole arrangement one of the most fantasti-
cally lucky deals anybody could have ever made. I felt almost like
I had stolen the property.

"In the days that followed, Dave Cooley and I spent a good deal
of time in the carriage, with Dave showing me the property lines,
and the different fields and streams that criss-crossed the property.
There were about 50 acres of pastureland, 150 acres of woodland,
and 400 acres of cropland.

"I asked him about the feeds, the seeds, the fertilizer, and that
kind of stuff when the time came to plant. The people on the farm
knew what to use. It was up to me to buy it, and see they had what
they needed. They knew how to farm, but I would have to see to
getting the things they needed.

"As we got deeper into winter I made excursions into Greenville.
I even joined the First Methodist Church, which was on my side

of town. I hadn't been to church since Ma died and they gave me a good warm feeling.

"I made friends rapidly in and around Greenville. During the fall and winter, I had several men who came calling on me. Some made improper advances I didn't appreciate; I invited them to leave with the comfortable knowledge that Dave was always in his quarters and I could call for help if they didn't behave. Mostly, though, they were young gentlemen of impeccable manners.

"The word rapidly spread I was a very wealthy young widow, which, as you know, was not so. That word got around; I really hated it because a woman in that circumstance is always afraid the man who actively courts her might be interested only in her money.

"I tried to squelch such rumors at every opportunity and allowed that I was a person of very modest means. Still, the word grew up that I was very wealthy. As a matter of fact, I had less than $10,000 in the bank, though I did have a beautiful farm all paid for. Already I'd been offered $45,000 for it, so I guess to a lot of people in that time I was wealthy.

"I gradually fell into a routine of going to the social events around Greenville, such as 'The Ladies Literary Society,' where we discussed books. Mark Twain's writings were very popular, although some of the ladies in polite society considered him rather vulgar.

"I went to Sunday school and church every Sunday. I was seriously considering buying a Model-T Ford that I could drive without having to get Dave up to harness and hitch the horse to my carriage every Sunday morning.

"They had a new Model-T Ford advertized in Greenville for $620. I asked Dave if he would enjoy the rest, but he said, 'Ma'am I'd rather hitch up Ol' Ned for ya. He's safer. I just don't think you'd look like the elegant lady if you're tryin' to drive a Model-T. You do look so dignified driving the carriage to church on Sunday morning, and I don't mind at all. I've been doin' it all my life for Mr. Rosco. I enjoy doin' those little things. It gets me out and gets my blood to circulating. No, ma'am, I'd rather you wouldn't buy no Model-T.'

"I was constantly amazed at all of the things Rosco and the others were so eager to do for me whom they'd never known before.

The west boundary of my land went all the way to the Mississippi River. There was a big marshy area that was dry only for a month or so out of the year, usually in August or September. When the fall and winter rains started, it became a big lake as the river went up. The current actually flowed through the marsh like it was the middle of the river. If you didn't know the difference, you'd think you were standing on the edge of the Mississippi, but it was really marshland most of the year and only dried out in early fall.

"The locals called it 'Crawfish Marsh' because there were a lot of crawfish in the area. The tenants could catch all the crawfish and catfish they wanted on the edge of the marsh, usually in a very short time. They'd even built a pier jutting out into the marsh so that when the river was up, they could fish from the pier. When I saw how much care they'd taken in building the pier, how well anchored it was, and how much hand labor it had taken to build it, it was clear they loved this place and the river. I learned about this when Dave was showing me all the different fields they plowed in the fall to get ready for next spring's cotton planting.

"As we stood at the pier I made the idle remark, "The next time you go fishing, I'd like to go with you." A few days later, in late November, there was an unusual warm spell. Dave told me a couple of families were going fishing and were thinking about having a fish fry on Saturday afternoon. I decided to go along with them, and we spent most of the day out on the pier fishing. The women got the fire going. They had a homemade steel oven to set over the campfire. They made bread and cooked beans. We were catching catfish about 8–10 inches long, mostly channel cats. I had myself one big time, the most fun I'd had since my mother died, including my marriage to Jeff Cannon.

"About two hours before sundown the fish fry started; I ate catfish and hush puppies till I thought I would pop. When the meal was finished, everyone sang hymns. I wanted to help them clean up, but they would have no part of it. I was the lady of the house; they waited on me hand and foot. Just at sunset, while they were finishing putting things in the wagon, I strolled out on the pier for one last look around. In the growing gloom, I saw what looked like a human body floating face up in the sluggish current of the river.

"I yelled for Dave, and he came running. Without giving it a second thought he looked where I was pointing and jumped into the river, grabbed the body, and pulled it ashore. By now the rest of our group was there. They dragged the man's body out of the river and turned him on his stomach. Dave jumped on his back and water squirted from his nose and mouth. He sputtered. Dave turned him over on his back. I could feel a weak pulse. He had a huge knot on his forehead that had already turned a deep purple.

"He had a handsome face with a fairly long beard. When I was sure he was breathing, I had Dave put him in the surrey and hold him while I drove the team to the house. The other families were hard on our heels. We carried him upstairs and put him in the bedroom next to mine. I asked the men to undress him and put him in bed while I stayed a discreet distance away.

"When they had all his clothes off, Dave pulled a money belt off and brought it to me. It was a duck-back canvas belt with double buckles on the side.

"'Ya want me to go bring the doctor, Miss Fanny?'

"'I don't believe there's anything a doctor can do for him that we're not doing. Why don't we wait until morning and see whether a good night's rest will bring him around. I'll look in on him from time to time during the night. I'll call you and Nancy if I need to.'

"I put a lamp on a chest of drawers at the head of the bed and stood back to take a close look at this tall stranger. He was truly a handsome man. I tried to imagine how he'd gotten into the Mississippi. Had he fallen overboard on a riverboat? Did the paddle wheel do that to his head? Had he been thrown overboard? His clothes looked expensive and fairly new.

"I opened the money belt, and was astounded by the amount of money there appeared to be. On the back of the belt was a book. I pulled it out, saw it was a diary, opened the first page and read, 'Case #59—The Private and Personal Diary of G. B. Balls. If found, the Pinkerton Detective Agency offers a reward to the finder. Please contact T. D. Bronski, Superintendent of Detectives, The Pinkerton Detective Agency, St. Louis, Missouri.'"

"Miss Fanny, is that how you met Uncle Will? You know he told me when he picked you up, you were a carnival girl, a travel-

ing carnival girl. You pulled him out of the Mississippi River? I
can't believe that. He said he picked you up at a carnival in
Tallapoosa. You were a carnie girl, somebody had just beat the hell
out of you, and you were running away from them."

"Gene, surely you've discovered by now your Uncle Will wasn't
born with a prayerbook in his mouth. He's a compulsive liar."

"Maybe it was another girl, maybe I got the names mixed up,
Miss Fanny."

"No, Gene, you didn't get the names mixed up. He told that
tale to the boys around Tallapoosa when he wanted to put me down,
when he was mad with me. Maybe he told it so many times he
came to believe it."

"Believe me, Gene, the first time I ever saw Will, we fished him
out of the Mississippi River at Greenville, on the backside of Green
Meadows."

"Please, please, go on."

"I got some warm water and began to bathe his face, especially
around the big blue knot on the right side of his forehead. I wondered if he had broken his skull. His breathing was shallow, but
regular. His pulse was a steady 60 beats per minute.

"Several times during the night I got up and went to look at the
sleeping giant. In between times I read the diary of G. B. Balls.
Until I finished reading the diary I thought it was Balls lying in my
bed. But then I asked myself the question, why so much money?

"Gene, there was $130,000, or maybe a little more, in his money
belt. Why would a Pinkerton detective need to carry that much
money? I began to doubt he was G. B. Balls, when I finished reading the last entry in the diary and realized it had been a year since
that entry had been made, I knew then that more'n likely it was
not Balls in my bed.

"He had a wallet in his hip pocket that had $1000 in it. He had
some paper that was soaking wet. It looked like a bill of sale, but it
was unreadable. I slept very little that night trying to bring out of
my memory the name G. B. Balls. It seemed vaguely familiar. I
had seen a newspaper, a magazine, with that name in it. But I read
mostly books and bought mostly books. I didn't read a lot of magazines. I didn't even take the newspapers on any regular basis.

"Then I remembered. We'd had a quilting at Nellie Nelson's house the week before. She was a great magazine reader. There been a picture in a detective magazine of G. B. Balls. I remembered thinking, 'what an odd name.' I must go to Nellie Nelson's house in the morning and see if she'll let me have that magazine.

"I put the money belt and the diary in the top drawer of my bureau. As soon as we finished breakfast the next morning, I asked Dave to hitch up the carriage. We headed for Nellie Nelson's to borrow a magazine.

"On the way to Nellie's house, I told Dave I didn't want anybody to mention I had a man in the house until I could find out who he was. There was some puzzling things he had in his money belt; I'd like to clear them all up before we let anybody know he's here. And I wanted Dave to pass the word on to the others. While in route, I had to think of something to tell Nellie to distract her from the fact I wanted that one magazine. So I decided I'd ask her to let me go through all her magazines, that I'd seen some that struck my fancy during my last visit. She was very gracious and I wound up taking home five or six."

Getting Acquainted

"I could not wait to get home to begin reading the *True Detective* story about G. B. Balls. As we bounced along in the carriage, I started reading what I hoped would lead me to the identity of the stranger now lying in a coma in my house.

"When I read how this tall stranger rose in the pulpit of the First Methodist Church in Plowshare, Kentucky, and accused his fiancé of copulating with her father, a charge that later turned out to be false, I hoped the stranger was not that person.

"All in all, it was one of the most fascinating stories I had ever read. It kept referring to a diary that was supposed to have been kept by G. B. Balls, the very diary I had just read in it's entirety.

"When I finished the story in the *True Detective*, I realized the key to the identity of Jesse Robinson, the absolute key, was the diary. Even before reaching home, I finished the story, and knew that Jesse Robinson was almost certainly the stranger in my house. And I wished fervently that I did not know.

"Even so, in order to establish once and forever whether the stranger in my house was Jesse Robinson, one would have to go to Evansville, Indiana, and persuade L. B. Pecker to draw another sketch, and I wasn't about to take that trip.

"When we arrived, I instructed Dave to go directly to the farmhouses and instruct each household that absolutely nothing was to be spoken about the stranger until they had my permission to do so. I did not like to threaten them, but if I heard any rumors before I told them it was alright, I would order them off the farm. It was most urgent that not one of them betray me in this matter.

"You see, Gene, in nursing Will, I fell in love with that unconscious zombie. I remember bending a straw, sucking it full of water, and forcing the water down his throat. I know he drank it, but he never stirred. I don't know if it was good or bad, nursing him, but gradually I fell head over heels in love with the giant lying unconscious in my bed. Only a foolish child could do such a thing.

296

It still embarrasses me now. Don't ask me how it's possible, I can't explain it. Sometimes to this day it makes me angry.

"After 11 o'clock the following night, when I knew Dave and Nancy were fast asleep in their quarters, I put out the light in his room. Clothed only in the darkness, I crawled beneath the covers, pressing myself firmly against his body and kissing him passionately, praying that he'd come alive, that he would live. But he continued only a slow rhythmic breathing; not one muscle stirred.

"I lay with my arms around him for hours, even crying and asking the Almighty how He could send me such a marvelous creature and not let him regain consciousness. It was a terrible ordeal.

"This went on for the next four nights. As soon as I was sure Dave and Nancy were asleep, I would blow out the light in his room, undress, crawl beneath the covers with him, press my body hard against his, and pray and cry that he would talk to me, that he would take his huge arms, and put them around me, and yes Gene, that he would love me as I loved him.

"Gene, you are blushing again."

"No, no, Miss Fanny. I'm not blushing, I'm enjoying the story."

"It's okay to blush, Gene. Some men can't. It's a charming quality. You should blush as long as you live."

"On the fifth night, I went in at 11 o'clock, put out the light, and once again crawled naked into bed with him. His eyes were open, though they had a some what vacant stare. I was thrilled!

"In a deep voice that I somehow knew I had heard before, he said, 'Who are you?'

"'I'm Fanny Hawk, Jesse Robinson.'

"Immediately his eyes clouded, 'Who called me that?'

"I knew he was frightfully upset that I'd called him that. He sat up in bed, raised the covers, looked underneath, and said, 'Get me some clothes. I'm hungry, do you have some food?'

"I went down, woke Dave and Nancy, asked them to fix him eggs, ham, and biscuits, with some coffee, and bring it up, explaining that he was now conscious. I'd stay with him until they brought the food.

"He was very unsteady on his feet, but he looked otherwise okay. I couldn't believe I was madly in love with this man as he stood shakily to his feet and asked me where my Ma and Pa were.

"'I don't have a Ma and Pa, I'm the lady of the house. I'm widow Cannon.'

"'Why, you're a child,' he said.

"'Jesse Robinson, I was married for over a year. I've been divorced, and I own this property. Shortly my servants will bring you some food.'

"He soon returned and fell in the easy chair. I sat facing him.

"'Jesse Robinson, are you guilty of all of the things that it says you are guilty of in this story?' I held up the *True Detective* for him to look at.

"'Young lady, I'll have you know that you don't know what you are talking about.'

"'Wait a minute, Jesse Robinson. If you'll remember you had G. B. Balls' diary in your money belt when we found you, along with an awful lot of money.'

"When I said that he grabbed his waist; the money belt was gone.

"'Your money is safe. I don't want any part of it. But there's no way you are G. B. Balls. The last entry in that diary was made over a year ago. G. B. Balls described you perfectly. All I'd have to do is go to Evansville, Indiana, which is not too far up the Mississippi, a little piece up the Ohio, and I'll find L. B. Pecker at a Standard Oil Station, and get him to draw me a picture. That's what G. B. Balls did. He states in his diary it's a perfect likeness; I know you must have read that diary many, many times after you killed him and took it.

"'When I found you, you were unconscious, nearly dead. You've been in that bed five days. I thought surely you would die. I have not notified the authorities; I thought I would let you explain before I did. But I want you to remember one thing. Though you're a huge, hard man and I'm a tiny woman, I've got people here in the house who can take care of you if you get any foolish ideas about doing to me what you did to Balls. I just wanted to get that out of the way. I am willing to listen to you explain why I shouldn't go to Greenville and tell the Pinkerton Detective Agency about you.'

"I sat in trembling, eager anticipation, praying that he would tell me something I could believe that.

"'What shall I call you, Miss?'

"'My servants call me Miss Fanny.'

"'Suppose I just call you Fanny, is that okay? You're such a child. Excuse me, you're so young. You should be flattered. Have you read any newspaper stories about this business, Fanny?'

"'No, I haven't.'

"'Since you've gone to the trouble to get this magazine, since you have G. B. Balls' diary, I'm sure when I finish my story you are going to check it out. So I am going to tell you the truth from the very beginning.

"'One thing that both Balls' diary and the detective story doesn't say is that I had a partner, a young lady named Kathy Taylor. She was in on it from the very beginning. As a matter of fact, she is the one who told me about this hideously ugly girl in Plowshare, Kentucky whose father was a rich minister.

"'Kathy and I were engaged to be married at the time. I was a poor man and Kathy's family was very wealthy until just a few years before. Her father started drinking and lost the family fortune. Kathy loved pretty things.

"'We were engaged to be married when she told me I should make love to Preacher Nelson's daughter. She even permitted me to move into the minister's house and told me to play up to the girl, figure out some way to get money out of them. As a matter of fact, while I was still in Plowshare after I became president of the bank, she came to my office, supposedly to borrow money, when in fact her business was to see how I was doing.

"'She was a greedy woman, Fanny; I'm a grown man. I'm 30 years old and I'm not making excuses for my behavior, but I loved Kathy Taylor. I loved her very deeply. Without her, I would have never even known about Josie Nelson. Of course, you read in Balls' diary how the whole business started; I don't have to go into that.'

"Nancy came in with a big plate of scrambled eggs, country ham, syrup, biscuits, and gravy. Will ate so much, he was embarrassed. I took a cup of coffee, with my heart fluttering the whole time I sat there. This giant had already convinced me everything was going to be alright. He was such a handsome fellow, so well spoken.

"I guess it's difficult to see how somebody could be in love with a person with whom you'd never even spoken. But Gene, that is

what happened to me. In looking back, I don't know if it was all
the hormones flowing, or what caused it, but I was desperately in
love with this tall stranger. I was not about to let him know that
until I knew more about him, but he had already told me enough
that I thought everything was going to be alright. I was sure hoping it would be.

"When he finished eating, Nancy and Dave took the dishes away.
I asked him whether he was strong enough to continue the story.

"'No, I feel wonderful. I must have slept for four or five days, but
the strangest thing, Fanny, the whole time I dreamed such an unusual dream. I dreamed there was a beautiful girl who came in, took
off all her clothes off, and snuggled up close to me every night,
night after night. It was the strangest feeling. She smelled so good.
How long have I been here?'

"I was mortified, but I tried not to show any change of expression. I said, 'You've been here five days; there certainly have been
no naked girls in bed with you for those five days. I don't know
about the past.'

"'If I tell you the 100 percent truth, Fanny, will you promise you'll
give me a chance to get away if you decide to turn me in to the
police? Just give me 24 hours notice. Will you promise me that?
And also give me time to recover my strength?'

"'I'll do that.'

"'Alright then, I'm going to tell you the total unvarnished truth.
Everything you read in the *True Detective* story about me is so, every
bit of it. Everything you read in G. B. Balls' diary is true. I already
told you about Kathy Taylor. I later married her just before we got
on a train going to St. Louis from Chicago. We were married, spent
our honeymoon in a pullman compartment. For a fellow as tall as
I am, that ain't the ideal place to spend a honeymoon. Now somebody as short as you are,' I blushed, 'it would be okay. I stole all of
the money they said, but I did it for my true love, Kathy Taylor.
She loved being rich better than anybody I've ever seen.

"'I don't see how you missed the story in the newspapers. It was
in all the newspapers in Texas. I read some stories she had given
the press in Texarkana, and those detective magazines are all over
the country.'

"While he was telling me his story, I felt so sorry for him it made me fall that much more deeply in love. The poor dear, to have put his faith in that money hungry woman, and her then do him that way. He was so conscience-stricken.

"'I started having nightmares about the people I had killed. Kathy didn't kill them, I killed them. It doesn't matter what her part was; we'll forget about that. I'm gonna have to answer to the Almighty himself, and I have these horrible dreams about Ebo.'

"'Ebo?'

"'Yeah. That's my name for the devil.'

"'I never heard that before.'

"'Well, that's my own private name.'

"'Ha, I've never heard of anybody having a private name for the devil.'

"I thought that sounded a little bit weird, like he was touched in the head, but maybe that terrible knot he had on his head, which was just now beginning to go down, had something to do with it. So far he had been most forthcoming in admitting these atrocious crimes. I had enough on him now to put him in the penitentiary for the rest of his life or probably get him hanged.

"'Well, that explains a lot of things, but how did you come to be floating in the Mississippi River?'

"'I left Brownsville on a shrimp boat. I went to Corpus Christi and bought a motorcycle with a sidecar. If you go to the newspaper offices and get the back issues of the newspaper for the last month, the whole story should be in the newspaper. It was big news in Texas, Arkansas, and probably Louisiana.

"'The Pinkertons found out about it. Everywhere I'd go in Texas, I'd read newspaper accounts that the Pinkertons were closing in on me from every direction.

"'I finally wound up on the banks of the Mississippi. I had been camped out there for about five or six days, maybe a week, I don't know how long. I woke up one morning with a big fellow in overalls holding my gun, telling me he was going to turn me over to the Pinkertons.

"'I tried to bargain with him. I tried to use the money you found in the money belt without telling him I had it on my person to buy my way out of his grasp, but he insisted on taking me in to the Pinkertons.

"'Fanny, when somebody undertakes to make me do something, I start seeing red streaks. I get mad and I do unreasonable things. It's probably going to be the death of me, but I am usually a pretty reasonable man until somebody tries to make me do something. I'll admit when I get drunk, I sometimes do things without provocation that I'm ashamed of. But when somebody tries to make me do something, it flies all over me. My Ma never could make me do nothing. My Pa never could make me do nothing. Now if you *ask* me to do something, it tickles me to death to do it. You try to *make* me do something, there ain't never been a Georgia mule as stubborn as I am, and I wish I wasn't that way.

"'He crawled in the sidecar of my motorcycle, pointed a shotgun at my head. When he sat down on the motorcycle, I asked him if I could ride up to the bank of the Mississippi for one last look. I enjoyed just sitting there looking at the river. He agreed.

"'As I eased off something inside of me took over. I eased up through the gears until I was making 45 miles an hour. Any damn fool with any sense would know to jump off of it would be death.

"'I rolled the throttle over against the stop. There was a little incline just as we went up to the bank of the Mississippi. I decided there wasn't no getting rid of this fellow, there wasn't no reasoning with him. I was gonna ride that motorcycle till just before it got to the water and jump off. Whatever he did was his own business, but I knew he wasn't gonna shoot me with the motorcycle going that fast.

"'We left the bank of the Mississippi going just as fast as that Harley would run. Right before it hit the water, I jumped off to the left. The last thing I saw was the motorcycle landing right in the middle of his back. Somehow he got to the water before it did. I'm satisfied he's dead, but I didn't kill him. He was killed in a motorcycle wreck.

"'Mind you, I ain't sorry. Miss Fanny, you judge me anyway you want to, I done wrong. I'm probably going to hell for it. I guess I am getting a taste of hell now. I have these awful nightmares where Ebo and his hounds chase me across a barren desert.

"'But since then, I've dreamed of this woman climbing in the bed with me, wrapping her arms around me, and pressing her naked body against mine. A wonderful dream, not the kind of dream I've had before. That's the story.

"'You promised me you would give me 24 hours. With God as my witness, Miss Fanny, that is the truth of how I got here in every respect. I tell you from the bottom of heart, I thank you for saving my life. If you'll give me my money belt back, I'll be glad to pay you for any inconvenience I've been to you. I'd like to stay here a day or two and get my wits back about me if you'd let me. I'm growing tired now, I'd like to go back to sleep if I could, Fanny.'

"I said good night to him and went back to my bedroom. I lay there for long hours, my body aching, and realized how much I missed snuggling up against him. I even blushed in the dark. So you see, Gene, he must have been partially conscious. He must have actually felt me press against him. Of course, I know nothing of medicine and things like that, certainly nothing of dreams, but he felt so wonderful. Oh, you're blushing again, my goodness."

"Miss Fanny, while you're talking about such things, you were married for how long?"

"Oh, I was married for six or seven months, I don't remember, a long time."

"Is it as wonderful, uh, uh, after you've been married that long, as it is the first time?"

"Oh you're talking about sex, Gene."

"Uh, yes ma'am."

"Oh sex is wonderful every time. The worse I ever had was wonderful. Oh my goodness Gene, you're blushing again."

"Miss Fanny, I really...I'm...I... I had a girl friend, but I don't understand. We had sex one night in the back seat of the car, and the next day she didn't want to ever see me again. I felt just awful. It was so wonderful, I can't understand what I did wrong."

"Maybe she's just playing hard to get, Gene. Maybe she wants you to beg her a little."

"Oh, I wish I knew that was so, if it was. She's so pretty and wonderful. I see her every day at work, but she acts like she don't even want to be around me."

"Why don't you walk up to her and say—what's her name?"

"Her name is Julie."

"Why don't you just walk right up to her and say: Julie, I really would like to go out with you again, I really, really would. What did I do wrong?"

"I'm afraid she'll get mad and say something terrible to me. I...I think maybe I'd rather just worry about what it is than to really know what I did wrong. It's a terrible pickle I'm in, Miss Fanny."

"I'll say it is, Gene, but the next time you see her you ought to walk right up to her and say, Julie, what did I do wrong? Can I do something to make it right? I would really like to see you again."

"Let me tell you, Gene, girls are in a terrible predicament. If they have sex with you, then you begin to think they're easy, even if they love you. They're afraid you'll tell other people. No girl wants a reputation for being loose. A girl is in a whole different position. Boys can't get pregnant. Nobody ever asks the boy if he's a virgin. It's only the girl who needs to be a virgin on her wedding night. Have you ever thought about how unfair that is? Nobody speaks of men as ex-virgins.

"I lay there most of the night thinking how he'd lied about his love for Josie. Was he lying about his love for Kathy? The monstrous lie he'd told in the pulpit of the church. I could understand doing some of these things for the love of a woman if he was that desperately in love with her, and how all of it began as an attempt to get money and wound up in murder and worse. That was understandable. But now was he really Will Jackson Johnson Jr? Was he telling me the truth, or was I going to be one of his victims?

"Sleep wouldn't come. I got up and crept back into his bedroom and listened to the slow rhythmic breathing coming from his bed. My physical desire for him was so strong I almost crawled in with him, knowing I'd wake him up and knowing what would happen.

"Then I heard a low moaning coming from the bed that gradually rose in volume until it was a blood-curdling groan, almost a scream. I backed out of his bedroom and returned to my own room grateful, because I truly don't know what I would have done had he not started groaning in his sleep. I guessed that Ol' Ebo he spoke of was chasing him across an endless desert. It was a terrible blood-curdling groan, I could now easily imagine Will being chased by Ol' Ebo.

"I wanted so much to believe him. The next morning I invited him down to have breakfast with us. He immediately struck up a friendly conversation with Dave. It was obvious he knew a lot about farming as he talked to Dave about growing cotton, corn, all of the things we grew.

"After breakfast, I rode into Greenville to the newspaper office. I asked the editor if I could look at some back issues of the *Greenville Chronicle*. The fact that I didn't buy the local newspaper was the reason for my ignorance. The back issues for a good month almost all had something about the chase after G. B. Balls' murderer.

"As I started out of the newspaper office, I looked at that day's paper. The headlines said, 'Body Discovered at the Mouth of Catfish Creek'. I picked up the newspaper to read the story; it said, 'A body that the Pinkerton Detective Agency now believes to be that of Jesse Robinson, alias Will Cotton, murderer of G. B. Balls, has been discovered caught on a snag at the mouth of Catfish Creek. Several days ago, a riverboat passenger reported that he had seen a motorcycle fly through the air near the New Orleans Queen Riverboat, landing in the river behind the boat.

"'At the time, little credence was given to the story told by the passenger. The captain thought he was hallucinating. Who ever heard of a motorcycle flying out of the woods along the banks of the Mississippi. But he duly marked the report, and now the Pinkerton Detective Agency has hired a salvage company to see whether they can find the motorcycle.

"'If the salvage company is successful, the serial number will tell the Pinkertons whether it is the motorcycle sold in Corpus Christi and believed to have been purchased by the infamous Jesse Robinson. If so, then the Pinkerton Detective Agency will at last be able to mark one of the most bizarre cases in modern times closed.

"'This reporter has been given permission by the salvage company hired by the Pinkerton Detective Agency to go along on their search. The spot marked by the captain's log is at a point just south of Arkansas City. We will leave Greenville at sunrise tomorrow morning. The captain of the salvage boat estimates that it could take up to a week to drag the entire area because of the shifting sands of the Mississippi.'

"I bought a copy of the newspaper to carry it home to Will. First thing Will said when he read the story was: 'If they declare this guy to be Jesse Robinson, they'll quit looking for me. The son-of-a-bitch tried to rob me, turn me in, and get me executed. It would serve him right if he gets the Pinkertons off of my back.'

"I was momentarily troubled by his attitude and that remark, but I let it pass. I was so in love with him I was ready to believe anything he said and forgive him for almost anything.

"Will rapidly became healthy and restless. He went out with Dave almost every morning. He actually began to act like a farm foreman, making suggestions here and there, nothing pushy. I would talk to Dave about Will's behavior. Dave liked him. He said he was knowledgeable about farming and would make me a good farm foreman. But Dave worried that he slept upstairs with me, and about what the people in the community would think. Every morning Will asked to ride into Greenville and get a copy of the newspaper to see whether there was any fresh news about Balls' case.

"A week after the first story appeared, I picked up a newspaper and the headlines read, 'Jesse Robinson's Motorcycle Discovered at the Bottom of The Mississippi River.'

"'Pinkerton checked the serial number of the Harley-Davidson against the bill of sale from the Harley-Davidson dealer in Corpus Christi and it checked. The Pinkerton Agency now suspects there's another alias for Jesse Robinson since the bill of sale was made out to Roddy Miles. The salesman has given a very accurate description of Jesse Robinson as the purchaser.

"'At this point in the investigation, the Pinkerton Agency assumes that the body discovered at Catfish Creek, and the motorcycle recovered from the bottom of the Mississippi, mark the end to one of the most gruesome crime sprees of modern times.

"'Having no idea who Will Cotton, alias Jesse Robinson, alias Roddy Miles, truly is, the Pinkerton Agency has turned the body over to the city of Greenville. City officials stated they expect to bury the body in an unmarked grave Monday. Thus will end a bizarre story that will perhaps be written of for many years to come.'

"When I carried the newspaper home and showed it to Will, he was ecstatic. But then he grew depressed. He said, 'You know, the Pinkerton Agency may have put this story in the newspaper so I'd relax and start appearing in public. This may be a trap set for me.'

"I insisted it wasn't, but he was adamant.

"'I thought two or three times that I had those sons-of-a-bitches off of my back, only to wind up with one in my hip pocket a few days later. I hope they truly believe this is the end of Jesse Robinson, but I'm going to continue to be very careful for some time to come.'

"Monday morning, Will asked me if it would be okay if he took the surrey and went to the cemetery to see whether they'd actually buried the body. Since the surrey had curtains, he could observe the burial without being observed. For some reason, I asked whether I could go with him, like I was asking permission. He agreed.

"It was a somber trip to the cemetery. Sure enough, about 9 o'clock, some city employees came up with a coffin in a wagon. They put the coffin in a grave that had already been dug and covered it up. When they finished, they already had a sign made.

"Jesse and I sat in the surrey until after the city workmen finished covering the grave and left. Then we drove up and looked at the sign. The sign said, 'Here lies the man who murdered G. B. Balls. Name unknown, but who lived under the aliases of Will Cotton, Jesse Robinson, and Roddy Miles. And God knows what else. May you burn in hell forever.'

"As we stood looking at the crudely lettered grave marker, Will turned to me and said, 'Fanny, I never thought about looking at my own tombstone. I certainly never expected it to be pasteboard.'

"We got in the surrey and started back to Green Meadows. Will talked about his Paw, about having a run-in with him at a very young age, and how he jumped on freight trains and rode all over the country. He seemed to want to reminisce. I never once got the feeling he was trying to show me his good side. But the more he talked, the more I realized that he was a lonely, that in a sense that he was searching for the right way."

"Miss Fanny, how can you say that? All of those people he killed?"

"Maybe I'm not saying it well, Gene. I guess what I mean is I was madly in love with him, and I wanted to think of him as a lonely, broken man. I guess that's what I mean. But that's the way I felt anyway.

"As we neared Green Meadows, he said, 'Fanny, I'm sure that you have to knock the boys off every time you go to town. But would you consider lettin' me take you to church Sunday?'

"'I thought you said you were going to lay low for a while. Even though the Pinkerton's case was closed, you thought they would still be looking for you.'

"'I'm sure they won't be looking for me in church.'

"'I would be delighted to accompany you to church, Will.'

"'I noticed there is an old run-down house that appears to be on your property, looks like it hasn't been lived in in 10 or 15 years. I would be willing to spend my money to fix it up if you would let me live here through a crop year, just to make sure all of this business with the Pinkertons has died down. When I take you to church, you can say that you hired me as your farm foreman and I'm living in the old foreman's home.

"'If you'll give me a week and the farmhands, I can have a couple of rooms ready to live in. I promise you, Fanny, I'll earn my keep. If you'll just let me have a place to stay, I'll spend my money to fix it up. I'll eat at the big house until I can get my own kitchen going, if that's alright with you, but I'd like to stay here in Greenville a little while to make sure that nothing else comes of this Pinkerton business. Then I'll be on my way.'

"I was delirious with happiness. From the fact that he wanted to stay around and had already asked me out, I was ecstatic. He was going to spend his own money. Even though I knew it was ill-gotten gains."

End of the Chase

"Will did carry me to services that Sunday. We told everybody in the congregation he was my new farm foreman, would be a regular at church, and that his name was Will J. Johnson, Jr.

"After the service was over, many of the young members of the church gathered around us, each eager to invite Will back and to tell us what a handsome couple we were. Most of the congregation had us married in their minds that very first Sunday.

"From time to time, I went to Will's house to see what progress was being made with the remodeling. In just a few weeks the house had become most livable even though he only had a bed, a chest of drawers, and kitchen and dining room furniture.

"Every time I went there and saw so little furniture, it gave me the feeling that he wasn't intending to stay there very long. I decided he didn't want to put new furniture in my house and then have to leave hurriedly because his past was catching up with him.

"For several weeks things went rather smoothly. He came over from time to time to take a meal with us. He took me to church every Sunday. He was the model of chivalrous behavior. I was profoundly in love with him, and it began to irritate me somewhat that he made never made any advances.

"One very cold night late in February when he had been there more than two months, I invited him to sit and chat with me in the parlor for a while after supper. We'd each had a glass of wine, and I was feeling a little bit mellow. I offered to serve him a drink. Even though the minister preached against liquor every Sunday, I thought it was a pretty nice thing to have around, though I couldn't quite forget that alcohol had cost me my virginity, and that I had vowed never to lose control again.

"Anyway, Will and I had a couple of drinks, and shortly he moved from across the room and joined me on the settee. Shortly he put his arms around me and kissed me a long passionate kiss that I only feebly resisted. He relaxed one arm and began to explore inside my blouse. I stiffened, pulled away from him, and told him to stop. I didn't really want him to. Then he said what I had been wanting to hear ever since the first time I laid eyes on him, 'Fanny, I'm in love with you; I want to marry you.'

"Suddenly I was frightened. It was terrifying that I loved him with such intensity I couldn't say, let's wait. I couldn't say, let me think about it. I simply said, 'Do you really want to?'

"I couldn't play hard to get, 'If you really want to, Will, nothing would make me happier.' He suggested we go upstairs consummate the marriage, but I firmly refused. I told him, 'No, if you want to get married, I want to get married. But I want to consummate my marriage after the vows.'

"'Very well,' he said. 'When? What about two weeks, at the church, three o'clock in the afternoon?' I agreed.

"Now it was my turn to plead for the truth if he hadn't told it. Immediately after agreeing to marry him, I said 'Will, I love you. If you haven't told me the truth about all your adventures, tell me now. I can forgive you anything—I love you that much—but tell me the truth. If there is anything you haven't been truthful about, please tell me now and we'll get all your past behind us.'

"He remained on the settee with me for several minutes. Two or three times it looked like he was going to say something, but he didn't. I waited. I was going to make certain I gave him every opportunity, and in my own mind that meant I wouldn't speak until he spoke. I wanted his past out of my mind.

"Finally he said, 'Darling, there's nothing else to tell. What I've told you is the way it is.' Saying that, he took me in his arms and we resumed our passionate affections.

"The next two weeks were the most hectic in my life, getting prepared for our wedding. Time passed swiftly, and soon we were married. I was deliriously happy. Will was kind, considerate, and even more attentive than my first husband, Jeff Cannon, had been.

"Nothing was ever said, but I knew Will was still wary of the Pinkertons. When the occasion arose that somebody needed to go into Greenville for something, he'd always have me go with Dave rather than coming himself. About the only place he was seen in public was at church on Sunday morning. He had a deep melodi-

ous voice; he sang in the choir. The people around us would sometimes stop singing just to listen to his voice. It seemed he knew
every one of the hymns.

"I suppose for a period of two or three months, I never once
thought about his past. One thing we both did though was look
forward each month for the *True Detective* to see whether the final
story about G. B. Balls would ever be printed.

"It was May when the story we'd been waiting for finally appeared, written by the reporter who'd done the previous ones. The
title was, 'G. B. Balls' Murderer Lies in a Pauper's Grave in Greenville, Mississippi?' There was a questionmark closing that sentence.

"The last couple of paragraphs in the story read, 'This reporter
does not believe the murderer of G. B. Balls lies buried in Greenville
for these reasons. There has been a young man missing from Arkansas City since the date the riverboat passenger reported seeing the
motorcycle come flying into the Mississippi River. The young man's
father says his son left home late the evening before with the cryp-
tic statement that he knew where he could make a pile of money.

"'This reporter would be the first to admit that this means little,
by itself. But the fact that the Pinkerton Detective Agency was
offering $25,000 for the apprehension of Jesse Robinson leads this
reporter to believe the young man thought he could take Jesse
Robinson in to the Pinkertons. Somehow, as Jesse Robinson has
been able to do in every instance, he managed to escape and send
the young man to eternity on a Harley-Davidson with a sidecar.
And made it look like that was the end of Jesse Robinson.

"'Another reason, inconsequential in itself, is that the body discovered at the mouth of Catfish Creek was wearing a pair of Lee's
overalls. Jesse Robinson never wore overalls. He always appeared
in dressy clothes, usually suits or woolen pants and blazers.

"'This reporter well realizes that these reasons are in themselves
insufficient to prove the body found was not Jesse Robinson's. But
taken collectively, along with Robinson's proven ability to outwit
the Pinkertons, they sow doubt in this reporter's mind that
Robinson is indeed buried in a pauper's grave in Greenville.

"'Before publishing this article I submitted it to T. D. Bronski,
Superintendent of the Detectives for the Pinkerton Detective

Agency and asked for comment. Mr. Bronski refused to be quoted on the matter. My belief is that Jesse Robinson remains the greatest embarrassment the Pinkerton Agency has ever suffered. They very much want to believe the end of the story lies in a pauper's grave, but this reporter has serious doubts.'

"When Will finished reading the story he looked at me and said, 'I should have guessed that some smart alec reporter would want to keep the G. B. Balls saga alive.' He fell into a deep depression. All the crops had been planted, and were growing remarkably well. It looked like a good year, but Will was now listless, though still kind, tender, and considerate toward me.

"Around mid-May on a Wednesday morning I was awakened by Will. He was already dressed. He said, 'Fanny, I want you to go into Greenville to the Harley-Davidson dealership and buy a motorcycle with a sidecar exactly like the one I had. I want you to put it in your maiden name, using the first name Travis. Since they know you in Greenville, you can say you're buying it for your brother.'

"He had already counted out $2000 and laid it on the bed, 'We've never talked much about finances. I don't know if you need any money; I'll leave with you whatever you need. Once you buy the motorcycle, I'd like you to sell this place and come to Tallapoosa, Georgia and live with me.

"'If you decide to do this, come to the hotel in Tallapoosa. I'll check frequently to see whether you've registered, and will look forward to seeing you when you get there. Darling, I love you more than anything in the world, but I can't stay this close to where the trail for Jesse Robinson ended. I hope you understand it has nothing to do with you. I love you, but I can't stay here any longer.'

"Dave said he could drive a motorcycle so I carried him with me, and with a heavy heart did as Will had asked. On the way I couldn't stop wondering why he didn't want to get a car, a truck, or some other vehicle. All of the previous stories had people looking for a rider on a Harley-Davidson with a sidecar. It seemed as if Will wanted to tempt fate.

"When I asked him about that, he said the Harley had saved his life. If he had been in a car, his rider could have turned the engine off, and he surely would have died. But the motorcycle had saved his life. A car would have delivered him to the Pinkertons, which would have been the same as killing him.

"I thought my heart would break when Will was ready to go. I couldn't stand the thought of living without him. He gave me the impression of being overwhelmed by grief, but as he said, it was better than dying.

"He made another request I bitterly resented. 'Fanny, pass the word that I just up, run off, and left you. That way you won't be tied to me if the Pinkertons decide to believe that magazine story and start looking for me. You can tell them I vanished, but only if they ask. Tell them you bought the motorcycle for your brother.'

"Unknown to me, Will had earlier driven the motorcycle off and come walking back. He told Dave and the others that he'd delivered the motorcycle to my brother. When he left, he described what he'd told them, making sure they were in the back field before he walked away, leaving me weeping like I hadn't since my mother died. I was devastated. It was almost as bad as the day I had escaped from Pa, maybe worse.

"I vowed to Will that as soon as I could sell the place, or even lease it to somebody, I would head for Tallapoosa."

"Miss Fanny, I need to go back and see about Uncle Will. I came because I thought you might like to know how really bad he is. I still want to hear the rest of the story, but I need to leave now?"

"Of course, Gene. You remember, you go by and see Julie. And you say to her what I told you to say, and see what happens."

I did what Miss Fanny suggested. I went by to see Julie late that day. Heading down the dirt road past her house, I saw a new, green Mercury, driven by a young, good-looking man, turning into her driveway. I passed right on by, watching Julie run out to his car, all the while wishing to god I hadn't followed Fanny's advice.

I drove on about a mile before I knew I had to go back. Then I turned around and went in roaring. Her visitor was sitting in the porch swing, and Julie faced him in a two-person glider. These seemed strange arrangements for lovers, but I was so distraught, I didn't want to think what it might mean.

Stopping by the hospital, I asked the nurses if I could see Uncle Will now. He was in a coma and not permitted any visitors. Dr.

King happened by the nurse's station, and I asked him if he was going to be able to save Uncle Will.

Dr. King, a kindly man, looked like he was trying to figure out what to say to me, finally said, "Son, Will's about spent. I'm trying to get some penicillin for him now. He's got heavy pneumonia, and if I don't get some in him in the next 24 hours, he's gonna die. From what they say about this penicillin, it'll cure the kind of pneumonia he's got, it'll pull him through. But if I were you, I wouldn't get my hopes up too much. Do you know how to pray son?"

"Well, my praying never did much good, I don't think. I've always started praying just before Ma or Pa started beating on me, and it never helped much. I guess I just ain't got the hang of it yet. I'm afraid if I'm all he's got praying for him, he's out of luck."

A flicker of a smile crossed Dr. King's face. "Sometimes, son, when you pray, the prayer gets answered and you don't ever know it. And sometimes, the answer is no."

I was going to ask Pa about this when I got home. Come to think of it, all this time I had been going to church, I had never heard it from a preacher either. Maybe doctors knew more about praying than preachers did.

It rankled me Uncle Will's story and Miss Fanny's didn't always match. If he was confessing to purge his shriveled, dying soul, how on earth did he expect to do that while lying? Of course, this whole business of living, dying, going to heaven, going to hell, was awful complicated for me. I didn't understand any of it.

Everybody was asleep when I got home. I was gonna talk to Pa about the prayer business, but I figured I'd see him in the morning. Since it was Saturday, and he wouldn't be going to work, I milked the cow, fed the hogs, and was done when Ma finished the breakfast biscuits. While we were eating, Pa asked if I was planning to see Will. I told him not till late afternoon, and mentioned Dr. King had told me not to get up my hopes that Will was going to live much longer. He didn't know whether he could save him or not.

Ma said, "Good."

I didn't feel like arguing with Ma, and just sat there silently. Pa came to my rescue, saying, "I want you to help me castrate the new litter of pigs; they're six weeks old today."

That was a chore I'd done many times, so I grabbed a bottle of turpentine, poured a few ounces in a bowl, and added a little kerosene. I then scooped up a handful of lard, worked the mix up into a paste, put it in a pint fruit jar, and screwed the lid on it so it I wouldn't spill as I headed for the hog pen.

When I got there, Pa was sitting on the fence rail, honing his knife on the whetstone he carried in his pocket. He pushed the sharp side of the knife blade back and forth on the stone at a 45° angle, occasionally twisting it over to sharpen the other side. With slow rhythmic strokes, occasionally stopping to spit on the stone for lubrication, he pulled a fine edge on the blade.

This ritual had been going on ever since I'd helped castrate my first pig, when I was six. Pa never castrated before he'd taken 30 minutes sharpening the knife sufficiently to shave the hair on the back of his arm. When he stopped honing, pushed the knife up his arm, and the blade came away coated with hair, it was ready. He wiped it on his britches leg, stuck it down into the witch's brew of antiseptic I'd just prepared, and ordered me to catch the first pig.

Seated on a two-and-a-half gallon bucket, I took each six-week-old male pig, put his shoulder between my knees and presented his rear end to Pa. One swift slice down the center of one side of the scrotum, popping the testicles out like a seed from an overripe peach, scrapped the cord, sliced it in two, dropped it on the ground, then just as swiftly repeated the process on the other side. Then stuck two fingers in the antiseptic and pushed the mix of lard and turpentine deep into the animal's wound. As he performed the same operation on each, I was thinking about all the fun the little fellows were going to miss.

God save me, I thought how, on that one night I'd had with Julie, it seemed for a brief moment that my entire purpose in life had been realized in one splendid moment.

Afterwards, as we sat watching the pigs to make sure they were alright, I brought up the subject of Uncle Will and what Dr. King had said about praying.

"Pa, Dr. King said that God answers all prayers, but sometimes the answer is No when we pray. I wonder why nobody ever said that to me before?"

"Son, many times that has been said by the preacher. You've heard it, but it just never was anything you could use before. There must be a reason the Almighty—at that moment—chose for you to hear that bit of information 'cause I've heard it many times, and he's right. All preachers make that point sooner or later; there're no unanswered prayers. Are you praying for Will's recovery?"

"Well, Pa, I've never had a whole lot of faith in prayer. Do you remember the time Ma got sick, went up to Grandpa's, stayed up there for three weeks, and I had to cook your meals and do the washing? Remember the first day you come home and the wood was wet? I didn't even have a fire in the stove and the corn bread cracked wide open 'cause I couldn't start a fire. That was the first day I'd ever prayed. Every which way I turned, nothing went right.

"I really prayed that day for the fire to start and somehow for the bread to get baked. It just never did. I prayed the hardest of all I guess that you wouldn't beat me up and you didn't. I'm still grateful 'cause I know I deserved it, but I just sort of lost belief in prayer."

"Did you ever have any belief in prayer?"

"Well, when the preacher gets down on his knees or the deacons in church, they pray for the sick not to die and all that, people still go ahead and die, people still get sick. It just seems to me like it don't work too good."

"But you've got to remember, son, all of them say 'if it be thy will.' Maybe God doesn't want this for Will, maybe it's his time to die. Maybe he's got things up in Heaven for him to do. There does come a time to die. Praying won't change that."

"Pa, I guess God knows his business, but it's an awful poor way to run things. You don't never really know if he said yes or no. It seems like maybe God could use some better way to communicate."

"Are you gonna let me have the car tonight to see Uncle Will?"

"Have you asked your Ma about it?"

"No, I'd rather ask you."

"Well, if it's alright with her, it's alright with me."

I hated it when Pa said that, "It's alright with me if it's alright with your Ma." He was just simply saying, "I ain't gonna get in the doghouse over it, but if you can persuade her then I won't stop you, I don't have any plans."

Then, of course, the first thing I went and said is, "Ma, Pa said I could have the car to go see Uncle Will tonight if it's alright with you. Will you let me go?"

"You're gonna wear the car out running back and forth over these dirt roads to see a son-of-a-bitch that everybody else in the country wishes was dead. Sometimes I think you're gonna grow up to be just like him."

"Ma, would you tell me what he ever did to you? Really, did he ever personally do anything to you?"

"He's scared the living hell out of me. I remember one time he come by the house drunk and he told Ma he was gonna kill my Pa. That scared me half to death; I cried all night long."

"Well, what happened?"

"Didn't nothing happen, but he scared the shit out of me."

"And that's why you hate him so bad?"

"Well, wouldn't you hate somebody to come by here and threaten to kill your Pa?"

"I don't think I'd hate him forever. That must've been 30 years ago."

"There's some things you don't ever forget."

"Ma, I don't think you ever forgot anything or ever forgave anybody. You go to church and you say the Lord's Prayer. Haven't you noticed it says, 'we forgive those who trespass against us'?"

"Get your ass out of here young man. You mess with me and you won't be going to see that son-of-a-bitch nor nobody else in my car."

"Can I go Ma?"

"I'll study about it."

I decided I'd go over to Harvey Wright's and see if I could get him to take me just in case Ma didn't let me have the car. I still had all that money of Uncle Will's, and thought about getting Harvey to take me to town to buy another car so I wouldn't never have to ask her again. I hated to have a fuss every time. If they were planning to use the car, it'd be different. Sometimes I was sure Ma just wanted to be mean.

So I tramped across the field to Harvey's house. I asked him if he would be able to take me up to Bremen if I couldn't get Pa's car. He said he had a date, but he could run me up there and come back by and pick me up, though it might be as late as 11:30.

On the way back home I kept thinking about the money in that old inner tube in the barn loft. If Ma knew there was that much money nearby, Lord she would have tore up the whole farm trying to find it. Then I thought about getting Harvey's Pa to go into town and put my new car in his name. Course I had no idea they'd sell a car to a young fellow like me who wasn't old enough to vote. But Uncle Will was so sick they wouldn't let me see him, and I didn't have his permission to spend the money. I guess I wouldn't buy a car unless he told me I could.

Which is one difference 'tween me and Uncle Will. If he was in my shoes, I'd bet the last catfish in Mississippi he'd go buy a car, telling them he was 21 years old. And he'd quit fooling around begging Ma to use ours every night. Maybe I ought to be more like him. But everybody'd want to know where I got the money, and I wasn't too good at lying.

I often thought I really ought to be just a shade more like Uncle Will. Nowadays, times are different—you've got tags for cars, you got telephones, the police have high-powered cruisers, you couldn't live the way Uncle Will lived. So that was my excuse for taking all that junkmouth off of Ma.

As soon as I walked in the door, she started in again.

"Where have you been? Why don't you tell somebody where you're going when you leave, and when you're coming back? Your Pa wants you to go down yonder and help him catch that old mule.

"You act like you're already full grown and can do just as you please. Let me tell you young man, you ain't a man of your own until you are 21 years old. Can you remember that? You gonna do what I tell you to do. When you leave here, you tell me where you're going and when you're gonna be back. Get your mind off of the ol' fart who's dying up there in Bremen and let him die. It serves him right."

I saw Pa down behind the barn. Ol' Jack was walking around him in a wide circle while Pa tried to lure him into the stable with an ear of corn. Ol' Jack was nearly as smart as Pa. Pa claimed he was smarter than me. Ol' Jack wasn't gonna let Pa get him in the stable with an ear of corn and then have to work all afternoon for that ear of corn. He was too smart for that, so we tried to hem him up in the corner of the pasture. A time or two he'd break and run a little piece, but he sure did want that ear of corn. Finally, I grabbed him in the nostrils as he ran by, and Pa slipped the bridle on him.

"You and your Ma having some more words?"

"Aw, yeah, I don't know why she's the way she is. It don't do nobody no good. Sometimes I think she hates herself."

"You may be closer to the truth than you think boy, but you've lived with her all your life. You ought not to let such a ....."

"Pa, what would you say if Uncle Will bought me a car so I wouldn't have to ask Ma every time I need to go somewhere?"

"I doubt he's got the money, son. He was pretty reckless with money. He had a lot, but it run through his fingers like quicksilver. I'd be surprised if he had money to buy any kind of car worth anything."

"Pa, he's got lots of money."

"How do you know?"

"He told me."

"Just remember, if he lets you buy the car, you're still gonna have to do what your Ma says as long as you live here. She ain't gonna let you have no peace of mind as long as you live in the house."

"Well, what would you say if I just up and moved out?"

"Son, according to the law you ain't a man of your own. You can't sign a legal contract till you get 21 years old. You are just seventeen. So, it's gonna be four years before you can have a car of your own or can legally do what you want to do. I think you're a pretty good boy, and I ain't got no problem with you moving out. You know how to behave yourself, but I've lived with your Maw for 18 years, and she's gonna have things her way, and you know it. So, you better ask her before you buy the car. She might even just throw you out, especially knowing it belonged to him."

"Why does she hate him so much, Pa?"

"Son, understanding your Maw is sort of like you was talking about earlier, about understanding God. I don't think men was meant to figure out women, especially your Ma. Don't go getting yourself disappointed thinking she's gonna let you do just as you please or you don't have to ask her for no car. If you buy it without asking her, it's gonna be a source of contention. My advice is, if

Will wants to buy you a car, go ahead and let him buy the car. Then park it the yard, and see what happens."

After helping Pa put the harness on Ol' Jack, I went into the barn loft to the old inner tube, took out my pocket knife, and cut a slit about three inches long. I fished out $2500, put the tube back in place, and started off to Harvey Wright's.

When I finally reached Harvey's house, I asked him to take me to town, told him I wanted to buy a new car, saying, "I'll let you go for a ride with me if you'll take me to buy it." He drove me to an auto showroom on Rome Street in Carrollton, where there was the prettiest emerald green Buick a fellow ever laid his eyes on.

I asked Billy Morrow, the owner of the place, "How much for that car?"

"You want the cash price or the credit price, young fellow?"

"I want the cash price."

"I've got a special today, I'll let you have that car for $1695. It's got a radio, white wall tires. You'd be a sport driving that pretty thing. You'd have to beat the girls off with a stick if you had it."

I felt sure he didn't think I had the money. His lower jaw dropped down about three inches when I pulled out a wad of money and started counting.

"Who do you want the bill of sale made out to, young fellow?"

"I want it made out to Will J. Johnson Jr.," I said as I finished counting out his money. Fifteen minutes later I pulled out of the Buick place in a new Roadmaster emerald green Buick with white sidewall tires and a radio that could you hear WSB in Atlanta on just as plain as if it was next door. Boy, did everybody turn their eyes when I drove through Carrollton.

When I drove up in the front yard, Ma was out in a flash. She started right up, "Whose car is this? Did you steal the thing?"

"Ma, this car belongs to Uncle Will, and he says I can drive it till he gets out of the hospital. I don't have to ask you to use that old beat up Ford no more."

"Where did that bastard get enough money to buy a car like this?"

"I don't know, Ma."

"I do. He stole the damn money, that's where he got it. That's the only way he ever had any damn money. And let me tell you one thing, young man, you may not have to ask me to use this car, but you've got to ask me if you can go. If I've got anything else for you to do, you'll do it. Do you understand that, young man? I'm still your Ma, and I'm still your boss, and don't you forget it. Unless you've got it in that thick head of yours to move out."

"I don't plan to move out, Ma, unless you make me. But sometimes you make it awful hard staying here. I give you half I make for the privilege of staying here, and I can do better than that at any boarding house in Carrollton, money-wise. And I wouldn't have to milk the cow, slop the hogs, and do all the chores I have to do around here."

"Young man, I can tell you right now, you're just about too big for your britches. Don't you get snotty with me."

" Ma, I'm on my way to the barn to milk the cow. And then I'm going to clean up, put me some Sunday clothes on, and I'm going to see how Uncle Will's doing. If Uncle Will still can't see me, I'm going back to see Miss Fanny."

"You mean that goddamn whore that that son-of-a-bitch lived with back when I was a girl?"

"Ma, I talked to Miss Fanny; she ain't no whore. She's a lady. I like her."

"You wouldn't know a whore from a pig's ass if you met one in the middle of the road. She's nothing but a straight-out carnival slut.

"If that's the likes of folks that you're hanging around with when you're away from home, I guarantee you, young man, you'll be in the penitentiary before you're 21. I don't know what in the hell this world is coming to."

By the time I walked out of the house, it was 4 o'clock in the afternoon. I sorely wanted to drive by Julie's house in that fine Buick, but then I thought I could drive it to work Monday, where she'd be sure to see it then. She might be out with her new boyfriend. I began to get a swelled head just at the thought of driving that big Buick to work and parking it in the General Shoe parking lot, of throwing a nonchalant look back over my right shoulder...I decided that would be even more fun than driving by Julie's house. She might not recognize me even if she was out in the yard, so I decided I'd save that thrill for Monday.

At about 5:30 I went out to the old Ford, opened the trunk, got the patching kit, and stuck it in my pocket. I wanted to put the rest of the money back in the inner tube. Ma yelled out the window, "What're you doing with that car? I thought you had one, and you didn't need to ask me no more...get out of there! What are you doing in the trunk of that car?"

I put the patching kit back, slammed the trunk down as hard as I could, and went on to the barn to milk. I could put the money under the floor mat of Uncle Will's new Buick.

I went to the hospital to see how Uncle Will was doing. He wasn't any better. The nurses were expecting penicillin the next morning. One nurse acted like she didn't think he'd last that long. So I decided to go back to Miss Fanny's.

"Miss Fanny, I didn't know what time you go to bed; Uncle Will is still in a coma, so I decided I'd come down here and get you to tell me some more about Greenville."

"Well, Gene, you gave me somewhat of a start. I wasn't expecting you to come at night time. But it will be an hour or so before I go to bed so I don't mind finishing the story. As a matter of fact, I'm delighted any time you want to come to listen to an old woman recount her life. I can't imagine why a young man like you would want to sit and listen to all of this stuff.

"Did you go by and see your Julie, and tell her what I told you?"

"Well, I went by to tell her, Miss Fanny, but another fellow in a new Mercury turned into her yard just as I got there. I'm thinking she's found her a boyfriend with a new car. So you know what I did? I took some of Uncle Will's money without his permission and bought a new Buick. It is a pretty thing.

"Now mind you, Miss Fanny, I put the car in Uncle Will's name. It's Uncle Will's, and he sort of gave me permission to spend his money. He didn't tell me I could buy a car, but he did say to take money for any expenses that I had because you know it was about to bust me flat for gas going back and forth to see him. Ma made me fill the car up every time I used it, and I give Ma half of my paycheck anyway. Will didn't tell me to buy no new car, but I did anyway. And you know what? I bought it because I think he'd have done the same thing. What do you think?"

"Well, there's not much doubt in my mind, Gene, that he probably would have. But you certainly don't want to pattern your life after your Uncle Will's."

"Oh, I don't want to kill anybody. No, I don't want my life to be like his. But I like him, Miss Fanny.

"I can't rightly say why I like him because I really don't know. One thing, when he says, 'Pete and Gabe,' referring to the archangels, it sort of sends a cold shiver up my spine. Anybody who has that much brass, I just can't help but like them. I ain't got that kind of nerve, Miss Fanny, I just ain't got the nerve to talk to folks the way he does and to say the things he does."

"He is a bold one, Gene, I'll tell you that. Or he was."

"Here I am, Miss Fanny doing all the talking and I come to hear about you and him."

"Where was I last time? Oh, I remember. I was crying my eyes out just after Will left. I was so lonely and depressed. I went to see my lawyer the next day and asked him about trying to sell the farm. Up to that point, I'd paid for everything I'd bought, and it looked like a good crop coming in. I told him my husband of only three weeks just up and left for no reason whatever. I decided that I was not a farmer and I'd like to sell out to somebody who would look after the black folks and bring the crop in. I would be willing to sell it at a good price.

"He asked me what I considered a good price. I told him I'd take $75,000 for it hoping I could come down to $60,000. It was really worth that much. I was amazed. He said, 'I'll give you that for it as it stands. I think I can sell it for at least $100,000 in a few weeks if you wait that long, but I'll give you what you ask for it today.'

"I told him, no. I'd take $75,000 for it; I was ecstatic I got my asking price. I told him I'd be out of the house within a week. I just wanted to keep it long enough to tell all of my friends good bye.

"I met him at the bank the following day and we closed the deal. I took $15,000 in cash and bought six $10,000 treasury bonds. I knew they'd be good anywhere in the United States, and there was no bank that was going bust and take my money. I went back home and got out the old suitcase I'd bought long ago in Rome, Georgia where I kept my money.

"When I got back, I gave each tenant family $500. I told them if anybody ever bought the property, it would help them get started somewhere else.

"In preparation for going east, I visited all my friends in the days that followed. Saturday morning, when I came down for breakfast, the chief of police from Greenville and a gentleman I didn't know were seated at my dining room table. Dave said, 'Ma'am, they came earlier, I asked them to wait until you got up. I told them you'd be up about now. I invited 'em into the living room.'

"The police chief of Greenville, Ezra Moon, introduced his companion as T. D. Bronski, Chief of Detectives of the Pinkerton Agency. My heart sank as T. D. Bronski began the interrogation.

"'Mrs. Johnson, we think the real name of the man you just married is Will something or other, but we don't think it's Johnson. We know that's the name he used when he first met you, and we know that's the name you married him under, but we're not so sure that that's his name. We think he has several aliases, among them, Jesse Robinson, Will Cotton, Roddy Miles, and God knows how many more. Are any of those names familiar to you?'

"As he spoke, I saw the *True Detective* magazines lying around over the room. 'Mr. Bronski, I have heard every single one of those names along with your name. They're in those detective magazines. Of course, I never thought I would really meet one of the characters out of a detective magazine. And I'm honored to do so.'

"'Mrs. Johnson, I need to ask you some questions. And I hope you will be forthcoming with me. If I feel that you are not being truthful with me, I can have Chief Moon arrest you as a material witness in a capital murder case. And we can hold you in jail for whatever amount of time we choose. I certainly don't want to do that to such a pretty young lady.

"'If, as you say, you have read these *True Detective* magazines, you no doubt noticed, the writer of those stories tried to put the Pinkerton Detective Agency in the worst possible light. More or less painted us as a bunch of stupid stumblebums. Now mind you, Mrs. Johnson, it is still my contention that Jesse Robinson lies buried in a pauper's grave here in Greenville. Two or three months ago you married a man who also fit the description we have of Jesse

Robinson. We know for an absolute fact that you settled in this community long before this tall stranger whom you later married came to this area. What we don't know is how you met this stranger or how he came to be in Greenville. Would you tell us about that?'

"'I was horrified. First of all, I didn't have the faintest idea that I could be arrested as a material witness, as he called it. Second, Will had not said anything about fabricating a story about how I met him. I guess we both thought I'd never face this situation. I had to think of something that sounded plausible right away and my mind just wouldn't seem to work. He repeated his question.'

"'Mrs. Johnson, where and how did you meet Will J. Johnson Jr.?'

"'Actually, I met him at the railroad station,' I lied. 'I went to the railroad station to pick up some fruit trees that I'd bought from a mail order house. A stranger helped me load them on the wagon.'

"'When we got the fruit trees in the wagon, we started talking. He told me he grew up on a farm in South Carolina, there didn't seem like there was any great future in farming so he took the job as sales representative for a shoe company. He was on his way to Dallas, thought he would call on some merchants here in Greenville since he had over a 4-hour wait for his train going west.

"'Maybe I was a little bit forward. I told him I was a widow looking for a foreman for my farm. When he told me how much he made, I told him I could match that sum if he would work for that. I told him I had a pretty nice house that needed repair, if he could repair it, I'd pay for the material and he could live in the house free of rent as he supervised my farm. On my part, I hate to say it was sort of love at first sight. I'm not usually that bold and forward. He rode out to the farm with me, looked it over, and agreed to take the job. That's the way I met him.'

"'During the time you knew him, Mrs. Johnson, he must have told you where he came from, about his family, and that sort of thing. He must have given you some mailing addresses.'

"'Yes, he did, only he doesn't have any living family. His mother and father both died and he was an only child. He grew up just outside of Charleston, South Carolina. He was 12 when his Pa died. His mother died the following year. He was taken in by the Lady of Perpetual Help Catholic Orphanage just outside of Charleston where he spent the next 4 years before he decided to strike out on his own.'

"I was not accustomed to lying; I'd about run out of anything else to say. I kept my eyes riveted on T. D. Bronski to see if I could detect whether he was believing what I was saying or not. I couldn't tell for sure, but I thought he believed what I told him."

"Miss Fanny, now he's got you doing it."

"What do you mean, Gene?"

"I mean Uncle Will's got you lying just like him."

"Well, I guess you're right about that, Gene, but I didn't think of it that way. I thought of it as protecting him. At that time, he'd convinced me all of the wrong he'd done was somebody else's fault. I claim my young age and immaturity for allowing him to persuade me of that fact, but that's the way I felt.'

"'Tell me, Mrs. Johnson, you have already sold this property. Doesn't it strike you as strange that Will J. Johnson Jr. would leave you three days after this magazine story appeared. Or at least after you bought the detective magazine?'

"'To tell you the truth, Mr. Bronski, the thought has not crossed my mind.'

"'We both read the *True Detective* stories about G. B. Balls in *True Detective* magazine, but not once did it occur to me or did he give any indication to me that he could possibly be Jesse Robinson, alias all of those other people.

"'I remember giving him the magazine with the first story about G. B. Balls after he came here. The magazine was already here, as you can see from the date on it. The only thing I remember him saying about the story when he finished reading it was, "I'd hate to be in that fellow's shoes when the Pinkertons catch him.'

"'I see. That, Mrs. Johnson, brings us to another question. Why so quickly after Will left you are you selling out and leaving? It looks to me suspiciously like you are going to meet him somewhere.'

"I'm sure I blushed when he said that out of anger and embarrassment for stumbling into or not expecting the question.

"I half shouted, 'Mr. Bronski, I'm beginning to understand why the magazine writer thinks the Pinkerton people are stupid. Let me tell you something, I was madly in love with Will. You know

Mr. Bronski, men seem to be able to discard women almost at will. Women don't find it quiet so easy. But then you couldn't know that, you're a man. If you're married, ask your wife about it. You men are so damn smart, you think you know everything, you can read minds. I'll tell you, I'd walk a rotten log through hell for that man, and I'm so depressed I don't think I can live another day. But I don't know why he left me.

"'When I sold the property, my lawyer advised me to get over the grief of losing my love before I sold it. I might even decide not to sell it. But the two months that I spent with him here were the happiest two months of my life. And you, sir, can go to hell. I am going back to my home to get away from those memories. I realize very well that in time I will heal, but it will surely take some time.'

"'Mrs. Johnson, I didn't mean to upset you, the man we're looking for murdered four Pinkerton officers in cold blood. We're almost certain of that. Even though we've never found the body of the fourth one. Also, it is a safe bet the man buried in the pauper's grave was murdered by Jesse Robinson, or else met his death as the result of knowing Jesse Robinson.

"'The undertaker tells me the body was so badly decomposed and nibbled on by the riverfish that there is no way we might identify the corpse for certain. The way the undertaker so graphically put it was, "His own mother couldn't identify him."'

"'Mrs. Johnson, you've convinced me that if you were married to Jesse Robinson, you're unaware of that fact. In the event we have other questions, can you leave a forwarding address where you plan to go?'

"'I haven't made up my mind yet where I'm going. I grew up in Newnan, Georgia. My Pa bet me against a $250 bet in a poker game and lost. So I don't think I'll be going back to Newnan.

"'My first husband abandoned me after six months for an old girlfriend whom he'd gotten pregnant. We lived in Virginia. I don't think I'll be going back to Virginia. I've been thinking about going down to the railroad station and buying a ticket to anywhere. And just find a place that looks promising to me and settle down there.

"'To answer your question, sir, I don't know where I'll go, I'm just going.'

"'Mrs. Johnson, when you get ready to leave town, would you at least do us the courtesy of coming by the police station to tell us where you finally decide to go just in case we'd like to talk to you in the future and cover some ground I may have forgotten this morning. We really think that Jesse Robinson lies buried in the cemetery, but in view of this story, we're going to have to stay alert for a while longer to prove one way or the other that Jesse Robinson is dead.'

"I promised I'd do that, and they left. I went to the window and watched them get in their car and drive away. I was not planning on leaving until the following Monday or Tuesday, but I went back to my bedroom and packed up the two suitcases that I was going to carry with me. I felt I'd better get out of Greenville while I could.

"Once I left, I was going to be a fugitive from justice. I couldn't help but think about T. D. Bronski's warning when he left the house, 'Remember, Mrs. Johnson, I don't think Jesse Robinson is still alive, but if he is, we can take a warrant for you for aiding and abetting the escape of a felon. So let me advise you to be very circumspect in your behavior. You wouldn't want to become a hunted criminal. If we felt like you were trying to elude us, we would take out a warrant for your arrest on the grounds that you aided and abetted a fleeing felon. Most judges would look upon your behavior as an admission of that fact.'"

Golden Gift

"I pretty well knew they were going to have a detective at the railroad station who would know my destination. About that time, Dave knocked at my door. He looked panic stricken.

"'Miss Fanny, there's more Pinkerton's down questioning the farm hands. They've done told them that we fished Mr. Will out of the Mississippi River.'

"'Dave, get the fastest horse we've got and hitch him up to the buggy. Take these two suitcases and I'll be down in a minute.' I told Nancy it might be two or three days before she saw Dave again and as soon as I could, I would send him home. She said, 'God bless you, child,' with fear in her eyes. Ten minutes later, I climbed into the buggy and we headed east at a gallop.

"I had Dave run the horse as fast as the beast could go, and stop and rest only when necessary. I had to get as far away from Greenville as I could, and I wanted him to last a long time. I'm not certain Dave understood exactly the trouble I was in, but he knew I was in trouble. I instructed him that, when he got back, and the Pinkerton's started questioning him, he tell them he'd had no idea I'd done anything wrong. That way he wouldn't be blamed for anything, and the detectives wouldn't cause him any trouble.

"Dave kept the horse at a steady trot mile after a mile. I began to take stock of my situation, but I couldn't really think of anything I'd done wrong. And yet, if the Pinkerton man was right, I was guilty of a crime, aiding and abetting a capital criminal. Suddenly a quotation from a poem my mother read to me once came to mind, 'To pluck a flower is to shake a star.' I'd thought, when she read that, what a terrible exaggeration it was, but now I wasn't so sure.

"It was about 15 miles east to Leland. We were there before noon. I asked an old man sitting on the front porch of the general merchandise store if there was a train station. He said if I hurried I could catch the 11:30 train going east, and pointed the way. Dave started whipping the horse, and in three minutes we were there.

"Rushing inside, I asked the ticket agent where the train was headed. He said it would be leaving in two minutes, and it was headed for Evansville, Indiana. I bought a ticket and got aboard just as the train started to move, feeling certain that I could lose my pursuers if I could get to a big city like Evansville.

"There were a few passengers on the train who tried to make conversation, but I just wanted to think, so I kept moving about. I considered my options and knew I'd have to cover my tracks well. Earlier I'd only needed to cover my own to keep the Pinkertons from following me to Will. Now it was a matter of staying out of jail myself if T. D. Bronski had declared me a fugitive for aiding and abetting a capital felon. I still didn't see how he could do that, because there was no way I could have known about Will. Maybe it was just an empty threat, but I couldn't afford to take the chance. Now I couldn't decide what I needed to do.

"It was well after dark when we got to Memphis. I gave my bags to a porter on the dock and asked him to call me a carriage to take me to a hotel, where I registered in the name of Sally Webb. As soon as I got to my room, I opened both suitcases—the big one that I'd had ever since Newnan and a much smaller one. Taking everything out of the larger one that I could do without, I put my bonds in my purse, along with $5000. The remaining $10,000 in cash I tied neatly in a paper sack and packed that into the smaller suitcase. It was now small and light enough that I could handle it easily. Leaving by the back door of the hotel, I caught a carriage, and told the driver to head east, I'd tell him where to stop.

"When we were two blocks from a large hotel, I had him stop, and walked the remaining distance. The hotel's name was the Newbuilt, but it certainly wasn't new. It seemed nice enough, so I paid a week's rent, went to my room, and fell in bed exhausted.

"When I awoke the next morning, I had begun to understand how Will felt as a fugitive from justice. I now knew I had to be very careful not to lead the Pinkertons straight to my darling.

"My room was on the second floor. I went down to the dining room to have breakfast at about 8 AM the next morning. Passing the desk, I picked up a newspaper where the headline said, 'Jesse Robinson Alive,' and read the story as I ate my breakfast.

"'The Pinkerton Detective Agency has reopened the case of G. B. Balls and his assailant, Jesse Robinson, as the result of an article that has just appeared in *True Detective* magazine. The writer had suggested the body in a pauper's grave in Greenville, Mississippi, thought to be Jesse Robinson might be someone else, and gave the following reasons.'

"Well, Gene, those reasons are the ones I told you about, so I won't repeat them. But the newspaper story had more.

"'It is now believed by the Pinkerton Detective Agency that Jesse Robinson married a Greenville woman by the name of Fanny Hawk about two months ago. He attended the First Baptist Church of Greenville, and sang in the choir on a regular basis. Though there is no solid proof, following the story's appearance, the man believed to be Jesse Robinson suddenly skipped town leaving his wife without any explanation.

"'When his wife was questioned by the superintendent of detectives, T. D. Bronski, she lied, saying she had met him at the railroad station. But her farmworkers reported they'd fished him out of the Mississippi River unconscious. The case of the Pinkerton Agency is strengthened by the fact his wife fled shortly after she was questioned, purchasing a railway ticket to Evansville, Indiana. Needless to say, the Pinkerton authorities are in vigorous pursuit.'

"As I finished reading the story and looked around the restaurant, it seemed that everybody was starring at me, just looking away as I caught their eyes. I felt there were signs all over the room, each pointing to me screaming, 'She's the one! She's the one!'

"Though I didn't think I stood out in a crowd like my giant Will, the paper had noted my exact height and weight as 5 foot 2 inches, 105 pounds, which made me most obvious.

"Feeling trapped in the hotel, I left with my suitcase at 9 o'clock and headed directly to the train station. This time I bought a ticket east to Knoxville, where I had once attended a finishing school. I was already aboard when it dawned on me that I knew a perfect disguise. So I got off the train with my bag and caught a carriage to a nearby dry goods store, where I told the clerk my grandfather had just died, and I needed to purchase some mourning wear for my grandmother, who was my size. I also purchased a walking cane.

"Since I hadn't checked out of the hotel, I went back to my room, and 30 minutes later, a bent hobbling old lady with a cane made her way downstairs, out the back door, and off to the railroad station in time to catch the 4 o'clock train to Knoxville.

"This time I got a Pullman compartment, since I didn't much care for sitting behind the heavy veils in those dark clothes all day long. Though I felt I had a perfect disguise, I still intended to take my time and cover a lot of miles before I finally headed for my rendezvous with Will in Tallapoosa.

"I spent better than a month wandering around the east coast on Pullman trains and in hotels until I was sick of them. Finally, I bought a ticket to Atlanta, and one from Atlanta to Tallapoosa, where I checked into the Old Oak Hotel under my maiden name, as Will had told me to do. I was frantic to know if Will was alright.

"True to Will's word, he knocked on my door less than 24 hours after I registered in the hotel. He put my bags in the side car of his Harley-Davidson and took me to the house you know all about on the banks of the Big Tallapoosa River.

"There we began our honeymoon all over again. It's fair to say that no woman has ever been happier than I was for the first couple of months. But Will was a restless soul. He'd go off and play poker in a roadhouse a few miles away two or three nights a week.

"In the beginning, I'd go to his poker games with him, and sit around and share a few drinks. But no other women came and it was a rather ill-kept place I didn't care for. I suggested to Will he should find better things to do with his time. With all the talent he had, it was such a waste to sit at a poker table night after night.

"One night he came home awful drunk and I started scolding him about the company he kept and how he was wasting his life. He went into a blind rage and beat me black and blue all over.

"The next morning, when he looked at me, he swore he couldn't remember anything that had happened, and I believed him. But I swore to Will several times that I'd leave if he ever did that to me again. He was so conscience-stricken for days he didn't leave the house, waiting on me hand and foot. As young and healthy as I was, it didn't take long for my bruises to heal, though my feelings were a mite slower.

"Then began one of the most exciting parts of my life. Will quit playing poker and drinking. We were at a party one night, and somebody started talking about Mayhayley Lancaster. She was an old fortuneteller living down in Heard County somewhere. She was supposed to have all sorts of powers, like telling the future and extrasensory perception. Her reputation stretched afar, and I made Will promise he'd take me to see her. I wanted to know my fortune.

"The following Saturday we headed out to find her house. It was an old broken down place with bales of cotton scattered about. Some of the bagging and bales had already rotted. There were several people ahead of us, each waiting on the front porch, I suppose, to have their fortune told. We giggled, talked to the other about Mayhayley, and speculated about how much she would charge for telling our fortunes. It was just generally a good time.

"Finally, it came our turn to see her. Will stuck out his hand and said, 'Mayhayley, tell me my fortune.'

"She was sitting behind a little table wearing an old army overcoat though it was very hot weather. She wore half-glasses, looking over them at his hand, one finger at a time. She touched his fingers. Suddenly she took a piece of paper, covered his hand, shielded her eyes, and refused to say another word.

"'Come on, Mayhayley, is it that bad?'

"She still refused to speak. Will pulled his hand off the table and dropped it down to his side. I was a bit frightened to stick my hand on the table, but I did. She began talking almost immediately. I was astounded by her first words, 'You're from Coweta County, and you're part Indian. Did you know that, child?'

"'No, ma'am.'

"'What is your maiden name, child?'

"'Hawk.'

"'Now I know what my vision means. Fanny Hawk, that's your name.'

"I was intrigued. I didn't know how she could know my first name unless she'd heard Will say it above the hubbub of the other people sitting on the front porch.

"'Have you ever heard of an Indian called Chief McIntosh?'

"'Of course, everybody around Arnco's heard of Chief McIntosh.'

"She looked me in the eye, 'Miss Fanny Hawk, you are Chief McIntosh's granddaughter at the 4th generation.'

"'How do you know that when I don't know that?'

"'Child, you are the first female offspring of Chief McIntosh for almost 100 years.'

"'How can you possibly know that?'

"'Child, do you ask the wind how it knows to blow?'

"'No, ma'am.'

"'Do you ask the sun how it knows to shine?'

"'No, ma'am.'

"'Do you ask the rain how it knows to fall?'

"'No, ma'am.'

"'Then don't ask a fortuneteller how to tell.'

"'Yes ma'am.'

"'What is your Pa's name?'

"I was so disturbed I couldn't think.

"'Was not his first name, Billy?'

"The moment she said it, I remembered that's what grandpa's first name was. He had died when I was a little girl, I remembered that.

"'His Pa before him—do you know what his name was?'

"'No, ma'am.'

"I was completely mystified by Mayhayley, and remain so to this day. She continued.

"'About 100 years ago, Chief McIntosh was the richest man in all of Carroll County. He was an Indian trader. Some said he was a slave trader. Some said he sold his own people into bondage. But the truth of the matter is, in 1825 he went to make peace with his brethren. But since they thought he'd betrayed them, they shot him so full of holes that it was said you couldn't place your hand anywhere on his body without covering at least two bloody wounds.

"'When I first started in this fortuneteller business, child, I had a vision of an Indian chief rising up from the dead so full of bullet holes you couldn't lay a hand on him without covering one. In my vision the dead chief said, "Mayhayley, my granddaughter of the 4th generation is coming to visit you. You'll be an old woman then, and you're going to tell her where I hid my gold—100 pounds of $20 gold pieces I've buried, and you must tell her how to find it.'

"At this point she stopped, pointed to Will, and said, 'Out.'

"Then she leaned across the table and said, 'Come close, my child, so you and only you can hear. These are the instructions the apparition gave me.

"'Walk along the railroad track going south from Carrollton until you can see the mighty Chattahoochee. The minute you can see the river in front of you, you will pass behind a little hill. Keep walking down the railroad track until the track begins to curve to the left. There is only one short stretch on the railroad track where you can see the Chattahoochee before the trestle crosses the river. At that point, go to the river bank. After about one mile, the river will start curving back to the left, and a high hill will lie ahead of you. On top of that hill there are two huge boulders sticking up from the ground, leaning against each other.

"'On the first day of fall, when the sun's orb is one finger above the horizon, go to the point where the shadow of the tops of the rocks meet. At that point, dig and you'll find your treasure.'

"Mayhayley looked at me expectantly over her half-glasses with a crazy wild-eyed look. 'Child, go and claim your birthright.'

"'Miss Mayhayley, you think I am going off to find gold that's been buried 100 years just because you dreamed of it?'

"'I did not dream, Fanny Hawk, I had a vision. If you don't go, you're a damn fool.'

"'Why don't you go if you believe there is gold buried there?'

"'I don't believe there is gold buried there, Fanny Hawk, I know there is gold buried there. Buried there by your grandfather of the 4th generation; it is yours not mine.'

"'Miss Mayhayley, that's the silliest thing I ever heard.'

"'How did I know your name before you came in this room, young lady?'

"'Well, I don't know, maybe somebody told you.'

"'Is there anybody here who knows you?'

"'Well, I didn't see anybody who does.'

"'That's not the name you bear now. I'll tell you how I knew Miss Fanny Hawk—because I saw your face in that same vision.'

"When she said that, Gene, that sort of sent a cold shiver up my spine. I was half beginning to believe what she said. She went on.

"'Have you ever known anybody else whose last name was Hawk?'

"'Well, nobody but my family. I can't rightly say, but I've never traveled that widely.'

"'It's a very rare name child. Let me tell you how your name got to be Hawk. When the great chief's bullet-riddled body was found, he had one finger pointing up at an eagle's nest. We now call them bald eagles, but in those days the Indians called them fish hawks. When your grandpa of the 4th generation was born, the last child of Chief McIntosh was named Little Fish Hawk.'

"'My name is not Fish Hawk, it's Hawk.'

"'But wait, child. The great Chief McIntosh made a deal with the white man to carry his people west and live on a reservation. When Chief McIntosh was murdered, that task fell to his eldest son, who didn't want his youngest brother to suffer the indignities of the reservation. So he carried his baby off to a white woman who was his mother and got her to promise she would name him Billy Hawk in the county records. Since he was half white and lived with a white woman, he grew up as white. Eventually he married a white woman and named his eldest Billy Hawk and so on.

"'Now that's how you came to be Fanny Hawk. Go and claim your birthright. But beware of your traveling companion; he'll only bring you heartbreak.'

"With that, I stood up and asked her how much I owed her.

"'You owe me nothing. You've taken a great burden from me. Go.'

"When we left Mayhayley's place, I told Will everything she'd said. As strange and foolish as it may seem, I now believed her. As strange and foolish as it may seem, Will did, too.

"I'm not one to believe in the supernatural or metaphysical. Will was much more superstitious and believed in that sort of thing a lot more than I did. But there were many, many tales told about Mayhayley—how she had solved murders, had told folks where lost things could be found. Many of the stories were substantiated by more than one person.

"As the days went by, we couldn't get our visit to Mayhayley off our minds. September came with a cool, rainy spell. Then the days turned warm and mellow. We couldn't stop dreaming about the treasure my distant grandpa had supposedly left me.

"About the middle of September we decided we'd see if we could find the place she described. We took Will's Harley south to Whitesburg, got on the Georgia Central track just to the east of Whitesburg, and started walking.

"Exactly as Mayhayley described it, the railroad started curving to the right. There was a point where you could see the river for about four or five steps. Then the railroad embankment blocked out your vision precisely as she'd described.

"We walked toward the river and proceeded downstream. Pretty soon the hill she'd described came into view. Even though it was thickly forested, it was easy to tell there was a bluff overlooking the river. We walked up to the top of the ridge, and sure enough, there stood two rocks leaning towards each other, forming an up-side down V with a sharp point.

"Near midday, the shadow cast by the rocks came to a sharp point, but only about 10 feet away from the boulders. We walked through the inverted V and turned back to see where the sun might come up. We tried to imagine where the point of that inverted V would be when the sun's orb was only one finger above the horizon.

"Because the ground fell away sharply, it looked as if it might be as far as a mile off. We kept walking away from the rock's arch to see whether any trees fell within the cone of the shadow. It appeared none were, even though we went on till it was difficult to see whether the rocks were there at all, they were so far away.

"We couldn't imagine a sharp shadow falling beyond where we trod. So we looked for arrowheads; we looked for anything that would remind us of Indians. This was supposed to have happened 100 years ago, and nature wouldn't likely hold scars that long.

"'Fanny, it's probably silly as hell, but let's go get us a tent and camp out for a week here. We can get us some ropes, picks, and shovels, and buy a Model-T truck for hauling out our treasure. But first, let's see if we can find an old lumbering road in.'

"We went back to Whitesburg and stopped at a blacksmith's shop, where the smithy was working on some plows. Striking up a conversation, we casually asked whether he was familiar with the spot on the north bank of the Chattahoochee where two rocks formed an inverted V.

"'Yeah, of course I am; that's on the land Chief McIntosh once owned. He was supposed to have buried a treasure down there somewhere. Folks have been looking for it near on to 100 years, and as far as I know nobody has ever found anything.'

"To take a vehicle in, according to the blacksmith, we needed to head toward Roopville. He gave us a rather complicated set of instructions, and we ran into several dead end roads, but eventually managed to ride right up to the foot of the hills where those leaning rocks came together.

"The next morning, we stopped at the Ford dealer in Carrollton and bought a new Model-T Runabout, as the dealer called it, guaranteed to haul 800 pounds up any hill in Carroll County, in addition to two grown men in the front seat, so the actual payload of the truck was 1200 pounds.

"Since I'd never driven a car or truck, I drove the motorcycle home. Will followed in the shiny new pickup. When we went through Tallapoosa, we stopped at the hardware store to buy some picks and shovels. Will and I decided we'd camp right on the river.

"While we were purchasing our camping supplies, he bought a coil of rope. By the time we got all our equipment loaded, Will started joking about finding 100 pounds of gold and not being able to bring it out. We'd have to make two loads because of our gear.

"Early the next morning we loaded all of our supplies on the Model-T—everything we imagined we might need for a week's stay camping out in the country—and headed for the Chattahoochee River below Whitesburg.

"It was around noon when we got there. Will immediately set about building us a lean-to much like the one he had built in Arkansas, with the open side facing the Chattahoochee. We wound up setting the tent up on the front side of the lean-to, with Will burying the edges by shoveling sand over them so no snakes or other critters could get in.

"This was the dry time of the year, so rain wasn't much of a consideration. Even so, Will dug a ditch about 30 or 40 feet long to make sure no water would collect if we had a late summer thunderstorm.

"All the time we were preparing our lean-to, Will kept talking about the gold we were going to find as if it were an accomplished fact. His attitude was infectious, and by the time we went to bed that night, I was totally confident we were going to find at least 100 pounds of gold, even though I knew it was very unlikely.

"The next morning we got up well before sunrise, fixed breakfast, went up on top of the hill, and headed away from the sun through the inverted V of the two boulders. As I recall, it was the 17th of September. We walked along in the shadow of the boulders until the orb of the sun just touched the horizon, bearing in mind Mayhayley's directions to dig at the point when the orb is one finger above the horizon.

"Gene, you don't think of the sun moving very rapidly when you just stand and watch it, but when you watch a shadow stretched that far away from something the sun is shining through, it's amazing how rapidly it moves.

"Will and I were walking along holding out fingers aimed at the sky and watching the shadow retreat as the sun moved higher. We agreed we would tell each other when we thought it was one finger above the horizon. The way we determined that was by holding our fingers directly in front of our faces, arms fully extended. The moment the bottom of the sun touched the top of my finger, we both marked the ground touched by the point of the shadow at that instant, and then stood and watched the shadow retreat. We drove a wooden stake to mark the point we'd decided would mark the 17th of September.

"Now we had a benchmark, a reference point for the next day. As the sun moved further south each day the shadow would move north, we didn't know how much. On the 18th we repeated the process, and the stake moved about 8 inches to the north. On the 19th it moved another 8 inches to the north.

"We suspected that each day, until the sun turned around, the point of the inverted V was going to move about 8 inches north, and not much to the east or west. So after three mornings we could guess where it was going to fall on the 20th and the 21st simply by measuring about 8 inches further along a straight line.

"We decided we would check this again on the first day of autumn, but in the meantime we were going to start digging at the exact spot we thought the point of the cone would fall on that day. We then laid out a cross centered on that point, making each leg of the cross three feet wide and five feet long.

"The first day we dug about a foot deep. The point of the cone of light actually fell inside our digging almost dead center. We'd dig a couple of hours, then rest a while, dig a couple of hours, rest a while, by the first day of fall we were probably two feet deep. As far as we could tell, the earth had never been disturbed.

"We began to wonder how deep a rich Indian Chief would dig to bury his treasure. Two feet was a mite shallow, but we were already beginning to feel like a convention of idiots doing this. Even though we enjoyed camping out, we decided to set an arbitrary depth of five feet. We didn't feel anybody would dig much deeper than five feet even to bury a treasure that was supposed to lie undiscovered for generations.

"On the first day of fall, it was cloudy in the east. The sun cast no shadow. Though we'd never know for sure exactly where the point of the cone fell, we remained confident we were in the right spot.

"We spent part of the morning digging and part resting. By midmorning the clouds began to thicken, and around noon looked ominous enough that we decided to build a new lean-to higher on the side of the hill.

"By late afternoon, a soft rain began to fall intermittently. We decided we'd better prepare our supper and eat soon since it's not easy to cook on a campfire in the rain. Later, Will went outside and did a little ditching to make sure the surface water would stay out of our new lean-to.

"Shortly after dark, lightning began to flash and thunder rocked the air as a full-blown storm of gigantic proportions rolled in. The lightning was almost continuous. Wind was whipping waves across the river. Water began to rush from the hillsides down into the river, which began to rise. It crept up on the sandbar, and across a tiny island out in the middle of the river where we could see some alder bushes during the lightning's more brilliant flashes.

"We watched logs and whole trees floating by, and eventually I saw a ferry barge coming around the bend. It was just a flat wooden barge about 20 feet long and 12 feet wide, just big enough to ferry a team of mules and wagon across the Chattahoochee.

"I grabbed Will by the arm, pointed upriver, and told him to watch. The next brilliant flash of lightning showed the barge closer, and it looked like there were three or four people all laying down holding tight to the chains that kept the wagons from moving.

"I yelled to Will, 'My God! What are people doing on that thing in this awful storm.' He yelled back to me he wasn't sure there was. We watched as each stroke of lightning showed the barge a little closer. Now it looked as though the barge might be easing toward our side of the river; if it ever got to the bank we could help the stranded people on the barge safely off.

"For a good minute there was no lightning, just a terrible blackness. Then another bolt of lightning revealed the barge almost abreast of us, but out near midstream again. A moment later it jammed hard against the little island, where it started slowly to rotate, trying to crab its way back into the mainstream.

"When the barge struck the island, one of the tiny figures was pitched overboard. Whoever it was grabbed one of the island's alder bushes and was now hanging on. Will jumped up and ran headlong for the river, never turning back, and dived in. As the lightning flashed, he crossed the turbulent stream. The force of the water seemed to be carrying him down, and I feared Will had to be awfully lucky to get safely to the island as the current swept him along. I stood there both praying for and cursing him for exposing himself to the raging floodwaters. With a lunge he finally caught one of the alder bushes near the person who'd fallen from the barge. It was only a boy, but Will was having trouble getting him to turn the alder bush loose. Finally he pulled the boy free and plunged back into the water. Seeing the current was going to sweep them at least 100 yards downstream, I ran to meet them where I imagined they'd land.

"Will fought the waters, taking long strokes with his right hand, and holding the boy in his left. The flood tossed him about like a cork on a fishing line, but he finally made it to the bank where I grabbed his right hand and dragged him onto the bank.

"The boy was spluttering and coughing from inhaling water. Will was totally exhausted, but managed to struggle to his knees. While he was gulping in air, I was screaming at him, 'Why did you do

such a stupid thing? You could have killed your fool self.' He was
so exhausted all he did was shake his head and heave for air.

"Will stayed on all-fours trying to catch his breath, and I kept
screaming at him, 'Don't do that no more.' He finally regained his
breath, and as he rested, we could see the barge still tossing in the
current. A huge log suddenly caught one edge of it, pushing it
straight up the in air. We now saw the other figures on the barge—
a woman and a baby. The barge cartwheeled back out to midstream,
tumbling off it's passengers, and was soon gone.

"We got back to the lean-to and lit two lamps. The heat from
the lamps took the chill off the child. We scrapped around and got
him enough dry clothes to make him comfortable for the night.
Will asked the young boy his name. 'Timmy Smith,' the boy replied. 'I want my Ma.'

"Very soon Timmy went to sleep. The next morning he told us
his grandpa lived in Whitesburg. Will decided we needed to take
him to his grandpa's house and explain what happened. Will also
didn't want his grandpa to know who we were. So, we decided we
would be Joe and Wilma Ashmore. We went to Timmy's grandpa's
house and told the old man about the previous night's tragedy.
We left Timmy's grandpa and grandmother crying, but it seemed
we could be of no further help.

"Miss Fanny," I interrupted, "Uncle Will never told me about
him doing nothing like that."

"No Gene, he wouldn't tell you about doing anything like that.
Will's done a lot of good in his life, but in his mind no amount of
good can make up for the bad, so he doesn't talk about it. Remember, this was less than six months from killing a bunch of Pinkertons
and other folks. That weighed heavy on his mind and on his heart—
he had the most god-awful nightmares that you've ever seen.

"I used to wake him up in the middle of those nightmares. The
sounds that came out of him you couldn't believe. I don't imagine
that groans straight out of Hell could be any more sorrowful than
his cries during those nightmares.

"The thing about Will, Gene, is he would save a life in an instant with total disregard for his own. But he would also take a life
if that person stood between him and what he wanted. He was al-

ways conscious-stricken after the fact, but I don't think he ever remembered that in his fits of rage.

"Maybe he'd mourn and cry as he buried you, but you were no less dead. I'm truly glad it's the Almighty who'll judge him and not me."

"Why's he still worried about going to Hell."

"As I said Gene, I'm glad the Almighty has to judge him, not me. Sometimes he could be the sweetest man on the face of this earth. But with a drink of liquor or a change in circumstances, he could be as mean and evil as Blue Beard. But I saw him put eight lives on the good side of his ledger in the time I was with him."

"Miss Fanny, if I were to take you to Dr. King's hospital, would you just go with me and speak to Uncle Will?"

"Gene, over these past weeks I've grown very fond of you. I'd almost do it just to please you, but if I go, I need to decide to go for myself. I don't want to see him lying in a coma. Let's see how it goes with him. I'll give you my answer soon.

"In the meantime, there's no way I can explain to you how it is from my perspective. When you're young and look ahead to the future, time seems to stretch out endlessly—there's no horizon, just an ocean of days. Well I've seen the other side of that ocean and watched it shrink behind me.

"I don't expect you to understand or even believe all that until you've lived another 40 or 50 years. But Will is spent, and there's not much more good or bad he can do if he survives this time. With the chronic lungs you say he's got, he sure won't survive next time. To you, two or three years is a long time, but to me and him, it's only a twinkling of an eye.

"Will's frozen in my memories the way he was 30 years ago. From what you say, he's far, far from being that person now. I don't know if I can handle the pain of seeing what the years have done to him.

"You may think, because I look old and wrinkled and wise, that somehow I've outlived pain. That's not so, Gene. When you cut me, I bleed, and when I bleed, I hurt."

"I'm sorry, Miss Fanny, I won't ask you anymore. If you want to go, you tell me. I'm sorry I interrupted you. Go ahead, you were...uh, uh, the next morning was a pretty morning."

"We decided we had to let the ground dry out a bit before we continued, but with all that water, it would be softer when we started again.

"The next morning while Will and I were looking at all the water still sitting in our two-foot-deep treasure pit, the water suddenly started draining out, rushing down into a sinkhole. In less than two minutes, and sounding like an underground waterfall, all the water had drained out of the cross and disappeared.

"Will immediately set about digging just beyond the north end of the cross, and shortly he was down to the level we had earlier reached. As he sank the pick deep into the ground, the earth caved in, and a hole as big as a 50 gallon barrel, maybe as big as two 50 gallon barrels, opened up.

"Of course the water had made a pool at the bottom of the new hole, but we could clearly see rotted bits and pieces of an old barrel with it's rusty metal bands. Will started yelling, 'By God she's right, by God she's right, she's right, she's right!' He jumped down in the hole, where the water came up to his knees. Clawing around in the muck with his hands, he presently brought up a handful of $20 gold pieces.

"Gene, I never believed in fortunetelling, but at that moment I was convinced. I grew dizzy as I thought. 'If we'd moved those stakes one foot short of where we put 'em, we'd have never have found it.' It was crazy, almost a divine intervention in my life. But then I remembered all the trouble money had gotten Will into.

"Before the day was out, we had counted over 5000 of those $20 gold pieces. We washed them and put them in two sacks. When we washed them they were as shiny as new. There were 5000 $20 gold pieces, a gift from my distant grandfather across almost a century."

Fortuneteller

"When we got back to our cabin on the river, Will took some steelyards we had and weighed the coins. The best the scales could show was something over 300 pounds. Can you imagine, 300 pounds of gold coins!

"That night we piled 5000 of those $20 gold pieces in the middle of the floor and played in the heap like two kids with new toys. Eventually, Will broke down and started sobbing great sobs. Holding him as tightly as I could, I asked why he was sobbing?

"'This is the only money I've ever had that somebody didn't get killed in the course of me getting the money. And it's not even mine—it's yours, left to you by your great grandpaw.'

"I told Will it was ours. That I'd agreed to 'till death do us part.' That I meant I'd forgiven him for everything he'd done. Sitting there in that little mountain of gold coins, holding him while he sobbed, was one of the happiest moments of my life. I guess that's hard for you to understand Gene, but at that moment he seemed so fragile, so childlike, it was easy for me to forgive him, and forget that both he and I were fugitives, wanted by the Pinkerton Detective Agency.

"We finally fell asleep. I really thought the whole business had been a dream until I raised up in bed the next morning and found my entire bedroom floor covered with gold coins.

"Will was already up. He had cooked breakfast; it was the smell of country ham and eggs that awoke me. Shortly, he brought me a tray. By this time Will already had his part of the treasure buried in glass fruit jars, in front of the house, where he could dig it up, take money out, cover it up again, and sweep the yard with a dogwood brush broom. You couldn't tell the earth had been disturbed until it rained. Then we'd have to do a little manicuring while the ground was still wet in the event somebody happened by. But we had nobody coming to see us—at least not very many folks.

"Will asked, 'What are we going to do with all this money?'

345

"'I'd like to have a big living room added to the house. The way the ground slopes away, it'd be high enough off the ground we could crawl under it and get at our money without ever having to worry when company comes they'll see fresh digging and wonder why.'

"'And then what, my love?'

"'Well, I'd like to bury it, wait, and save it so we can give our children a good education, and a good start in life or business if they don't want an education.'

"'Oh, it's our children now.'

"'I'd like to have a few, wouldn't you Will?'

"'Sure,' he said without much enthusiasm.

"'It doesn't sound to me like you want children. Why?'

"'They're too damn much responsibility, and the way I've lived my life, the way I've been on the run for the past two years, I might be havin' to leave again.'

"So the subject sort of died. But then he said, 'There's one thing I'd like to do. I'd like for us to go back to that fortuneteller, that Mayhayley Lancaster, she's so damn smart. Let's not tell her a thing, just walk in the same as before and see if she says anything about us finding the treasure. The more I think about that woman, the more I think she just got lucky. There ain't no way anybody could possibly know about a treasure buried 100 years. It just ain't possible. It's spooky, people seeing the future and the past like that.

"'That would be pure and simple proof, if we went back and sat before her in the same fashion. I bet she won't even remember us, much less the story. What do you say? When we get the room built, let's go back and see Mayhayley.'

"I agreed. We immediately got a contractor and had the room built. It turned out to be high enough off the ground that you could very easily swing a short handled mattock to dig up and bury money. Of course my money in cash was in a checking account in a bank in Tallapoosa except for $500 that I kept in my purse around the house. Will had his buried for reasons of his own, mostly I guess because he didn't trust banks, but also 'cause it was ill-gotten.

"I felt that the chances of being discovered here were insignificant, but every time we went to Tallapoosa we'd step by the drugstore to look for any new magazines with stories about Balls' murder.

"It had been months, and there'd been nothing. We checked on a fairly regular basis, bought dozens of magazines and newspapers. But there's always that itch at the back of your neck when you're a fugitive from justice. You never rest quite as easily as before.

"We stored all those coins in our bedroom closet until the new living room was finished. Will bought some old Army surplus ammunition boxes that had once been used for machine gun rounds. It took four of those to hold the coins."

"Miss Fanny, is that the metal box buried with the fruit jars?"

"Sure was, Gene."

"Well how come Uncle Will didn't know what it was?"

"I'll get to that, Gene, I'll get to that.

"I was in the position that there was no way I was going to carry that many gold coins and put them in the bank, so I buried them along with Will's. I'd given him half the money, we buried it all together, along with his fruit jars, under the house."

"But he never mentioned that, Miss Fanny, he told me he had no idea why a metal box would be buried with his fruit jars."

"Did he ever explain why he had more money than he thought?"

"No ma'am."

"Like I told you Gene, I'm coming to that.

"We planted a garden and grew our own vegetables. We'd go fishing and catch our own fish. We settled down into a domestic routine with which I was very comfortable, but I kept getting the feeling Will wasn't happy.

"We'd go to Tallapoosa and buy the detective magazines. Sometimes I'd go alone, and when I'd bring them back Will would seem disappointed that there was nothing about G. B. Balls. If there had been, of course it would mean he'd be back on the run. I began thinking he was bored with me, and liked life on the run. But that didn't make any sense.

"Two months after we moved into our new living room, we decided it was time to put Mayhayley Lancaster to the test. I was completely sold she'd had a vision. I even began to think of myself as part Indian, of Chief McIntosh as my great ancestor.

"Will offered to bet his half of the gold she wouldn't say anything about us having already discovered the gold.

"I was almost tempted to bet with him, but what he said made sense. It was really a fantasy world, a congregation of coincidences that let us find the money. Even the storm that raged all night and soaked the ground enough to cause the cave-in couldn't shake my feeling that she'd truly had a vision and I was somehow destined to have Chief McIntosh's treasure. It doesn't make any sense, but that's the way I felt.

"The 4th generation daughter of a great Indian chief, claiming his ancient treasure after all his other offspring had perished on a reservation in Oklahoma where even he was no longer known—I felt almost like an Indian princess straight out of the schoolbooks.

"We set off once again to Heard County to see Mayhayley. Once again, we had to sit on the front porch benches, waiting our turn. People think flies are gone come the first frost, but when we have warm spells they often return by the millions. As I recall, it was sometime in early December when we were there, and I had never seen as many flies.

"When we finally got into the room with Mayhayley she was using a peach tree limb with the dried leaves still on it to shoo off the flies. No sooner were we seated than she took one look at Will and said, 'I told you, I will not see you, I will not read your palm. You are evil, you are not good for the Indian princess.'

"She turned to me and said, 'Miss Hawk, I'm surprised he's still with you. Where've you hidden the Chief's gold? I know you found it—I had another vision.'

"I looked at Will.

"'You are a foolish girl to give him half of it. It'll do him no good. But if you use it right, it can bring you great happiness, child. Your little test has only confused you, has it not? You came here to see if I'd know. Now get out the holy scriptures and read what it says about, 'oh ye of little faith.' And be gone.'

"I walked out of that room feeling like a suck-egg dog caught in the hen house. But I was troubled by her prediction about me and Will, and carried a heavy heart from that house. On the way home, I kept wishing we hadn't gone there. She'd put me in a deep depression. Will tried to cheer me up, but now I totally believed what she said, and so I believed we had no future. Sometimes, when I look back, I wonder if that visit was the beginning of our separation, the beginning of the end of us, so to speak. That's where the final breakup all started."

I looked at the clock on the mantle; it was five minutes till ten.

"Good Lord, Miss Fanny, I got so carried away with your story. I've got to go. When can I come back?"

"Gene, you come back any time. I'm just a lonesome old woman who lives till the day my grandchildren come see me, and I enjoy these little sessions I think as much as you do."

I jumped in Uncle Will's new Buick and tore out to Bremen. Since it was already after 11 o'clock, I didn't figure I'd catch it any worse from Ma if I got home at 12:30 or if I got home at 11:30.

So I went up to Dr. King's hospital to see if Uncle Will was any better, the nurse told me he'd had his first shot of penicillin about a hour before. Since it was supposed to be a miracle drug, he should be better in the morning, which would be Sunday. If the penicillin was going to do any good, it would act pretty quickly.

Of course I wanted Uncle Will to get well, but it seemed like the older I got, the more disagreement me and Ma had. I even toyed with the idea of leaving home and moving in with Uncle Will, but that would be a terrible blow to Pa. Pa hadn't done me any wrong, and I didn't know if I had the nerve to do that.

As soon as I walked in the door Ma said, "*You*, young man, sit down, we are gonna have a talk! Mr. Smarty Pants, you finally got too big for your britches. As long as you stick your feet under my table, you're going to do what I tell you to do. You know your deadline to get home is 11 o'clock. Have you been back over yonder to see that slut in Alabama?

"You think, young man, you're grown, but I'll tell you right now, you're 17 and you've got four years before you're gonna be old enough to do as you please. I'm telling you right now, you're gonna stay at this house for one week. You're not gonna leave except to get up and go to work. When you get back, you're gonna do your chores. And you ain't driving that new car to work, you're gonna ride with Harvey Wright just the way you've been riding. I'm telling you right now, young man, your wild way of doing just as you please has suddenly come to a stop! You hear me, I mean stop!!

"You ain't been the same since the first time you went to see that son-of-a-bitch in the hospital who ought done be dead. Somebody ought to have shot the bastard 50 years ago. You've gone as wild as he is. That damn slut over in Alabama who shacked up with him down on the river ain't nothing but a street whore! I ain't aiming for my younguns' to wind up in no such fashion."

"Ma, Miss Fanny is one of the nicest people I've ever seen. I wish some times you were as nice as she is."

"You wish I was as nice as that goddammed slut! I ought to take a broom and beat the living shit out of you. Ain't nothing but a goddammed whore ever had anything to do with that no good son-of-a-bitch anyhow. The Bible says hell takes hold of a whore's feet."

"Ma, what's the Bible got to do with anything? You're always quoting the Bible; that don't even make sense to me. What's taking hold of a whore's feet..."

"There you go smart-mouthing me again. You are just tempting me, ain't you?"

"Ma, you're gonna wake Pa up. You know he gets ill when he gets woke up in the middle of the night. Why are we always doing this to each other? Can't we just be friends?"

"You only want to be friends if I let you do just exactly as you damn well please—associate with whores, whorehoppers, and drunks. Now you want to be friends! Why didn't you think about that before you started doing every goddammed little thing both of them asked you to do? You'd do anything in the world they asked you to do, and you won't do nothing I want you to do!"

"Ma, I'm gonna be 18 soon, old enough to be drafted. You know they're still drafting folks into the army."

"Yeah, you'd like that wouldn't you? You could be in the army then you wouldn't have to do what Ma tells you to do any more. Is that what you think, young man? Well you may find out the army is a tougher boss than I am. If you want to go in to the army so damn bad, why don't you sign up? You're 17; you can sign up, I'll be glad to sign the papers and get you in."

"Ma, could you just tell me one thing? Why is it every time we try to sit down and have a conversation, it winds up in a cuss fight? I don't like to fight with you. All I want you to do is to let me..."

"All you want me to do is to just let you do as you damn well please—and that ain't never happening as long as you stick your feet under my..."

"Ma, you've done said that 40 times. I give you half of my pay check to pay for the food that goes on the table. I've checked around with other people at the shoe factory; they don't give their Ma's half of their paychecks. Their Ma's don't want half their paychecks. Their Ma's let them spend it all. I don't understand why I have to give you half the paycheck just to live here. I could live somewhere else. If I had my own one room apartment, I could live cheaper."

"Well, get your ass out young man."

"Okay, Ma, I'm gonna rent an apartment. When Uncle Will gets out of the hospital, I'm gonna let him move in with me."

"You are gonna what?"

"I can rent an apartment with the money I give you every week. I won't have to milk the cows, won't have to slop the hogs, won't have to get in the stovewood, won't have to get in the firewood, won't have to plow the garden, and won't have to listen to you raise hell every time I want to go somewhere or do something."

"You're just gonna up and leave us like that are you? Nobody to get in the firewood, nobody to get in the stovewood, nobody to milk the cow, nobody to slop the hogs, and it'll all be for your Pa to do when he gets home after a hard day's work."

"Ma, it wouldn't break your arm to do some of it."

"I ain't able to do it, you know yourself I ain't able to do it. I haven't been able to work since you was born. Somehow you strained something in me when I was giving birth to you. I ain't never been the same since, and now you're gonna go off and leave me with all these things to do. Oh death, where is thy sting?"

"Ma, you've been threatening me with dying every since I was six years old. You seem as healthy to me now as you ever did."

"That's all you know, boy. I'm as good as dead. I went to the doctor last week. He told me there's a sharp knife laying up for me."

"Ma, don't start trying to get me feeling sorry for you, and talk me out of it. I've made up my mind. You done pushed me too far. I'm moving out."

"Well, I'll tell you right now, young man, with all this strain and all this worry that you are putting on me, don't be surprised if your Pa don't come get you in the middle of the night and tell you I'm dead, and it's your fault. I want you to remember that as long as you live, my death is on your head.

"If you'd rather spend my last days with that drunken, whoring, son-of-a-bitchin' Will than with your own dear Ma, well you just get your ass out and get out now. For that slut over in Alabama, I want you to tell that bitch one thing your Ma said. She's a slut, a tramp, a whore, and your Ma hopes she burns in hell. You tell her that. Now get out!"

"I'm gonna get my clothes."

"No, hell, you ain't gettin' a damn thing. You get your ass out of here, get in your big fancy car, and get away from here right now. And I'll tell you something else, them two are gonna have you in the penitentiary before you get 21 years on you. You mark my word."

Furious, I got up and stomped out of the house while the echoes of Ma's swearing died away. It was late Saturday night, and I didn't have anywhere to go. So I went out on a lonely dirt road between Carrollton and Bremen, crawled over in the back seat of the new Buick, and slept like a baby.

The sun was way up in the sky when I woke up. I remembered it was Sunday morning. I couldn't wait for Julie to see that big fine Buick, but I didn't want to wait until Monday morning. I just had to have a place to live before I could go see her.

So I went to McPherson Street in Bremen where I saw a sign that said 'Apartment for Rent.' I stopped, went in, and talked to the landlord. It was a small duplex apartment with two bedrooms. He asked me how old I was. I told him seventeen. "You're just a boy," he said, "I can't rent you that apartment. Where do you work?"

"I work at General Shoe in Carrollton."

"Why don't you go to Carrollton and rent something.'

"I got an uncle who's sick that I'm gonna live with when he gets better; he's in the hospital. I just thought he'd like Bremen better. It's only twelve miles, I don't mind driving to Carrollton to work."

He thought it over a minute. "When is your uncle getting out of the hospital?"

"I don't know, they are giving him some new medicine that's supposed to be a miracle drug. He may die."

"Son, you look clean enough and you speak well enough; I just don't want to rent to two bachelor males. I've had problems with males before. I've got a friend, though, who has a house sittin' out in the woods' edge on Bush Mill Road. Why don't you go see him? It's the first house after you turn right on Bush Mill. Talk to him."

I couldn't imagine why he wouldn't rent to me and Uncle Will. But I went over to see the guy who had the place on Bush Mill Road, and he rented it to me, no questions asked, for $30 a month. I paid him with Uncle Will's money, he handed me the key. It was a nice snug little place, but. there was one thing I had forgotten—there wasn't a stick of furniture. Nothing had been said about that, there was no place open on Sunday to buy furniture. Uncle Will was probably gonna be madder than hell at me.

I decided I'd better go to the hospital and see how he was before I spent all of his money. Of course, there was no way I could spend all of it, but I didn't want to make him mad by taking too many liberties.

Arriving at the hospital, I stopped at the nurses desk to ask how he was. They said he'd just had a good breakfast—that penicillin was truly a miracle drug. I went in. He looked more fit than I'd seen him since he'd been in the hospital.

"Well, Uncle Will, you're looking good this morning."

"Yeah, Nephew, I feel good. That's some powerful medicine Dr. King's got. How long have I been out of the world?"

"I don't know, Uncle Will, it's been several days. I thought you was a goner for sure."

"How's my favorite nephew?"

"Well, there's a lot of things that's happened while you haven't been able to talk to me. There are some things I want to ask you about. But first, I done spent a bunch of your money while you was unconscious. I bought you a new car; I rented you a house. I want to move in with you. I left home last night. Me and Ma got in a fight, and I just up and left."

"Did you tell her you was gonna move in with me?"

"Yes sir, I told her that."

"She didn't like that, I bet."

"No sir, she told me to give you a message that you was gonna have me in the penitentiary before I was 21 years old. The funny thing about it, she don't like Fanny Hawk, either. Ma's sort of peculiar, but Miss Fanny seems like a wonderful person to me."

"She is, Nephew. She's a wonderful, wonderful, person and don't you ever forget it, no matter what your Maw says. By the way, did she ever decide whether she was gonna let me come to see her or not?"

"No sir, I asked about that just last night. She said you hurt her bad, Uncle Will, and she ain't really sure yet whether she wants to ever see you again or not. She knows you've changed and probably ain't the same man you was then, but the hurt goes awful deep and she don't know whether she wants to open up old wounds.

"What'd you do to her, Uncle Will? It must be awful."

"That's the funny thing, Nephew, I don't remember doing a thing in the world to her. I just woke up one morning, and she was gone. That's the truth."

"She ain't never told me anything except you beat her up and hurt her bad, but never gave me any details. But you're lookin' good now. When's Dr. King gonna let you go home? Is it alright to rent the house and spend your money? There's one little thing I overlooked; we ain't got no furniture, and there ain't no place open today."

"Oh yeah, Nephew, you can go down to Will Maxwell's place at Bowdon Junction. He's started opening on Sunday, and he's got some real good, cheap furniture down there. You can go down there, spend my money, and get us set up for housekeeping, because they tell me maybe I'm gonna be home by Wednesday or Thursday.

"In the meantime, instead of me talking to you and you sitting here, I'd like for you to go sit up with Miss Fanny. If we're gonna have a place of our own, I'd like to fix it up pretty nice and invite her over. I'm glad you set everything up, Nephew. Does Miss Fanny seem like she's softening any? If you had to guess, do you think she's gonna let me see her again? I'd really like to see her."

"Uncle Will, I don't know how to judge her. I really like her, I hope she will. I've told her you've changed a lot."

"Did you tell her I've got one foot in the grave and the other on an alligator snout?"

"No sir, I didn't tell her nothing like that; I told her you was pretty sick."

"Well, that's what you saying ain't it? The old man has one foot in the grave on the other on a banana peel?"

"I've heard that."

"Well, I thought I was a goner for sure, Nephew. Boy, I'm telling you, I had some more fearsome nightmares. The doctor and nurses say that's just fever getting in my head, but I'll tell you, Nephew, ain't no damn fever gonna do stuff like that to you. I mean, I'm telling you, when I was about to start under I could see Ol' Ebo standing there with his pitchfork and twitching his tail just like a tomcat watching a parakeet. You ever see that?"

"Yes sir."

"Every time, when my breath wouldn't hardly come and them nurses were sticking needles in me, that old tail of Ebo's would twitch. That's enough to scare the hell out of you, Nephew. I mean scare you, because you know once he gets his hands on you, he's got you forever.

"I don't want to go into that right now. He ain't gonna get me today. I'm feeling pretty good. They say about two more doses of that penicillin, and I'm gonna be healed up and haired over. You run along and get some furniture. Has the house got electricity?"

"Yes sir, that's the first thing I noticed. It's got electricity in it."

"Well, spend whatever money is necessary. Fix it up nice and go see Fanny. Every chance you get, put in a good word for me."

"Yes sir."

I went to Bowdon Junction like Uncle Will said, and asked Mr. Maxwell about buying the furniture and getting it to the house in Bremen. I told him what all I wanted.

"Son, if you buy that much furniture we'll take it up there and set it up in the house ourself."

So, I spent nearly $700, and bought a whole house full of furniture. I bought the finest Maxwell's Furniture Store had. By 2 o'clock in the afternoon I had the beds made, and the house looked like a million dollars. I decided Uncle Will ought to have the big bedroom. There was a bathroom next to it with a tub, a shower over the tub, a commode, and a sink.

I was a pretty good cook; I could just imagine me and Uncle Will living there, not having nobody to fuss at me. I really thought I was going to enjoy my newfound freedom.

I decided I'd go see Miss Fanny and tell her the good news about my move. I didn't want to wear out my welcome, but I decided she liked me well enough she wouldn't think I was imposing on her.

On the way down, I had to pass Julie's road, so I decided I'd at least drive by her house and see what she was doing this Sunday afternoon. She was sitting on the swing, swinging away. As soon as I saw that, I pulled Uncle Will's shiny new Buick into her yard. I thought her eyes would pop right out of her head.

She jumped down and leaned in the window. "My goodness, you've moved up in the world. Whose car is this?"

"It's mine."

"Aw," she said, "go on; it ain't your car. How can you afford a car like this? You don't make no more money at General Shoe than I do. You can't afford no car like this. There ain't nobody who'd be fool enough to loan you the money to buy a new Buick. Go on."

I said, "No, it's mine, I had a rich uncle who died and left me a pile of money. You wouldn't believe how much money he left me." Her eyes got as big as saucers.

"I even bought myself a house. Would you like to go see it?"

"I know you are putting me on; I want you to know I ain't believing none of this. Let me go ask Ma."

When she said that I thought my heart would turn over in my body. God, I was so in love with her.

"Ma said I could go with you if you'll get me back home in time for church tonight." She jumped in the car and I tore back out to Highway 78.

"When I got to where I would turn to go to Miss Fanny's, I went right instead to go back to my new house. About ten minutes later, I was pulling out the key, proudly unlocking the front door and saying, "Now you see, I didn't tell you no lie."

She just couldn't get over what beautiful furniture it was, how it all smelled new and wonderful. She went into the bedroom where I had just so nicely made the bed, sat down, and started rubbing the bedspread. I sat down beside her, put my arms around her shoulders, and gave her a big kiss. I gently laid her down on the bed; she wiggled up, got comfortable, and made no effort to try to stop me from taking her clothes off.

We left the bedroom in time for me to get her home before church. Not a word was said till we got almost to her house. Then she broke the silence, "I'm sorry I'm so easy, Gene. I know you would have married me if I hadn't of been so easy, wouldn't you?"

I didn't know how to answer that question; she was probably right. But I felt awful. I didn't love her anymore, didn't want to marry her anymore, and didn't understand it. I felt terrible, and showed it.

She patted me on the back and said, "I understand, I know."

"No, you don't understand. I love you, I don't love you. I want you, and I know it's wrong. Can I come back to see you next Sunday, one more time?"

"No, Gene, I just can't see you again, and I mean it this time."

I no longer felt like going on over to see Miss Fanny. I just went back to the new house and went to bed.

The Buick didn't seem so shiny as it had before. I realized how little I understood about how the world worked. I wanted to talk to Miss Fanny, I wanted to talk to Uncle Will, and I wanted to ask a lot of questions.

Monday morning I got up, made myself breakfast, and went to work at General Shoe. I was still depressed. My love affair had ended for reasons I didn't understand.

When I got to work, lots of people turned their heads to stare at the new Buick. They came around and talked about what a beautiful car it was and how lucky I was. I was there when Julie came in, she didn't speak. She parked in her regular parking place and went inside the factory. It was a terrible letdown.

Always before, I could think about going home, fussing and fighting with Ma, seeing my brothers and sister, or doing the chores. Now, when I got off work, all I had to look forward to was that newly furnished house with nobody to talk to and nothing to do.

We went to work at 7 AM and got off at 3:30 with 30 minutes off for lunch. That afternoon I went by the hospital to see Uncle Will. He was still feeling good, and encouraged me to go see Miss Fanny.

Now that he was feeling better, he seemed to have forgotten about confessing his sins. Dr. King had promised him he would go home on Friday, or before. Uncle Will urged me to try to persuade Fanny to let him visit her, or even come to see him the following Saturday, after he got home from the hospital.

When I left the hospital, I was depressed for reasons I didn't understand. I started off to Muscadine, then changed my mind and decided I'd go back to the house where Fanny and Will had lived, dig up the treasure again, and see what was in that metal box.

One time, Miss Fanny had begun to tell me why there was more money in the glass jars than Will thought there was. I couldn't remember why she hadn't finished, but the way the story was developing, I'd opined that some of that gold from Chief McIntosh still laid buried in the tin box. But I wasn't sure.

Maybe I was still suffering from my sadness about Julie, but not really wanting to see anybody, I went back to the old house.

When I was passing Mr. Webster's house, I remembered how he'd showed an abnormal interest in what I was doing there, so I just went on by. Less than half a mile off, I found an old logging road that turned right. I worked my way down to the river.

It was tough going through briars, canes, and underbrush. Within 10 minutes I was at the bend of the river where Uncle Will and Miss Fanny had lived. It was probably no more than an hour before dark, so I crawled under the house straightaways. Everything looked exactly as it had when I'd left it earlier.

Since I hadn't brought any tools from the car, I started digging into the loose sand with my hands, shortly felt the outline of the metal box. Feeling all the way around, I uncovered it about four inches. It seemed exactly like one of those square ammunition boxes Miss Fanny described. I took hold of the handle on top and tugged. It popped off, rusty, I guess, from all those years lying there under the sand, alternately getting spring-flooded and summer-scorched.

I reached around the metal box with both hands, and tried to roll it over in the hole. It resisted, and so I pulled harder until suddenly the box came in two; it had rusted almost tissue-thin. I heard the tinkle of coins as they poured out of the box into the hole. Even in the twilight under the house, I could see the shine of gold.

I picked up a big handful of them coins, poured them from hand to hand, and listened to the sweet clink of gold striking gold. Nothing else on earth sounds that way.

I didn't have anything but my pockets to carry that gold away in, but I was wearing a long sleeve shirt. Tying a knot in the sleeves, I filled both arms full of gold coins. When I picked the shirt up, it was so heavy it started to tear, so I put about half the coins back in the hole. Then I tore the hem off of the shirt and tied the sleeves so the coins couldn't spill out while as I went back to the car. I certainly didn't want any gold coins scattered along the way, maybe making a body curious where they come from. Just as the sun went down, I covered up my trove, crawled out from under the house, and started down the Tallapoosa to where I had parked the car.

It was almost dark when I got in the Buick and started back to Bremen. Much elated, I felt very, very rich. But I had another problem—how was I going to get rid of all of those gold coins. They didn't really belong to me, but to Miss Fanny Hawk. Was I a thief even though she hadn't told me yet what was in the box? In the meantime, what was I going to tell my conscience?

By the time I got back to Bremen, I'd worked myself into a lather. I couldn't decide whether to go by the hospital and tell Uncle Will what I'd discovered, or wait until I saw Miss Fanny the next night. Either way, what was I to do with all those coins?

So I went to my new rented house and scattered them out on the bathroom floor, much as Miss Fanny had described she and Uncle Will doing in their bedroom when they'd first discovered Chief McIntosh's gold all those years ago. I ran my bare feet through the gold coins, then I counted them. There were 400 as new and shiny as Miss Fanny had said, even though they'd laid amoldering in the ground for all those years.

Eventually I took a gallon milk jug, poured the milk out, scooped the coins in, which filled that jar almost full. Exploring the toolshed behind the new house, I found a pick and shovel, crawled up under the house, and buried the jug deep. Just as Will, I had a treasure nobody knew about.

Later I lay in bed thinking about the story Uncle Will had told me about his life, and specially about how Ol' Ebo had stood twitch-

ing his tail waiting to claim his soul. About how Will had hurt
Fanny Hawk, how he had once told me that all his troubles sprung
from his wanting money he wasn't willing to work for. And here I
had taken 400 coins that certainly didn't belong to me and had
buried them where nobody but I knew where they were. How was
I different from Uncle Will? I hadn't killed anybody, I had stolen
the coins and Ol' Ebo might already be snaking through my worm-
hole straight to the heart.

I tried to tell myself they didn't belong to anybody, I found them.
Fanny'd told me about the metal box, so I knew I had no claim to
those coins.

I fell into a troubled sleep. Dreams are funny creatures. The first
thing I saw, when I drifted off to sleep was Ebo, exactly as Uncle
Will had described him, his ebony luster as black as a quarter past
midnite. Such a fearsome creature I'd never before beheld. He stood
before me, with fire and smoke drifting out of each nostril; when
he opened his mouth to speak to me, it flickered fiery red as if a
volcano were boiling somewhere in his belly.

"So Will didn't convince you, did he, Gene? Seems like some of
you can't be convinced, until you've drunk the piss-trough dry.
You wouldn't listen to your Ma, just like Will. And you took all
that gold, just like Will. It can't be long before you murder, just
like Will. Now I'm going to show you what I showed Will."

Every fiber of my body resisted. And suddenly I was pulled from
awful depths of Ebo's fiery breath as my cheap alarm clock sum-
moned me to go to work. God, it was a powerful ease on my heart
when I realized it was a dream. But then, while I was making my
preparations for work, a new depression fell over me.

Later that day, when I saw Julie across the plant, I felt wicked
and dishonest, like a thief. I smiled sickly at her and waved, but
she turned away as if to show contempt. While a hundred machines
seemed to run like hogs to slaughter all around me, everyone else
seemed to be laughing and talking.

About 15 minutes before the whistle blew for quitting, I figured
out a solution to my problem. Mayhayley Lancaster was still living—I'd go see her. I knew she'd never seen me, and I wanted to
learn whether she could tell my fortune.

The minute the whistle blew announcing the end of the shift, I was out the door like a flash. I jumped in the Buick and headed for Heard County. I didn't know where Mayhayley Lancaster lived, but I knew when I got in the general neighborhood of Ephesus, somebody could point me in the right direction.

Sure enough, when I asked how to get to Miss Mayhayley's house, they told me. I found my way there while the sun was still an hour and a half high. The house was almost exactly as Miss Fanny had described it. There were still rotting bales of cotton lying around in the yard. The smell of jute, which is what the bagging was made from, was strong about the house, as were many other strange odors. There was an old hound dog, powerful rotted with mange, laying up under a tree; two cars were parked in front.

I walked up on the rickety front porch where some old pine benches leaned along the wall. A swing hung by chains from the roof of the porch, and a young couple slowly glided back and forth. I asked, "Are you waiting for Miss Mayhayley?" They both nodded.

Having nothing else to say, I asked them if you had to have an appointment to see her. They didn't think so, because they didn't have one. They'd just walked in while she was talking to somebody else and she'd told them to go out, sit in the swing, and she'd talk to them later. They had been sitting there for 30 minutes.

They introduced themselves as Susie something-or-other, and as Ray, no last name. I said, "I'm Gene. Do you know how much she charges?" Ray said, 'I hear she don't charge nothing, but she'll take a gift. I'm from Randolph County, Alabama. We're here to find out where my grandpa's milk cow has wandered off too. We've hunted her all over, and gramps thinks Miss Mayhayley will know where she is. So we come to find out."

Soon a man emerged from Mayhayley's house with a scowl on his face. "Miss Mayhayley said for you young folks to come in. But she ain't nothing but a god-damned witch, I'll tell ya that. I ain't believing nothing the hussy says. I ain't never been as insulted in my life." Saying that, he walked off, got in one of the cars, and left.

I tried to imagine what Miss Mayhayley might have said. According to Miss Fanny, she refused to even talk to Uncle Will, he hadn't gotten mad, and stomped out the way that fellow did.

I was growing faint-hearted about even seeing her. If she was the know-all, see-all, fortuneteller folks claimed, she was gonna know I stole some gold even though I wasn't yet sure who the gold belonged to. I didn't have long to worry. Susie and Ray came out after only a few minutes, and Ray said, "Don't you pay any attention to what that fellow said. She called the man's name that grandpaw thought stole his cow. We are gonna go over to his house and see. If he's sold it, we are gonna tell him Mayhayley Lancaster said he stole grandpaw's cow and see what he says to that."

That boosted my courage tremendously as I went into a dark and dreary room. Mayhayley was sitting there in an old army overcoat, just a little bird of a woman. I was shocked! I never had in my life seen anyone that skinny. Age, arthritis, or something had curled her hands, they were little more than claws. I didn't know whether to sit, speak, or what. Finally she said, "Well, what did you come for young man?"

"I come to talk to you."

"Well sit," she said. "Give me your right hand, give me your left hand.' As she ran her small, crippled fingers about over the lines of my hands, suddenly she stiffened. 'These hands have stolen gold."

I jerked my hands away, folded my arms in front of me, and covered my hands. "That don't do no good youngun'. I've seen all I need to see. What I can't understand, youngun', is why you didn't steal it all, you just stole part of it. Couldn't you tote it? Ha!

"You don't believe, youngun', I read the past, know the future. I even know whose gold it is, youngun'. It's Chief McIntosh's gold, what he gave to Fanny Hawk, his 4th generation granddaughter. Silly girl, she divided it with her lover, an evil man named Will. That Will's a thief, a murderer, a robber—and he's your blood kin."

I was terrified by that scrawny little woman. I recoiled, turned my chair clear over. The back of my head hit the floor with a thud. I stood up to right my chair, and she commanded, "Sit!" So I immediately sat down again, rubbing the back of my head. Then she looked at me with those beady little eyes and said, "Why didn't you steal it all?"

"Well, I didn't think I stole any. I thought I was just picking it up for the rightful owner."

"Then why did you rebury it if you didn't steal it? Does anybody know where it is but you and me?"

In this short time the old woman had convinced me beyond a shadow of a doubt that she not only could see the past, and see the future, but she could read my mind. I wanted out of that place. I no longer doubted one single word Fanny Hawk told me about Mayhayley. And I didn't doubt that it was Chief McIntosh's gold I had dug up and carried to Haralson County.

She was foolish to give him any part of that gold and I told her so. I told her he would walk off and leave her, which he did. I said, "Miss Mayhayley, that ain't what Fanny says. She says she left him."

"She ain't done tellin' yet, is she youngun'?"

"No ma'am, she ain't done tellin' yet."

"I'll tell you, he left her just like I told her he would."

I swallowed hard. "But I'll tell you this, youngun', the gold you left moldering in the ground—you're never going to see it. It will lie moldering in the ground long after you are dead."

"I know exactly where it is. I can go and dig it up tomorrow."

"When you go there next time youngun', you can't find it. I promise you, you can't find it. You ain't going tomorrow and you ain't going the next day, you ain't going for months. But when you do go, you ain't gonna be able to find it. Take Mayhayley's word for it youngun'."

"Miss Mayhayley, how can you know that?"

Then she said exactly what Fanny Hawk told me she had said to her years and years before I was ever born. "Youngun' do you ask the wind if it knows how to blow? Do you ask the rain if it knows how to fall? Do you ask the sun if it knows how to shine? Do you ask the fire if it knows how to burn?"

"Miss Mayhayley, I truly believe every word you've told me. I don't know how, I don't understand, but I believe you. But tell me, am I gonna be like Uncle Will?"

"No youngun' you're gonna have a lot of trouble, mostly caused by yourself, but you're gonna live a long life. Your last days are gonna be your happiest days."

"Miss Mayhayley, I need to know, did I steal the gold?"

"Of course you did. And you're gonna give it back."

Will Restored

As Dr. King had promised, Uncle Will got out of the hospital Saturday, and I drove him to our new place on Bushmill Road. He looked it over, saying I'd done a good job buying all the furniture.

That night, I counted out the money I had left from what I'd found, $19,000, and gave it to him. Then I asked if he wanted to tell me more of his story; he said he didn't.

"I feel better now, and I'm not going to die right away. But, Nephew, you gave me a lot of company coming and listening to me. Soon as I gain my strength back, I'm going down to visit Fanny to see if I can't talk her in to marrying me and coming back here."

Uncle Will had sensed that I'd be lonesome living there with him, so Monday, when I got home from work, I found he'd gone and bought an enormous radio and record player. He had an aerial installed on top of the house, so we could pick up WSB in Atlanta just as plain as anything. Even WSM in Nashville, came in as clear as yesterday, and we could hear the Grand Old Opry.

We spent a lot of time listening to Lum and Abner, Jack Benny, George Burns, Bob Hope. Every night we had a program we'd waited all week to listen to. All in all, I enjoyed my new growed-up life, except I was homesick once and a while.

After a couple of weeks away from home, I couldn't stand it any longer, and so went by on Saturday morning.

"You've just totally abandoned your family? Your gonna live the rest of your life with that sorry no-good son-of-a-bitch? Him and that street-walking whore of his. You just abandon your family to the mercy of the world. Nobody to do the chores, nobody to split the wood. Just let us starve to death. I've never understood how a person can let their own family down the way you have.

"The sting of a serpent is nothing compared to a thankless child. That's in the Bible. You cannot imagine the grief you've caused your poor Ma, your brother and sister, and your Pa. What possesses you to take up with that scoundrel and that whore?"

"Ma, let's don't fight. All I want to do is to take the kids to the show tonight. I'll bring them back as soon as the show is over. I don't want to fight with you. And I don't look at those people the way you do. They're old, and Fanny Hawk is good people. Uncle Will is no harm to anyone. He's paid for his crimes."

"You can't pay for the kind of stuff he did; you've got to burn in hell for it, and he knows it. That's why he called you, he's trying to soothe his conscience. I tell you right now, he's going to hell. There ain't no question in my mind. It serves the son-of-a-bitch right, and that woman. She ain't nothing but a carnival whore."

"Ma, she said she wasn't no carnival whore. She's never been to a carnival in her life. Will got drunk and told that tale on her. She says that ain't so, she's never spent a day in a carnival."

"You believe that lying bitch more than you believe your own Ma, I guess."

"Ma, there's no reason for her to tell me an untruth. What reason has she got?"

"Like I said, young man, you believe that bitch before you would your own Ma. I'm telling you, she's a carnival whore. And she's probably got every filthy social disease that can be had."

"You mean venereal disease, Ma?"

"Well, you can call it anything you want to, but I promise you, if you stick your little dick in her, it's liable to rot right off. I'll tell you that, young man."

"Ma, Adrian and Cornelia are probably sitting right behind that door listening to every word you say..."

"Well, they've got to learn it sometime. You start whoring around and you are going to get things that ain't good for you. They might as well know it now as ever."

"Ma, can I take them to the show? I'll pay for it."

"You're damn right you'll pay for it if you take them. If you'll have them back here at eleven o'clock."

At that moment, the kids busted through the door where they'd probably been sneakin' and listenin' to everything that was said, and started getting ready to go.

Suddenly, Ma started crying, heaving great sobs. They gathered around and asked her what was wrong. I knew that was the wrong thing to do, and sure enough she started telling them that she was going to be dead in a few days. That their big old brother was just worrying her plumb to death. That they were going to be orphan children, and it was all their big brother's fault.

We finally managed to get out of the house in time for the 7 o'clock show at the Strand Theater in downtown Bremen. This was usually a double feature—a cowboy picture, one B-grade detective picture, along with a newsreel, a serial, and a cartoon, all for the price of 10 cents.

Uncle Will gained strength rapidly, and the weeks flew by. It had been two or three months since I'd seen Miss Fanny, so one Saturday morning I told him that I was going to see her. When I knocked on Miss Fanny's door, she hugged me warmly.

"Gene, it's been a long time. I decided that something bad had happened to Will and you weren't going to see me any more."

"I've been trying to get back, Miss Fanny, but one thing or another kept me from it. Uncle Will got out of the hospital; he's pretty fit now. Every day he talks about coming down to find out whether you'll see him again. He wants to make amends for any wrongs he's ever done you. And I'm here to try to work out the details."

"Before you say you won't talk to Uncle Will, there's something I need to ask you. There was more money buried in the glass jars than he'd remembered. What he thought was about $9000 turned out to be $23,000, and you said you knew why. You also said you left him. But Mayhayley Lancaster says he left you. You ain't finished telling the story, and I can't hardly wait to see why you said you left him, and she says he left you. That woman knows more than any person has got a right to know about other folk, including me. And I know she ain't never seen me before."

"Gene, that's no big problem. Actually, one night he'd been off playing cards with the boys again, came home drunker than a lord, and beat me within an inch of my life. I'd already told him if he ever did that again, I'd leave him, and that I'd never come back. And I meant it.

"I knew it was the liquor that was doing it, but I was determined not to spend the rest of my life wondering when he was going to come home and whup me again.

"Will told you that I wasn't there the next morning when he came to with his hangover. Is that right?"

"That's right, Miss Fanny."

"Well, I took a quilt, and an old army blanket, crawled up under the house and slept until daylight. We had the Model-T truck Will'd bought. Back then they didn't have good headlights like now, and the lights on the Model-T were little better than kerosene lanterns. I knew I couldn't see how to get to a hotel at night, though I'm sure Will thought I had. The next morning, after it got to daylight, I drove to Tallapoosa and checked into the hotel. I had them hide the Model-T, and asked the desk not to let anybody know I was registered. I stayed there a whole week, waiting for my black eyes to get back in some reasonable condition so I could go out in public again.

"In the meantime, there were some things at the house I wanted, but I didn't dare go back when Will was there. So I got one of the bellhops to drop by the roadhouse where Will spent a lot of his time to see whether he could find out where he was and what he was planning to do. Will had already told the boys at the roadhouse he'd left me. You see, Will was one of the biggest liars in the world, especially when he was drinking. Sometimes it didn't make sense why he'd tell a lie, but the lie always served some purpose in his head. A lot of times, nobody else could figure out what that purpose was, but he'd tell you a lie in spite of anything.

"Of course, he'd already told them he'd picked me up as a carnival girl, so they thought I was a tramp. The only reason Miss Lancaster would've thought Will left me is that he must have gone back to get his fortune told after I left and told her the same lies he'd told everybody else, what a tramp I was and how he'd left me.

"When the bellhop told me he'd gone on a trip out of state, I guessed that he'd be off somewhere else getting himself in trouble. You see, the G. B. Balls business was never dead settled, and the detective magazines kept hashing the story over and over again whenever they'd run out of other things to write.

"As soon as my face healed to where I could be seen in public, I bought a ticket to Atlanta. I, too, was the subject of a manhunt, though things had cooled off quite a bit. People do forget those gruesome murders and stories pretty quick, probably because fresh killings and mayhem hop up and take their place regular, and the old ones just become less horrifying as time goes on.

"So I went to Atlanta and bought a nice house on Peachtree Battle, a fancy, exclusive section. With my distant grandfather's gold, and the money I had from selling my plantation in Mississippi, I was very wealthy by the standards of the day. I could afford servants and all of the things that made living easy.

"Then the Great Depression hit. One bank where I had a lot of money failed, and I lost about $15,000 or so dollars. But I had some money in another bank that didn't.

"When Roosevelt declared the Bank Holiday in '33 right after he came into office, even though my other bank didn't fail—I had maybe $20,000 there—I was temporarily caught short of funds. So, I took a train back to Tallapoosa. This was years and years later. Once there, I went back to the old house down at the river bend. The place was all grown over. It was as if nobody had been in that house since I left. The furniture was the same. It was right spooky.

"Well, I crawled under the house and dug up my gold. It was still there. When I'd left, I thought I had enough money to last forever, and had only taken half. That's when I discovered the fruit jars with Will's money in them. I didn't count it, I just borrowed a big handful. Then I took the rest of my own gold and left his.

"When I got back to Atlanta, I found I'd taken $4000 that didn't belong to me. That was Will's paper money. But the years went on, and I was rearing a daughter. I had enough to live comfortably. You can't imagine what $4000 was worth in 1933. You could live a year on maybe $700 and have servants.

"Then along about 1939, the war clouds piled up over Europe. You remember the war ended only three or four years ago. Well you must have been only nine or ten when it started."

"I was 11, Miss Fanny."

"In 1939, I decided I'd go back for more because a collector's market for gold coins had developed. They'd been out of circulation since '33, and a lot of people were buying them. They were afraid of the war and didn't know what was going to happen. Everybody was collecting gold coins in those days—you couldn't own gold bullion because it was illegal. But gold coins were collector's items, and you could own all you wanted.

"Roosevelt set the price officially at $35 an ounce. But there's been a black market in gold for more than that ever since he set the price. In 1939, you could sell a $20 gold piece for maybe $55. Since the war ended, there hasn't been such a tremendous demand for 'em, but you can still get a premium for them as collector's items.

"So I went back to the house once again—I don't know how Will is going to explain all this business to you—but I went back, I couldn't tell whether anybody had been by since my last visit. Then I dug up 500 of the coins I'd given Will from my inheritance. I figured he was dead, and couldn't imagine him letting that gold lie under the house along with the money if he wasn't. Exceptin' if he was out robbing and stealing from somebody else, or had gotten caught and was off in the penitentiary.

"At that time, 'cause I was going to earn a good size premium over the face value of the coins, I carried the extra money you found, put it in those jars, and covered it up. That's why you found more money than Will thought there was. I'd left his gold, except what I paid for, stuck in that old ammunition box.

"I love my flower garden here, and I can keep myself busy at it. The grandchildren can ride their bicycles all day up and down these dirt roads and never have to worry about a car crackin' their bones. I plan to stay here till I die.

"But let's not talk about dying; that's a long way off, I hope. Well, Gene, I've pretty much covered Will, and I guess now I won't be seeing you very much."

"I'd like to come visit with you regular, and I still'd like you and Uncle Will to get back together. But I got my notice to go be examined for the army next week. I think I'm going to Columbus, where they've been sending folks lately. If I pass I may get drafted. But I'm gonna powerful miss you and Uncle Will, as well as my brothers and sisters, if I get drafted."

"Well, if you go dig up his gold and take it to him, he can afford anything he wants."

"Have you made up your mind to see Uncle Will, Miss Fanny, or do you want me to quit asking?"

"No, no, Gene, ask away any time you want to. I just don't know yet. I was surprised to see you when you walked in. And sometimes I do get wicked lonesome. Of course, I got neighbors, I go visiting back and forth, but I got right used to you coming and sitting with me for a while and if you'd pressed me when you first came by, I'd have told you I was ready to see Will. I'm younger than him, but I'm getting on toward blue heaven."

"Miss Fanny, I don't think Uncle Will'd hurt a fly. He's been through a lot. Even with the pneumonia cured, he's still got asthma. He ain't gonna be running no foot races again, I promise. I wish, if you can find it in your heart, you'd at least see him and talk to him."

"Well, Gene, if I do that, I know we'll get back together. I just know we will, because he could talk me into anything back when we was young. You know how I helped him cover up that murder I knew he was guilty of. I sure did some careless things just because I loved him so much, then him turn on me the way he did.

"To ease your mind a bit, Gene, I promise I'll let you arrange for me to meet him somewhere before you go off to the army. That's the best I'm gonna do, so once you know you're going in the army, you come here. Even if it isn't right away, I'd like for you to come visit me now and again, and let me know how he's doing.

"If I was you, Gene, I'd go get that money for sure. I'd go there today and dig it up before somebody accidentally discovers it. The way it looks to me, those gold coins are worth a lot of money, and Will may live long enough he's gonna need more than $19,000 or whatever it was you said he had left."

I wanted to tell Miss Fanny I'd already dug up 400 coins. If they were worth as much as she said they was, $50 or $60 each, that was another $24,000. That would last a long time. But I let it pass. I didn't tell her I now had some gold buried under our house—I was calling it "our house" now—and I hadn't told Uncle Will either. I didn't think it was gonna be long till he died.

I'm ashamed of myself now for thinking such thoughts, but if I thought them, then the gold certainly wouldn't be stolen. If I didn't tell him nothing till he died, and he was probably going to die while I was in army, I wouldn't know anything about it, and then when I got out of the army, I'd have myself a pile of gold.

I quit the hateful job at General Shoe and got me one at Dryden Brothers Lumber Company in Bremen, driving a truck. After I was accepted for military service, I was awfully busy. The months seemed to fly by.

Uncle Will never got to the point where he was ready to tell me any more of his life, and acted embarrassed when I asked him about it. So I finally quit askin'. When the Chinese Communists invaded South Korea, it had been so long since I'd been examined for the army, they called me back to make sure I wasn't broke yet, and told me I'd be inducted on September 1, 1950. I was to go to the courthouse in Buchanan to swear in for military service.

On Friday night before I was supposed to leave, I went to see Miss Fanny. I reminded her she said she'd see Will before I left. She picked the following Sunday. If I'd have Will there at 10 AM Sunday morning, she'd talk to him about getting back together. If they couldn't, she'd at least sit down and chew air with him a spell.

When I told Uncle Will she'd see him at 10 o'clock Sunday, he got like a worm on a hot rock. He couldn't be still. He started telling me how grateful he was for all the things I had done for him. How I had saved his life when Ol' Ebo was chasing him.

"Uncle Will, she didn't say ya'll were gonna get back together. She said she'd talk to you about it, and that's all she said. She wants me to tell you she's gonna fix you some Sunday dinner. I 'spect I'll just put you out the door, and go off somewhere while ya'll talk."

He was so antsy waiting for Sunday morning to come, I had to get away from him. Saturday night I went back to visit with Ma, and passed on the news that I was going off to the army next week. Told her the way fighting was going on over in Korea, I'd probably have to go to there.

"Well you might as well go to Korea—you ain't worth nothing to us here. You done abandoned your family for them folks up in Haralson County. The scrapings of the earth they are; you abandoned a perfectly wonderful family."

Will woke me up before daylight the next morning, all shaved and shined with his Sunday meetin' clothes on, and wanting me to take him right then. I grumped, "Uncle, Fanny said 10 o'clock. It's barely 7."

"Well it'll take us 30 minutes to get there."

"That's right, but that still leaves two and a half hours. I don't think we ought to go this early. Let's go down to the bus station cafe, take some breakfast, read the newspaper, see how the war is. We can still be down to Miss Fanny's about the time she says."

So we went to the bus station cafe and ordered some scrambled eggs, country ham, and coffee. He kept looking at the clock over the door. Finally, at 9 o'clock, I said, "Okay, I don't guess it'll kill Miss Fanny if we get there 15 minutes early. Let's go."

When we got in sight of Miss Fanny's, there was a Cadillac parked in her front yard. I remembered once meeting her daughter Caroline, a tall, good-looking woman I'd guessed to be in her 30s. There were two kids playing out in the front yard.

When we drove up, they stood and stared at us like we were two creatures from the moon. I said, "They must be Miss Fanny's grandchildren." I realized the moment I said it, I'd never mentioned them to Uncle Will.

"You never told me she had any grandchildren."

"I just met her daughter, Caroline, one time."

He pushed in front of me and knocked on the door. Fanny opened the door, he towered over her, but straightaways grabbed her powerful like I'd never seen anybody grabbed before and gave her a long hug. He held his head down and seemed to squeezed the very life out of her. Tears run down their faces like split levees. They must have embraced five minutes.

When he finally let go, her tears had soaked the front of his white shirt. All the time me and Caroline stood there looking at each other and then at them. Finally she cleared her throat and said, "Will, meet your daughter, Caroline."

At that instant I was kicking myself for not realizing how much she looked like Uncle Will. She was tall, slender, and purty enough. But it never once crossed my mind, that she might have been my uncle's daughter. Now it all come to me. I knew why Miss Fanny'd felt hurt so bad all those years ago. She'd been pregnant with his child when he beat her up. That would be a powerful hurt.

Then they called the grandchildren in and introduced them to their grandpaw. Both of them liked him from the first, we all sat down loud as a cloud of yellowjackets at a reunion picnic. Later when the dishes were done and put away, Miss Fanny said, "How about we all drive over and look at the house on the river where me and Will used to live when we were young?"

So we all piled in the car and went to Josh Webster's house. I got out and asked Mr. Webster, who was sitting on his front porch, if it would be alright if we went and looked at the old place.

"Sure it's fine with me lad. You won't hardly know it when you get there, but go right ahead."

As soon as we reached the bottom of the little hill on the winding log road below his house, I saw what he meant. The scrub trees had been cut down, the broom sage had been turned under with a tractor, and the land had been run over by a smoothing harrow, we could see all the way to the river. The house was gone.

We got out of the car and started across the plowed furrows toward the riverbank. When we arrived, Miss Fanny and I recollected Mayhayley Lancaster's prediction, and stared at each other in astonishment. I couldn't believe she could have known what was going to happen. With all the trees gone and the house gone, there was no way we'd have any idea where the gold was buried.

I tried using the little hill behind where the house had been as a reference point, along with the riverbank. But when I tried to imagine the house where I thought it should be, it didn't seem right. Anywhere I mentally placed the house, it still didn't look right. Miss Mayhayley was right. That gold was going to lie moldering in the ground for no telling how long.

"Fanny, after all the boy has done for us, the least we can do is invite you to come spend the night with us at our house, and then we'll see him off at the bus station in the morning. Gene needs somebody to give him a good send off, and right now he ain't on too good terms with his Ma and his Pa."

"Uncle Will, me and Pa get along fine. It's me and Ma that don't. But that's okay. I'd rather ya'll just stay here. I've got less than a mile to walk to the bus station. I'll see you on my first leave."

"Okay nephew, we'll see you on your first leave."

On Monday morning, I rode a bus to Columbus where I was inducted into the United States Army. We took a train trip through

Savannah to Fort Jackson, South Carolina. There I began inten-
sive infantry basic training for fourteen weeks.

Ma even told me she and Pa would take me to Terminal Station
in Atlanta. All the way up, it was one continual lecture on how
I'd failed the family and how I could make it up now if I'd sign
over an allotment to the family and help them with their bills.
Did I love that son-of-a-bitch more than I did them? Did I make
an allotment to him? There'd be nothing for me to do with my
money once I got overseas. It was one continuous harangue. About
the time we got to Terminal Station, Pa finally told Ma to hush.
She shut up like a clam with lockjaw and sulked the rest of the
way to Atlanta, which gave us both a little peace.

I was a country boy gone to the city for sure. As soon as I got on
the train I joined a poker game and lost what money I had. So I
wired Uncle Will and asked him to send some money to me at
Camp Stoneman.

He wired it ahead by Western Union, so when I arrived, I had a $50
check waiting for me with the following message:

"Nephew, keep your money in your pocket. STOP. I am beginning to regret not teaching you how to play poker. STOP. When
you get back to Georgia I'll teach you the finer points of the game.
STOP. Ain't no use in going broke in a poker game if you know
what you are doing. STOP."

I never did figure out how he knew 'xactly how I went broke. It
was probably just a wild guess.

I was overseas almost a year, and didn't get a lot of mail from home.
Miss Fanny wrote me every once in a while, and Uncle Will would
occasionally scribble a few lines. They seemed mighty happy, and I
was proud for them. Not once did they mention, either one of them,
the confession Uncle Will had started and never finished.

One night along in January, when it was cold and I could hear
the distant rumble of artillery, the mail truck came just before dark.
There was a letter from Ma. Usually Ma's letters were telling me
to make my Class E allotment bigger. I was already sending all the
money home the army would allow me.

I got promoted rather rapidly. Pretty soon I was a Sergeant First
Class. Every time I'd get a promotion, she'd write and tell me how

they were starving to death and needed money. I didn't have any use for the money, so every time I'd get around the Pay Master, I'd up the amount I was sending home. I was sending home $140 a month out of my pay, which was all that was permitted.

I ate supper and went in my tent. At that time we were living in squad tents. We had a generator with one bare naked light in the tent. I sat down under the light to read the only letter I got, it started off as usual.

> Dear Gene,
>
> You can't imagine how tough times are here. We just got more bills than we can pay. We just paid our property tax. It was $21. We are gonna be lucky to have biscuits to eat by the end of the month.
>
> I've been meaning to ask you, you never did tell us who you made the beneficiary of your life insurance. I don't know whether you made it to us, or not.
>
> Bill Garnet got killed the day before yesterday. His Ma got the telegram. I talked to Mrs. Garnett, and she said Bill's insurance sure was gonna help them out. It let them finish paying for their place. At least they'd have a home as long as they lived.
>
> Love,
>
>
> Ma
>
> PS: If you made Will the beneficiary of your insurance, you ought to change it. With $10,000 we could pay off our place.